MW01620989

The Psychology of
COURAGE

The Psychology of COURAGE

MODERN RESEARCH ON AN ANCIENT VIRTUE

EDITED BY
Cynthia L. S. Pury and Shane J. Lopez

American Psychological Association • Washington, DC

Published by
American Psychological Association
750 First Street, NE
Washington, DC 20002
www.apa.org

To order
APA Order Department
P.O. Box 92984
Washington, DC 20090-2984
Tel: (800) 374-2721;
Direct: (202) 336-5510
Fax: (202) 336-5502;
TDD/TTY: (202) 336-6123
Online: www.apa.org/books/
E-mail: order@apa.org

In the U.K., Europe, Africa, and the Middle East,
copies may be ordered from
American Psychological Association
3 Henrietta Street
Covent Garden, London
WC2E 8LU England

Typeset in New Century Schoolbook by Circle Graphics, Inc., Columbia, MD

Printer: Maple-Vail/Manufacturing Group, York, PA
Cover Designer: Mercury Publishing Services, Rockville, MD

Library of Congress Cataloging-in-Publication Data

The psychology of courage : modern research on an ancient virtue / edited by Cynthia L. S. Pury, Shane J. Lopez.
p. cm.
ISBN-13: 978-1-4338-0807-4
ISBN-10: 1-4338-0807-2
1. Courage. I. Pury, Cynthia L. S. II. Lopez, Shane J.

BF575.C8P75 2010
179'.6—dc22

2009047845

British Library Cataloguing-in-Publication Data
A CIP record is available from the British Library.

Printed in the United States of America
First Edition

APA Science Volumes

Attribution and Social Interaction: The Legacy of Edward E. Jones

Best Methods for the Analysis of Change: Recent Advances, Unanswered Questions, Future Directions

Cardiovascular Reactivity to Psychological Stress and Disease

The Challenge in Mathematics and Science Education: Psychology's Response

Changing Employment Relations: Behavioral and Social Perspectives

Children Exposed to Marital Violence: Theory, Research, and Applied Issues

Cognition: Conceptual and Methodological Issues

Cognitive Bases of Musical Communication

Cognitive Dissonance: Progress on a Pivotal Theory in Social Psychology

Conceptualization and Measurement of Organism–Environment Interaction

Converging Operations in the Study of Visual Selective Attention

Creative Thought: An Investigation of Conceptual Structures and Processes

Developmental Psychoacoustics

Diversity in Work Teams: Research Paradigms for a Changing Workplace

Emotion and Culture: Empirical Studies of Mutual Influence

Emotion, Disclosure, and Health

Evolving Explanations of Development: Ecological Approaches to Organism–Environment Systems

Examining Lives in Context: Perspectives on the Ecology of Human Development

Global Prospects for Education: Development, Culture, and Schooling

Hostility, Coping, and Health

Measuring Patient Changes in Mood, Anxiety, and Personality Disorders: Toward a Core Battery

Occasion Setting: Associative Learning and Cognition in Animals

Organ Donation and Transplantation: Psychological and Behavioral Factors

Origins and Development of Schizophrenia: Advances in Experimental Psychopathology

The Perception of Structure

Perspectives on Socially Shared Cognition

Psychological Testing of Hispanics

Psychology of Women's Health: Progress and Challenges in Research and Application

Researching Community Psychology: Issues of Theory and Methods

The Rising Curve: Long-Term Gains in IQ and Related Measures

Sexism and Stereotypes in Modern Society: The Gender Science of Janet Taylor Spence

Sleep and Cognition

Sleep Onset: Normal and Abnormal Processes

Stereotype Accuracy: Toward Appreciating Group Differences

Stereotyped Movements: Brain and Behavior Relationships

Studying Lives Through Time: Personality and Development

The Suggestibility of Children's Recollections: Implications for Eyewitness Testimony

Taste, Experience, and Feeding: Development and Learning

Temperament: Individual Differences at the Interface of Biology and Behavior

Through the Looking Glass: Issues of Psychological Well-Being in Captive Nonhuman Primates

Uniting Psychology and Biology: Integrative Perspectives on Human Development

Viewing Psychology as a Whole: The Integrative Science of William N. Dember

APA Decade of Behavior Volumes

Acculturation: Advances in Theory, Measurement, and Applied Research

Aging and Cognition: Research Methodologies and Empirical Advances

Animal Research and Human Health: Advancing Human Welfare Through Behavioral Science

Behavior Genetics Principles: Perspectives in Development, Personality, and Psychopathology

Categorization Inside and Outside the Laboratory: Essays in Honor of Douglas L. Medin

Chaos and Its Influence on Children's Development: An Ecological Perspective

Child Development and Social Policy: Knowledge for Action

Children's Peer Relations: From Development to Intervention

Commemorating Brown: The Social Psychology of Racism and Discrimination

Computational Modeling of Behavior in Organizations: The Third Scientific Discipline

Couples Coping With Stress: Emerging Perspectives on Dyadic Coping

Developing Individuality in the Human Brain: A Tribute to Michael I. Posner

Emerging Adults in America: Coming of Age in the 21st Century

Experimental Cognitive Psychology and Its Applications

Family Psychology: Science-Based Interventions

Inhibition and Cognition

Measuring Psychological Constructs: Advances in Model-Based Approaches

Medical Illness and Positive Life Change: Can Crisis Lead to Personal Transformation?

Memory Consolidation: Essays in Honor of James L. McGaugh

Models of Intelligence: International Perspectives

The Nature of Remembering: Essays in Honor of Robert G. Crowder

New Methods for the Analysis of Change

On the Consequences of Meaning Selection: Perspectives on Resolving Lexical Ambiguity

Participatory Community Research: Theories and Methods in Action

Personality Psychology in the Workplace

Perspectivism in Social Psychology: The Yin and Yang of Scientific Progress

Primate Perspectives on Behavior and Cognition

Principles of Experimental Psychopathology: Essays in Honor of Brendan A. Maher

The Psychology of Courage: Modern Research on an Ancient Virtue

Psychosocial Interventions for Cancer

Racial Identity in Context: The Legacy of Kenneth B. Clark

The Social Psychology of Group Identity and Social Conflict: Theory, Application, and Practice

Strengthening Couple Relationships for Optimal Child Development: Lessons From Research and Intervention

Strengthening Research Methodology: Psychological Measurement and Evaluation

Transcending Self-Interest: Psychological Explorations of the Quiet Ego

Unraveling the Complexities of Social Life: A Festschrift in Honor of Robert B. Zajonc

Visual Perception: The Influence of H. W. Leibowitz

Contents

Contributors

Carl Andrew Castro, PhD, Colonel, U.S. Army Medical Research and Materiel Command, Fort Detrick, MD
Peter Fischer, PhD, Department of Psychology, University of Graz, Graz, Austria
Dieter Frey, PhD, Department of Psychology, Ludwig Maximilians University, Munich, Germany
Tobias Greitemeyer, PhD, School of Psychology, University of Sussex, Brighton, England
Sean T. Hannah, PhD, Colonel, U.S. Army, Director of the Army Center of Excellence for the Professional Military Ethic, United States Military Academy, West Point, NY
Melinda Key-Roberts, PhD, U.S. Army Research Institute, Fort Leavenworth, KS
Ted Kimmey, Jr., BS, First Lieutenant, U.S. Army, Kaiserslautern, Germany
Kristin Koetting, PhD, Psychology and Research in Education, Rockhurst University, Kansas City, MO, and Live What You Wear®, LLC, Leawood, KS
Paul B. Lester, PhD, Captain, U.S. Army, Arlington, VA
Shane J. Lopez, PhD, Clifton Strengths School, Omaha, NE
Dennis McGurk, PhD, United States Army Medical Research Unit and Walter Reed Army Institute of Research, Heidelberg, Germany
Silvia Osswald, PhD, Central Psychological Service of the Bavarian police, Munich, Germany
Stephanie E. Petersen, PhD, private practice, Houston, TX
Cynthia L. S. Pury, PhD, Clemson University, Clemson, SC
Daniel Putman, PhD, Department of Philosophy, University of Wisconsin–Fox Valley, Menasha
S. J. Rachman, PhD, University of British Columbia, Vancouver, Canada
Heather N. Rasmussen, PhD, University of Kansas, Lawrence
Christopher R. Rate, PhD, Lieutenant Colonel, U.S. Air Force, Behavioral Sciences Branch, Joint Military Information Support Command (JMISC), MacDill AFB, FL
William P. Skorupski, EdD, Department of Psychology and Research in Education, School of Education, University of Kansas, Lawrence
Charles B. Starkey, PhD, Department of Philosophy and Religion and Rutland Institute for Ethics, Clemson University, Clemson, SC
Patrick J. Sweeney, PhD, Colonel, U.S. Army, Department of Behavioral Sciences and Leadership, United States Military Academy, West Point, NY
Gretchen R. Vogelgesang, PhD, George Mason University, Arlington, VA
Cooper R. Woodard, PhD, Wheaton College, Norton, MA
Monica C. Worline, PhD, University of California, Irvine, School of Social Ecology and Merage School of Business, Irvine
Ya-Ting Yang, PhD candidate, University of Kansas, Lawrence

Foreword

In early 1988, the American Psychological Association (APA) Science Directorate began its sponsorship of what would become an exceptionally successful activity in support of psychological science—the APA Scientific Conferences program. This program has showcased some of the most important topics in psychological science and has provided a forum for collaboration among many leading figures in the field.

The program has inspired a series of books that have presented cutting-edge work in all areas of psychology. At the turn of the millennium, the series was renamed the Decade of Behavior Series to help advance the goals of this important initiative. The Decade of Behavior is a major interdisciplinary campaign designed to promote the contributions of the behavioral and social sciences to our most important societal challenges in the decade leading up to 2010. Although a key goal has been to inform the public about these scientific contributions, other activities have been designed to encourage and further collaboration among scientists. Hence, the series that was the "APA Science Series" has continued as the "Decade of Behavior Series." This represents one element in APA's efforts to promote the Decade of Behavior initiative as one of its endorsing organizations. For additional information about the Decade of Behavior, please visit http://www.decadeofbehavior.org.

Over the course of the past years, the Science Conference and Decade of Behavior Series has allowed psychological scientists to share and explore cutting-edge findings in psychology. The APA Science Directorate looks forward to continuing this successful program and to sponsoring other conferences and books in the years ahead. This series has been so successful that we have chosen to extend it to include books that, although they do not arise from conferences, report with the same high quality of scholarship on the latest research.

We are pleased that this important contribution to the literature was supported in part by the Decade of Behavior program. Congratulations to the editors and contributors of this volume on their sterling effort.

Steven J. Breckler, PhD
Executive Director for Science

Virginia E. Holt
Assistant Executive Director for Science

Preface

We've always been drawn to stories of people acting with valor and intrigued to know why and, more important, how they do so. As psychotherapists, we heard daily accounts of people rising to the occasion to overcome adversity and improve their lives. The strength they demonstrated sounded like, looked like, and felt like courage. We each went to the literature in the early 2000s to learn more about this strength, and we each made the same discovery: most researchers did not examine everyday courage in their work. While philosophers have speculated about courage for centuries, the assembled psychological research on courage easily fits into a briefcase. But this situation is changing. A small but growing body of scholarly work now demystifies the courage that all people possess and call on in time of need.

We assembled many of the researchers and practitioners behind this body of work for the 2007 Courage Summit, a conference sponsored jointly by the American Psychological Association and Gallup which was held on October 3, 2007. To the best of our knowledge, it was the first conference dedicated solely to presenting research and theory about the psychology of courage. Using the conference as a springboard, we asked the presenters as well as other top courage researchers to give us their best thinking on the topic. You hold the results in your hands.

We would like to thank Gallup and the American Psychological Association for their generous support. Cindy Pury thanks her colleagues at Clemson University for numerous hallway conversations about conference planning, book editing, and courage, and Shane Lopez for his collaboration and encouragement. A special thanks to Craig, Alice, Theresa, and Emily for their support, encouragement, and love. Shane Lopez thanks Cindy Pury for her collaboration, Alli and Parrish for their love and support, and all the courageous people who have shared their stories.

The Psychology of COURAGE

Introduction

Cynthia L. S. Pury and Shane J. Lopez

While Wesley Autry was waiting for a subway, a fellow passenger had a seizure and fell onto the tracks and into the path of an oncoming train. Autry asked a bystander to keep an eye on his children, then dove onto the tracks and held the other man down while a train passed over them, missing them by a few inches (Buckley, 2007; "Rescuer pins fallen man," 2007).

A group of African American high school students sat down at a segregated lunch counter in downtown Greenville, South Carolina, in 1960. As expected, the management at the store told them that they were not allowed to sit at the Whites-only counter; many stayed and were arrested. Their case made it to the Supreme Court, where, along with other sit-in protesters from around the country, they won a landmark civil rights case ("Civil rights pioneer," 2009; Peterson v. City of Greenville, 1963).

Film critic Roger Ebert feared attending his first Alcoholics Anonymous meeting but went anyway, and then continued to attend often enough that he came to consider himself a member and recently attained 30 years of sobriety (Ebert, 2009). Ebert currently blogs about living with the side effects of cancer surgery that has left him mute (Ebert, 2008a) and missing part of his jaw (Ebert, 2008b). Yet he describes each challenge inspirationally, with humor and post-traumatic growth.

Though these dramatic and high-profile instances of courage catch the popular imagination, other, more everyday examples of courage exist. The cheerleader who breaks the fall of a teammate during a failed basket toss; the colleague who takes responsibility for an error at work; the transfer student who willingly steps outside of his or her comfort zone—each of these people exhibit everyday courage (e.g., Pury, Kowalski, & Spearman, 2007; Worline, 2004).

Courage has been denoted as an important virtue in many cultures and across time. It is one of a limited set of human qualities and behaviors singled out in statues, monuments, and awards; its opposite, cowardice, is considered to be a failing, and rituals and institutions exist to promote courage in many cultures (Peterson & Seligman, 2004). However, psychologists' research into courage has been extremely limited. Although studies of fear and related constructs are well-researched, courage has rarely been a topic of study until recently. A recent PsycINFO search (April 19, 2009) found 22,496 hits for *fear* and *avoidance* and only 251 hits for *courage, bravery,* or *valor*. As with other positive psychology constructs, psychologists' interest in courage is growing: Over half of the hits for courage have been published in the past decade.

We believe that the time has come to create a starting place for researchers, students, and others interested in psychological research on this important virtue. The contributors to this volume play an important role in the developing science of courage. They represent the fields of social psychology, clinical and counseling psychology, management and leadership, military psychology, and philosophy. Each has published multiple works dealing with the psychology of courage, and each brings a fresh and exciting perspective to studying this ancient virtue. For this volume, we have asked them to review their best work on the topic, present new data, and speculate on the future of courage research. Their chapters answer three fundamental questions about any new area of inquiry: What is it? How does it come about? How can understanding it improve individual lives, organizations, and society? Our purpose in addressing these questions goes beyond the academic: We hope to inspire psychologists and other behavioral and social scientists to consider courage in their work, whether it be basic research or applied practice.

Part I of this book, What Is Courage?, examines ancient and modern answers to the question posed by Plato in *Laches* (trans. 1961): The protagonist, Socrates, asked esteemed warriors how to define courage and ultimately came up empty-handed. In Chapter 1 of this volume, Daniel Putman describes the philosophical history of courage and outlines three types of courage—physical, moral, and psychological—that are used by psychological researchers today. In Chapter 2, Shane J. Lopez, Heather N. Rasmussen, William P. Skorupski, Kristin Koetting, Stephanie E. Petersen, and Ya-Ting Yang examine common features of courage and explain how they differentiate among types of courage. Next, in Chapter 3, Christopher R. Rate presents an empirically derived definition of courage that involves three major requirements: willingness and intentionality, risk or difficulty to the actor, and noble or moral motivation. Finally, in Chapter 4, Cynthia L. S. Pury and Charles B. Starkey propose a distinction between courage as an accolade and as an action, and describe the implications of this distinction for theory and research.

Part II, Basic Research and Theory, provides a cross-section of work on courage today. In Chapter 5, S. J. Rachman, the patriarch of modern courage researchers, describes his work on courage and its ties to emotion theory. In Chapter 6, Cooper R. Woodard examines empirical distinctions between types of courageous action and their links to the existential concept of authenticity. In Chapter 7, Sean T. Hannah, Patrick J. Sweeney, and Paul B. Lester look at courage from the perspective of the cognitive affective processing system approach to personality. Finally, in Chapter 8, Silvia Osswald, Tobias Greitemeyer, Peter Fischer, and Dieter Frey examine moral courage and its distinction from helping behavior using the perspective of social psychology.

Part III, Applied Research and Theory, presents three chapters on courage in a variety of specific contexts. In Chapter 9, Dennis McGurk and Carl Andrew Castro explore courage on the modern battlefield. In Chapter 10, Paul B. Lester, Gretchen R. Vogelgesang, Sean T. Hannah, and Ted Kimmey, Jr. take an organizational leadership approach to examine the transmission of courage from a leader to his or her followers. In Chapter 11, Monica C. Worline presents research on the effects of witnessing other people acting courageously at work.

Finally, in Part IV, Chapter 12, Cynthia L. S. Pury, Shane J. Lopez, and Melinda Key-Roberts discuss the future of courage research, noting that there are countless opportunities for researchers to make discoveries about courage and its significance.

As the editors of this volume, we have found these chapters enlightening and, yes, encouraging. As a field, psychology knows very little about courage: what it is, where it exists, what its implications are, and how (or even when) to foster it. We believe that the research reviewed in these chapters represents a fundamental beginning to a serious science of courage, and we hope they inspire you to consider adding to the field's growing knowledge.

References

Buckley, C. (2007, January 3). A man down, a train arriving, and a stranger makes a choice. *New York Times.* Retrieved from http://www.nytimes.com

Civil rights pioneer remembers Woolworth's sit-ins. (2009, September 13). *WYFF4.* Retrieved from http://www.wyff4.com/news/20878205/detail.html

Ebert, R. (2008a, October 24). I think I'm musing my mind [Web log post]. Retrieved from http://blogs.suntimes.com/ebert/2008/10/i_think_im_musing_my_mind.html

Ebert, R. (2008b, November 19). Siskel & Ebert at the jugular [Web log post]. Retrieved from http://blogs.suntimes.com/ebert/2008/11/siskel_ebert_the_jugular.html

Ebert, R. (2009, August 25). My name is Roger, and I'm an alcoholic [Web log post]. Retrieved from http://blogs.suntimes.com/ebert/2009/08/my_name_is_roger_and_im_an_alc.html

Peterson v. City of Greenville, 373 U.S. 244 (1963).

Peterson, C., & Seligman, M.E.P. (2004). Strengths of courage: Introduction. In C. Peterson & M. E. P. Seligman (Eds.), *Character strengths and virtues: A handbook and classification* (pp. 197–212). Washington, DC: American Psychological Association.

Plato. (1961). *Laches* (B. Jowett, Trans.). In E. Hamilton & H. Cairns (Eds.), *The collected dialogues of Plato, including the letters* (pp. 123–144). Princeton, NJ: Princeton University Press.

Pury, C., Kowalski, R., & Spearman, J. (2007). Distinctions between general and personal courage. *Journal of Positive Psychology, 2,* 99–114.

Rescuer pins fallen man as subway passes over them. (2007, January 3). The Associated Press. Retrieved from http://www.msnbc.msn.com/id/16444249/

Worline, M. (2004). *Dancing the cliff edge: The role of courage in social life* (Unpublished doctoral dissertation). University of Michigan, Ann Arbor.

Part I

What Is Courage?

1

Philosophical Roots of the Concept of Courage

Daniel Putman

Many studies in psychology over the past 50 years, including the Milgram (1974) shock experiment and Latané and Darley's (1970) studies of the bystander effect, have had courage as a critical component. However, in these studies courage was not the focus of analysis; rather, the focus was on obedience and conformity, with issues about courage lingering in a tantalizing way in the background. Not until very recently has the character trait of courage been studied directly by psychologists.

The concept of courage itself has roots as deep as some of the earliest human writings. Western cultural self-understanding is grounded in literature about Achilles and Odysseus; sagas of courage range from the ancient Greeks to innumerable books, movies, and television shows today. Usually the courage displayed has been what is called *physical courage,* that is, overcoming a fear of death or physical harm for the sake of a noble goal such as defense of country or family. However, much literature also depicts what is called *moral courage,* that is, overcoming fear of social ostracism or rejection in order to maintain ethical integrity. The courage of Gandhi or Martin Luther King, Jr., to stand up for a higher moral standard is a combination of physical and moral courage. Within the past 150 years the literary tradition has also praised a third form of courage, what I call *psychological courage* (Putman, 2004). Psychological courage is overcoming the fear of losing the psyche—the fear of psychological death. Today stories (in print or on screen) often relate the courage of the addict overcoming his or her addiction or the person abused as a child overcoming deep psychological fears to become a loving and productive adult. Although physical, moral, and psychological courage frequently overlap, they are useful ways of dividing up this critically important character trait.

In this chapter, I explore four philosophical traditions that have been instrumental in developing the concept of courage. The first three are represented by Western philosophers whose schools of thought have been highly influential. The fourth perspective is that of Eastern philosophy, especially Zen Buddhism. To some degree each of the four traditions reflects a different dimension of courage. The Western philosophers are Aristotle (the school of thought being

Portions of Chapter 1 were adapted from "Wisdom of Stoics" in *Psychological Courage* (2004) by Daniel Putman with permission of Roman & Littlefield Publishing Group.

the Aristotelian tradition), Epictetus (and the Stoic tradition), and Jean-Paul Sartre (and the existentialist tradition). Along with the Buddhist perspective they represent a cross-section of the philosophical analysis of courage and have established the foundation for the scientific study of this virtue.

Aristotle

In his writings on ethics, Aristotle (trans. 1985) analyzed courage through his discussion of the practical virtues. In doing so, he talked about what is referred to today as physical courage. To convey the lasting power of Aristotle's analysis, I must provide some background on what Aristotle means by *virtue.* If one examines human life, it becomes obvious that survival as a social being requires certain actions. If people did not defend themselves or their family or friends in dangerous situations, then nothing else could be achieved. If early humans had not outwitted predators, or if they had not been willing at times to face real physical dangers, we would not be here today. Aristotle saw in his experience in Athenian society that noble goals, such as defense of family or way of life, could not be achieved without what is called in English *courage.* Besides courage, Aristotle also noted several other critical virtues that seem to ring true throughout history. For example, without generosity or sharing of some type, people could not function together. Without temperance or some control over desires, long-term projects in society or the stability required for raising a family would be nearly impossible. Courage is important simply because the environment poses real dangers to people and those they love. Courage and the other virtues are necessary for human beings to develop *happiness,* the vague English term usually used for the Greek term *eudaimonia,* perhaps better translated today as a full and rich life (trans. 1985, pp. 1115a20–1121a10).

Aristotle looked at courage and other virtues and noticed something unusual about them. They tend to be a *mean* between two extremes. This term is often misunderstood. He was not referring to some kind of arithmetical mean. An example using temperance will clarify his point. Consider a 5-year-old child and the linebacker for a professional football team. Both go into a restaurant. Both clearly have vastly different needs and desires when it comes to food. However, for each of them, the mean for their desires with regard to food will be somewhere between the two extremes. The child can overeat (a problem in Western society) or undereat (a different problem for many in Western society). Likewise, the football player can overeat or undereat, depending on what his body needs. The mean will clearly be different for each one, but this does not turn Aristotle's idea into relativism, another common misperception. There actually *is* a best amount for each person to eat, but it will differ because of the actual differences between the two people. People have some sense of this, I believe, when they go into restaurants, although they may not always be conscious of it. Temperance with regard to food is a real virtue (Aristotle, trans. 1985, pp. 1117b23–1119b20).

Courage is the mean between the two extremes of *cowardice* and what is usually translated as *rashness.* Cowardice is easy to comprehend: It is running away or avoiding the danger. Rashness is facing danger in a careless way or in a manner that masks other motives. An example similar to what Aristotle had in mind is the soldier who, because he or she wants to look brave, acts in an impetuous but foolish way. This is not courage. A more everyday example is someone who drives extremely fast on the freeway and thinks he or she is being brave in doing so. (Alcohol can easily distort the mean.) As Aristotle pointed out, "the attitude to frightening things that the brave person really has is the attitude that the rash person wants to appear to have; hence he imitates the brave person where he can" (trans. 1985, pp. 1115b30–32). Aristotle also pointed out that some extremes are much more common than others. With regard to temperance, overindulgence of desires is more common because the natural tendency of desires is toward satisfaction. With regard to courage, cowardice is more common because the natural reaction to fear or danger is self-protection. However, both extremes, cowardice and rashness, are vices (1985, pp. 1109a1–19).

As with temperance, the mean for the other virtues varies from person to person. Consider anger. A parent who wants to be a good parent will express anger toward a child depending on the child's personality and what the child has done. Overreaction and underreaction are both negative, and parents know that. The parent will also respond knowing his or her personal tendencies with regard to anger. (The parent may have a problem regarding anger control.) All these elements factor into acting with the appropriate degree of anger. The same variability applies to courage. If there is a potentially dangerous situation, such as helping to save a drowning person in a fast-moving river, there are big differences in the mean for courage on the part of the excellent swimmer, the mediocre swimmer, and the nonswimmer. It might be rash for the nonswimmer to jump in; in fact, doing so might make the situation much worse. However, it might be cowardly for the excellent swimmer not to help because he or she is too afraid to try. As alluded to with regard to the child and the parent, the facts of the situation also affect the mean. If the person is in relatively shallow water (e.g., a child thrashing about), courage might be the same for swimmer and nonswimmer. If the person drowning is in deeper water, the appropriate act for each individual would likely be different. However, Aristotle emphasized that the mean is real even though it involves both personal and situational variables.

Aristotle's rich analysis of the virtues also involves the critical distinction between acts and traits. It is one thing to say that an act was courageous; it is quite another to say a person is courageous. Character, Aristotle argued, is primarily composed of habits, and habits are composed of acts that the person performs on a regular basis (trans. 1985, pp. 1103b7–25, 1105b6–20). On reflection, this may seem obvious, but it is not at all obvious in the way that courage is presented in the media, nor is the achievement of being a courageous person or a temperate person or a generous person an easy task. Part of the problem is that, frequently, the actual act others see may be done from character or it may be an isolated act never to be repeated again. People know this about themselves. If I tend to overindulge in sugar and know it, I may grit my teeth and pass up the rich cake at the wedding reception. To an observer this may look like a great sign of temperance in character (and I may bask in this false glory), but I know the act was an isolated one. To change who I am with regard to my desire, I need to practice the mean until it becomes a more or less natural tendency. This is hard to do, but no talk about character change is accurate until that occurs. The same is true for courage. Overcoming fears must become a habit for someone to be justifiably called a courageous person. An isolated courageous act is certainly to be praised, but being a courageous person is what maximizes one's chance to grow and develop throughout one's life.

A final issue Aristotle raised concerns acts that look courageous but are not. I already alluded to impetuous acts, but Aristotle refined this point by claiming that five types of actions frequently give a false impression of courage. First are acts done because of fear (trans. 1985, pp. 1116a30–1116b3). Such acts seem counterintuitive, but they are actually quite common. People may do things that look courageous because they are afraid of their supervisors or they are afraid of being talked about negatively. So a soldier who acts against danger primarily because of fear of reprisal if he or she does not do the act is not acting courageously. Of course, motives are frequently mixed. Any particular person may act from several motives, such as a desire to do the right thing, fear of losing reputation, or fear of punishment. However, if fear for self dominates the motive, the act is not courageous (or, rather, not fully courageous). Fear on behalf of someone else is a different story; such fear, such as for a family member, motivates actions that put oneself in danger, and the actions are for a noble cause. Such acts are courageous according to Aristotle, whereas actions done out of fear for oneself are not and may often be a form of cowardice. As Aristotle bluntly said, "However, we must be brave because it is fine, not because we are compelled" (1985, pp. 1116b2–3).

Aristotle then raised the issue of expertise (trans. 1985, pp. 1116b4–23). A professional soldier may look brave to an outsider in certain circumstances but may not be because the soldier's expertise allows him or her to make the distinction between actual danger and perceived danger, a distinction not apparent to the outsider. But Aristotle also attacked in this context mercenaries who may have a great deal of expertise and look brave in certain nondangerous situations but turn and run when real danger meets them. What Aristotle called "citizen troops" are much more likely to be truly courageous because they are fighting for a noble goal. Aristotle's third point concerns acts that look brave but are based only on emotions (1985, pp. 1116b24–1117a10). Making a decision and having a noble goal are essential ingredients to courage for Aristotle; otherwise one would call all animals courageous if they defended their territory by instinct. Instinct and emotions alone are not courage. The next example of acts that only appear courageous involves actions done by people who are overconfident. This is not courage because, as Aristotle said, "they think they are stronger and nothing could happen to them" (1985, pp. 1117a13–14). Such a person is different from someone who realistically trusts his or her own character because, for the overconfident person, the reality of the danger is downplayed and his or her own strength is overplayed. Acts done with such distorted judgments are not courageous. The final type of act is done out of ignorance (trans. 1985, pp. 1117a23–29). If a person does not understand the situation, he or she cannot be courageous, even though he or she may appear so when doing the act.

Many of these points have been debated extensively in philosophy since Aristotle's time. Other related questions have been raised, such as whether one needs to actually feel fear to be courageous and whether one can be courageous for a goal that the individual perceives as noble but society does not. Can a Ku Klux Klan member or a Gestapo member be courageous? Despite the many fascinating issues left under discussion, no philosopher would disagree that Aristotle's analysis of courage is brilliant and is a founding document, so to speak, for the analysis of courage in Western civilization.

Epictetus and the Stoics

Aristotle's analysis conceives of courage as active; it assumes that the agent will be facing dangers and will need to act in a decisive way at critical moments. Then as now this is the most common image of the courageous person. For example, the Medal of Honor given to Jason Dunham for throwing his helmet and himself over a grenade to protect his fellow Marines illustrates exactly the kind of physical courage Aristotle was talking about (Phillips, 2005).

However, courage can also have a distinctly passive quality to it. No philosophers have done a better job of analyzing this element of courage than the Stoics. The major spokesmen for this long-lasting, extremely influential tradition are Marcus Aurelius, the Roman Emperor, and the remarkable Epictetus, a former slave turned philosopher. Before I discuss courage for the Stoics, however, it is important to understand the Stoic view of human life.

In contrast to Aristotle's assumption of the active agent, the Stoics claim that people have little or no control over most things that happen to them in life. The universe works as it does independent of one's wishes. Hurricanes, earthquakes, diseases, and bad genes affect the lives of millions of people. Moreover, the thoughts and actions of other people are almost always beyond control. The person who resents his or her neighbor's success in life or the drunk driver who just happens to be on the road at the same time as someone's child—in all such cases one has little or no control over the thoughts and actions of others. Granted, we humans have come a long way in controlling nature from the time of the Stoics. We no longer have to sit passively by while disease wipes out our family and, even for events that we cannot directly control, we have some measure of prediction. Yet cancer, earthquakes, and the general fragility of life remind us that we are still prone to nature's whims. As far as other people go, some progress has been made in understanding why people do the things they do and some very limited ability to control some of the most destructive human actions has been found, yet, all in all, the thoughts and actions of other people are as unpredictable and uncontrollable today as they were in 100 AD for Epictetus. In fact, with the current population pressures and the anonymity of large cities, people's thoughts and actions may well be less predictable (Putman, 2004).

In light of all this, how do people respond to events in life? A key point of the Stoics is that most people waste an enormous amount of their lives being resentful, hostile, or frustrated over events that are already completed or over which they have no control. What a person is doing in these cases is giving one's life away to the event or person. Suppose a person's car is vandalized one night by a group of teenage boys. Many people would not only be upset at the incident but also would be upset for a long time and develop thoughts to match their frustration (perhaps about teenagers). Then, whenever a similar situation or even the thought arises, the initial frustration gets renewed. Millions of people have axes to grind, abiding resentments, and chips on their shoulders because of real or imagined slights. In response, the Stoics ask some simple questions: Why are you allowing someone else to dictate your life? Why waste the precious moments you have in negative and irritating emotions over events that are either past in time or over which you have no control? Why give your freedom of thought and expression to some long-gone vandals (or, far more seriously, to the torturer in front of you)? Maintain your freedom. Your life is your own (Putman, 2004).

This overview offers a clue to the Stoic view of courage. Courageous acts from the Stoic perspective may involve everyday garden variety issues such as resisting peer pressure. As Epictetus said about "friends" who are pressuring him to get money so that they can have some,

> If I can get it while keeping self-respect and trustworthiness and high-mindedness, show me the way and I will get it. But if you demand that I lose the good things that are mine so that you may acquire things that are not good, see for yourselves how unfair and inconsiderate you are. Which do you want more, money or a self-respecting and trustworthy friend? (Epictetus, trans. 1983, #24)

People generally agree with this ideal, but acting with integrity under social pressure is incredibly difficult for most people. This defense of one's self-worth and maintaining one's internal freedom in the face of external pressure is what the Stoic concept of courage is about.

Compared with the Aristotelian approach, the Stoic view of courage seems at first to be more reactive. This is somewhat deceiving. The act of Stoic courage is still a choice made after understanding the facts of the situation. Probably one of the best modern examples of this is Vice Admiral James Stockdale's experience as a North Vietnamese prisoner of war for 8 years, 4 of them in solitary confinement. Stockdale attributed much of his ability to survive to the Stoics. It was because of Stoic wisdom that he was able to keep reminding himself that, no matter what was done to him, he would do his utmost to maintain his inner freedom and control (Soccio, 2001). This is truly courage. A much more everyday example would be the choice a person must make in the face of bullying or gossip. The Stoics are not saying people should never respond actively. Sometimes active courage against the bully is best for all parties. What they are saying is that, in many circumstances, courage may involve accepting that the problem lies in the doer and that real courage may involve maintaining one's inner freedom and self-worth in the face of circumstances either beyond one's control or beneath one's dignity as a person. Again the question must be raised: Is it worth giving away one's life for hours, days, or years to whatever external force may be acting on one's self? Courage to maintain one's inner freedom and dignity is still a choice.

As a former slave Epictetus was well aware that it is impossible to avoid pain in life. The question is how to deal with it. That pain can be physical, but often what life forces people to deal with has to do with loss of integrity or psychological pain. The Stoic view of courage ties closely into the other types of courage mentioned at the beginning of the chapter: moral courage and psychological courage. Moral courage can be highly active, such as defending integrity by fighting to improve a highly sexist or prejudice-filled workplace. However, often it has a more reactive quality to it, such as *not* responding to hatred with hatred or *not* participating in something unethical by simply saying "no." Again, it depends on the situation. Not doing anything can be an act of cowardice, but saying "no" can also be an act of real courage. A great example of the Stoic ideal in moral courage was exhibited by some of the people in the famous Milgram (1974) shock experiment in which participants were told to shock the "learners" (who actually worked for Milgram and were not shocked) up to 450 volts if the learners got memorized word pairs wrong. The amazing number of people who went all the way to 450 volts masks the fact that some of the participants chose to say "no" to the experimenter under strong social pressure because they refused to hurt an innocent human being (Milgram, 1974). These people are not who society usually calls heroes; nevertheless, compared with the large majority who cave in under social pressure (even the pressure of one man in a white lab coat), these individuals deserve credit for real courage in the Stoic meaning of the term. (In the first 10 versions of the experiment reported by Milgram [1974], 102 out of 400 subjects broke off before 195 volts, what the machine labeled "very strong shock," but only 9 broke off before 135 volts, labeled as "strong shock.") These individuals who courageously contradicted the experimenter are similar to those who maintain moral integrity by saying "no" in the face of pain or death.

Finally, I want to tie the Stoic view of courage into what I earlier termed *psychological courage.* I say more about psychological courage later in this chapter in a discussion of existentialism, but two points stand out here for those facing anxiety and psychological fears. First is the preciousness of the moments one has. One of the most striking characteristics of anxiety is the amount of time and energy it can take up. For example, people who feel undesirable socially may spend much of their lives avoiding experiences during which that anxiety will occur. Their lives are constrained by a series of *not*s: not there, not with that person, not that job. The Stoics would say that a person in that situation is basically forfeiting his or her life. That person has given control of his or her life to anxiety. The Stoics would urge that person to make choices to take back his or her freedom and self-worth. The choice to seek help can be a true act of courage (Putman, 2004).

The second major point I want to raise about the Stoics and psychological courage is their emphasis on one's decisions about one's emotional state. This is very different from the way people think today. At one point Epictetus said, "Remember that what is insulting is not the person who abuses you or hits you, but the judgment about them that they *are* insulting. So when someone irritates you be aware that what irritates you is your own belief" (trans. 1983, #20). So, if someone steps on a person's foot and that person gets angry, that person's anger is his or her choice. A person is in fact free to respond any way he or she likes. Westerners have a hard time with this claim, especially given what is known about the lasting impact of some early childhood experiences. The Stoics' ideas may need modification, but it is far too easy to dismiss their point. Many situations in which people think emotions force them to act are actually situations in which they do have a choice. The moment of reflection recommended by the Stoics may provide the psychological space to make that choice.

One last point regarding the Stoics is especially relevant in a society dominated by immediate gratification. Highly pleasure-oriented Western society, which always talks of freedom, may actually block it. The Stoics say that people who are hedonists—pleasure-seekers—have given up their freedom to whatever pleasure happens to be in front of them at the moment. Freedom means responsibility of personal choice and there is an inverse relationship between the ability to choose one's life and the degree to which one is led around by one's emotions and desires. I am certainly not advocating the Stoic extreme about emotions here. Epictetus and other Stoics often sound cold and are too aloof from the pain around them. They seem to get little joy out of life. Nevertheless, I believe the fundamental Stoic point is a powerful one: If a person realizes his or her thoughts, actions, and responses are literally his or hers to decide, a person may find he or she actually has more options in real life (Putman, 2004).

Sartre and the Existentialists

The Aristotelian and Stoic traditions dominated philosophical discussions of courage for well over 1,700 years. Medieval philosophers were especially good at adding to and modifying Aristotle's analysis. Saint Thomas Aquinas (trans. 1960) added the instructive point that courage includes patience. This is a useful way of differentiating courage from rashness. Among other things, the rash person lacks patience. In the 1700s David Hume raised two interesting issues about courage. First, observing courage tends to cause it to spread among the observers. So if one person can be courageous, the spirit of that act (through what Hume called *sympathy*) can increase the level of bravery in those around that individual (Hume, 1777/1975). This is clearly true in times of war. Second, Hume (1777/1975) pointed out that excesses beyond the mean in courage can destroy other virtues. So societies, or parts of societies, in which courage becomes *the* virtue and is taken beyond the appropriate level can in many circumstances destroy or block virtues such as generosity, kindness, or understanding. Put in more modern language, these other virtues might be considered "soft." Hume's point can be put another way. It takes psychological courage to accept aspects of oneself that those around one may ridicule. If physical courage is pushed to the extreme in certain cultures or subcultures, there can be enormous social pressure against the expression of other interpersonal virtues. It takes psychological courage to live a well-rounded life in such cases. Psychological courage can help people face the fear of opening up to others.

Courage is again an important side issue in two of the most influential modern moral theories: John Stuart Mill's utilitarianism and Immanuel Kant's formalist or deontological perspective. For Mill, an act is right if it produces the greatest good for the greatest number in a situation. A courageous act that did not perform this function, that is, an act that was performed for self-centered or narrow goals would by Mill's account simply not count as ethical (Mill, 1863/1957). Now, it is important to note the word *situation* here. A person with a terminal illness who struggles against pain simply to see another sunrise would be acting courageously in that situation because the greatest number is one: the ill person. A mother defending her family against a flood may see many others suffering also but be unable to help families other than her own. Acts on behalf of her family, the greatest number possible in this case, would be courageous. Many cases of utilitarian courage include putting one's own life in danger for the greater good. One of the most cited examples of this involved the Dutch boat captains in World War II who helped Jewish families escape and often had to lie to the Nazis to achieve that good. These were truly courageous acts. What would not count for Mill would be to knowingly avoid a realistic greater good yet do something that looks courageous. This would be another one of those courageous "look-alikes" first mentioned by Aristotle. These are often very difficult cases. A soldier who saves himself and his best friend in a bold act when he knows he could have saved more with a different act did act courageously, but, as Mill would argue, his act was not the most ethical one because he knew he could have done more. One of the biggest problems in such cases, and one that plagues many veterans, is what *know* means in those situations of intense warfare: Did I actually *know* at the time I could have done more? If so, what could I have done? Forgiving oneself may involve having the psychological courage to work through many internal fears and anxieties carried over from the original situation. For many veterans the need for psychological courage replaces the former emphasis on physical courage. War and battle produce traumas and fears that require great courage to face.

Immanuel Kant argued that certain acts are right or wrong in themselves and that people have certain duties that have nothing to do with consequences (Kant, 1785/1964). For example, people have a duty to tell the truth even if the consequences will be bad. Similarly, a parent has a duty to be a good parent even if he or she does not feel like it at the time. Without my going into the background argument Kant made, it seems clear that courage, especially moral courage, would be a factor in many such situations. For example, I may want to lie to someone because, if I do not, my reputation will be damaged among my peer group, or, conversely, I may want to lie because it will greatly increase my reputation. It takes a great deal of courage to tell the truth in such cases. In the Milgram experiment the reason people stopped was often put in Kantian terms: "The moment the subject insists he wants to leave the experiment, I respect his judgment" (Milgram, 1974). Acting on such a Kantian principle required courage to safeguard the dignity of the other subject.

Though courage is an important virtue lying behind much moral theory, there is one school of modern thought for which courage is absolutely central: existentialism. Existentialism is my third example of the roots of courage in Western philosophy. This approach, which emphasizes at its core individual responsibility and having what is called *authenticity,* is usually considered to have started with the 19th-century Danish philosopher Soren Kierkegaard. For Kierkegaard courage was the central fact of life in facing up to the falseness and superficiality of mass society. This critique runs all through the existentialists but is developed most clearly in Jean-Paul Sartre.

Freedom and courage are intimately linked for Sartre. Sartre argued that humans have no a priori essence, that is, nothing exists in us that forces one to be anything or that is fulfilled if one does or does not do certain things. Human beings have no fixed essence. If humans have no essence ahead of time, then what people do will determine who they are. This has been phrased in a couple of ways. One is "you are your choices." A person literally is what he or she chooses to do. A somewhat more technical phrase is "existence precedes essence" for humans (Sartre, 1946/1957). In the animal world, essence precedes existence. The instincts (or biological essence) of a squirrel determine its actions. However, because humans have self-awareness, we may have biological tendencies but we are always capable of choosing our actions; these actions (existence) precede and establish what we become (essence). We may not think we are free to choose, but those restrictions are ones we put on ourselves in our mind. I may not think I can stop to help that injured person by the highway because I have an important meeting to get to, but of course I can stop. I let the meeting function as an excuse for not acting. Sartre really does not care whether I stop or not. What he objects to is the cowardice of running away from one's free choices by making excuses that act as absolute blocks to one's actions.

Such running away from free choices is called by almost all existentialists *inauthentic*. An authentic choice is one in which a person recognizes and accept his or her freedom to choose. An authentic life is one in which a person consistently accepts his or her freedom to choose and have a life that he or she constructed based on those free choices. Sartre gave many examples of such absolute freedom, but one of the most powerful is the ability to choose even death. Sartre was in the French Resistance in World War II and discussed the daily choice between dying and betrayal (Sartre, 1949/1965). When humans can choose death, even in the face of the biological drive for self-preservation, then all the little excuses they give themselves every day to avoid making choices are trivial in comparison.

Courage of all types is at the heart of authentic choices. Sartre's World War II example is physical courage combined with moral courage in the face of death, but psychological courage plays a major role here also. When people realize that they are actually free to choose in a situation, it creates what Sartre called *anguish* or what has often been called *existential anxiety* (1946/1957). Put another way, despite all the talk about freedom, most people really do not like making their own choices. They would rather have somebody else or society (or any number of possible sources) do it for them. (Milgram's experiment is again relevant.) When they do realize they have a choice, it creates a type of tension because *they* are responsible. That tension or sense of unease is existential anxiety. A good example of this might be put this way: If a person does not have existential anxiety before he or she gets married, he or she should not get married. Unless that person is marrying for reasons that other people or society have given him or her, that person will realize that this is his or her choice and it should create existential anxiety. The key is to face that anxiety courageously and work through it to make the best choice one can. The same would hold for a major life choice, such as a career. Making an authentic choice early in life may save a person from looking in the mirror 20 years later and realizing that his or her life has not been his or her own. Making authentic choices without excuses and working through existential anxiety is psychological courage in action.

One of the most common ways people avoid choices and responsibility is through self-deception. This lying to oneself Sartre called "bad faith" (1943/1965). Thanks in large part to Sartre, philosophy now has a rich literature on self-deception. Some issues raised are whether self-deception is even possible

(Can a person actually lie to him- or herself?), whether self-deception is ever moral (Isn't denial in some cases the best course at the time?), and how people deal with self-deception. I close this section with some analysis of this third point and the role courage plays in facing the truth. Much of this is based on Sartre's ground-breaking work on freedom, self-deception, and courage.

People have many clever ways to avoid making choices and deceiving themselves. One is willful ignorance (Martin, 1986). People may deliberately not want to know something because, if they do know it, it means they would have to exercise their freedom and make a choice. A parent of a child who consistently gets in trouble may do everything possible to remain ignorant of the details. That way it is easier to let the situation ride and not have to face any tough choices. Such an individual does not want to face the fact of his or her freedom and would rather remain blissfully ignorant (we all are, in fact, prone to this). To actually come to grips with the issue, the person must have psychological courage.

Another technique has been called *systematic ignoring* (Martin, 1986). Here the individual is aware of the evidence but avoids thinking about it because it would require acknowledging responsibility and making choices. Two of the techniques to do this are blocking and distraction. Every time the problem area comes up in thought, the person represses it so quickly (with just the slightest tinge of emotional awareness) that he or she quickly again feels safe. Distraction is also common. If the topic happens to come up in conversation, the person might distract from it by quickly changing topics or if it comes up in his or her thought process, he or she immediately distracts him- or herself, perhaps by having another drink or doing another report for work. Indeed, one of the most common ways for the modern person to maintain self-deception is to keep busy all the time. If a person constantly seeks the latest pleasures or keeps working all the time, he or she never has to sit down and think about what he or she has done in life or what choices he or she has to face. The goal of this behavior is not genuine pleasure or productive work but to run away from facing one's life. Overcoming tendencies to block or distract can take enormous psychological courage.

A third technique people often use is rationalization (Martin, 1986). Here the upsetting situation or information is allowed into consciousness, but people hide its significance with phony reasons that take away their choices and responsibility. People often do this by hiding behind their roles. To go back to the roadside accident example mentioned earlier, I may say something to myself along the lines of "I am a carpenter, not a doctor. I can't do anything. But of course I can try; I just don't want to make that decision." People develop all kinds of rationalizations. Common ones are giving responsibility to some group ("Society expects it"), claiming helplessness ("I'm not a doctor. What can I do?"), or hiding behind a claim to innocence ("It's not my fault!"). In all these cases people are avoiding existential anxiety by covering up the fact that they actually do have a choice or some responsibility. Courage is the central virtue in overcoming the human tendency to rationalize and allowing people to grapple with fears involved in making choices.

Granting that existentialist philosophers often disagree among themselves, are often inconsistent, and often make assumptions that can be questioned, they are still owed a huge debt of gratitude for raising consciousness about the role of courage in everyday decision making. Sartre said at one point that people are "condemned to be free" (1946/1957). Whereas other philosophers view such decision-making power more as a gift than as a condemnation, Sartre was completely accurate in pointing out that this freedom, whether gift or condemnation, is something people very often try their hardest to avoid. People are simply afraid of life's decisions and responsibilities far too much. People easily become experts at psychological cowardice. For the existentialists, courage is the virtue that allows people to express fully their unique human freedom.

An Eastern Perspective on Courage

Before I close, a brief note about courage and Eastern philosophies is in order. Physical and moral courage are central to the practical philosophy of Confucius. *Jen* (good will), *yi* (justice), and *te* (power of moral principle) have no substance unless performed in both easy and difficult situations. Many of the writings of Confucius emphasize firmness and integrity in the face of negative social pressures to do wrong (Confucius, trans. 1992). The remaining major Eastern perspectives (Hinduism, Taoism, Buddhism) emphasize expanding and deepening mental awareness. Though they differ about the goal of increasing awareness (e.g., Brahman in Hinduism, the Tao or nature in Taoism), for all of them positive actions are not the focus of attention per se but follow from greater awareness.

A case in point is Buddhism. Zen is a useful example of the relationship of courage and awareness. Zen points out that the vast majority of human thinking is rooted in stereotypes of one degree or another about the past or future. For example, a word such as *student* or *rose* gives rise to a concept based on past experience that then provides a tool for dealing with future experiences of students or roses. This is necessary for functioning in the social and natural worlds. It has deep evolutionary roots in the need to survive. However, one then constantly has a disconnect between one's thought process and where one actually is at the moment—the now. A metaphor used innumerable times in Zen is balancing a pencil on one's finger and putting the index finger of one's other hand on top of the pencil at the balance point. One's mind is constantly going left or right on that pencil scale, concerned about the past or future, but one is actually living at the balance point, the moving current moment. An excellent example of this in practice is the sense of wonder experienced at something new: the first flower in spring, the first snow, a newborn child. Very soon thereafter, however, as Zen writers note, one's mind narrows and one now "knows" about these things (Chodron, 1991). Flowers, snow, and children become categories of thought and one lives in one's patterns of thought, not in the actual moments of one's life. A major goal of meditation and part of Zen's metaphysical belief is that being able to live fully in the now unites a person with the world around him or her, temporarily abolishes the illusion of "self," and has a deep and resounding spiritual quality.

However, aside from the metaphysics, what does this have to do with courage? In many cases self-discipline and self-reflection are more important than courage, but in many other situations courage is critical because people are afraid to let go of concepts that give comfort or reinforce personal needs. An example is the way someone may stereotype another person—one's spouse or "boss," for example. In a relationship, one clings to old images and stereotypes, what one writer called our *superstructure* (Beck, 1989). One clings to the past because it is genuinely frightening to give up one's own ego needs and security level to actually be with the person in front of one, to see how he or she actually is or has become. Understanding of the other cannot grow unless old images can be modified or discarded and people are often afraid to do that. Routines and preestablished thinking are so easy. Being in the moment and breaking down old ways of thinking, especially when it comes to other people, can take enormous courage.

One might notice a relationship between the Zen emphasis on openness and courage in thinking and the existentialist emphasis on avoiding self-deception. The difference is that self-deception is one particularly destructive way of living in one's own thought patterns. The Zen point is broader. Being open to the flower one is standing in front of, being open to the person who, after 15 years, one thinks one "knows," and being open to a drinking problem that, right now, is ruining one's life are all part of the same process for Zen. It is a process of living in the now, being aware of what is actually around and within oneself, and acknowledging that reality. Many people who may be courageous when it comes to physical courage are terrified of being open psychologically to individuals or facts that threaten them in the moment. Courage for Zen, and for much Eastern thought, is primarily psychological courage. Death of the psyche, which people fear will occur if they increase their awareness and change their habitual thought patterns, may be as terrifying for many as the fear of physical injury or death. Courage in the Zen tradition means facing that fear.

Summary

The concept of courage thus has a long and rich history in philosophy. Aristotle's analysis of physical courage, with its emphasis on making a difference through action, is still one that inspires modern ethicists. By adding the dimension of maintaining personal integrity in the face of factors in the world that cannot be controlled, the Stoics brought moral courage to the forefront. Courage was not just something soldiers need to be concerned about. All people must deal with the pains and difficulties of life and how a person handles those is a function of courage. The existentialists pushed the concept to the heart of human life. Courage is not just about acting or reacting to the environment. It is about who a person is going to *be*. Finally, Zen emphasizes the courage it takes to be open to the moment, to overcome the constant fear of giving up thought processes that have become comfortable and routine. Zen pushes psychological courage to the forefront. Into this framework comes the scientific study of courage. What exactly is this thing called *courage* that philosophers have praised for 2,500 years? That is the subject of the remainder of the volume.

References

Aquinas, T. (1960). *St. Thomas Aquinas: Philosophical texts* (T. Gilby, Trans.). New York, NY: Galaxy Books.

Aristotle. (1985). *Nicomachean ethics* (T. Irwin, Trans.). Indianapolis, IN: Hackett Publishing.

Beck, C. (1989). *Everyday Zen: Love and work* (S. Smith, Ed.). San Francisco, CA: Harper-SanFrancisco.
Chodron, P. (1991). *The wisdom of no escape*. Boston, MA: Shambhala.
Confucius. (1992). *The essential Confucius* (T. Cleary, Trans.). San Francisco, CA: Harper-SanFrancisco.
Epictetus. (1983). *The handbook of Epictetus* (N. White, Trans.). Indianapolis, IN: Hackett.
Hume, D. (1975). *Enquiries concerning human understanding and concerning the principles of morals* (3rd ed.). Oxford, England: Clarendon Press. (Original work published 1777)
Kant, I. (1964). *Groundwork of the metaphysic of morals* (H. S. Paton, Trans.). New York, NY: Harper & Row. (Original work published 1785)
Latané, B., & Darley, J. (1970). *The unresponsive bystander: Why doesn't he help?* New York, NY: Appleton-Century-Crofts.
Martin, M. (1986). *Self-deception and morality*. Lawrence: University Press of Kansas.
Milgram, S. (1974). *Obedience to authority*. New York, NY: Harper & Row.
Mill, J. S. (1957). *Utilitarianism*. Indianapolis, IN: Bobbs-Merrill. (Original work published 1863)
Phillips, M. (2005). *The gift of valor*. New York, NY: Broadway Books.
Putman, D. (2004). *Psychological courage*. Lanham, MD: University Press of America.
Sartre, J. P. (1957). *Existentialism and human emotions* (H. Barnes & B. Frechtman, Trans.). New York, NY: Citadel Press. (Original work published 1943 and 1946)
Sartre, J. P. (1965). *The philosophy of Jean-Paul Sartre* (multiple trans.). New York, NY: Random House. (Original work published 1936)
Soccio, D. (2001). *Archetypes of wisdom* (4th ed.). Belmont, CA: Wadsworth.

2

Folk Conceptualizations of Courage

Shane J. Lopez, Heather N. Rasmussen, William P. Skorupski, Kristin Koetting, Stephanie E. Petersen, and Ya-Ting Yang

Courage is a universal virtue lauded throughout the course of history, across Eastern and Western cultures, and by women and men from all walks of life. Personal narratives, historical accounts, and folk conceptualizations of courage have helped create a shared though basic understanding of the phenomenon; common knowledge facilitates daily conversations about the virtue.

Despite thousands of years of discussing courage, the canon of world literature and the scholarship in theology, philosophy, psychology, and associated health fields have not gone too far beyond the question that Confucius examined with his disciples and that Socrates posed to Laches: "What is courage?" This core question has sparked many other investigations into courage, and literature addressing these issues seems sparse and disjointed (for essays, see Mack, 2004, and for reviews, see Lopez, O'Byrne, & Petersen, 2003; O'Byrne, Lopez, & Petersen, 2000; Peterson & Seligman, 2004; Snyder & Lopez, 2007). Our consideration of the literature focused on the distinctions between forms of courage (physical, moral, and vital; proposed in O'Byrne, Lopez, & Petersen), and our examination of the construct targeted the commonalities of our implicit theories about the virtue.

The Many Forms of Courage

Efforts to construct a socially relevant view of courage transported it from the heart of the brave soldier on the battlefield to the experience of daily life of every person. Accordingly, two groups of scholars (O'Byrne, Lopez, & Petersen, 2000; Peterson & Seligman, 2004) developed similar expanded classifications of forms of courage. O'Byrne, Lopez, and Petersen identified three forms of the virtue: physical, moral, and vital. Physical courage involves the attempted maintenance of societal good by the expression of physical behavior that is grounded in the pursuit of socially valued goals (e.g., a firefighter saving a child from a burning building). Moral courage is the behavioral expression of authenticity in the face of the discomfort of dissension, disapproval, or rejection (e.g., a politician invested in a "greater good" voting in an unpopular manner in a meeting). Vital courage refers to the perseverance through a personal struggle or disease or disability, even when the outcome is ambiguous (e.g., a child with a heart transplant maintaining her intensive treatment regimen even though her prognosis is uncertain).

Peterson and Seligman's (2004) values in action classification presents courage as a core human virtue made up of the strengths of authenticity (i.e., representing oneself to others and the self in a sincere fashion), enthusiasm/zest (i.e., thriving or having a sense of vitality in a challenging situation), industry/perseverance (i.e., taking on tasks and challenges and finishing them), and valor (i.e., taking physical, intellectual, and emotional stances in the face of danger).

Both systems of classifying courage are based on a basic assumption: The construct of courage may be best understood by focusing on the shared and unique dimensions of the different types or forms of courage. With this assumption in mind, we distill the literature on physical, moral, and vital courage, and we consider implicit theories of courage in light of this classification system.

Physical Courage: The Battlefield and Beyond

Andreia, or military courage, defined the "brave soldier" in ancient Greece. Finding the rugged path between cowardice and foolhardiness distinguished a soldier as courageous and hence more valuable to the force. That disposition to act appropriately in situations involving fear and confidence on the battlefield seems to be universally valued throughout history (Rorty, 1988). It is believed that military courage is a subtype of physical courage, but this hypothesis has yet to be empirically examined.

In 20th century America, fiction writers became the primary purveyors of courage, and their writing fueled a fascination with the virtue. Ernest Hemingway marveled at the physical courage displayed in a variety of arenas (the battlefield, the open sea, the bull-fighting arena), and his writings seem to mirror the fascination that Americans had with staring danger in the face and persevering. In fact, the "Hemingway code" (i.e., living a life characterized by strength, knowledge, and courage) provided a code of conduct for many Americans.

Physical courage became the focus of Jack Rachman's research after he realized that the strength was the mirror image of the fear associated with physical jeopardy, and some people deal with the perceived danger better than do others. Rachman (1984) worked with various military personnel to gather information on the nature of courage. He found that the courageous persevere and make a quick physiological recovery. He also suggested that courageous acts are not necessarily confined to a special few, nor do they always take place in public. In regard to this latter point, his formal research augmented what he observed about the inner battles and private courage displayed by his psychotherapy clients. In light of his work in the field, lab, and therapy office, he concluded that there clearly was more to courage than *andreia* and related physical conquests over danger.

Moral Courage: Doing What Is Best and Authentic

It is apparent from the writings of Plato on Socrates' moral courage that a person can display physical as well as moral courage. As Putman (1997) noted, Socrates endured in the fight to protect Athens from conquest, but he fought a more difficult battle when he defended "a greater moral good *against* society" (p. 1).

John F. Kennedy was fascinated by courage. He spent years gathering stories of statesmen who followed their hearts and principles when determining what was "best" for the American people—even when constituents did not agree with their decision making or value their representation. Although Kennedy himself was a military hero, he lauded moral, or political, courage in his *Profiles in Courage* (1956).

Authenticity and integrity may be the fulfillments most closely associated with the expression of personal views and values in the face of dissension and rejection. Exactly when should one take a stand? Rosa Parks said that she took a seat at the front of a bus because it was time to do so. Others (e.g., Finfgeld, 1998; Shelp, 1984) have maintained that in a health care context, providers display moral courage in part by being truthful and straightforward. This form of courage can take on still another face when an individual stands up to someone with power over him or her (e.g., boss) for the greater good, and individuals displaying moral courage often are at risk of social disapproval (Putman, 1997).

Vital Courage: Fighting for Life

In our estimation, vital courage is at work as a person battles personal struggles and illness (through surgery and medication) and perseveres with efforts at change and with treatment and counseling regimens. Health professionals use their expertise and, sometimes, vital courage to save lives or to improve the quality of life of those they serve. Many researchers have examined vital courage (though not calling it such), and their work has captured the phenomenon that captivates people when hearing about someone facing life adversity or chronic illness.

Haase (1987) used a phenomenological approach to study the subjective experiences of courage in nine chronically ill adolescents and to uncover the essential structure of courage in the face of illness. Through this process Haase found that the "lived experience" (p. 69) of courage is an interpersonally assigned attribute that results from living in a specific manner (i.e., developing personal awareness, successfully dealing with "minisituations" of courage, building on episodes of courage) through the experience of having a health condition. Finfgeld (1998), in interviews about courage with middle-aged and older adults with illnesses, concluded that being courageous is a lifelong process involving factors such as significant others, values, and hope. Participants in Finfgeld's (1995) study indicated that struggle or threat elicited courage in their lives and that courageous behavior has the potential for creating a sense of equanimity, personal integrity, and absence of regret about one's life.

Psychological courage, as Putman (1997) described it, is strength in facing one's destructive habits. This form of vital courage may be quite common as everyone struggles with psychological challenges in the forms of stress, sadness, and dysfunctional or unhealthy relationships. In light of these threats to psychological stability, people stand up to their dysfunction by restructuring their beliefs or systematically desensitizing themselves to the fears. Putman went on to say that in pop culture, many physically courageous and morally courageous icons are presented in literary works and movies, but there are few exemplars of psychologically courageous individuals. It is also possible, however, that vital courage is new relative to moral and physical courage, which have been acknowledged since ancient times.

The Purpose of Mixed-Methods Examination of Folk Conceptualizations of Courage

Classic literature and scholarship have provided us with broad and basic information on courage, and classification systems seem to have become appropriately expansive and detailed to organize our knowledge. In an effort to build our knowledge base, we designed four interconnected studies to examine folk conceptualizations (i.e., implicit theories) of courage to identify common characteristics and to explore how different forms of this universal virtue are manifested in daily life. Implicit theories, which are personal constructions about phenomena that reside in the minds of individuals (Furnham, 1988; Sternberg, Conway, Ketron, & Bernstein, 1981), can, and often do, spark the development of explicit, scientific theories. Though implicit theories can be inconsistent in the explanation of phenomena, they tend to be fairly descriptive of types of phenomena (Furnham, 1988) and can account for both personal and social aspects of constructs and associated affective reactions and behavioral choices. Indeed, collection and examination of implicit theories has been successful in generating further research and theory development for constructs such as intelligence and wisdom (Clayton, 1982; Sternberg, 1985).

Data collection procedures included open-ended questions, focused discussions, a repertory grid, and a Web-based survey (in that order) with the goal of systematically narrowing the scope of ideas shared by participants. Data reduction procedures moved from open coding to grounded theory analysis to grid examination to factor analyses. Participants included graduate students, professionals, and community samples on three continents. Study 1 (Ten Questions on Courage) was an exploratory study that examined the answers to questions such as "What is courage?" Study 2 (The Focus Group on Courage) used ground-theory methodology to examine the facilitated discussion of professionals considered to be "observers of courage." Study 3 (The Repertory Grid Examination of Courage) used personal construct psychology tools and technology to examine descriptions of courage. Study 4 (The Web-Based Scaling Project) used information gained from the first three studies and exploratory factor analysis to summarize participants' views of courage.

Study 1: Ten Questions on Courage

The scholarly examination of the construct has not produced what could be considered a comprehensive operationalization of courage. Therefore, the purpose of Study One: Ten Questions on Courage was to initiate our exploration of implicit theories on courage and to summarize the folk concepts via open coding.

Method

PARTICIPANTS. The first sample consisted of American students in a graduate-level class in education ($n = 38$). The second sample of participants from India and Greece (and the Greek portion of Cyprus) were contacted primarily because those countries are the origin of several philosophers who have historically discussed courage (i.e., Ancient Greek philosophers and Indian philosophers of Hindu and Buddhist traditions). Colleagues who had contacts in India and Greece identified potential participants. A total of 14 Indian individuals (males = 5, females = 9; mean age = 31.58; $SD = 6.52$) and 12 Greek individuals (males = 10, females = 2; mean age = 27.64; $SD = 1.74$) completed the questionnaire. Graduate students completed the survey in class, and the international participants submitted the survey via e-mail.

PROCEDURE. The two-part survey had a qualitative section and a quantitative section, each consisting of five questions or requests. The qualitative section consisted of (a) What is courage?; (b)What is courage NOT?; (c) Tell me about one time you displayed courage; (d) Tell me about a time when you were less than courageous; and (e) Tell me about an event that exemplifies courage in your mind.

An existing measure of courage—five items used in a Gallup Organization survey examining the wellsprings of life—was used to see how people rate themselves on a brief courage scale. The five items are (a) I have taken a stand in the face of strong resistance; (b) I sometimes call for action while others talk; (c) Challenges increase my determination; (d) I can keep cool while others are freaking out; and (e) I express my courage several times a day. Response options ranged from *strongly agree* (1) to *strongly disagree* (5).

Results

Two independent raters used open coding to summarize the answers to the five qualitative questions into themes. In the open coding process (Strauss & Corbin, 1998), data were broken down into concepts (units of meaning), labeled (typically with words close to those used by the participants), and interrogated (gaps filled). The coded units of meaning were compared with one another, and slowly the concepts were grouped into larger categories. As additional data were considered, these coded concepts were compared with existing data and categorized (or recategorized). (For a review of the qualitative data, see Table 2.1.)

The major themes that surfaced in response to the question "What is courage?" across samples included (a) taking risks even in the face of possible failure, negative consequences, or uncertainty; (b) possessing a particular attitude; and (c) defending beliefs. The theme of "inner strength" emerged only for the Indian sample.

One major theme emerged from the three samples in response to the question "What is courage NOT?": "hiding, backing down, or giving up." "Not standing up for morals" surfaced only for the Indian sample in response to "What is courage NOT?" whereas only the Greek sample answered "taking the easy route"

Table 2.1. Major Themes From Study 1 Qualitative Responses

Participants	What is courage?	What is courage NOT?	A time you displayed courage?	A time when you were less than courageous?	An event that exemplifies courage in your mind?
Graduate student sample $n = 38$	(1) taking risks even in the face of possible failure, negative consequences, and/or uncertainty, (2) a particular attitude, (3) facing challenges, and (4) defending beliefs	(1) weakness, (2) action or behaviors with no risk involved, (3) no strong beliefs or convictions, (4) selfish reasons for action, (5) fear/panic/self-doubt, and (6) hiding/backing down/giving up/avoidance	(1) moving into new situation alone, (2) saving someone, (3) keeping positive attitude during a difficult time, (4) challenging self or another (like a boss), and (5) childbirth/raising children	(1) refraining from taking action or engaging in confrontation, (2) giving into family/peer pressure, and (3) not taking a stand for a belief	(1) saving a life, (2) standing up for beliefs, (3) living with disability/disease, and (4) keeping a positive attitude at difficult times
Asian Indian sample $n = 14$	(1) taking risks even in the face of possible failure, negative consequences, and/ or uncertainty, (2) a particular attitude, (3) facing challenges, (4) defending beliefs, and (5) inner strength	(1) weakness, (2) action or behaviors with no risk involved, (3) selfish reasons for action, (4) hiding/backing down/giving up/avoidance, (5) no inner strength, and (6) not standing up for morals	(1) moving into new situation alone, (2) saving someone, (3) challenging self or another (persons and government), (4) helping another through illness, and (5) true to self (inner strength)	(1) refraining from taking action or engaging in confrontation and (2) giving in to fear, avoidance	(1) saving a life, (2) standing up for beliefs, (3) overcoming tragedy/disaster, and (4) soldiers going to war
Greek sample $n = 12$	(1) taking risks even in the face of possible failure, negative consequences, and/or uncertainty, (2) a particular attitude, and (3) defending beliefs	(1) hiding/backing down/giving up/avoidance, (2) and taking the easy route	(1) taking a stand, (2) engaging in physically courageous acts, and (3) taking difficult route/making difficult decisions	(1) not following through on an action and (2) not taking a stand for a belief	(1) physical acts of courage and (2) standing up for morals or beliefs

for this particular question. (See Table 2.1 for themes associated with personal examples of courage or lack of courage.)

With regard to descriptions of events that exemplify courage, similar themes across the three samples included standing up for beliefs and physical acts of courage, specifically saving a life. Only the graduate student sample from the Midwestern university answered "keeping a positive attitude in difficult times" as an event exemplifying courage.

Means and standard deviations are reported for the quantitative questions (see Table 2.2). Mean responses across the groups ranged from 1.42 (*strongly agree / agree*) to 3.0 (*neutral*). Comparisons between the samples should be made with caution because the groups do not have equal sample sizes and the number of participants is low. Thus, only trends in the data are reviewed here. For each of the questions, the mean for the Asian Indian sample was higher (closer to neutral) than the mean of the Greek and the American graduate student sample with the exception of "I can keep my cool while others are freaking out." Accordingly, the Asian Indian participants were least likely to endorse the response that they express their courage several times a day, whereas the American graduate student participants were most likely to agree with that statement.

Discussion

Participants' conceptualizations of what courage is (and is not) seemed to be fairly consistent across cultures. Though some participants framed it as an attitude, others considered it an "inner strength." The participants collectively highlighted the role of risk in the face of uncertain or negative outcomes and described courage as rising to the occasion that demands such. These findings are consistent with those deduced from another study (Philips, 2004), which suggested that courage involves facing risk or overcoming fear for a noble purpose.

Means for quantitative questions indicated that, on average, all participants were neutral or affirmative when asked if they possessed or demonstrated

Table 2.2. Means and Standard Deviations From the Well-Springs Measure

Item	American Graduate Student Responses $n = 38$ Mean (*SD*)	Greek Responses $n = 12$ Mean (*SD*)	Asian Indian Responses $n = 14$ Mean (*SD*)
I have taken a stand in the face of strong resistance.	1.79 (0.70)	1.66 (0.89)	2.43 (0.85)
I sometimes call for action while others talk.	1.92 (0.49)	1.66 (0.65)	2.57 (1.09)
Challenges increase my determination.	1.71 (0.65)	1.42 (0.90)	2.43 (1.09)
I can keep cool while others are freaking out.	1.92 (0.71)	2.58 (0.99)	2.07 (0.92)
I express my courage several times a day.	2.52 (0.76)	2.83 (1.19)	3.0 (0.78)

Note. 1 = *strongly agree;* 2 = *agree;* 3 = *neutral;* 4 = *disagree;* 5 = *strongly disagree.*

courage. Americans were most likely to report courageous behavior; Asian Indians were least likely to do so. In general, these results suggest that ordinary people may see themselves as being capable of courageous behavior (Lopez, O'Byrne, & Petersen, 2003; Putman, 2001; Woodard, 2004). Effects of humility and social desirability on responding are unknown.

Limitations of the Study

The study was exploratory in nature. Participants were members of convenient samples and, therefore, the thematic findings may not generalize to all groups.

Study 2: The Focus Group on Courage

Study 1 demonstrated that participants were capable of accessing and sharing their folk conceptualizations of courage. In Study 2, we attempted to examine the conceptualizations of the construct in more depth by inviting "observers of courage" to participate in a facilitated discussion. The questions posed to the focus group were determined on review of the literature and the results of Study 1.

Method

PARTICIPANTS. A focus group consisting of six members from various professions (graduate student in school counseling, middle school teacher, former college basketball coach and educational leader, long-time Catholic priest, Navy Captain and Reserve Officers' Training Corps commander, philosopher studying Martin Luther King, Jr.) participated in a guided discussion about courage in daily life. These individuals (all Caucasian and long-time residents of the Midwestern United States) were invited to participate because they were believed to be frequent "observers of courage" given their biographies and vocations. The group was led by a trained focus group facilitator and lasted 1 hour.

The proceedings were taped via video camera. The audio of the tape was then transcribed and reviewed for accuracy.

PROCEDURE. The text from the focus group was subjected to a three-part analysis (open coding, axial coding, and collaboration and consolidation), following the ground theory approach outlined by Strauss and Corbin (1998). Open coding involved two researchers independently identifying the significant categories discussed by the focus group participants. Each response was examined and a theme extracted from the text. After every unique response had been identified, prevalent themes of development, risk, training, whether people or actions are courageous, and forms of courage emerged. Once the categories were identified, a second round of coding, axial coding, extracted details about the structure of these categories. Axial coding is a line-by-line analysis of the text that examines the "who, what, why, how" questions for each of the themes already identified.

Finally, the two researchers met to complete the collaboration and consolidation phase of the analysis. Through review and discussion, the researchers found that their individual efforts were consistent.

Results

The themes and related details identified through coding are described in this section. Verbatim responses are shared to exemplify the types of comments that contributed to the identification of the theme.

DEVELOPMENT OF COURAGE. The participants described the development of courage as being dependent on a strong system of personal values. For instance, "It's what the person is made of; they may be influenced by circumstances in one's life, but there's an inner core of values that becomes evident when circumstances call for courageous actions." Values and associated courage were believed to be modeled and reinforced by others in society and by one's culture.

PRESENCE OF RISK. Participants noted that people exhibit courage in the face of risk and that risk could be construed in terms of adversity or fear. Over the course of the discussion, the group identified numerous exemplars of courage (e.g., Winston Churchill, Lt. Col. Doolittle, Martin Luther King, Jr.) and contended that the experience of adversity bonds them all ("In talking about that list, it seemed like there was some kind of adversity. The people are put in difficult situations."). Furthermore, participants noted that adversity encourages or demands people to rise to the occasion ("I think of Winston Churchill. In the absence of war he was an awful prime minister; in the presence of war he was superlative."). With regard to a courageous response to adversity, one participant stated, "Think about all the people with severe multiple disabilities that, despite that, have made important differences in the world and in the lives of others."

Courage and fear were inextricably linked in the comments of the participants, as exemplified by statements such as "fear immobilizes . . . courage does the opposite. It allows us to put feet to whatever we believe in" and "I think they are connected. There is something in overcoming the fear that is inherent in the exercise of courage." The group also agreed that courage does not banish fear ("I think courageous people can still be afraid.").

EFFECTS OF SPECIALIZED TRAINING ON COURAGE. Specialized training, such as that completed by military personnel or lifeguards, may foster the development of courage. Participants argued that training for a job that requires regular acts of facing adversity or fear serves to link responsibility to the *job* of being courageous. In other words, as participants explained, some specialized training organizes action and instills skills ("you have the tools for courage by virtue of training") and provides "tools to deal with the unimaginable." There was some discussion that training potentially obligates a first responder (e.g., firefighter and police officer) to face adversity or fear in a manner that is different than would be expected by someone without a special background.

Courageous Acts and Courageous People. "How can you say a person is characteristically courageous if that trait of character never had an opportunity to be manifested?" Participants grappled with this question throughout the discussion hour and did not reach consensus about whether courage was a character trait or a descriptor of an action. Both views about courage were endorsed: (a) some people act courageously throughout their lives as a result of a value system they possess or because of training and (b) other people practice "situational courage" or commit a courageous act when a dire situation demands it.

Forms of Courage. The participants specifically discussed "situational courage," "ordinary courage," "visionary courage," and "moral courage." Situational courage involves an "extreme circumstance that pushes people" to self-sacrifice. This is contrasted with ordinary courage that involves meeting the "demands of each day." Visionary courage requires "thinking you can make a difference" and "buck[ing] the accepted way of seeing the world." Similarly, the description of moral courage emphasized standing up for what one believes despite being backed by "very few people."

Across the types of courage, participants proffered that there were private and public displays of courage. Private courage is displayed by those unsung for their acts whereas public courage often carries the "hero" tag.

Discussion

Participants in Study 2 noted that courage is built on a bedrock of values, is modeled and reinforced by others in society and by one's culture, and is made more possible if a person engages in specialized training. Contemporary courage theorists and researchers have commented on how values, or more specifically moral education and moral habits, set the stage for courage and how training facilitates the manifestation of courage. Pears (2004) argued that people are more capable of courage if they have had an adequate moral education. Similarly, Cavanaugh and Moberg (1999) described a cognitive developmental process by which courage becomes a good moral habit over time as people act deliberately and consistently to approximate the virtue. Then, when a situation demands courage, the moral habits can be strung together. Also commenting on the development of courage, Haase (1987) proposed that developing personal awareness and building on successful attempts to overcome adversity can foster courage in every person.

Specialized training received by first responders and military personnel does appear to facilitate the development of cognitive, emotional, and physical skills needed in overwhelming, life-threatening situations (Rachman, 1978, 1984, 2004). Participants in Study 2 did not address training associated with courage other than that needed for valor. They did discuss but did not resolve whether a first responder needs to do more than is required of him or her by duty or obligation to be considered courageous.

The group of courage observers certainly considered risk to be a precursor to courage and their discussions framed risk in two ways: adversity and fear. Comments about adversity seem to suggest that a cognitive appraisal of a bad situation takes place and then courageous action is chosen. The topic of fear introduced emotion into the focused discussion for the first time. Participants appeared to believe that fear is present when courageous action is taken and that fear is not resolved as a result of courage.

With regard to the ongoing debate about whether the unit of analysis for courage should be people or actions (for a discussion, see Lopez, O'Byrne, & Petersen, 2003), the group was split. That is, some participant commentary suggested that people are courageous as a result of a value system they possess or because of specialty training, and other comments indicated that all are capable of courageous acts when dire situations arise and future research should focus on acts rather than actors. (There was consensus that the social context influences courage, as discussed later.)

Participants' comments generated descriptions of forms of courage that included "situational courage," "ordinary courage," and "visionary courage." These add to the list that we have proffered (moral courage, physical courage, and vital courage) and to the forms discussed elsewhere (e.g., intellectual courage, military courage, political courage, psychological courage, social courage). Though little consensus was reached about the most prevalent forms of courage, the participants' discussion along with the literature review suggest that people have expanded their view of courage beyond that which takes place on the battlefield.

Study 2 participants also made a distinction between public and private forms of courage. This breakdown is supported by the findings of Asarian (1981) and Pury, Kowalski, and Spearman (2007). Asarian described two forms of courage—assertive/determined and dignified acceptance—that parallel the public and private forms, respectively. In making the distinction, Asarian discussed how the social context is an important aspect to consider in the examination of courage. Courage often is not recognized or experienced as courage without other individuals interpreting it as such. Without outside observers, courage easily can go unrecognized by the courageous actor; this could undermine the development of courage in the actor. Pury et al. distinguished general courage (actions that would be courageous for anyone; akin to public courage) from personal courage (actions that are courageous only for the particular actor; akin to private courage). Actions rated as high in general courage involved more confidence, less fear, and fewer personal limitations; personal courage was exhibited despite more fear and greater difficulty.

Study 2 and the work of Asarian (1981) and Pury et al. (2007) suggest that more examination of the influence of the social context on defining courage and deriving benefits from courage is needed.

Limitations of the Study

The focus group was semi-structured by questions derived from the findings of Study 1; because of these restrictions (and despite the fact that spontaneous interaction was encouraged) important aspects of the participant's experiences may not be included in the findings. Because of the nature of the data gathering, reported attitudes offered in a group setting may differ from actual attitudes. In addition, because of the number of participants, nature of the interview, selection process, and demographics of the current sample (all of the participants were Caucasian and long-time residents of the Midwest), these results cannot be generalized to all observers of courage.

Study 3: The Repertory Grid Examination of Courage

Over the course of the first two studies, we gathered numerous descriptors of courage that were subjected to thematic coding. Another method for exploring individuals' unique perspectives on courage involves having participants share their perspective on how two descriptors of courage are alike in a way that differentiates them from a third. Personal construct theory (Kelly, 1955, 1963, 1977) and its repertory grid allows for examination of the verbal construction of courage. In Study 3, we asked participants to tell us what courage is and what courage is not by completing a computer-based grid (Idiogrid; Grice, 2002) juxtaposing elements and constructs. This methodology also allowed us to consider cross-sectional differences (by age and sex) in conceptualizations of courage. The purpose of Study 3 was to further explore how courage is conceptualized and to examine how conceptualizations differ among young adults and older adults (baby boomers and older) and across men and women.

Method

PARTICIPANTS. Research participants included 49 young adults (18–22 years old) recruited from undergraduate courses offered at a large Midwestern university and 44 adults of the baby boom generation (according to the U.S. Census Bureau, those born between 1946 and 1964, when the number of births was substantially higher than in the period before or after) and beyond recruited via a snowball sampling technique. There was a large difference between the return rate of questionnaires for the younger and older samples. One hundred percent of the younger adults returned questionnaires (with 19 ultimately discarded from analyses because of an unusable grid), whereas 20% of the older adults returned questionnaires (with 16 discarded from analyses).

The majority of the student participants (71%; n = 34) were male; all were single. The majority (81.3%; n = 39) self-identified as Caucasian/White. Others indicated they were African American (14.6%; n = 7), Asian American (2.1%; n = 1), or Latino (2.1%; n = 1) (and one respondent did not provide information about race or ethnicity). Of the older participants (ages ranging from 43 to 84), 50% were male and 50% were female. The majority (68.2%; n = 30) reported they were married, and the remainder (31.8%) described themselves as single, divorced, or widowed. The vast majority of respondents (93.2%; n = 41) self-identified as Caucasian/White. One respondent reported being biracial, one African American, and one Asian American.

PROCEDURE. The repertory grid allows for the elicitation of elements (i.e., situations that exemplify courage) and constructs (i.e., descriptions of how the situations are alike or different from each other) before participants rate each element on the bipolar constructs. (The elicited repertory grid allows for participants' own views of courage, in contrast to supplying elements or constructs for participants to rate. By eliciting the participants' own courageous situations the grid was considered more personally meaningful, and eliciting constructs offered participants the chance to consider more personally salient descriptors on which to rate the elements.) Participants were asked to describe eight situations that represent courage ("List eight situations that exemplify courage to you."), then constructs were obtained through the triadic elicitation method. Respondents were instructed to consider a grouping of three situations and to identify how two of these are similar and different from the third ("You will be given 3 of the situations you listed above. Each time, think of a similarity between 2 of them, but not the third, then think of how the third is different. . . . Consider Situations B, E, and F from above. How are two of these alike in some important way, and in what way is the third situation different?"). The resulting descriptor word (i.e., construct) occupies one construct pole, and a description of the third "different" situation represents the other construct pole.

Each element was then rated with a 7-point scale (ranging from –3 to +3) for the set of constructs (i.e., which construct pole best describes the element?). The zero option on the scale allows the participant to indicate that the construct does not apply to the element, whereas the negative and positive numbers represent the emergent and implicit poles of the construct, respectively.

Elements and constructs are described subsequently (see Tables 2.3 and 2.4). The repertory grid summary indices of extremity (percentage of extreme ratings used suggests personal meaningfulness and significance of a construct;

Table 2.3. Summary Table of Elements Listed by Participants

Category	Total *N*
Stand for beliefs	147
Health issues	94
Rescue/safety	79
Occupations with risk	60
Educational/professional issues	47
Independence	43
Family issues	40
Public speaking/performance	40
Activities with risk	40
Perseverance/goals	34
Honesty	32
Relationships	31
Religious activities	13
Fear	9
Fight crime	8
Kindness to others	5

Note. *N* represents the total number of elements listed. Eighteen elements were mentioned only once.

Table 2.4. Summary Table of Constructs Listed by Participants

Category	Description	Total *N*
Self versus other	Does the situation involve oneself or others (or others in addition to oneself)?	57
Emotions	Feelings about a situation, such as fear or excitement	50
Beliefs, values	One's beliefs, value system, or morals	46
Consequences, outcomes	Consideration of the consequences of a situation or action	43
Risk, danger	Evaluation of the risk or danger involved in a given situation	42
Personal attributes	Such as patience, independence, responsibility, or selflessness	34
Decisions, choices	The need for a decision to be made in a situation	32
Helping, rescue	Act of helping another person or rescue of another	29
Persistence, determination	The determined effort demonstrated by a courageous actor	28
Harm, pain	The harm that is possible given the danger of a situation (i.e., death or physical injury)	25
Setting/location	Where a courageous action takes place, such as one's job; everyday action versus infrequent	23
Challenge level	Evaluation of the task as easy or difficult	16
Skills	Suggestion of skills or training being necessary to a courageous act	11
Action (passive versus active)	Evaluation of one being more active or passive in a situation	11
Strength	Suggestion of strength as a component to the situation	10
Honesty	Suggestion of honesty as a component to the situation	10
Permanent versus temporary	Evaluation of the situation being temporary or more permanent	9
Control	Amount of control one might have in the situation	6
Confrontation	Confrontation as part of a situation	5
Past event	Recall of an event that has happened in the past	3
Perception of others	Suggestion that the view of others besides the actor is a component of the courage	3
Patriotism	Pride in one's country as part of the situation	2
African American history	Courageous situation reflecting such history	2

Note. *N* represents the total number of participants who provided a given response. Ten additional elements were mentioned by only one respondent.

Neimeyer, Neimeyer, Hagans, & Van Brunt, 2002), matching (proportional measure of cognitive complexity; Bieri, 1955), intensity (degree of integration or differentiation; Fransella & Bannister, 1977), and ordination (the extent constructs differentiate among grid elements; Landfield & Cannell, 1988) also are considered. Finally, results of analyses of variance evaluating the differences in the grid summary indices across age and sex are reported.

Results

Participants identified 740 situations that exemplify courage (i.e., elements) with 507 unique constructs distinguishing the elements. Grid summary indices suggested that participants viewed the constructs as personally meaningful (extremity), demonstrated cognitively complex views of courage (matching), revealed a high degree of differentiation or tightness among constructs (intensity), and indicated that numerous constructs and elements successfully differentiated among each other (ordination). Analyses of variance were used to evaluate the differences across age groups (i.e., older and younger) and sex (i.e., male and female) for each grid summary index. There was one significant main effect of age for extremity analysis, F (1, 90) = 6.12, $p < .05$, whereby the responses of the older group of adults revealed that these participants considered courage more personally important and meaningful than did the younger participants. There were no additional significant main effects or significant interactions.

For analysis of elements provided by participants, categories were determined through a review of elements of courageous situations. Each element was viewed as an individual unit and compared with another to determine groupings according to similar content and theme. If an element did not match a given group already noted, then that element established a new group (see Table 2.3). Those courageous situations (i.e., elements) most frequently noted among all participants involve standing up for one's beliefs, dealing with health issues, and pursuing safety of oneself or another. These situations reflect all three of the aforementioned forms of courage (i.e., moral, vital, and physical courage, respectively). Younger adults most frequently listed situations related to standing up for one's beliefs, rescuing of another, and managing relationships (such as beginning or ending a relationship). In contrast, older adults most frequently listed situations related to dealing with health issues, followed by standing up for one's beliefs and rescuing of another.

Two undergraduate students independently coded all participant responses for the courageous situations for form of courage and achieved a 67.84% agreement rating (502 out of 740 responses). They then worked together to reach consensus on the remaining 238 responses on which they did not originally agree. Out of 740 responses, 351 were coded as moral courage, 216 as vital courage, and 173 as physical courage.

For analysis of constructs provided by participants, constructs were listed on individual note cards with the participant number of all who listed that particular construct. Constructs were considered according to the number of participants listing them, rather than the number of times they were listed. (The section of the repertory grid eliciting constructs allowed for use of repeated constructs by participants, and for that reason constructs were counted based not on the number of total occurrences but on the number of participants listing a given construct.) Table 2.4 summarizes the constructs. Those constructs most frequently noted involve oneself versus others (participant in the courageous situation), emotions (e.g., fear), beliefs and values, consideration of consequences, and evaluation of risks. Older adults most frequently noted the consequences or outcomes of a situation, along with whether the situation involved oneself or others, followed by beliefs and values and the risk or danger associated with a situation. Younger adults, though, most frequently noted emotions and involvement of self versus others, followed by the personal attributes necessary to act courageously and beliefs and values.

Discussion

Participants in Study 3 considered courage to be a personally meaningful construct and were sophisticated (i.e., cognitively complex) in describing what courage is and is not. No differences in approaches to describing courage existed across men and women, but the responses of the older group of adults revealed that these participants considered courage more personally important and meaningful than did the younger participants. Though it has been demonstrated that children and adults see courage differently (Szagun, 1992; 5- and 6-year-olds likened courage to the difficulty of the task at hand and being fearless, 8- and 9-year-olds likened courage to subjective risk taking and overcoming fear, and 11- and 12-year-olds reported that being fully aware of a risk at the time of acting is a necessary component of courage), little more is understood about true differences in how traditional college students see courage compared with their parents' and grandparents' generations and whether these cross-sectional differences are or are not associated with developmental trajectories.

Those courageous situations (i.e., elements) most frequently noted among the participants involve standing up for one's beliefs, dealing with health issues, and pursuing safety of oneself or another. Situations depicted moral, physical, and vital courage. Review of these situations suggests that both young adults and older adults see courage as something that could be beneficial to others (e.g., rescuing another) and themselves (e.g., standing up for personal beliefs), but, generally, elements involving dealing with health issues (addressing health problems, facing death of self or of loved one, providing care to others, quitting unhealthy behaviors) were listed by the older participants (81% of the time).

Those constructs most frequently used to distinguish among the situations involve the participant in the courageous event, emotions such as fear, beliefs and values, consideration of consequences, and evaluation of risks. These construct themes suggest behavioral, emotional, and cognitive aspects of courage.

Limitations of the Study

Limitations of this study have to do with the sampling procedure, the return rate for the older group of participants, and the difficulty of the repertory grid measure. The sampling procedure was different for the two groups; the younger participants could be considered a convenience sample, whereas the older participants were solicited via a snowball technique. There were more favorable conditions for the younger group completing the grid test (i.e., requesting participation from classes of individuals with time provided to complete if interested); the older participants typically completed it in private. This was particularly problematic because the repertory grid task is somewhat complex, tedious, and academic in nature. Anecdotal reports suggest that some older adults, working without the guidance of a proctor, found the task confusing. Neither the younger nor the older adult samples are considered representative of their respective peer groups, and hence generalizability of the findings may be limited.

Study 4: The Web-Based Scaling Project

Over the course of Studies 1, 2, and 3, participants shared nearly 800 descriptions of exemplars of courage, and in Study 4: The Web-Based Scaling Project we wanted to determine how "courage-like" their depictions of courage would be when rated by another group of participants. Furthermore, we wanted to be able to tell a more concise yet representative story of the implicit theory data. Therefore, we completed three data reduction procedures: We identified unique examples of courageous situations, subjected ratings of those courage stems to exploratory factor analysis, and considered the extent to which our classification system accounts for the findings from the factor analysis.

Method

PARTICIPANTS. This online study was completed by 130 participants. The majority (71.5%, $n = 93$) were female, ranging in age from 18 to 74 ($M = 38.74$, $SD = 13.11$). Over half of participants were currently married (56.6%, $n = 73$). Nearly one quarter (24%, $n = 31$) were never married. The remaining were in a committed relationship (though not legally married; 9.3%, $n = 12$), separated or divorced (7.8%, $n = 10$), or widowed (2.3%, $n = 3$). (One participant did not provide data on this item.)

Participants were asked an open-ended question about their race and ethnicity. The majority of respondents (76.1%, $n = 99$) self-identified as Caucasian/White. Others indicated they were Latina/Hispanic (6.2%, $n = 8$), multiethnic or biracial (3.1%, $n = 4$), African American (5.4%, $n = 7$), or Asian American (0.76%, $n = 1$). One participant (0.76%) indicated he or she was "other" (even though no such category was listed), and 10 respondents did not provide information on their ethnicity.

PROCEDURES. For the final study, we reviewed comments and responses from the previous three studies. We incorporated these participant-generated responses into stems to determine the extent those stems exemplified courage. After we deleted many stems to avoid redundancy, our final survey instrument included 73 stems, followed by 10 demographic questions. Participants were asked to consider for each stem, "To what extent does the behavior or characteristic exemplify courage?" and to respond based on the following scale: 1 = *Not at all*, 2 = *Barely*, 3 = *Somewhat*, 4 = *Mostly*, and 5 = *Very much*.

Participants were solicited via e-mail using a snowball technique and asked to complete the online measure. The e-mail requesting participation included a

URL link to an explanation of the study, then participants were directed to the informed consent page. After they read the informed consent, if participants agreed to participate, they selected the "I agree" button, which then directed them to the electronic (Zoomerang) survey.

Results

An exploratory factor analysis was conducted on the responses to 73 items related to courage. Examination of a scree plot of eigenvalues indicated that a five-factor solution would provide a balance between parsimony and satisfactory explanatory power for the model. The five-factor solution accounted for 48.96% of the total variance. The item stem with the highest mean rating was "Risking own life to protect others" ($M = 4.81$, $SD = 0.51$), indicating that most respondents found this stem genuinely exemplified courage. The item stem with the lowest mean was "Finishing what one has started" ($M = 2.62$, $SD = 0.99$). Thus, it was determined that all item stems exemplified courage to a moderate to a high degree.

The extent to which courage stems and factors reflected forms of courage was further examined using an additional comparative procedure. Two of the researchers independently coded each of the 73 stems as one of three types of courage conceptualized in our previous studies (physical, vital, or moral). Again, items had been extracted from participants' responses from Studies 1, 2, and 3. Out of the 73 items, 10 were coded as physical courage, 12 as moral courage, and 51 as vital courage. (We believe this disparity in the number of items reflecting each form of courage is attributable to the similarity among examples in both the physical and moral categories and the diversity of courageous situations in the vital courage category.) After coding each item independently, researchers compared results and found that they initially agreed on 67 out of 73 (92% agreement). Researchers came to a consensus on the six items they did not initially agree on.

After we coded for form of courage, a repeated measures analysis of variance was conducted by treating courage stems as the unit of analysis. Factor loading was a within-subject factor with five levels, and the researcher-supplied item coding (physical, vital, or moral for each item) was a between-subjects factor. A full-factorial model was considered, and main effects—$F\,(1, 122) = 5.15$, $p < .001$ for Factor Loading and $F\,(1, 122) = 10.53$, $p < .001$ for Coding—and the interaction were statistically significant. The existence of a statistically significant interaction, $F\,(1, 122) = 10.53$, $p < .001$, between Factor Loading and Coding indicates that there was a systematic relationship between the pattern of factor loadings and the researcher-supplied coding for each item. This pattern is clearly visible in Figure 2.1, the physical representation of the interaction.

Discussion

The results of Study 4 lend strong support to the existence of three factors of courage (as described in the literature review) but also indicate that the concept of Vital Courage may be more complex than originally conceived (i.e., we may be able to potentially subdivide the construct into other, related subcomponents).

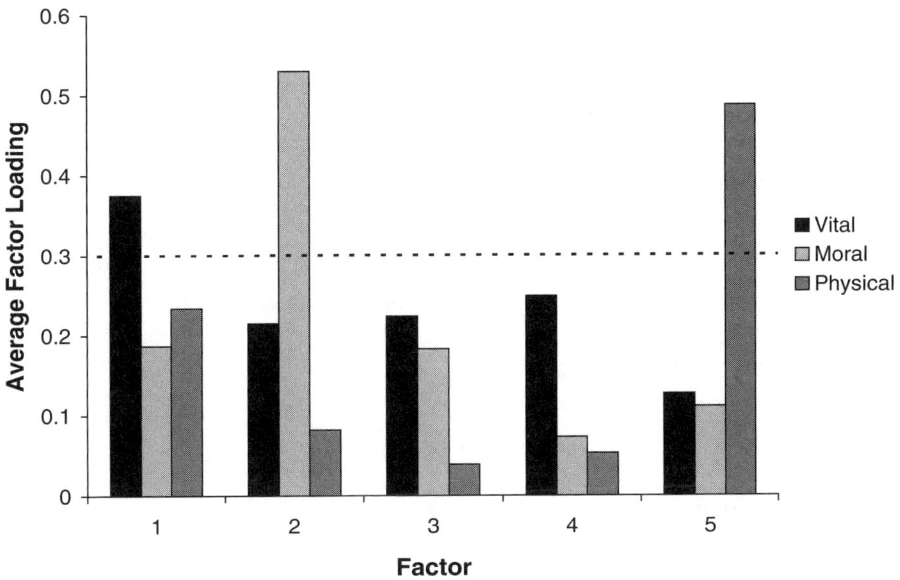

Figure 2.1. Average factor loadings by factor and type of courage. Values above the dotted line indicate average loadings greater than 0.3.

For Factor 1, the average factor loadings were highest for items associated with Vital Courage; for Factor 2, the average factor loadings were highest for items associated with Moral Courage; and for Factor 5, the average factor loadings were highest for items associated with Physical Courage. For Factor 3, average factor loadings were approximately equal for Vital Courage and Moral Courage items, indicating that this factor, which resembles perseverance, may be associated with some related aspect of these two types of courage. Factor 4, like Factor 1, was dominated by Vital Courage items, but the average loadings were not as high. This indicates that Factor 4 may be tapping into some aspect of Vital Courage, possibly overcoming personal and interpersonal struggles, that is structurally distinct from the other areas.

Limitations of the Study

Although we collected more than 800 examples of courage, our final list of unique stems included only 73 items. It is possible that this list is representative of the full spectrum of courage, but it is more likely that additional sampling across more diverse groups (in the first three studies) would have yielded more unique examples of the virtue.

General Discussion

Across history and cultures, courage has been regarded as a great virtue because it helps people face their challenges. Over the centuries, efforts to construct socially relevant views of courage have been fruitful yet incomplete. This series of studies tapped into the folk conceptualizations of courage in an effort to identify common characteristics of people's implicit theories about the virtue and to explore how courage manifests itself in daily life. Characteristics of courage (presence of risk, a developmental process for courage, socioenvironmental influences on courage) that were identified in two or more of the four studies are discussed here. First, we consider two findings that were supported by direct or indirect evidence across the four studies. It became apparent, on the basis of the folk conceptualizations, that courage is not necessarily the province of the special few, nor is courage always exhibited in public. Furthermore, in line with our expectations, participants distinguished among forms of courage. Convergence of findings across these four studies hopefully will help guide the development of explicit theories on courage.

Courage of the Many, in Its Many Forms

Findings from Studies 1, 2, and 3 suggest that participants saw themselves and other ordinary people (i.e., those folks not necessarily considered heroes) as capable of manifesting courage. Across survey responses (Study 1) and response generation tasks (Study 2 and Study 3), participants acknowledged the presence of courageous behaviors in self and others in addition to the often-celebrated behavior of some cultural heroes. Responses in the first three studies suggest that courage does not always take place in public; an example of private or personal courage (Pury et al., 2007) was repeatedly given. In light of the consensus among folk conceptualizations, explicit theories about the courage phenomenon should account for how courageous behavior is manifested in the lives of all people, in public and behind closed doors. With regard to the many forms of courage, it appears that individuals draw clear distinctions among moral, physical, and vital courage (Studies 1, 3, and 4) and propose alternative forms (e.g., intellectual courage, social courage; Study 2) that warrant further investigation. Indeed, it appears that there may be fine distinctions between how the different forms of courage look and act in the world and these findings are in line with our literature review and proposed classification system. More important, these results provide evidence for past suppositions (O'Byrne, Lopez, & Petersen, 2000) about how focusing theoretical and empirical examinations on forms of courage will do more for promoting development of explicit theories and further understanding of courage than will focusing on it at the universal virtue level.

Common Characteristics of Courage

The common characteristics of courage represent a convergence of data across the mixed-methods examination of folk conceptualizations. Presence of personal risk, courage (as a personal asset) developing over time and experience, and the influence of socioenvironmental context on the manifestation of courage were identified by two or more groups of our participants. These characteristics should be carefully considered as researchers move toward the development of new courage theories, models, and assessments.

Presence of personal risk (which was framed as a fearful situation or adversity in Study 1) has been acknowledged a core component of courage (or courageous actions) in Studies 2 and 3 and most scholarly discussions of the virtue (e.g., Mack, 2004; Putman, 2001; Rachman, 1984). How people become aware of and process personal risk has been considered (e.g., Woodard, 2004), and this topic warrants closer examination.

With regard to the development of the personal asset of courage over time and experience, our participants (Study 2; Study 4, Table 4) acknowledged the role of specialized training or successful experiences. On this front, we know most about how to train first responders to rise to the occasion (Rachman, 2004), some about how to foster vital courage in medical patients (Haase, 1987), and little about how to inculcate moral courage. It does appear that knowledge of optimal human development, character enhancement, and self-regulation and motivational models may bear on this developmental process, and theoretically grounded explanations for the development of courage should be interwoven into new explicit theories of courage.

The final common factor of courage identified by our participants involves the influence of socioenvironmental context on the manifestation of courage (see Studies 2 and 3). Courage researchers have considered the role of the bystander effect on courageous behavior (e.g., Fischer, Greitemeyer, Pollozek, & Frey, 2006; Greitemeyer, Fischer, Kastenmüller, & Frey, 2006) and the role that perceptions of actors and observers have in defining courage (Asarian, 1981). In future explicit conceptualizations of courage, theoretical tenets need to be developed to address the role other people have in facilitating and defining courage; furthermore, the ways in which social and environmental characteristics of a community or work setting might make "doing the right thing" more probable need to be more carefully considered. In short, what sets the stage for courage to emerge or to flourish needs to be explored. There are possibly conditions that are conducive to displaying courage or that liberate a person to demonstrate courage. For example, then-U.S. Senator Barack Obama (2006) stated, "The longer you are in politics, the easier it should be to muster such courage, for there is a certain liberation that comes from realizing that no matter what you do, someone will be angry at you" (p. 134).

Future Directions

Historical writings, Eastern and Western philosophy, and folk conceptualizations have provided rich descriptions of the phenomenon of courage. These operationalizations and recent courage research reveal subtle differences and considerable, meaningful overlap. Given what is known about the distinctive forms and common factors of courage, we (the diverse courage research community) can develop explicit theories of the virtue and move forward with associated research that results in a deeper understanding of what "rising to the occasion" is all about.

As research on courage moves forward, all perspectives on theories of courage need to be considered. Little is known about feminist perspectives on the virtue (Asarian, 1981) and about traditional Eastern views on the best in people (Yang,

2006). Furthermore, the personal and communal sequalae of courage (hypothesized as inspiration, renewed energy, prosocial motivation) warrant careful study.

A Final Note on Courage

In September 1985, the American television news anchor Dan Rather surprised everyone by ending a national broadcast with one word: "Courage." When asked why he ended the report of the news in this way, Rather (1993) stated, "I want to hear the word. I want to hear it praised, and the men and women who have courage elevated."As courage research and related media shed light on the best in people, it will be interesting to note whether segments of society come to expect courage from the many rather than from the few.

References

Asarian, R. D. (1981). The psychology of courage: A human scientific investigation. *Dissertation Abstracts International, 42,* 2023.

Bieri, J. (1955). Cognitive complexity-simplicity and predictive behavior. *Journal of Abnormal and Social Psychology, 51,* 263–286. doi:10.1037/h0043308

Cavanaugh, G. F., & Moberg, D. J. (1999). The virtue of courage within the organization. In M. L. Pava & P. Primeaux (Eds.), *Research in ethical issues in organizations* (pp. 1–25). Stamford, CT: Jai Press.

Clayton, V. (1982). Wisdom and intelligence: The nature and function of knowledge in later years. *International Journal of Aging & Human Development, 15,* 315–321. doi:10.2190/17TQ-BW3Y-P8J4-TG40

Finfgeld, D. L. (1995). Becoming and being courageous in the chronically ill elderly. *Issues in Mental Health Nursing, 16,* 1–11. doi:10.3109/01612849509042959

Finfgeld, D. L. (1998). Courage in middle-aged adults with long-term health concerns. *Canadian Journal of Nursing Research, 30,* 153–169.

Fischer, P., Greitemeyer, T., Pollozek, F., & Frey, D. (2006). The unresponsive bystander: Are bystanders more responsive in dangerous emergencies? *European Journal of Social Psychology, 36,* 267–278. doi:10.1002/ejsp.297

Fransella, F., & Bannister, D. (1977). *A manual for repertory grid technique.* London, England: Academic Press.

Furnham, A. (1988). *Lay theories: Everyday understanding of problems in the social sciences.* New York, NY: Pergamon.

Greitemeyer, T., Fischer, P., Kastenmüller, A., & Frey, D. (2006). Civil courage and helping behavior: Differences and similarities. *European Psychologist, 11,* 90–98. doi:10.1027/1016-9040.11.2.90

Grice, J. W. (2002). Idiogrid: Software for the management and analysis of repertory grids. *Behavior Research Methods, Instruments, & Computers, 34,* 338–341.

Haase, J. E. (1987). Components of courage in chronically ill adolescents: A phenomenological study. *ANS. Advances in Nursing Science, 9*(2), 64–80.

Kelly, G. A. (1955). *The psychology of personal constructs.* New York, NY: Norton.

Kelly, G. A. (1963). *A theory of personality: The psychology of personal constructs.* New York, NY: Norton.

Kelly, G. A. (1977). Personal construct theory and the psychotherapeutic interview. *Cognitive Therapy and Research, 1,* 355–362. doi:10.1007/BF01663999

Kennedy, J. F. (1956). *Profiles in courage.* New York, NY: Harper and Brothers.

Landfield, A. W., & Cannell, J. E. (1988). Ways of assessing functionally independent construction, meaningfulness, and construction in hierarchy. In J. Mancuso & M. L. G. Shaw (Eds.), *Cognition and personal structure* (pp. 67–90). New York, NY: Praeger Publishers.

Lopez, S. J., O'Byrne, K. K., & Petersen, S. (2003). Profiling courage. *Positive psychological assessment: A handbook of models and measures* (pp. 185–198). Washington, DC: American Psychological Association. doi:10.1037/10612-012

Mack, A. (Ed.). (2004). Courage. *Social Research: An International Quarterly of the Social Sciences, 71*(1).

Neimeyer, G., Neimeyer, R., Hagans, C., & Van Brunt, D. (2002). Is there madness in our method? The effects of repertory grid variations on measures of construct system structure. In R. A. Neimeyer & G. J. Neimeyer (Eds.), *Advances in personal construct psychology: New directions and perspectives* (pp. 161–200). Westport, CT: Praeger Publishers.

Obama, B. (2006). *The audacity of hope: Thoughts on reclaiming the American dream.* New York, NY: Crown Publishing.

O'Byrne, K. K., Lopez, S. J., & Petersen, S. (2000, August). *Building a theory of courage: A precursor to change?* Paper presented at the 108th Annual Convention of the American Psychological Association, Washington, DC.

Pears, D. (2004). The anatomy of courage. *Social Research: An International Quarterly of the Social Sciences, 71,* 1–12.

Petersen, S. E., Lopez, S. J., Frey, B. B., & Krieshok, T. S. (2005, August). *A repertory grid evaluation of a multidimensional theory of courage.* Poster session presented at the annual meeting of the American Psychological Association, Washington, DC.

Peterson, C., & Seligman, M. E. P. (2004). *Character strengths and virtues: A handbook and classification.* New York, NY: Oxford University Press.

Philips, C. (2004). *Six questions of Socrates.* New York, NY: Norton.

Pury, C. L. S., Kowalski, R. M., & Spearman, J. (2007). Distinctions between general and personal courage. *Journal of Positive Psychology, 2,* 99–114.

Putman, D. (1997). Psychological courage. *Philosophy, Psychiatry, & Psychology, 4*(1), 1–11. doi:10.1353/ppp.1997.0008

Putman, D. (2001). The emotions of courage. *Journal of Social Philosophy, 32,* 463–470. doi:10.1111/0047-2786.00107

Rachman, S. J. (1978). Human fears: A three systems analysis. *Scandinavian Journal of Behaviour Therapy, 7,* 237–245.

Rachman, S. J. (1984). Fear and courage. *Behavior Therapy, 15,* 109–120. doi:10.1016/S0005-7894(84)80045-3

Rachman, S. J. (2004). Fear and courage: A psychological perspective. *Social Research: An International Quarterly of the Social Sciences, 71,* 149–176.

Rather, D. (1993, September 29). Remarks at the 48th annual conference of the Radio-Television News Directors Association, San Francisco, CA.

Rorty, A. O. (1988). *Mind in action: Essays in the philosophy of mind.* Boston, MA: Beacon Press.

Shelp, E. E. (1984). Courage: A neglected virtue in the patient-physician relationship. *Social Science & Medicine, 18,* 351–360. doi:10.1016/0277-9536(84)90125-4

Snyder, C. R., & Lopez, S. J. (2007). *Positive psychology: The scientific and practical explorations of human strengths.* Thousand Oaks, CA: Sage.

Sternberg, R. (1985). Implicit theories of intelligence, creativity, and wisdom. *Journal of Personality and Social Psychology, 49,* 607–627. doi:10.1037/0022-3514.49.3.607

Sternberg, R. L., Conway, B. E., Ketron, J. L., & Bernstein, M. (1981). People's conceptions of intelligence. *Journal of Personality and Social Psychology, 41,* 37–55. doi:10.1037/0022-3514.41.1.37

Strauss, A. L., & Corbin, J. (1998). *Basics of qualitative research: Techniques and procedures for developing grounded theory* (2nd ed.). Thousand Oaks, CA: Sage.

Szagun, G. (1992). Age-related changes in children's understanding of courage. *The Journal of Genetic Psychology, 153,* 405–420.

Woodard, C. R. (2004). Hardiness and the concept of courage. *Consulting Psychology Journal: Practice and Research, 56*(3), 173–185. doi:10.1037/1065-9293.56.3.173

Yang, Y.-T. (2006). *Conceptual paper on Eastern perspectives on courage.* Unpublished manuscript, University of Kansas, Lawrence.

3

Defining the Features of Courage: A Search for Meaning

Christopher R. Rate

Courage. The word conjures up countless images of boldness, bravery, heroism, perseverance, and endurance. The following excerpt is descriptive of one such image.

> THE PRESIDENT [The Honorable George W. Bush]: The Medal of Honor is awarded for an act of such courage that no one could rightly be expected to undertake it. Yet those who knew Michael Monsoor were not surprised when he did. . . . On Saint Michael's Day—September 29, 2006—Michael Monsoor would make the ultimate sacrifice. Mike and two teammates had taken position on the outcropping of a rooftop when an insurgent grenade bounced off Mike's chest and landed on the roof. Mike had a clear chance to escape, but he realized that the other two [Navy] SEALs did not. In that terrible moment, he had two options—to save himself, or to save his friends. For Mike, this was no choice at all. He threw himself on the grenade and absorbed the blast with his body. One of the survivors puts it this way: "Mikey looked death in the face that day and said, 'You cannot take my brothers. I will go in their stead.'" ("Remarks by the President," 2008)

Branding Courage

Notable pioneering researchers (e.g., Evans & White, 1981; O'Byrne, Lopez, & Peterson, 2000; Peterson & Seligman, 2004; Shelp, 1984; Szagun, 1992) have conceptualized courage in myriad ways; courage is not reserved and characterized solely for physical actions. Other common conceptualizations or brands of courage found in the literature are labeled moral courage and, more recently, psychological or vital courage. Other lesser reported brands have also been identified.

This chapter is based, in part, on a presentation for the American Psychological Association–sponsored conference, the 2007 Courage Summit, and doctoral dissertation work completed at Yale University. A special thanks goes to Drs. Bob Sternberg, Frank Seitz, Jeff Jackson, Cindy Pury, Shane Lopez, Cooper Woodard, Linda O'Hara, Marcia Johnson, Jeff Sonnenfeld, and Victor Vroom for their mentorship, guidance, comments, critiques and suggestions throughout the process of conducting these studies and writing this chapter.

Physical Courage

The courageous act depicted at the beginning of this chapter—willingly sacrificing one's life for a friend—is illustrative of physical courage, which is often characterized as the overcoming of fear of death or physical harm in the face of risk (Lopez, O'Byrne, & Peterson, 2003; Putman, 1997). By far, it is the most prototypical definition put forth by modern lexicons (Kidder, 2005); however, it is not the only one.

Moral Courage

On December 1, 1955, in Montgomery, Alabama, Rosa Parks displayed moral courage when she refused to give up her bus seat to a White man because she felt it was time to take a stand for civil rights. Putman (1997) defined this moral courage as the absence of fear while defending deeply rooted morals despite the risk of social disapproval. Lopez et al. (2003) similarly defined moral courage, stating that "authenticity and integrity may be the fulfillments most closely associated with the expression of personal views in the face of dissension and rejection" (p. 187).

Psychological or Vital Courage

Lopez et al. (2003) described vital courage as thriving in the face of physical and mental illness. Putman (2001) also attributed this type of courage to the person recovering from alcoholism, emphasizing that the relationships between the dimensions of courage are just as critical in determining the success or failure of the person recovering from alcoholism as they are for the military soldier.

Other Brands of Courage

Several other brands of courage also have been proposed. Bauhn (2003) described two types of courage: courage of creativity (May, 1978) and courage of conviction. Pury, Kowalski, and Spearman (2007) also described two types of courage: general and personal. Greitemeyer, Fischer, Kastenmüller, and Frey (2006) described a brand of courage labeled *civil courage.*

In general, brands or types of courage seem to emerge when conceptualizations of courage are contextually restricted rather than when its common underlying structure is focused on. For instance, if a "type" of risk is perceived as either physical or moral, then courage is defined with the corresponding brand, that is, physical or moral courage. This parsing of courage into brands may hinder the ability to find a consensus definition common to all types. The focus is removed from identifying core dimensions common among all brands and is placed on what is unique to each type or brand.

Therefore, it would appear that there is no clear consensus understanding of the concept. People are able to identify courage or certain courageous acts when they see them—as exemplified by the actions of Congressional Medal of Honor winners such as Navy SEAL Michael Monsoor, civil rights leaders such as Dr. Martin Luther King, Jr., and Rosa Parks, early explorers such as Captain Ernest Shackleton and Ferdinand Magellan, and the young mother of five children, twice diagnosed with leukemia, thriving in the face of this physical illness. Unfortunately, these examples do not readily translate to an adequate articulation of a definition of courage.

In the context of previous discussions of conceptualizations and brands of courage, Lopez et al. (2003) correctly asserted that

> though we have been able to parse out the different types of courage by establishing between-brand differences, we have been less successful at determining the elements or components [features] of courage. Thus, what is common to all brands remains unclear. (p. 189)

The search for the meaning of courage has certainly been influenced by cultural zeitgeists and scholarly domains (philosophy, classic literature, and so on). As such, the theoretical conceptualizations of courage reflect these influences. The numerous brands of courage may, in fact, obfuscate an understanding of its meaning.

In our investigation, my colleagues and I uncovered no empirical studies that have examined the adequacy of the numerous conceptualizations of courage and compared them in any systematic way. Conducting a content analysis of the definitions and then directly comparing them would seem like a logical step toward reaching a consensus definition and understanding the features of courage underlying all types of courage. So, rather than focus on the nuances that differentiate one type of courage or one conceptualization of courage from another, I focus on commonalities of these conceptions—the core dimensions of the courage construct.

Proceeding from theoretically to empirically based conceptualizations of courage, a thorough analysis of the definitions would greatly enhance the field's understanding of a global framework underlying all conceptualizations of courage. This type of analysis would provide a conceptual understanding of courage based on the cumulative knowledge and works of pioneering researchers and laypeople alike. Therefore, in the search for the meaning of courage and its defining features, two important questions must be asked:

- Can the common features and dimensions of courage be determined first?
- Do these features adequately communicate what people think courage is, that is, their implicit theories of courage?

In this chapter, I seek to address these questions to establish a parsimonious yet heuristically useful definition of courage. The first section briefly addresses the theoretical conceptualizations of courage, including its historical development and recent conceptualizations, followed by a section discussing the current methodologies used to discover the dimensions of courage. After establishing this foundation I then describe our efforts to (a) identify scholarly definitions of courage and extract their underlying features; (b) examine these features for their reliability; and (c) propose a global conceptualization of courage, providing testable features for subsequent studies. Finally, I describe our successful attempt to directly compare the adequacy of several conceptualizations of courage through a vignette study investigating the extent to which people actually use the previously identified features of courage in their evaluations of other people's courageous acts. This process leads us to our goal: a better understanding of courage and what it means—from an observer's perspective—to act courageously.

The Search Begins: Theoretical Perspectives of Courage

The word *courage* is grounded in Western and Eastern ancient philosophical traditions, and the search for its meaning was once the proprietary domain of philosophers. "Tell me if you can, what is courage?" In *Laches,* the Ancient Greek philosopher, Plato (trans. 1987), recorded the dialogue between Socrates and two Athenian generals, Nicias and Laches, focusing on the answer to this very question.

Historical Development

The Ancient Greeks, namely, Socrates, Plato, and Aristotle, called it *andreia* (pronounced ahn-DRAY-a; Aristotle, trans. 1987; Plato, trans. 1987). Though it is translated as courage, the Ancient Greek meaning of *andreia* is "manliness." The ancients considered courage as something that fell within the traditionally masculine aspects of virtue. The display of *andreia* was typically found in the overt actions of the soldier on the battlefield (Aristotle, trans. 1987). In accord with the Ancient Greeks, Saint Thomas Aquinas (trans. 1922) also identified courage, using the Latin word *fortitudo,* with manhood. For Aquinas, "every courageous act involves a willingness to die and that endurance is courage's defining mark" (Yearly, 1990, p. 118). However, it was the martyr rather than the battlefield warrior Aquinas exemplified as possessing the purest form of courage (Peterson & Seligman, 2004).

Yet even prior to the ancients' philosophical treatises on courage, the 4th century BC Confucian thinker Mengzi (Mencius) had already engaged in this discourse. Mengzi's category of *da yong,* "great courage," depicts courage as directed toward morally praiseworthy ends, resulting from a continuous process of self-cultivation. With long practice of self-cultivation, virtuous persons are able to choose moral action undeterred by any difficulty or danger (Ivanhoe, 2002).

Today, *andreia, fortitudo,* and *da yong* are translated as "courage," but over several centuries the word *courage* has taken on different meanings. Through its evolution, many definitions of *courage* have become outdated. For example, meanings implied by the definition of courage as "spirit, liveliness, lustiness, vigour, vital force or energy," that is, anger, pride, confidence, boldness, sexual vigor, and inclination, are now obsolete. These meanings were typically found in literary texts (e.g., Chaucer, Shakespeare) dating from the mid-16th and 17th centuries (*Oxford English Dictionary,* 1989).

Today, there is ample discussion of the meaning of courage, with empirical scientists, politicians, and laypeople all entering the debate. The growing body of literature in recent years indicates a remarkable increase in interest and intrigue in the quest to answer the question "What is courage?" Defining courage in terms of character strengths of human goodness and excellence (i.e., bravery, persistence, integrity, and vitality), the positive psychologists endeavor to view courage through the lenses of positive subjective experiences, positive individual traits, and institutions that enable positive experiences and positive traits (Peterson & Seligman, 2004; Seligman & Csikszentmihalyi, 2000). On the other hand, other notable researchers have argued, as is our stated position, that courage is better construed as an attribute of the act than as an attribute of the person (Pury et al., 2007; Rachman, 1990; Rate, Clarke, Lindsay, & Sternberg, 2007; Rate & Sternberg, 2007; Walton, 1986). Although this literature is growing at an accelerated rate, it actually says little about the meaning—nature or form—of courage (Harris, 2000; Srivastva & Cooperrider, 1998; Walton, 1986).

In many ways, the field has ended up where Socrates began; following several attempts to define courage and describe its nature, Socrates and his two interlocutors failed, regrettably, to reach a consensus definition. Socrates lamented this fact: "Then . . . we have not discovered what courage is." One may wonder whether Socrates and Plato would be surprised—despite their unsuccessful attempts to fully understand courage—that similar discussions persist over 2,000 years later.

Conceptualizing Courage

One would think that conceptualizing courage would be easy, right? To illustrate the difficulty in reaching a consensus definition, Table 3.1 lists 20 select definitions (see Rate, 2007, for an expanded table), each espoused to define or describe courage or courageous acts. This list contains representative definitions from modern lexicons, philosophical treatises, literary works, and social science investigations.

Despite the myriad definitions, courage researchers seem to acknowledge the multidimensional nature of courage, identifying dimensions such as intentionality, fear, risk, and noble purpose. For example, my colleagues and I (Rate et al., 2007) carefully executed empirical testing to determine the essential features of people's implicit theories of courage, describing courage as (a) a willful, intentional act, (b) executed after mindful deliberation, (c) involving objective substantial risk to the actor, (d) primarily motivated to bring about a noble good or worthy purpose, (e) despite, perhaps, the presence of the emotion of fear. The numerous definitions of courage provide a rich foundation from which to build, yet there is no operational definition of this construct on which to base sound explicit theories. All of the attempts to define courage have not quite advanced the domain to an agreed-on conceptual definition.

Investigating Courage: Implicit-Theory Methodologies

Implicit- and explicit-theory approaches to research exemplify two complementary components approaching a more nearly complete operational and universal definition of courage from different angles. Explicit theories are constructions

Table 3.1. Select Conceptualizations of Courage: From Lexicons to Literature

Source	Definitions and Descriptions
Lexicons	
American Heritage Dictionary	The state or quality of mind that enables one to face danger, fear, or vicissitudes with self-possession, confidence, and resolution (2006).
Compact Oxford English Dictionary	Ability to do something that frightens one; strength in the face of pain or grief (2005).
Merriam-Webster Dictionary	Mental or moral strength to venture, persevere, and withstand danger, fear, or difficulty (2005).
Philosophy	
Bauhn	Courage is "a disposition to confront fear (rather than being fearless), and . . . it is essential to the advancing of the personal good of the agent as well as of the common good of human communities" (2003, p. 9).
Comte-Sponville	Courage is the "ability to confront, master, and overcome fear, which assumes that fear either exists or might reasonably exist; and the risks that we incur must be in proportion to the ends we seek" (2001, p. 51).
MacIntyre	Courage is "the capacity to risk harm or danger to oneself" (1981, p. 192).
Walton	Courage consists of three characteristics: "1) careful presence of mind and deliberate action, 2) difficult, dangerous, and painful circumstances, and 3) a morally worthy intention . . . at the agent's personal risk and suffering" (1986, p. 3).
Social Sciences	
Gould	Courage is revealed in three dimensions: (a) fear; (b) appropriate action; and (c) a higher purpose (2005).
Kidder	Moral courage is defined as the intersection between three elements: (a) principles, (b) danger, and (c) endurance; moral courage is "a commitment to moral principles, an awareness of the danger involved in supporting those principles, and a willing endurance of that danger" (2005, p. 7).
Kilmann, O'Hara, & Strauss	A courageous act in an organization includes five essential properties: (a) member has free choice to act; (b) member experiences significant risk; (c) member assess the risk as reasonable; (d) member's contemplated act pursues excellence or other worthy aims, and (e) member proceeds despite fear with mindful action (2005).
O'Byrne, Lopez, & Petersen	Dispositional psychological courage is the cognitive process of defining risk, identifying and considering alternative actions, and choosing to act in spite of potential negative consequences in an effort to obtain "good" for self or others, recognizing that this perceived good may not be realized (2000, p. 6).

Table 3.1. *(Continued)*

Source	Definitions and Descriptions
Peterson & Seligman	Emotional character strengths (bravery, persistence, integrity, and vitality) "that involve the exercise of will to accomplish goals in the face of opposition, external or internal" (2004, p. 29).
Putman	"Facing our deep-seated fear of psychological instability" (1997, p. 1).
Rachman	"Willing and able to approach a fearful situation despite the presence of subjective fear and psychophysiological disturbances" (1990, p. 12).
Rate, Clarke, Lindsay, & Sternberg	Courage is described as (a) a willful, intentional act, (b) executed after mindful deliberation, (c) involving objective substantial risk to the actor, (d) primarily motivated to bring about a noble good or worthy purpose, (e) despite, perhaps, the presence of the emotion of fear (2007).
Shelp	The disposition to voluntarily act, perhaps fearfully, in a dangerous circumstance, where the relevant risks are reasonable appraised, in an effort to obtain or preserve some perceived good for oneself or others, recognizing that the desired perceived good may not be realized (1984, p. 354).
Woodard	Courage is defined as the "ability to act for a meaningful (noble, good, or practical) cause, despite experiencing the fear associated with perceived threat exceeding the available resources" (2004, p. 174).
Worline, Wrzesniewski, & Rafaeli	Courage (in organizational settings) "involves risk, has been freely chosen, demonstrates considered assessment of consequences, and pursues excellence within the circumstances where it occurs" (2002, p. 299).
Literature	
Kennedy	Political courage: men whose abiding loyalty to their nation triumphed over personal and political considerations (1956, p. 21).
McCain & Salter	Defined courage as an "act that risks life or limb or other very serious personal injuries for the sake of others or to uphold a virtue—a standard often upheld by battlefield heroics but one that is certainly not limited to martial valor" (2004, p. 14).

of psychologists that are based, or at least tested, on data collected from people performing tasks presumed to measure the construct under investigation. In contrast, implicit theories are people's cognitive constructions. Such theories need to be discovered rather than invented because they already exist. The goal in research on implicit theories is to find out and document the form and content of people's informal theories. With the notable exception of Rachman and his colleagues (see Cox, Hallam, O'Connor, & Rachman, 1983;

McMillan & Rachman, 1987; and Rachman, 1990), the researcher's tool of choice is the use of one or more implicit-theory methodologies to further the understanding of courage and its dimensions. In the search for people's implicit notions of a psychological construct (e.g., courage), three prominent research methodologies are generally implemented (Bluck & Glück, 2005):

- *Descriptor studies.* Descriptor-rating studies typically focus on the perceived characteristics of courage. That is, this methodology is aimed at describing courage as viewed by laypeople (see O'Byrne, Lopez, & Petersen, 2000; Rasmussen, O'Byrne, Petersen, & Lopez, 2005; Rate et al., 2007; and Woodard, 2004).
- *People's own lives.* The second line of inquiry asks laypeople to describe whom they consider to be courageous or to describe a time in which they recall being courageous. This methodology puts courage within the context of laypeople's lives (see Finfgeld, 1995, 1998; Greitemeyer et al., 2006, Haase, 1987; and Pury et al., 2007).
- *Experimental studies.* In the third methodology, laypeople are generally presented with information or descriptions of a target individual and then are asked to evaluate the person's courage (see Evans & White, 1981; Greitemeyer et al., 2006; Rate et al., 2007; Szagun, 1992; and Szagun & Schauble, 1997).

A comprehensive review of the literature has revealed a mere handful of empirical studies comparing differing notions of the construct of courage. Because it is difficult to create laboratory environments or conditions in which to reproduce meaningful courage or courageous behavior (Deutsch, 1961; Greitemeyer et al., 2006; Pury et al., 2007), the researcher's tool of choice, at this point, seems to be implicit-theory methodologies. These three lines of research or variations of the same are all focused on discovering people's conceptions of courage. Most of the existing research accordingly relies on case studies, interviews, or responses to hypothetical scenarios (Peterson & Seligman, 2004).

The current implicit- and explicit-theory studies of courage provide a good understanding of the psychological construct of courage while serving as a launching point to further investigate courageous acts. The priority of establishing a consensus definition of courage is not merely a humanistic or intellectual exercise. A concise, operational definition is necessary to proceed with developing or training this construct and its underlying features in individuals and organizations. Unfortunately, the problem of a consensus definition of courage has not been completely resolved. A more precise understanding of the meaning of courage will clear the path for future advances in the evaluation of courage and courageous acts.

An Empirical Search for the Meaning of Courage

The notion that one must search for the meaning of courage is a puzzling prospect. One sees what one *thinks* is a courageous act, but cannot define courage. What is courage?

From the Ancient Greeks and Chinese sages to present-day philosophers and psychologists, scholars have wrestled with this question. There is no consensus definition of courage. In fact, no significant attempts have been made to reach consensus. New or modified definitions of courage periodically pique interest in the construct, yet, more often than not, they result in increased ambiguity about what courage means (Miller, 2000). The paucity of empirical research illuminating this issue has resulted in a failure to generate consensus-driven definitions of courage, although recent investigations into implicit theories of courage have begun to address this question.

Searching for Features of Courage

Building on our initial line of research investigating implicit theories of courage (see Rate et al., 2007), my colleagues and I launched the first-ever examination of the commonalities, that is, the common features, of various conceptualizations of courage. To ascertain these features of explicit and implicit conceptualizations of courage, we used content-analysis methods to examine select definitions of courage to see whether they converged on a limited set of extracted features. This study was essential to understanding and analyzing conceptualizations' shared features, capitalizing on their similarities and at the same time assessing the variability of these features within definitions of courage. From this investigation we were able to conceptualize a comprehensive theoretical framework for understanding and analyzing definitions of courage. This framework, based on the extracted features of courage, provides a springboard for future investigations to explore whether each of these testable features is necessary to the core meaning of courage and to examine the adequacy of definitions of courage. Not all definitions were created equal.

Our theoretical population of interest included all the definitions and descriptions of courage and courageous behavior. As a practical matter, however, it was necessary to obtain a sample from this population. The primary criterion for inclusion in this study was that the definitions were explicitly stated in the authors' works. The sample was an accumulation of scholarly definitions from modern lexicons, philosophical works, English literature, and the social sciences. Using methods to capture the implicit structure of courage from folk tales and myths, as demonstrated by the work of anthropologist Joseph Campbell (1949) in his development of the heroic "monomyth," was beyond the scope of the present study. At some point, many of the explicitly stated definitions became redundant. This was particularly true for the lexical definitions. Therefore, the sample of interest was limited to 49 definitions (see Rate, 2007) of which a select sample are listed in Table 3.1.

Following an exhaustive search of the literature and the collection of published definitions of courage, we used the technique of emergent coding, as described by Stemler (2001), to extract the dominant themes that emerged from the definitions. Stemler described the procedures for emergent coding by two researchers as follows: (1) Review the material of interest and establish a set of features that form a checklist; (2) Compare notes and reconcile differences; (3) Independently apply coding; (4) Check reliability of coding; and

(5) Repeat if reliability is not acceptable. After several iterations, we reached consensus on the presence of seven major features: (1) External Circumstances, (2) Cognitive Processes, (3) Motivation Toward Excellence, (4) Affect/Emotion, (5) Volition, (6) Behavioral Responses, and (7) Characteristic/Trait/Skills/Abilities.

1. *External Circumstances.* This feature is defined as objective conditions or facts that determine or must be considered in the determining of a course of action. These circumstances are external in that they are from outside of the "self" and exist apart from cognitive processes (i.e., they are present regardless of one's perception or awareness). Examples of this feature include objective dangers, difficulties, and risks.
2. *Cognitive Processes.* This feature includes a wide range of cognitive processes. Examples of this feature include perception of danger, awareness of risk, appraising or assessing risk, problem solving, and identifying alternatives. Cognitive processes associated with volition are not included in this feature. Volition is considered as a stand-alone facet (see later section).
3. *Motivation Toward Excellence.* This feature focuses on one's moral impetus for acting. One's actions are directed toward, for example, the good of others, a noble purpose, or worthy aim.
4. *Affect / Emotion.* This feature is best exemplified by the presence of emotions such as fear. The presence of this feature is weakened with equivocations (e.g., "perhaps fear") and is absent when qualifiers such as "no" are used without the respective affect.
5. *Volition.* This feature is defined as an exercise of one's will. Volition could arguably be considered an example of a cognitive process. However, its uniqueness and importance in defining courage suggest it should be included as an individual feature. Examples of this facet include "willing," "voluntary," "deliberate," and "freely chosen" actions.
6. *Behavioral Responses.* This feature is described as reactions in response to specific stimuli (such as external circumstances or emotions such as fear). These responses or "acts" can be categorized as active or passive, and are illustrated by the following descriptors: facing, confronting, persevering, and enduring, and so on.
7. *Characteristic / Trait / Skills / Abilities.* This final feature encompasses the aspects of definitions of courage that attribute the concept of courage to an individual. This feature is exemplified by elements such as ability, capacity, and disposition. In addition, descriptors such as "quality of X," "state of X," "X strength," or "strength of X" are indicative of attributes rather than any process that "X" may imply. For example, the descriptors "quality of mind or spirit," "quality of will," or "strength of mind" refer to attributes rather than cognitive processes or exercises of volition. Also included in this feature are other elements appropriately attributed to an individual's character, whether occurring naturally or through development and experience (e.g., confidence, grace).

Interrater Reliability. To further validate the seven major features of courage and to establish their reliability, we asked independent experts to complete a rating task establishing the degree to which the seven major features were present in a particular definition. These experts were used to guard against any shared meaning we may have generated that would have produced artificially elevated reliability scores that would be unlikely to be replicable by other outside investigators (Krippendorff, 2004). The purpose of assessing rater agreement in this study was to identify the extent to which raters agreed when attempting to apply the seven major extracted features to various definitions (i.e., reproducibility—the extent to which ratings produce the same results by multiple raters), not to measure whether raters come to a "correct" conclusion about the degree to which the major features are present (i.e., accuracy; Stemler, 2001). Interrater agreement was assessed in several ways: (a) interrater agreement of the principal investigators, (b) interrater agreement among the expert raters, and (c) interrater agreement among all raters combined. In each case, the interrater agreement and reliability defined as consensus, consistency, and measurement were found to be quite good (Rate, 2007).

Coding of the Definitions. Using the major features extracted through emergent coding and tested for reliability, expert raters coded the definitions of courage. Table 3.2 describes the percentage of definitions in which the particular features are present. For instance, the feature Volition is included in only 29% of the definitions, whereas External Circumstances is present in 78% of the definitions.

There is, however, a great deal of variability across the definitions of courage. The number of features incorporated in a definition of courage approximates a normal distribution. In other words, very few definitions emphasize only one feature or all seven features. Figure 3.1 displays the number of unique features per definition.

As indicated earlier, not all definitions of courage are created equal. This should surprise very few, given the myriad definitions of courage and the absence of consensus. If a consensual definition had already been reached by the sages and researchers producing definitions of courage, then we would have predicted that our study's data would reveal that all definitions were basically saying the same thing. This was not the case. Our study revealed that definitions of courage are quite varied in the number and type of content (i.e., major extracted features) they include.

Table 3.2. Percentage of Definitions in Which the Features of Courage Are Found

Facet	% of Definitions
External Circumstances	77.6
Cognitive Processes	38.8
Motivation Toward Excellence	44.9
Affect/Emotion	51.0
Volition	28.6
Behavioral Responses	85.7
Characteristic/Trait/Skills/Abilities	55.1

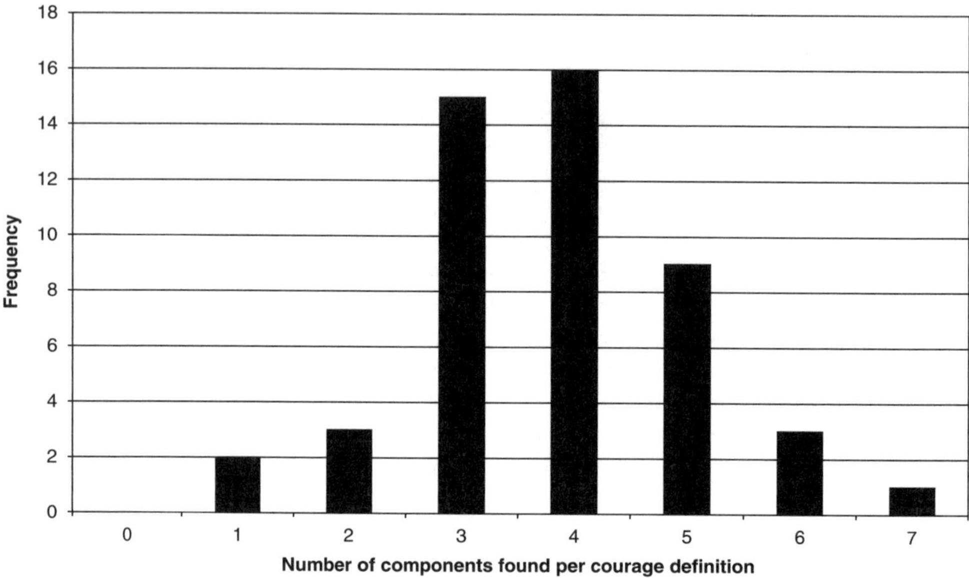

Figure 3.1. Frequency chart showing the number of unique features found per definition.

Using content analysis as a tool to determine a global conceptualization of courage, we have been able to identify differences and similarities between definitions. This content analysis allows for the systematic evaluation of the features of numerous definitions of courage. In essence, this analysis permits the pooling of the numerous explicit and implicit conceptualizations of courage to ascertain a more universal conceptualization of courage (see Figure 3.2).

The interactional nature of this conceptual framework is an abstract one and could be used to further an understanding of numerous other psychological constructs. However, we use it, specifically, to approach the construct of courage from multiple psychological perspectives. The framework does not suggest where the process of defining courage begins or ends, nor does the framework specify a process flow from one feature to another. It does, however, provide a more universal perspective of the major features of courage and their possible interaction with each other. The features do not exist in a vacuum. The framework suggests that the features interact in some unspecified manner and are correlated with each other. This framework also suggests that the core features of courage are among the seven features. Which features are necessary to the core definition of courage is an exciting but empirical question that remains a challenge for future investigations. Accordingly, the relative contributions of each of the seven features need to be empirically established in regard to courage and courageous acts.

LIMITATIONS. One of the limitations of this study was that rater agreement solely addresses the interrater agreement across the major themes or features. There are possible thematic elements within each major feature that could fur-

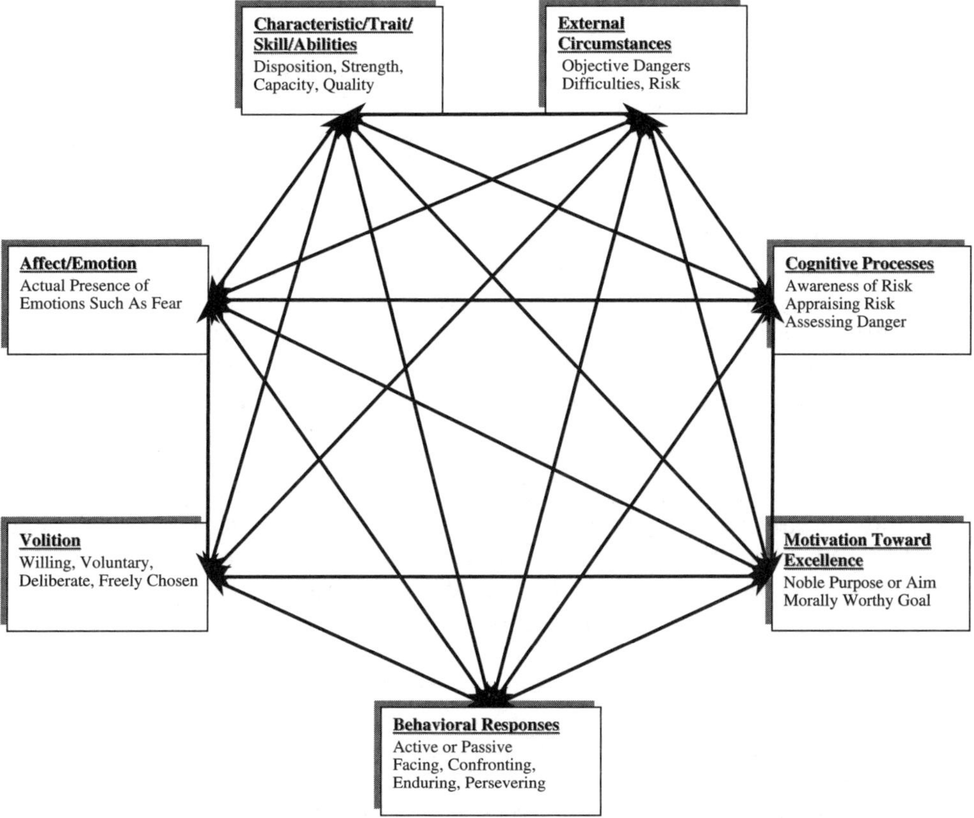

Figure 3.2. An interactional framework for understanding courage.

ther illuminate the meaning of courage. These elements may influence the manner in which we type or brand courage (Lopez et al., 2003).

Although our search for definitions of courage was as exhaustive as practical, other definitions or descriptions of courage exist. A different set of features could potentially emerge from a different sample of definitions. We are, however, confident the major features extracted in this study would be effective in describing these definitions as well.

Testing the Adequacy of Courage Definitions

The question now remains, "So what?" Although we were able to identify the major features of a global conceptualization of courage, the previous analysis does not address the adequacy of the definitions, nor whether the features are necessary to the meaning of courage. Our follow-up study explicitly allows the comparison of definitions to determine the extent to which people actually use the emergent features of courage in their evaluations of other people's courage. The results of this study allow us to directly compare existing definitions of courage, and ultimately to generate the most parsimonious yet heuristically useful definition(s) of courage.

Nearly 300 participants (active-duty Air Force officers and officer candidates from the United States Air Force Academy) rated 30 vignettes. The vignettes described scenarios of varied situations and individual behaviors. Vignettes were developed, in part, from real-world events, whereas other scenarios were entirely fictitious. In both cases, specific feature manipulations were used to ensure each vignette was developed with varying levels or degree of presence of five features (i.e., External Circumstances, Cognitive Processes, Motivation Toward Excellence, Affect/Emotion, and Volition) that emerged from our content analysis. It is important to note that in the development of this vignette study, we intentionally excluded the measurement of the features Behavioral Responses and Characteristic/Trait/Skill/Abilities. The rationale for excluding the former feature was that it was regarded as the manifestation of courage rather than an underlying feature of the construct. The latter feature was excluded because it presumes that courage is a dispositional attribute of an individual. Many researchers argue, as we also assert, that it is tenuous at best to attribute a dispositional courage to an individual based on a single event (Rate et al., 2007; Walton, 1986), and the scenarios depicted by the vignettes are, in fact, one-time occurrences of courageous acts.

In real life, an observer's assessment of an individual's courageous behavior would be largely subjective and require the observer to make certain inferences (e.g., level of fear or cognitive awareness of the individual). Therefore, we maintained the ecological validity of the vignettes by avoiding overly formulaic scenarios. Vignettes were descriptive of physical, moral, and social situations; however, this study did not explicitly compare whether different "brands" or "types" of courageous behavior were perceived as more or less indicative of courage than were others. The following is a typical vignette used in this study (see Rate, 2007, for other examples):

> Bob was fishing on the Colorado River, enjoying the quiet outdoors, when he noticed two young boys playing and swimming upstream near the opposite bank. He was very concerned about the river's strong current. Without warning, one of the boys was pulled underwater by the current and swept downstream towards Bob. Instinctively, Bob dove into the river in an attempt to save the struggling boy. Just before they reached the churning rapids, Bob reached the boy and pulled him to safety on the river bank.

In an effort to ensure independence of feature and courage ratings, one half of the participants were asked to evaluate the presence of the five features in the vignettes. The other half of the participants evaluated the vignette protagonist's level of courage. Principal component regression analysis revealed that levels of attributed courage could be predicted at a high level if people's ratings of the five features are known.

The present study continues to refine our search for the meaning of courage by building on the foundation established in our previous study, which described seven features extracted from select conceptualizations of courage. We ascertained which features people actually use in their evaluations of other people's courage (i.e., External Circumstances, Motivation Toward Excellence, and Volition). These identified features were used to qualitatively compare conceptualizations of courage in regard to their adequacy in denoting the core meaning of courage. Finally, the features that were predictive of courage represented a parsimonious and heuristically useful definition of courage.

Three features meet the condition of necessity; that is, if an act is courageous, then by definition (a) the action was freely chosen, (b) the actor seeks to bring about a noble purpose, and (c) the act is attempted or accomplished at substantial risk to the actor. If one of these features is absent, then the act is not courageous. By itself, each feature is insufficient to define courage; however, in combination, the three features satisfy the condition of sufficiency. On the basis of these results and the conditions of necessity and sufficiency, conceptualizations of courage should include the features of External Circumstances, Motivation Toward Excellence, and Volition. The remaining two major features, Affect/Emotion and Cognitive Processes, may be described as contingency factors (i.e., factors that may be highly associated with courage and present in a specific scenario but not necessary for an act to be attributed as courageous). In fact, our studies revealed statistically significant correlations between courage and Cognitive Processes, Affect/Emotion, and Observer Fear, but their contributions to the predictive model of courage were tenuous at best. Even after the removal of these three components from the regression model, the R^2 values (.80) remained stable for the main and cross-validation samples.

COMPARING DEFINITIONS OF COURAGE. Once again we concluded, "Not all definitions are created equal." This was true in our first study, with regard to the number and type of features in each conceptualization. It also remains true in terms of each conceptualization's adequacy in defining courage. Referring back to our content analysis, we noted that only 28.6% and 44.9% of the conceptualizations of courage included the features of Volition and Motivation Toward Excellence, respectively. Only 9 of 49 definitions (18.4%) incorporated both of these features and External Circumstances, and 81.6% failed to include one or more of these features. In fact, every lexical definition analyzed in this study inadequately conceptualized courage. However, seven of these nine definitions also included other features (e.g., Cognitive Processes and Affect/Emotion) that could be interpreted as leading to an overly restrictive conceptualization of courage.

Illustrating this point, Kilmann, O'Hara, and Strauss (2005) defined a courageous act as including five essential properties: (a) member has free choice to act (Volition); (b) member experiences significant risk (External Circumstances); (c) member assesses the risk as reasonable (Cognitive Processes); (d) member's contemplated act pursues excellence or other worthy aims (Motivation Toward Excellence); and (e) member proceeds despite fear (Affect/Emotion) with mindful action. This definition not only consists of our three core features of courage but also includes features that were found not to contribute to the prediction of courageous behavior. Therefore, this particular definition would be considered overly restrictive. Assume, for example, that if all other features were present, an individual who acted without fear would not be considered courageous. This is simply not supported by our results. Overall, however, the conceptualizations of courage that were rated in our content analysis study as having the strongest presence of External Circumstances, Motivation Toward Excellence, and Volition were also deemed to be overly restrictive in defining courage based on the results from the current study.

Only two conceptualizations of courage were limited to the set of three features. In one conceptualization, Peterson and Seligman (2004) described courage as emotional character strengths "that involve the exercise of will [Volition] to accomplish goals [Motivation Toward Excellence] in the face of opposition, external or internal [External Circumstances]" (p. 29). Although this description of courage consists of the parsimonious set of features, our expert raters considered the presence of Motivation Toward Excellence particularly weak because of the absence of a moral qualifier of the particular goals. These same raters also found the second conceptualization of courage posited by Klein and Napier (2003) to be similarly weak, this time in regard to presence of the feature Volition.

An Empirically Based Conceptualization of Courage. The results of the present study clearly indicate the need to reassess the myriad conceptualizations of courage. Words matter, the meanings of words matter, and people's understanding of the constructs behind these meanings matters. Therefore, to adequately capture and articulate people's notions of courage, researchers should ensure that their conceptualization of courage is both parsimonious and heuristically useful. When asked to articulate this conceptualization, researchers should not give contingency factors undue influence, resulting in overly restrictive conceptualizations. With the present study as a basis to ascertain a more concise meaning of courage, we would recommend revising the conceptualization of courage advocated by Rate et al. (2007). Courage consists of three major features (i.e., Volition, External Circumstances, and Motivation Toward Excellence) and is best described in lay terms as (a) a willing, intentional act (b) involving substantial danger, difficulty, or risk to the actor, (c) primarily motivated to bring about a noble good or morally worthy purpose.

Summary. The examination of the major features of courage extracted from scholarly conceptualizations has provided the support for an empirically driven conceptualization of courage. The current study clearly revealed the essence or core of courage to include the features External Circumstances, Motivation Toward Excellence, and Volition. Use of our model of courage to evaluate other conceptualizations (definitions/descriptions) of courage revealed that over 80% of the conceptualizations omitted one or more of these features. The remaining conceptualizations tended to be overly restrictive in that they included too many features. Although three features may constitute the core of the concept of courage, features such as Fear and Cognitive Processes may represent contingency factors influencing the expression of courageous action. Investigations of such contingency factors remain essential when considering developmental interventions to promote individual or organizational courage.

The search for the meaning of courage can take different directions. Continued investigation and validation of the core features of courage would be useful. Clarifying the influences of contingency factors and peripheral influences on courage and courageous behavior would be useful as well. Regardless of one's chosen path, as Ralph Waldo Emerson quite eloquently stated, "There is always someone to tell you that you are wrong. There are always difficulties arising which tempt you to believe that your critics are right. To map out a course of action and follow it to an end requires courage" ("Courage Quotes," n.d.). The search continues.

Why Does Courage Matter? Our Conclusion

Why are we studying courage? It could not be that we were simply interested in one of 30 virtues, 300 person attributes, or over 3,000 abstract concepts in the human language. Why should we be interested in courage in particular? Simply put, it is increasingly difficult to face an unpredictable future—sure to offer challenges with varying levels of risks, fears, and moral decisions—without being able to call on courage if needed. People need to know what, in fact, courage is in order to call on it. The future may not be as bleak as some predict, but those who believe in increasing entropy as a measure of increasing societal disorder have little assurance that it will not be. What is needed is an understanding of what people think courage is, and how to promote and train courage in individuals and organizations.

Recent headlines and publications illustrate the broad interest in courage and courageous behavior. Courage is examined in the contexts of patient–physician relationships (Bunkers, 2004; Finfgeld, 1995, 1998; Shelp, 1984), military service and leadership (Cox et al., 1983; Gole, 1997; Miller, 2000), politics (Kennedy, 1956), business and management (*Fast Company,* 2004; Johnson, 2005; Klein & Napier, 2003; Meisinger, 2005, Rate & Sternberg, 2007), and organizations (Cavanagh & Moberg, 1999; Kilmann et al., 2005), to name just a few. As the literature suggests, this construct is important to a vast number and variety of people: not just the military member, firefighter, or police officer, but also to business managers and leaders, to academic scholars, and to the ordinary citizen.

We proposed a parsimonious and heuristically useful definition of courage that emerged from a vignette-rating task. This conceptualization comprises three features that can be described as (a) a willing, intentional act, (b) involving substantial danger, difficulty, or risk to the actor, (c) primarily motivated to bring about a noble good or morally worthy purpose. Not all conceptualizations of courage are equal. Over 80% omitted one or more of the identified core features, and the remaining conceptualizations tended to be overly restrictive.

A multiple-perspective approach to the investigation of courage could provide a clear and consensus understanding of the answer to the question, "What is courage?" To date, however, the search for a scientifically acceptable and generally agreed-on meaning of courage continues. Though a consensus conceptualization of courage is a goal of our investigation, we realize that science, in general, is not determined by popular vote, and there will always be reasonable, differing perspectives on courage.

Do we now know what courage is? We are, arguably, closer than we were before our search began. As we review the literature that covers a variety of theoretical and empirical approaches to people's conceptions of courage, we find at least some support for the core or essence of courage (namely, risk, volition, and morally worthy purpose). These core features emerge, regardless of the empirical methodology. We have shown that explicit and implicit definitions converge.

Our current search for the meaning of courage has provided partial answers to the question, "What is courage?" Those seeking to behave in a courageous way may find it useful to know what is considered courageous, but also what is not. It will always be difficult to resolve whether any particular act is or is not courageous, because there may always be disagreement, for example, as to what is a noble or worthy purpose or the influences of peripheral factors. Even though people may agree conceptually on a definition of courage, in its application, courage becomes a construct perceived through the lens of the individual and is, at least in part, influenced by his or her personal experiences and biases. This should not, however, deter continuing investigation of the core meaning of courage, its contingency factors, and peripheral influences. The culmination of this search for the meaning of courage is simply the beginning of another. It would seem regrettable if we and our colleagues now abandon, as did Plato, the pursuit of courage and its meaning, particularly now, when courage seems so much in demand.

References

American Heritage Dictionary (4th ed.). (2006). Boston, MA: Houghton Mifflin.

Aquinas, T. (1922). *The summa theologica. Literally translated by the Fathers of the English Dominican Province.* London, England: Burns, Oates, & Washbourne.

Aristotle. (1987). *The Nicomachean ethics* (J. E. C. Welldon, Trans.). Amherst, NY: Prometheus Books.

Bauhn, P. (2003). *The value of courage.* Lund, Sweden: Nordic Academic Press.

Bluck, S., & Glück, J. (2005). From the inside out: People's implicit theories of wisdom. In R. J. Sternberg & J. Jordan (Eds.), *A handbook of wisdom: Psychological perspectives* (pp. 84–109). New York, NY: Cambridge University Press.

Bunkers, S. S. (2004). Socrates' questions: A focus for nursing. *Nursing Science Quarterly, 17,* 212–218. doi:10.1177/0894318404266318

Campbell, J. (1949). *The hero with a thousand faces.* Princeton, NJ: Princeton University Press.

Cavanagh, G. F., & Moberg, D. J. (1999). The virtue of courage within the organization. In M. L. Pava & P. Primeaux (Eds.), *Research in ethical issues in organizations* (pp. 1–25). Stamford, CT: JAI Press.

Compact Oxford English dictionary (3rd ed.). (2005). New York, NY: Oxford University Press.

Comte-Sponville, A. (2001). *A small treatise on the great virtues* (C. Temerson, Trans.). New York, NY: Metropolitan Books.

Courage Quotes. (n.d.). Retrieved January 15, 2007, from http://quotations.home.worldnet.att.net/courage.html

Cox, D., Hallam, R., O'Connor, K., & Rachman, S. (1983). An experimental analysis of fearlessness and courage. *The British Journal of Psychology, 74,* 107–117.

Deutsch, M. (1961). Courage as a concept in social psychology. *Journal of Social Psychology, 55,* 49–58.

Evans, P. D., & White, D. G. (1981). Towards an empirical definition of courage. *Behaviour Research and Therapy, 19,* 419–424. doi:10.1016/0005-7967(81)90131-5

Fast Company. (2004, September). The courage issue.

Finfgeld, D. L. (1995). Becoming and being courageous in the chronically ill elderly. *Issues in Mental Health Nursing, 16,* 1–11. doi:10.3109/01612849509042959

Finfgeld, D. L. (1998). Courage in middle-aged adults with long-term health concerns. *Canadian Journal of Nursing Research, 30,* 153–169.

Gole, H. G. (1997, Winter). Reflections on courage. *Parameters: US Army War College Quarterly,* 147–157.

Gould, N. H. (2005). Courage: Its nature and development. *Journal of Humanistic Counseling, Education and Development, 33,* 102–116.

Greitemeyer, T., Fischer, P., Kastenmüller, A., & Frey, D. (2006). Civil courage and helping behavior. *European Psychologist, 11,* 90–98. doi:10.1027/1016-9040.11.2.90

Haase, J. E. (1987). Components of courage in chronically ill adolescents: A phenomenological study. *ANS. Advances in Nursing Science, 9,* 64–80.

Harris, H. (2000, February). *Courage as a management virtue.* Paper presented at the Ninth Annual Meeting of the Association for Practical and Professional Ethics, Arlington, VA.

Ivanhoe, P. J. (2002). The virtue of courage in the Mencius. In B. Darling-Smith (Ed.), *Courage* (pp. 65–79). Notre Dame, IN: University of Notre Dame Press.

Johnson, P. (2005, May 9). Five marks of a great leader. *Forbes, 175,* 31.

Kennedy, J. F. (1956). *Profiles in courage.* New York, NY: Harper and Brothers.

Kidder, R. M. (2005). *Moral courage.* New York, NY: Morrow.

Kilmann, R. H., O'Hara, L. A., & Strauss, J. P. (2005). *Developing and validating a quantitative measure of organizational courage.* Manuscript submitted for publication.

Klein, M., & Napier, R. (2003). *The courage to act: 5 factors of courage to transform business.* Palo Alto, CA: Davies-Black.

Krippendorff, K. (2004). *Content analysis, an introduction to its methodology* (2nd ed.). Thousand Oaks, CA: Sage.

Lopez, S. J., O'Byrne, K. K., & Petersen, S. (2003). Profiling courage. In S. J. Lopez & C. R. Snyder (Eds.), *Positive psychological assessment: A handbook of models and measures* (pp. 185–197). Washington, DC: American Psychological Association. doi:10.1037/10612-012

MacIntyre, A. (1981). *After virtue.* London, England: Duckworth.

May, R. (1978). *The courage to create.* New York, NY: Bantam Books.

McCain, J., & Salter, M. (2004). *Why courage matters: The way to a braver life.* New York, NY: Random House.

McMillan, T., & Rachman, S. (1987). Fearlessness and courage in paratroop veterans of the Falkland war. *The British Journal of Psychology, 78,* 375–383.

Meisinger, S. R. (2005). The four Cs of the HR profession: Being competent, curious, courageous, and caring about people. *Human Resource Management, 44,* 189–194. doi:10.1002/hrm.20063

Merriam-Webster dictionary. (2005). Springfield, MA: Merriam-Webster.

Miller, W. I. (2000). *The mystery of courage.* Cambridge, MA: Harvard University Press.

O'Byrne, K. K., Lopez, S. J., & Petersen, S. (2000, August). *Building a theory of courage: A precursor to change?* Paper presented at the 108th Annual Convention of the American Psychological Association, Washington, DC.

Oxford English dictionary (2nd ed.). (1989). New York, NY: Oxford University Press.

Peterson, C., & Seligman, M. E. P. (2004). *Character strengths and virtues: A handbook and classification.* New York, NY: Oxford University Press.

Plato. (1987). Laches (J. H. Nichols, Jr., Trans.). In T. L. Pangle (Ed.), *The roots of political philosophy: Ten forgotten Socratic dialogues* (pp. 240–268). Ithaca, NY: Cornell University Press.

Pury, C. L. S., Kowalski, R. M., & Spearman, J. (2007). Distinctions between general and personal courage. *The Journal of Positive Psychology, 2*(2), 99–114. doi:10.1080/17439760701237962

Putman, D. (1997). Psychological courage. *Philosophy, Psychiatry, & Psychology, 4*(1), 1–11. doi: 10.1353/ppp.1997.0008

Putman, D. (2001). The emotions of courage. *Journal of Social Philosophy, 32,* 463–470. doi:10.1111/0047-2786.00107

Rachman, S. J. (1990). *Fear and courage* (2nd ed.). New York, NY: Freeman.

Rasmussen, H. N., O'Byrne, K. K., Petersen, S., & Lopez, S. J. (2005). *Differences in courage between cultures: An international perspective.* Unpublished manuscript.

Rate, C. R. (2007). What is courage? A search for meaning (Doctoral dissertation, Yale University, 2007). Available from ProQuest Dissertations and Theses database. (AAT 33293368).

Rate, C. R., Clarke, J. A., Lindsay, D. R., & Sternberg, R. J. (2007). Implicit theories of courage. *The Journal of Positive Psychology, 2*(2), 80–98. doi:10.1080/17439760701228755

Rate, C. R., & Sternberg, R. J. (2007). When good people do nothing: A failure of courage. In J. Langan-Fox, C. L. Cooper, & R. J. Klimoski (Eds.), *Research companion to the dysfunctional workplace: Management challenges and symptoms* (pp. 3–21). London, England: Edward Elgar.

Remarks by the President at Presentation of Medal of Honor. (2008, April 9). *Business Wire.* Retrieved from http://www.enewspf.com

Seligman, M. E. P., & Csikszentmihalyi, M. (2000). Positive psychology: An introduction. *The American Psychologist, 55,* 5–14. doi:10.1037/0003-066X.55.1.5

Shelp, E. E. (1984). Courage: A neglected virtue in the patient-physician relationship. *Social Science & Medicine, 18,* 351–360. doi:10.1016/0277-9536(84)90125-4

Srivastva, S., & Cooperrider, D. L. (Eds.). (1998). *Organizational wisdom and executive courage.* San Francisco, CA: New Lexington Press.

Stemler, S. (2001). An overview of content analysis. *Practical Assessment, Research & Evaluation,* 7(17). Retrieved from http://PAREonline.net/getvn.asp?v=7&n=17

Szagun, G. (1992). Age-related changes in children's understanding of courage. *Journal of Genetic Psychology, 153,* 405–420.

Szagun, G., & Schauble, M. (1997). Children's and adults' understanding of the feeling experience of courage. *Cognition and Emotion, 11,* 291–306. doi:10.1080/026999397379935

Walton, D. N. (1986). *Courage: A philosophical investigation.* Los Angeles: University of California Press.

Woodard, C. R. (2004). Hardiness and the concept of courage. *Consulting Psychology Journal: Practice and Research, 56,* 173–185. doi:10.1037/1065-9293.56.3.173

Worline, M. C., Wrzesniewski, A., & Rafaeli, A. (2002). Courage and work: Breaking routines to improve performance. In R. Lord, R. Klimoski, & R. Kanfer (Eds.), *Emotions at work* (pp. 295–330). San Francisco, CA: Jossey-Bass.

Yearly, L. H. (1990). *Mencius and Aquinas: Theories of virtue and conceptions of courage.* Albany: State University of New York Press.

4

Is Courage an Accolade or a Process? A Fundamental Question for Courage Research

Cynthia L. S. Pury and Charles B. Starkey

Courage has been described as a human virtue by philosophers across time and cultures (e.g., Dahlsgaard, Peterson, & Seligman, 2005; Miller, 2002). It figures prominently in positive psychology's science of virtue (e.g., Peterson & Seligman, 2004), and interest in courage as a topic of psychological study has grown with the field of positive psychology. However, what psychologists mean by the term *courage* has varied, and this variation has important consequences for understanding the construct. We therefore asked ourselves the following questions: Do we see courage as rare, lofty, and worthy of societal acknowledgment, which we view as part of *courage as an accolade,* or do we see courage as something that occurs many times in the typical person's life, a process, perhaps *the* process, by which people overcome subjectively felt risks for compelling reasons? Though desirable, most of the acts that fall under this second type of courage, which we call *courage as a process,* may pass unnoticed by observers and are not typically deserving of societal recognition.

Courage can be defined in many ways. Norton and Weiss (2009) described courage as "persistence or perseverance *despite having fear*" (p. 214, emphasis in the original). Pury and Woodard (2009) defined it as "the intentional pursuit of a worthy goal despite the perception of personal threat and uncertain outcome" (p. 247). Peterson and Seligman (2004) defined courage as "emotional strengths that involve the exercise of will to accomplish goals in the face of opposition, external or internal" (p. 29). Finally, in the most comprehensive study of the definition of courage, Rate, Clarke, Lindsay, and Sternberg (2007) used a multimethod approach to develop a definition of courage as "(a) a willful, intentional act, (b) executed after mindful deliberation, (c) involving objective substantial risk to the actor, (d) primarily motivated to bring about a noble good or worthy end, (e) despite, perhaps, the emotion of fear" (p. 95).

The first two definitions focus on courage as a process. In Pury and Woodard's (2009) work the definition is general. Pury and Woodard highlighted the importance of the worth of the goal and two unknowns—risk to the actor and completion of the task—without any particular behavioral or emotional response described. Norton and Weiss's (2009) definition is directed at the specific case of predicting performance during an exposure-like exercise for phobias.

Norton and Weiss described a specific behavior, persistence, and a specific emotional response, fear, which are particularly well-matched to the demands and obstacles of exposure therapy.

Peterson and Seligman (2004) characterized courage as a character strength, a trait-like concept. Like a trait, a strength is obvious to external observers: Their definition describes courage as a strength that succeeds in accomplishing a goal, a more obvious marker than merely pursuing a goal. As with a trait, a strength needs to be present in a wide array of circumstances: Their definition allows for broad goals and broad obstacles. Their resulting definition describes results obtained in a wide array of circumstances, the type of broadly observable actions one expects from traits.

Rate et al. (2007) studied the criteria used by laypeople to determine the courageousness of an action. Rate and his colleagues provided the most detail about the motivation of the act (worthy) and the nature of risk required (objective and substantial), and included the stipulation that the act must be voluntary and fully considered, thus requiring a clear internal causality. Their definition shares much in common with the requirements for many bravery awards (e.g., The Carnegie Medal, Carnegie Hero Fund Commission, 2009b; The Courage in Journalism Awards, International Women's Media Foundation, 2008; The George Cross, Hebblethwaite, n.d.) by requiring that both the goal of the action and the risk to the actor be substantial. Their definition best captures the idea of courage as an accolade, as indicated by the overlap between their definition and common requirements for awards for courage.

Two very distinct concepts of courage—as a psychological process and as an accolade—share the view that courage involves acting in the face of internal or external resistance. However, they also differ in important ways, and each of the previous definitions falls short when attempting to use it in research with a different object of study. To illustrate this, imagine that two separate suspicious packages are found. In each case, a person who believes it to be a bomb warns others of the danger, picks up the package, and runs with it to an empty area. The bomb squad finds that one package contains a bomb whereas the other contains harmless wires. Would the two actions be labeled later as equally courageous? Probably not, according to Rate et al.'s (2007) requirement of objective risk. Were the same processes at work in both actors before they knew if there was really a bomb in their package? Probably. Thus, to avoid semantic disputes and misunderstandings, it is important to identify and explicitly distinguish between the various applications of the term *courage*.

In this chapter, we focus on one particular distinction: the distinction between courage as an accolade and courage as a process. We discuss what we know about courage as an accolade and argue that calling an action courageous constitutes an illocutionary act, defined later. We explore the evidence for this view and explore differences between courage as an accolade—a type of illocutionary act—and courage as a process. We then discuss the implication of this distinction for trait notions of courage, and end with implications for understanding courage and the future of courage research.

Courage as an Accolade: An Illocutionary Act View

We believe that in many cases the function of calling a particular action or actor courageous is not merely providing a description, but rather conveys the approval by either an individual or a larger social milieu, and encourages the behavior involved. We propose that here courage is chiefly an accolade that is a form of illocutionary act. One of the most important contributions of J. L. Austin, an influential linguist, was to bring to light the fact that language has multiple functions beyond referring to things in the world. Austin (1975) defined illocutionary acts as statements that go beyond simply informing the listener or reader; they are normally uttered with the intent of changing something. For instance, exclaiming "The dog is rabid!" does not merely describe a feature of something in the world but serves to influence people's behavior by encouraging them to avoid the dog. Similarly, by calling an action courageous, the speaker is typically not only describing a feature of the act but also praising an action as good, noble, or worthwhile to the end of encouraging such behavior. Here, following Rate et al. (2007), from the speaker's perspective real risks were taken in pursuit of a goal that was worth the potential cost.

Public Praise

What is the evidence for this view? First, the hypothesis that labeling something as *courageous* has the function of an accolade predicts that society will commonly praise courage in a tangible and public way. Indeed, awards for courage are quite common. This labeling is frequently quite public: A LexusNexis Academic search of news wire services for *courage* and *award* returned 999 hits for 2008, 994 hits for 2006, and over 1,000 hits (the search limit) for 2007, 2005, and 2004. Many of these stories are about recipients of some particular award for courage or bravery: The Anne Frank Award for Moral Courage, the Australian Bravery Awards, the Courage to Come Back Awards, the Children of Courage Award, the Arthur Ashe Courage Award, the Profile in Courage Award, the Courage in Journalism Award, and a multitude of others appear in the results.

As described previously, these awards commonly prescribe a particular level or type of risk, or both, faced in the course of pursuing, and typically achieving, a particular goal, and in this way are consistent with the criteria for the accolade of courage discussed in the literature discussed earlier. For example, the Australian Bravery Decorations are awarded to those who "selflessly put themselves in jeopardy to protect the lives or property of others," making a "deliberate choice to go from a place of safety to danger or remain in a perilous position to provide help" (Australian Government, 2008). The Courage in Journalism Award recognizes women who

> exhibit extraordinary strength of character, bravery and perseverance in reporting the news; have a strong commitment to press freedom and [are] well-respected journalists who have shown a commitment to journalism exemplified by a willingness to continually put their life or their freedom at risk to produce a body of work in the face of government oppression, political

> pressure, physical danger or other intimidating obstacles. (International Women's Media Foundation, 2008)

The Courage to Come Back Awards honor people who have "inspired others as they have courageously battled back from illness, adversity or injury. Through [the Courage awards], British Columbians are acknowledged for their accomplishments, positive attitudes and willingness to give back to their communities" (Coast Mental Health Foundation, 2008). Each of the awards discussed in this section specifies a particular level of goal or accomplishment (e.g., protecting another, reporting the news, enhancing the recovery of others) and a focus on the level of risk the person faced in striving for that goal (putting oneself in danger or remaining in danger, putting one's life or freedom at risk, or the variety of conditions covered by the Courage to Come Back Awards). Nomination instructions make it clear that awards are determined on a clear statement of the magnitude of both the risks and the goals.[1]

Other evidence is found in a more permanent form, namely, modern statues and monuments that commonly commemorate acts of courage, most often military courage, such as the World War II Memorial in Washington, DC, and the Tugu Negara in Malaysia. Other monuments celebrate moral courage, such as the Civil Rights Memorial in Montgomery, Alabama, and the Nelson Mandela bust in London. The inscriptions attached to these public sculptures are suitably monumental and commonly describe a debt owed to the honorees. One example is the quote by Harry S. Truman inscribed on the World War II Memorial: "Our debt to the heroic men and valiant women in the service of our country can never be repaid. They have earned our undying gratitude." Some describe the specific goals pursued by the honorees: "the cause of peace and freedom" for the Tugu Negara, and justice and righteousness for the Civil Rights Monument. They frequently also include a description of the risks incurred by the honorees, such as Nelson Mandela's imprisonment dates inscribed on his bust in London. Psychological or vital courage is rarely commemorated in a monument, and when it is, the disability is prominently featured: A statue of Helen Keller in Cleveland, Ohio, reads "Here I am not disenfranchised. No barrier of the senses shuts me out." On the wall behind a bronze statue of Franklin D. Roosevelt in a wheelchair at the Roosevelt Memorial in Washington, DC, is an inscription from Eleanor Roosevelt suggesting that his disability was a wellspring for later greatness.

In all these cases, the individuals or groups honored with a monument are, almost by definition, cultural icons who have overcome extreme risks pursuing and often attaining a good that is extremely valuable to society. Pury, Kowalski, and Spearman (2007) described such actions, in pursuit of very good goals against very severe risks, as "monumental courage" (p. 100). These monuments and awards demonstrate that though courage is commonly praised, extremely high levels of courage garner the highest praise.

---

[1]Each of these awards also exemplifies a commonly described type of courage (e.g., Lopez, O'Byrne, & Petersen, 2003; see Chapter 1, this volume). The Australian Bravery Award exemplifies physical courage, the Courage in Journalism Award moral courage, and the Courage to Come Back Awards psychological or vital courage.

Endorsement of Goals and Appreciation of Risk

If calling an action or person courageous is an accolade and not merely a description of the act or the psychological state of the actor, then people should be less willing to call an action courageous if they devalue or disagree with its goals or consider its risks trivial. There is ample anecdotal evidence consistent with this prediction. Comedian Bill Maher, shortly after terrorists used hijacked airplanes in suicide attacks against the World Trade Center and Pentagon, stated on his television show that "We [the United States] have been the cowards, lobbing cruise missiles from 2,000 miles away. That's cowardly. Staying in the airplane when it hits the building, say what you want about it, it's not cowardly" (quoted in Breznican, 2002). Public outcry ensued, with Maher's show rapidly losing advertisers and eventually being cancelled.

Other anecdotal evidence is provided by the experience of examining questionnaires about courage. In our lab we have collected nearly 1,000 narrative answers to the request "Describe a time in your life when you believe that you acted courageously." In coding the data, nearly every person working on the coding, from the first author of this chapter to first semester research assistants, encountered narratives that left them with a gut response of "That's not courage!" These incidents normally involved cases in which the ethical choices pursued by the participant were different from those that the coder would make; for example, in a case of breaking up with a boyfriend because of family pressure, the coder believed the morally better choice was to stay. Other actions that were questioned as courageous involved those in which the risks were judged too small to warrant the label of courage; for example, a coder who grew up in South Africa was unimpressed by narratives of encounters with vicious dogs. Unlike lions or hyenas, dogs are unlikely to hunt humans for prey.

Laboratory studies provide at least partial support for this view. Erin Jenkins and the first author of this chapter (Jenkins & Pury, 2009) examined the relationship between endorsement of goals and ratings of courage. We asked 149 college students (86 female, 63 male; mean age = 18.7, *SD* = 1.1) to read a variety of scenarios about a female actor performing an action that might be seen as courageous, then to rate the courageousness of that action. The first three scenarios were control scenarios about three different actors; the actor in the first scenario stands up for someone being teased, in the second wants to dive off of a high platform but changes her mind, and in the third saves a child from drowning. In the fourth and final scenario, half of the participants were randomly assigned to read about an actor who is strongly pro-choice and half about an actor who is strongly pro-life. In both conditions the actor has friends and family who strongly support the opposite position. The actor participates in a contentious abortion protest supporting her beliefs, in the process identifying herself and her beliefs to disapproving friends and family.

After reading each scenario, participants answered questions about the courage of the actor, but only the final scenario was analyzed. An overall Courage Index was computed from the mean of three questions: "Compared to the actions of most other people, how courageous was this action?" "To what extent was (the main character) rising to the occasion when she demonstrated on behalf of her beliefs?" and "To what extent was (the main character) brave when demonstrating on behalf of her beliefs?" These items were rated on a 0 to 10 scale where 0 was *not at all* and 10 was *very much*. Perceived morality of the actor's actions was assessed by asking, "How moral are (the main character's) actions?" Respondents rated perceived morality on a 0 to 10 scale where 0 was *extremely immoral* and 10 was *extremely moral*. The participants' own views toward abortion and toward free speech were assessed with items derived from a previously developed scale using a 1 (*not at all*) to 5 (*extremely*) scale (Britt, 2003). The extent to which the participant supported the views of the protesters (Support of Views) was calculated separately for each experimental group: For the group that read about the pro-choice protester, pro-life scores ("To what extent would you label your attitude toward legalized abortion 'pro-life'?") were subtracted from pro-choice scores ("To what extent would you label your attitude toward legalized abortion 'pro-choice'?"). For the group that read about the pro-life protester, pro-choice scores were subtracted from pro-life scores. One item assessed views toward free speech: To what extent would you say that you are for free speech?

The mean of three items assessing the importance of abortion and the mean of three items assessing the importance of free speech were used to create an Importance Index for both abortion and free speech: "How important would you say the issue of legalized abortion (or free speech) is to you personally?" "How much do you personally care about the issue of legalized abortion (or free speech)?" and "How important is the issue of legalized abortion (or free speech) compared to other issues?" Participants whose Abortion Importance Index was higher than their Free Speech Index were labeled the Abortion group (n = 65), whereas those whose Free Speech Importance Index was equal to or higher than their Abortion Index were labeled the Free Speech group (n = 83).

For both groups, rated morality of the main character's action was significantly and positively correlated with the Courage Index (Abortion $r = .48, p < .01$; Free Speech $r = .38, p < .01$). For the Abortion group, whose attitudes toward abortion are more important than their attitudes toward free speech, Support of Views was significantly correlated with the Courage Index ($r = .33, p <.01$), whereas attitude toward free speech was not significantly correlated with the Courage Index ($r = -.02, p > .1$). For the Free Speech group, the results were reversed: Support of Views was not significantly correlated with the Courage Index ($r = -.14, p > .2$), whereas attitude toward free speech was significantly and positively correlated with the Courage Index ($r = .26, p < .02$). Thus, perceived courageousness of the protester was related to belief in her cause for participants whose beliefs on abortion were strongest, whereas perceived courageousness was related to belief in free speech for participants whose beliefs on free speech were strongest. For both groups, perceived morality had a strong correlation with perceived courageousness.

This relationship between morality and perceived courage may be developmental in nature and may reflect increasing cognitive complexity. Children increasingly use internal mental processes in their view of courage, with younger children viewing courage as acting without fear, whereas older children and adults view it as acting despite fear (Szagun, 1992; Szagun & Schäuble, 1997).

Whereas the courage attributed to taking obvious, physical risks declines with age, taking more subtle risks, such as the social risks encountered in overcoming peer pressure, is seen as more courageous with increasing age. Actions taken for morally good goals are seen as increasingly courageous with age, whereas actions taken for morally bad reasons are not.

Thus, it appears that for adults, calling an action courageous is dependent on one's view of the morality and risks involved in the situation.

Outcome: Was the Action Worth the Risk?

If calling an action courageous is an act of praise, it follows that the act is deemed worthy of praise. This in turn entails that acting is perceived to be worth the risk involved. Accordingly, this theory predicts that actions failing to meet their goal should be less likely to be praised because the risks involved are perceived to be less worthwhile than the risks involved in actions that succeed. Some awards for courage have an explicit requirement that the action was successful. For example, the Courage in Journalism Award requires that awardees "produce a body of work in the face of government oppression, political pressure, physical danger or other intimidating obstacles" (International Women's Media Foundation, 2008).

Other awards specifically state that the intended goal need not be attained; for example, the Carnegie Medal requires that nominees "save or attempt to save" the life of another (Carnegie Hero Fund Commission, 2009b). However, in practice the award may be made much more often to those who succeed than to those who fail: Inspection of the narratives posted for the 74 acts for which at least one Carnegie Medal was awarded in 2008 (Carnegie Hero Fund Commission, 2009a) revealed that in 66 cases (89%), all of the victims were rescued. In eight cases (11%), at least one of the victims died during the incident. Moreover, cases of failed or incomplete rescue are significantly associated with the death of the rescuer ($\chi^2 = 19.45, p < .01$). Of the cases in which at least one victim died before rescue, seven incidents (88%) also led to the death of at least one would-be rescuer, whereas of the 66 cases of rescue, only 11 (15%) also involved the death of at least one rescuer. There was only one instance of an award being made to rescuers who lived who did not save every victim; in that case, one victim died and the other two were saved. Thus, at least in 2008, awards were made only in instances of successful rescue or when a would-be rescuer died trying.

The awarding of the Carnegie Medal, or any award for courage, depends on a variety of idiosyncratic factors (e.g., Becker & Eagly, 2004). It may be that some of these factors make it more likely that successful actions will be honored for these idiosyncratic reasons rather than because successful actions are seen as more heroic, or it may be the case that attempted rescues are typically successful, and the high death rate among rescuers in failed attempts merely reflects more extreme (and less worthwhile) risks. What happens in more scientifically controlled situations?

When asked to describe their own courageous action (Pury et al., 2007) or the action of another (Pury & Hensel, 2010, Study 1), participants nearly always described an action that improved the situation and did not make it worse. In both cases, to answer the question, participants needed to select an action that they believe is courageous: Even if it is their own behavior, selecting and writing about that action is, in effect, labeling it as courageous. (It is interesting that participants in the self condition frequently appear proud of their actions: One participant in an ongoing study recently asked the first author if she would publish his narrative because he was very proud of what he had done and wanted others to know.)

As with the Carnegie Medal, other factors, such as a high base-rate of success for intentional actions, might lead to an overrepresentation of success. To examine this possibility, Pury and Hensel (2010, Study 2) asked participants to rate the courageousness of a variety of scenarios, drawn from physical, moral, and psychological courage. Two independent variables—Outcome and Cause—were manipulated. Outcome was manipulated by ending the scenarios with the action improving the situation or making it worse. Cause, which was orthogonal to Outcome, was manipulated by attributing the Outcome to internal or to external factors. For example, in one scenario the main character encounters a person being teased by a crowd and steps in to tell the crowd to stop. In the Internal Success condition, the actor is talented at persuasion and the crowd stops. In the External Success condition, other people also notice the situation and come to help disperse the crowd. In the Internal Failure condition, the actor is not very persuasive, and the crowd continues to harass the victim. In the External Failure condition, the crowd contains some leaders who incite them to continue harassing the victim. In keeping with the proposition that success contributes to the labeling of courage, participants rated successful actions as significantly more courageous than unsuccessful actions. Although this effect was attenuated for externally caused outcomes, it was not eliminated. Moreover, participants were also asked to provide their own definition of courage at the end of the study. Only 15 of the 153 participants mentioned outcome and, of those 15, 14 stated clearly that intent, not outcome, matters for courage. Data from those 14 showed the same pattern of results: Despite their stated definition, they still rated successful actions as more courageous than unsuccessful ones.

Saying that an action is courageous, then, is more likely for actions that end with success than with failure. This is in accordance with Peterson and Seligman's (2004) trait definition but not Rate et al.'s (2007) accolade definition.

Elevation and the Praising of Courage

It might be that the positive feelings aroused by the moral quality and happy ending that characterize actions judged as courageous also lead people to draw other people's attention to such an action through the behavioral expression of the emotion of elevation. Elevation is characterized by feeling emotionally touched, experiencing physiological sensations of goosebumps and tearfulness, with a desire to help others and, most important for the accolade view of courage, to tell others about the action (Haidt, 2000, 2003; Silvers & Haidt, 2008). Observing or being reminded of a courageous act taken by another commonly produces elevation, although elevation can also be elicited by acts of great charity or love. The core trigger of elevation appears to be witnessing someone else acting in a morally beautiful manner. Observation of courage in the workplace has been linked to a changed sense of possibility at work and inspiration, outcomes one would expect if the participants felt elevation (Worline, 2004). This sense of inspiration and elevation may explain some of the desire to laud acts as courageous.

Constant and Changing Heroes

Because morality includes both evolved and culturally determined features (e.g., Hauser, 2006), there may be cultural differences in exactly what type of acts are deserving of public praise. Moreover, the degree to which acts are seen as heroic, or extremely high in courage, may vary with changes within a culture. For example, Barczewski (2007) traced the change in public perception of the heroism of Robert Falcon Scott and Ernest Shackleton, two contemporary Antarctic explorers from Great Britain in the early 1900s. Scott's final expedition and death in Antarctica, seen as the epitome of a "stiff upper lip" mentality and a devotion to a lost cause, was extensively praised during the first part of the 20th century. Shackleton returned from his failed expedition with little fanfare. More recently, however, admiration of Scott's heroism has declined in favor of Shackleton, whose flexibility and optimism saved his entire party.

This approach leads to a hypothesis, which to our knowledge has not been tested, that some actions should seem courageous across most times and cultures, an expanded version of general courage (Pury et al., 2007) that might be called *universal courage*. These actions should be those that evoke evolutionarily driven responses to both the goal and the risk. For example, goals that are part of universal courage should include those that preserve society or the fundamental rules underlying society, save genetic kin, and save children (particularly from the perspective of the parents). Risks that should be part of universal courage include risk of death or physical injury and risk of social rejection (e.g., Nesse, 1990; Nesse & Ellsworth, 2009). Actions pursuing one of these goals despite one of these risks should be seen as courageous in most places and at most times. Actions involving more culturally bound goals or risks should be seen as more courageous in cultures that value those goals or fear those risks than in those that do not.

We propose that most traditional instances of physical courage, in which a person risks his or her life on behalf of another person or the society, and moral courage, in which a person risks social rejection (up to ostracism) to defend fundamental rules of society, might be prototypes of universal courage. On the other hand, psychological courage, in which one risks emotional well-being for a personal growth or wellness, may be a culturally bound type of courage that may be limited to cultures placing an emphasis on personal growth and inner life.

Differentiation From Courage as a Process

How do people come to act courageously? This is the key question that theories and studies of courage as a process seek to answer. Note that this question is fundamentally different from "Was that a praiseworthy instance of courage?", the tacit question posed by courage as an accolade. In this section, we explore the difference between examining how courageous actions are taken and determining if such actions are worthy of the accolade *courage*. This difference is analogous to the difference between understanding a cartwheel from the perspective of a kinesiologist and understanding it from the perspective of a gymnastics judge. Though both observe people tumbling, the kinesiologist explores the physics, biomechanics, and acquisition of the skill to complete a cartwheel effectively. Because of these interests, all levels of cartwheel ability are suitable for research and the results may be used to help individuals at all levels improve their performance. In fact, failed cartwheels may be especially useful in learning the conditions needed for successful performance. Internal states such as dizziness due to vestibular and ocular disparity are of interest, as are techniques such as spotting developed to cope with them. In fact, kinesiology provides the discoveries and the tools to develop additional techniques. The gymnastics judge, on the other hand, is interested in grace, form, and adherence to competition rules. Instances of flawless execution, garnering a perfect 10, are of most interest, and the emphasis is on how much the individual's performance deviates from the expected form. Inner states and techniques to deal with them are of limited interest.[2]

Though the kinesiology approach to cartwheels involves physics and biomechanics, the process approach to courage has underlying psychological mechanisms. For example, Lord (1918) used the relatively new mechanism of "sentiments" to explain courage, proposing that courage occurs when the base sentiment of fear is overcome by another more noble sentiment. The idea of acting in opposition to the internal state of fear is a key component for many theories regarding the process of taking courageous action. Current process approaches, particularly those from clinical traditions, emphasize fear but largely ignore the more noble sentiments, as described later.

Fear and the Process of Courage

Fear on the part of the actor is a questionable part of courage as an accolade. Rate et al.'s (2007) data suggest that fear might or might not be required to call an action courageous and, indeed, in some of the definitions used in their study the absence of fear was a requirement. It is difficult to imagine a citation for valor including the statement "She was terrified, but then she got over her fear and jumped into the water to rescue him." A search of Carnegie Medal data from 2008 (Carnegie Hero Fund Commission, 2009a) for the words *fear, afraid, terrified,* and *worried* found that those words were never used in the description of the 74 courageous actions for which medals were awarded.

In contrast to its questionable role as part of courage as an accolade, fear plays a very prominent role in the conception of courage used in psychotherapy, a field that aims to change behavior by understanding and altering the process

[2]One important difference between judges of cartwheels and observers of potentially courageous actions is that a gymnastics judge is likely to consider a poorly done cartwheel a cartwheel, whereas observers of actions that do not measure up to the standards of courage might not consider those acts courageous.

by which people experience and interact with themselves and the world. Analytic theorists (e.g., Bacha, 2001; Gans, 2005) have described courage as a helpful and possibly necessary part of engaging in the psychotherapeutic process. According to this approach, it requires psychological courage (Putman, 2004) to face unpleasant facts in the service of emotional recovery. Facing such facts is essential to this process, but often is a source of intense fear and anxiety. Bacha (2001) proposed that facing these facts might be a part of therapeutic change, including being willing to examine one's underlying psychological structures, mourning the past and accepting that some possibilities are lost, and moving from the familiar to the unfamiliar. The disclosure and confrontation of pain in psychoanalytic group work, according to Gans (2005), requires courage from patients that should be acknowledged by therapists. Gans also noted that the type of courage he describes is neither universal nor absolute, and that therapists need to learn to become more attuned to patients' courageousness in treatment. It is presumed that therapists would not need to increase their awareness of courage that easily fits the courage as accolade model.

Similarly, existential courage, or the courage to accept one's own limited existence and move past the fear of nonbeing, is a key feature of existential theory (Tillich, 1958) and therapy (Medina, 2008). Medina proposed that the courage emerging from existential treatment is best thought of as "everyday courage" and has five key components: being, self-hood, choice, faith, and creativity.

Though the fear described by psychoanalytic and existential theorists is thought to be common to all clients (and perhaps to all human beings), fear as studied by cognitive–behavioral therapists has a specific target and primarily affects clients with anxiety disorders. Rachman (1990) described his research into courage as stemming from observations of clients undergoing exposure therapy for phobias. Despite enduring great fear and even panic during exposure exercises, clients recovered remarkably quickly and were willing to face their feared situations again and again. Recent reconceptualizations of cognitive–behavioral therapy (CBT; e.g., Arch & Craske, 2008) have reframed the cognitive piece of CBT as a way to facilitate exposure exercises rather than having a direct therapeutic benefit. Likewise, in acceptance and commitment therapy (ACT) for anxiety disorders (Eifert & Forsyth, 2005; Hayes, Strosahl, & Wilson, 1999), acceptance of anxiety symptoms facilitates clients' ability to act with anxiety or to engage in meaningful life activities despite anxiety.

All of these treatments involve taking action that will increase a subjective sense of risk (and the objective chance of having an unpleasant panic attack) in pursuit of increased mental health—the prototypical case of psychological courage (Putman, 2004). Courage, operationalized as a measure of behavioral approach in the face of fear in general and panic attacks specifically, was investigated as a possible mediator between panic disorder and phobic avoidance (Schmidt & Koselka, 2000), but no effects were found. Norton and Weiss (2009) developed a longer measure focusing on persistence in the face of fear in general. When given to individuals high in spider fear immediately prior to a behavioral approach test, their measure predicted approach distance to taxidermied spiders above and beyond fear measures.

Fear is not, however, always observable in others under ordinary circumstances. Rachman (1990) originally proposed that courage occurs when someone experiences the physiological and subjective sense of fear but not the behavioral component. Testing this idea, he brought individuals decorated for bravery into the lab and found that their physiological and subjective fear response to laboratory stress was less than that of individuals in similar jobs who were not decorated for bravery. In our view, this is not surprising because the accolade view has little to say about fear but much to say about performance.

Fear does, however, seem to play a strong role in courage as a process seen from the inside. Pury et al. (2007) asked participants to describe a time they acted courageously. Then they asked them how courageous the act was compared with their own typical action, which they called *personal courage,* and how courageous this act was for people in general, which they called *general courage.* Though self-reported fear before and during the action had a significant and positive correlation with personal courage, it did not correlate with general courage. Confidence, on the other hand, was significantly and positively correlated with general courage but not with personal courage. Acts that were high in personal courage commonly involved overcoming personal limitations or facing fears that were particular to the individual, whereas acts that were high in general courage were described as actions that would be risky for anyone. We propose that general courage is likely to be related to the courage as accolade view: What can be externally observed in the situation and would others comment on its merit? Understanding personal courage, on the other hand, may offer a view of the process people use in overcoming fear and personal limitations—the type of courage that might be profitably encouraged in psychotherapy.

Noble Emotions and Courage

A similar view of the importance of emotions and related states in the process of taking courageous action emerges from Greitemeyer, Fischer, Kastenmüller, and Frey (2006; Studies 2 and 3). Using a retrospective self-report method, they examined differences between instances of civil courage (support of social and ethical norms despite the risk of a social cost) and helping behavior. They found that the process of taking a civilly courageous act, compared with typical helping behavior, differed in important ways, including feeling more responsible and more competent, being aware of moral norms, experiencing anger, and experiencing the fear-related expectancy of more negative social consequences. Several of these differences, most notably the moral emotion of anger, feelings of responsibility, and, particularly, awareness of moral norms, are tied to Lord's (1918) idea of a more noble sentiment overcoming fear.

This idea of overcoming fear or other emotional turmoil for a good cause finds specific voice in the commitment phase of ACT (Eifert & Forsyth, 2005; Hayes, Strosahl, & Wilson, 1999). Commitment exercises are explicitly tied to achieving a meaningful goal in the client's life that is conceptually separate from exposure therapy's goal of symptom reduction, although in practice they may result in similar outcomes (Arch & Craske, 2008). Such exercises may be seen as instances of psychological courage in its purest form: Clients are asked to perform meaningful actions despite their symptoms. ACT also features the results orientation of the accolade model of courage: Clients are told not to try but to succeed.

ACT also explicitly ties participants' goals and values to commitment exercises. In our lab, we have found that when participants are asked to describe anything they did to increase their courage, they commonly list strategies of reminding themselves about the value of the goal they are pursuing. In fact, this strategy is the most commonly used, reported by 48% of participants, compared with emotion-focused coping, problem-focused coping, or a combination of strategies (Pury et al., 2006). We believe that more research on the subjective experience of the goals and the risks of courageous action, including efficacy to reach goals without engendering risks, will yield the most complete picture of courage as a process.

Other Differentiations of Courage as an Accolade and Courage as a Process

Aside from fear, there are several other differences between these two approaches. First, studies of the process of courage are likely to fall far short of the high bar of accolade courage for several reasons. First, much of the interest in courage as a process comes from psychotherapy. Though some awards for psychological or vital courage do exist (e.g., the Courage to Come Back Award), these are rare and commonly include a stipulation that the nominee's recovery goes above and beyond what is expected, to the extent that he or she is an inspiration to others. However, one very likely early application of understanding courage as a process is envisioned by Norton and Weiss (2009): predicting who will remain in exposure therapy or other treatments in which fear needs to be overcome. It is both unlikely and undesirable for society at large to celebrate the successful completion of an exposure exercise with a medal. However, it is clearly in exposure therapy clients' best interest that they do so. Moreover, a process mode can help answer the important question of how a client can best overcome his or her fear to reach the desired goal of improved mental health.[3] Second, the subjective experience of the actor is a key component in studying process courage in a way that it is not in studying accolade courage. If one is to "get inside someone's head" as that person takes a courageous action, then one needs to start with understanding that person's experience of the risks and the goals involved. Rachman's classic work on decorated bomb disposal operators (Rachman, 1990) is an excellent example: His fearless yet award-winning bomb disposal operators clearly meet the standards required for a courageous accolade but may not be a good example of courage as a process, at least if fear is required. Thus, though they earned accolades for observers' perceptions of their behavior, their internal state may be less fearful than that typically seen, or at least expected, in a process view. For internal states, then, the process view of courage may have more stringent requirements than does the accolade view.

Next, the final chapters of Lord's (1918) monograph on courage stand as a cautionary tale for keeping the two types of courage distinct. Although his initial premise seemed to be to elucidate courage as a process that explains how fear

[3]Although entering into or staying with an emotionally threatening treatment might be described by some as personal growth rather than courage, we, like Putman (2004), believe that the label of *courage* is appropriate because it captures the psychological burden and the risks that the actor must overcome in addition to the positive direction in which the actions take him or her.

may be overcome by more noble sentiments, his monograph ends by muddling this process approach with an accolade approach. He divided the noble sentiments into lower, higher, and higher still sentiments, including a very high rating for support of a lost cause (similar to Barczewski's, 2007, analysis of Anglo-American attitudes in the early 20th century). He ended by reassuring his World War I–era readers that Allied soldiers are more courageous than German solders because the cause they fight for is a higher, and thus a more noble, one. Thus, although his model of courage is one that could have led to testable hypotheses (e.g., increasing the strength of noble sentiments should lead to an increase in courageous action, increasing the strength of fear should require stronger noble sentiments to overcome it), instead it reaches a conclusion that, 90 years later, seems nationalistic at best.

Finally, a common criticism of contemporary courage-as-process research is that the actions studied do not rise to the level of true courage. We would argue that such criticism confounds courage as an accolade with courage as a process. The aim of process studies is to find out how humans overcome fear or other responses to risk to do something for a meaningful reason. From the social risk in asking for a raise to the risk of the unknown in traveling to strange places to agreeing to the risk of pain in undergoing many medical procedures, there is abundant evidence that humans overcome minor to moderate risks for meaningful goals all the time. There is also evidence that sometimes they do not: They do not ask for a raise, they cancel travel plans, or they avoid needed medical procedures. Though some of these acts of cowardice simply result in lost opportunities, others can have much more serious effects. Do we believe that people pursuing acts of everyday courage deserve medals, awards, or even praise from others? No. But we do believe that people's lives can be enhanced by understanding the processes that help them choose to follow their goals instead of their fears, particularly when those fears are less than rational.

The extent to which the processes underlying everyday courage parallel or differ from those of monumental courage remains to be seen. However, just as research on depression has progressed at a more rapid rate and benefitted by not limiting acceptable participants only to those hospitalized for recent suicide attempts, we believe that casting a wide net and including acts of everyday courage in our study of the process of courage will benefit science and society.

Differentiation From Courage as a Character Strength or Personality Trait

If there is a trait of courage, it should mean that more courageous people should be more likely to take courageous action than less courageous people. The problem, as outlined earlier, is determining exactly what type of action qualifies as courageous. Do we mean that the courageous person is more likely to take actions that garner the accolade of courage, or more likely to take actions that are characterized by the process of overcoming fear for a good reason?

One approach to looking for the personality trait of courageousness embraces the accolade model. A group of courageous individuals, determined by their status as acclaimed courageous by others, is compared with a group of less courageous individuals. Moral exemplars, for example, are by definition deserving of accolade. Walker and Hennig (2004) argued that moral exemplars are not all the same and that at there are at least three moral prototypes: just, caring, and brave. Compared with just and caring, brave exemplars were seen as more dominant and extraverted. Multidimensional scaling revealed five clusters of typical traits of brave exemplars: dedicated (driven, persistent), confident (self-assured, independent), self-sacrificial (principled, noble), heroic–strong (tough, gallant), and intrepid (gutsy, risk-taking). The clusters were described by the main dimensions of agency and selflessness. Walker and Frimer (2007) compared individual difference variables among winners of the Canadian Medal of Bravery, an award for civilians who have saved others despite extreme danger; winners of a parallel award for long-term humanitarian service (a caring group); and a matched control group. Compared with the control group, both the brave and caring groups were higher on agency and communion, were more likely to have themes of redemption in their life stories, identified more helpers in their early lives, and had more secure attachments. Compared with the brave group, the caring group was more nurturing, generative, and optimistic. In other words, there was evidence for a core of personality traits and life experiences that leads one to notable moral achievements, but there were few specific markers for doing so through acts of physical courage rather than through volunteerism, and the markers that were found were all higher in the caring volunteer group.

These two studies together indicate that though outside observers have different traits in mind for brave actors compared with just or caring ones, measured individual differences between brave and caring exemplars are not great. In part, this may be due to the selection process for their brave exemplars. Winners of the Bravery Medal, like winners of the Carnegie Medal, are selected on the basis of a single physically courageous act of short duration. Traits, on the other hand, reflect differences that persist across multiple acts and over time.

Fagin-Jones and Midlarsky (2007) examined courageous action of longer duration by comparing Holocaust rescuers with a matched control group. To control for the effect of being honored for one's courage, they included in their rescuer group only people who had not yet been honored by the primary award for Holocaust rescuers, Yad Vashem, but instead had been identified to the researchers by survivors. Compared with the matched control group, the rescuer group was higher in social responsibility, altruistic moral reasoning, empathic concern, and risk taking. Three of these traits—social responsibility, altruistic moral reasoning, and empathic concern—likely relate to the moral goal of the action, whereas risk taking may reduce or reframe the fear experienced in response to the personal risk component.

The previous three studies used an explicit accolade model to select courageous people: Participants thought of exemplars, won an award for bravery, or were eligible for an award even though they had not been officially nominated. Peterson and Seligman's Values in Action system (Peterson & Seligman, 2004) takes a slightly different approach, although we propose that they too have an implicit accolade model. They proposed four character strengths, similar to personality facets, that make up the larger virtue of courage (one of six superordinate virtues in their model): bravery, or not giving in to threats or setbacks; integrity, or staying true to one's inner self; persistence, or not giving up; and vitality, or being energized. To develop their system, Peterson and Seligman made extensive use of paragons and other ways in which values and strengths appear in cultures worldwide.

Not all of these strengths characterize courageous action as seen from a process view of courage. Whereas persistence, bravery, and integrity, along with the noncourage strengths of hope and kindness, are characteristic of a courageous act from the actor's point of view, vitality is not (Pury & Kowalski, 2007). Perhaps the difference in findings for hope, kindness, and vitality are due to the infusion of the process approach in Pury and Kowalski's methodology.

Finally, several scales have been developed specifically to measure courage as a trait. Both the Woodard-Pury Courage Scale-23 (WPCS-23; Woodard & Pury, 2007) and the Munich Civil Courage Instrument (MuZI; Kastenmüller, Greitemeyer, Fischer, & Frey, 2007) ask participants to rate their likelihood of action in a variety of situations: a broad range of situations for the WPCS-23 and a more narrow range of civil courage situations for the MuZI. In both cases, the goals and the risks of the action are described in most items. An additional measure, the Courage Measure (CM; Norton & Weiss, 2009), asks participants to make self-ratings of their courageousness and their willingness to act in the face of fear. The goal of the action, however, is purposely vague.

Items on the first factor of the WPCS-23, actions taken to help oneself or one's job, do not fall within the prototypical range of accolade courage (e.g., "I would talk to my supervisor about a raise if I really needed one") but measure a more clinically relevant level of personal or everyday courage. (The other factors—acting on one's beliefs, acting despite or on behalf of specific others, and acting on behalf of family concerns—are more likely to measure the type of courage that rises to accolade standards.) Likewise, the CM measures willingness to face fear, with no mention of the noble purpose required by courage as an accolade.

Although efforts are under way to validate each of these measures, they are still a work in progress as of the time this chapter was written. Efforts at validation should include careful attention to both types of courage, and it may be that some measures are better at predicting one type of courage than another. For example, measures that are focused on courage as pursuing morally good goals despite objective risk might have better predictive power for winning awards for bravery or taking ostensibly high courage jobs, such as police officer or firefighter. On the other hand, measures that focus on overcoming fear for personally important reasons might predict how well someone will do in therapies that demand direct confrontation with upsetting material, in rehabilitation after a physical injury, or in coping with threatening organizational change.

Proposed New Types of Courage and an Integration of Courage as an Accolade and as a Process

At the intersection of courage as an accolade and courage as a process, we should find people who pursue a meaningful or important goal despite personal risk and the fear it might bring. Both meaning and risk are subjective and based on the actor's understanding of the situation in the moment, and in many cases the actor's valuing of the goal, understanding of the risk, and their relative importance are the same as those of most outside observers.

However, in what we call *foolish courage,* most rational outside observers should agree that the goal is not worth the risk. For example, running into a burning building to save a child is courageous; running into a burning building to save a favorite computer is probably not. What about running into a burning building to save a pet? The appraised courageousness of this action probably depends on the observer's opinion about pets. Such actions occasionally surface in the media: A news story in early 2009 recounted the rescue of a couple who were trapped on a steep hillside while trying to retrieve their child's toy. From the outside, the benefit—retrieving a lost toy—was probably not worth the risk of falling off a cliff. From the inside, however, it is entirely possible that the parents underestimated the steepness of the cliff or placed a higher value on the toy than most observers would place on it. Evidence from prospect theory (Thaler, 1980), for example, suggests that the endowment effect might cause them to overvalue their child's toy.

A more destructive case of the process of courage that is misaligned with the accolade view is what we call *bad courage.* In bad courage, what seems to the actor like a subjectively good goal is actually a bad one from either society's or an objective point of view. Former terrorists, for example, describe the process of planting bombs in the language of the process of courage (Silke, 2004). The reaction to Bill Maher's comment on the courage of the 9/11 terrorists confounds the process of courage, in this case, bad courage, with the inherent morality endorsed by the illocutionary act of labeling courage. Likewise, suicide attempts may be seen as instances of bad courage, in which the harm is done to the self rather than to society; one promising observation in this area is that the presence of anxiety disorders, with an increase in uncomplicated fearfulness and sensitivity to risk, seems to mitigate the risk of suicide in affective disorders (Nakagawa et al., 2008, 2009).

Finally, as discussed earlier in this chapter, everyday or personal courage also may be at odds with an accolade view of courage. Many of the things people, particularly people in therapy, fear are idiosyncratic and actions that they take to overcome those fears may not rise to the level of courage required for an accolade. Similarly, many of the goals a person pursues are likewise more meaningful to that person than to the general population, and some of the things a person values may have little to no meaning in a broader population. A quick look at the variety of awards for courage described on the Internet makes it clear that most of these awards are given to those who overcome risks and difficulties to strive for the goals endorsed by the sponsoring organization: a free press, wellness and inspiration of others, courage in sport. Depending on the observer, the goal pursued by winners of these particular accolade may or may not seem worthy of the description "courage."

Foolish courage, bad courage, and personal courage may very well follow the same underlying processes as do acts more commonly seen as courageous: The extent to which they are seen as courageous by specific others may depend on the ability of the observer to empathize with the actor's view of the rewards and the threats. The intersection of accolade and process includes many possible courageous actions in which the actor is pursuing morally good goals that society endorses and the person finds meaningful in the face of great personal risk that causes him or her fear.

Some actions are more firmly in the realm of courage as an accolade than of courage as a process. An internal whistleblower who believes that her company's nonretaliation policy will protect her job but is later forced out anyway has accomplished a morally good goal of reporting wrongdoing while facing an objective risk, but the risk was far greater than she thought. A soldier who enters a "berserker" state and kills large numbers of the enemy without a thought for his own life is more strongly motivated by a sense of injustice than by the desire to attain military objectives and is not fully aware of the risk to himself (Shay, 1994). However, he may accomplish a goal desired by his society and clearly faces a substantial objective risk. Rachman (1990) called his decorated bomb disposal technicians fearless rather than courageous, subscribing to a process model, yet society's accolade model clearly disagreed.

On the other hand, some actions are more firmly in the realm of courage as a process than as an accolade. In these actions, the actor's internal perception of the value of the goal or the magnitude of the risk (or both) may be magnified or even reversed. Asking for a raise may seem far riskier to someone who is deeply insecure about his worth to the company than it would seem to most observers. Risking physical safety to save a rare comic book from a house fire may be an extremely meaningful goal for the comic book collector but may be something that society at large would call foolish. Overcoming fear to plant a bomb to fight for freedom strikes one as bad courage, but terrorists describe their actions in just such terms (Silke, 2004).

Confounding process and accolade courage can stunt the practice of both. If awards for courage switched to process standards for making awards, then committees would be burdened with guessing exactly how much risk or fear the nominees experienced before taking action. Actions would most likely be considered for their intent, not their outcome, and people who tried and failed to save others would be given awards in the same proportion as actual rescue attempts succeed or fail. This would almost lead to a true cheapening of courage, such that all who do the thing they fear most for a good reason might be eligible to get one, whether they succeeded or not, whether they overcame a raging river or a cockroach, or whether they were trying to stand up for oppressed people or to get ahead in their own career.

If accolade standards are applied to courage as a process, even stranger things happen. In the comic movie *Monty Python and the Holy Grail* (Jones, 1975), one knight, Sir Robin, is doggedly followed by a minstrel who attempts to remind the knight of his bravery. Unfortunately for Sir Robin, the minstrel does so by serenading him with a list of increasingly gruesome injuries that the knight has not yet encountered but, according to the minstrel, does not fear. Of course, the increasingly graphic descriptions lead to the opposite effect, and Sir Robin flees at the first sign of danger (albeit "bravely," according to the minstrel). The comedic premise of this segment rests on the tension between the accolade model followed by the minstrel and the process model Sir Robin needs.

In our own experience as well as that of several other courage researchers, research on the process model, particularly research designed to look at actions high in personal courage that are most relevant to a therapeutic or coaching context or everyday courageous actions, is commonly dismissed as "not really about courage" by reviewers. Such common but smaller actions may touch the lives of more people in aggregate than rare but monumental courage. This dismissal may occur when accolade standards are applied to a process approach. We think this is a mistake. Process research does not seek to give awards to participants for the smaller acts of courage studied. It does not claim that the acts studied arouse the same intensity of emotions as do acts of monumental courage.

Process research does, however, propose that it is valuable to learn about times when people might "chicken out" on a good goal but do not. It also seeks to understand this process from the inside out, with an ultimate goal of helping people to change their behavior. An accolade definition of courage is inappropriate to this goal for several reasons. First, an accolade model, by definition, looks at courage from the outside in, seeking objectivity. Therapeutic and coaching approaches are guided by the particular individual experience of the client and need to look at the process from the inside out, seeking an understanding of the subjective world of the individual. Second, the more common an accolade becomes the less it is worth; thus, the accolade model directs us to study rare and extreme acts. However, if the process of courage is common, then studying its rarest form will give us only a skewed picture of the process, as with studying depression only in people who are currently hospitalized and under suicide watch. Finally, the accolade model studies the behavior of praising an action, whereas the process model studies how the action is taken.

In what ways is the process of taking an everyday courageous action similar to taking a monumental courageous action? Do magnitude, clear moral good, and objective risk matter more than the divisions among physical, moral, and vital or psychological courage (Lopez et al., 2003)? We suspect not, but it is a worthwhile methodological consideration for future research.

Conclusion

In this chapter, we proposed that many of the apparent differences and difficulties of courage research may be resolved by considering two decidedly different ways to look at courage: as an accolade and as a process. As an accolade, courage is typically reserved for actions that are rare and monumental; as a process, courage extends to actions that occur every day and are less extreme. The trait of courage, studied from an accolade perspective, offers information about people who have performed at an extraordinary level and how they are different from the rest. The trait of courage, studied as a process, offers information about the continuum of a strength for meeting a variety of risks, including those that are risks only to the specific actor. Each approach can yield interesting answers to important, but fundamentally different, questions.

References

Arch, J., & Craske, M. (2008). Acceptance and commitment therapy and cognitive behavioral therapy for anxiety disorders: Different treatments, similar mechanisms? *Clinical Psychology: Science and Practice, 15,* 263–279.

Austin, J. L. (1975). *How to do things with words.* Cambridge, MA: Harvard University Press.

Australian Government. (2008, October 13). *Australian bravery decorations.* Retrieved from http://www.itsanhonour.gov.au/honours/awards/medals/bravery.cfm

Bacha, C. (2001). The courage to stay in the moment. *Psychodynamic Counselling, 7,* 279–295.

Barczewski, S. (2007). *Antarctic destinies: Scott, Shackleton and the changing face of heroism.* London, England: Continuum.

Becker, S. W., & Eagly, A. H. (2004). The heroism of women and men. *American Psychologist, 59,* 163–178. doi:10.1037/0003-066X.59.3.163

Breznican, A. (2002). Bill Maher to tape final episode of "Politically Incorrect." *The Associated Press State and Local Wire.* Retrieved from the LexisNexis database.

Britt, T. W. (2003, September). *Dispositional attitude strength: Assessment, correlates, and manipulation.* Paper presented at the annual meeting of the Society for Southeastern Social Psychologists, Greensboro, NC.

Carnegie Hero Fund Commission. (2009a, March 27). Awardee announcements 1998-present. Retrieved from http://www.carnegiehero.org/awardees_press.php

Carnegie Hero Fund Commission. (2009b, March 27). Requirements for a Carnegie Medal. Retrieved from http://www.carnegiehero.org/nominate.php

Coast Mental Health Foundation. (2008). Annual Courage 2009. Retrieved from http://coastmentalhealth.com/courage-2009.html

Dahlsgaard, K., Peterson, C., & Seligman, M. (2005). Shared virtue: The convergence of valued human strengths across culture and history. *Review of General Psychology, 9,* 203–213. doi:10.1037/1089-2680.9.3.203

Eifert, G., & Forsyth, J. (2005). *Acceptance and commitment therapy for anxiety disorders: A practitioner's treatment guide to using mindfulness, acceptance, and values-based behavior change strategies.* Oakland, CA: New Harbinger.

Fagin-Jones, S., & Midlarsky, E. (2007). Courageous altruism: Personal and situational correlates of rescue during the Holocaust. *The Journal of Positive Psychology, 2,* 136–147. doi:10.1080/17439760701228979

Gans, J. S. (2005). A plea for greater recognition and appreciation of our group members' courage. *International Journal of Group Psychotherapy, 55,* 575–593. doi:10.1521/ijgp.2005.55.4.575

Greitemeyer, T., Fischer, P., Kastenmüller, A., & Frey, D. (2006). Civil courage and helping behavior: Differences and similarities. *European Psychologist, 11,* 90–98. doi:10.1027/1016-9040.11.2.90

Haidt, J. (2000). The positive emotion of elevation. *Prevention & Treatment, 3,* Article 3.

Haidt, J. (2003). Elevation and the positive psychology of morality. In C. L. M. Keyes & J. Haidt (Eds.), *Flourishing: Positive psychology and the life well-lived* (pp. 275–289). Washington, DC: American Psychological Association. doi:10.1037/10594-012

Hauser, M. (2006). *Moral minds: How nature designed our universal sense of right and wrong.* New York, NY: Ecco.

Hayes, S., Strosahl, K., & Wilson, K. (1999). *Acceptance and commitment therapy: An experiential approach to behavior change.* New York, NY: Guilford Press.

Hebblethwaite, M. (n.d.). George Cross database: The decoration. Retrieved from http://www.gc-database.co.uk/decoration.htm

International Women's Media Foundation. (2008). Courage in journalism award nomination form. Retrieved from https://www.iwmf.org/couragenomination.aspx

Jenkins, E., & Pury, C. L. S. (2009). [The role morality plays in attributing courage: The Bill Maher effect.] Unpublished data, Clemson University.

Jones, T. (Director). (1975). *Monty Python and the Holy Grail* [Motion picture]. Culver City, CA: Sony Pictures.

Kastenmüller, A., Greitemeyer, T., Fischer, P., & Frey, D. (2007). Das Münchner Zivilcourage-Instrument (MüZI): Entwicklung und Validierung [The Munich *Civil Courage* Instrument (MüZI): Development and validation]. *Diagnostica, 53,* 205–217.

Lopez, S., O'Byrne, K., & Petersen, S. (2003). Profiling courage. In S. J. Lopez & C. R. Snyder (Eds.), *Positive psychological assessment: A handbook of models and measures* (pp. 185–197). Washington, DC: American Psychological Association. doi:10.1037/10612-012

Lord, H. G. (1918). *The psychology of courage.* Boston, MA: John W. Luce.

Medina, M. (2008). Everyday courage: Living courageously without being a hero. *Existential Analysis, 19,* 280–298.

Miller, W. I. (2002). *The mystery of courage.* Cambridge, MA: Harvard University Press.

Nakagawa, A., Grunebaum, M., Oquendo, M., Burke, A., Kashima, H., & Mann, J. (2009, January). Clinical correlates of planned, more lethal suicide attempts in major depressive disorder. *Journal of Affective Disorders, 112,* 237–242. doi:10.1016/j.jad.2008.03.021

Nakagawa, A., Grunebaum, M., Sullivan, G., Currier, D., Ellis, S., Burke, A., . . . Oquendo, M. A. (2008, June). Comorbid anxiety in bipolar disorder: Does it have an independent effect on suicidality? *Bipolar Disorders, 10,* 530–538. doi:10.1111/j.1399-5618.2008.00590.x

Nesse, R.M. (1990). Evolutionary explanations of emotions. *Human Nature, 1,* 261–289. doi:10.1007/BF02733986

Nesse, R.M., & Ellsworth, P. (2009). Evolution, emotions, and emotional disorders. *American Psychologist, 64,* 129–139. doi:10.1037/a0013503

Norton, P. J., & Weiss, B. J. (2009). The role of courage on behavioral approach in a fear-eliciting situation: A proof-of-concept study. *Journal of Anxiety Disorders, 23,* 212–217. doi:10.1016/j.janxdis.2008.07.002

Peterson, C., & Seligman, M. E. P. (2004). Strengths of courage: Introduction. In C. Peterson & M. E. P. Seligman (Eds.), *Character strengths and virtues: A handbook and classification* (pp. 197–212). Washington, DC: American Psychological Association.

Pury, C. L. S., & Hensel, A. D. (2010). Are courageous actions successful actions? *The Journal of Positive Psychology, 5*(1), 62–72. doi:10-1080/17439760903435224

Pury, C. L. S., & Kowalski, R. (2007). Human strengths, courageous actions, and general and personal courage. *The Journal of Positive Psychology, 2,* 120–128. doi:10.1080/17439760701228813

Pury, C. L. S., & Woodard, C. (2009). Courage. In S. J. Lopez (Ed.), *The encyclopedia of positive psychology* (Vol. 1, pp. 247–254). Oxford, England: Wiley-Blackwell.

Pury, C., Kowalski, R., McRae, T., Kentera, J., Arnold, C., Becht, C., & Starkey, J. (2006, October). Getting up the nerve: Self-reports of deliberate attempts to increase courage. In C. Pury (Chair), *Symposium: Courage.* Symposium conducted at the 5th Gallup International Positive Psychology Summit, Washington, DC.

Pury, C. L. S., Kowalski, R. M., & Spearman, M. J. (2007). Distinctions between general and personal courage. *The Journal of Positive Psychology, 2,* 99–114. doi:10.1080/17439760701237962

Putman, D. (2004). *Psychological courage.* Lanham, MD: University Press of America.

Rachman, S. (1990). *Fear and courage* (2nd ed.). New York, NY: Freeman/Times Books/Holt.

Rate, C., Clarke, J., Lindsay, D., & Sternberg, R. (2007). Implicit theories of courage. *The Journal of Positive Psychology, 2,* 80–98. doi:10.1080/17439760701228755

Schmidt, N., & Koselka, M. (2000). Gender differences in patients with panic disorder: Evaluating cognitive mediation of phobic avoidance. *Cognitive Therapy and Research, 24,* 533–550. doi:10.1023/A:1005562011960

Shay, J. (1994). *Achilles in Vietnam: Combat trauma and the undoing of character.* New York, NY: Atheneum/Macmillan.

Silke, A. (2004). Courage in dark places: Reflections on terrorist psychology. *Social Research, 71,* 177–198.

Silvers, J. A., & Haidt, J. (2008). Moral elevation can induce nursing. *Emotion, 8,* 291–295. doi:10.1037/1528-3542.8.2.291

Szagun, G. (1992). Age-related changes in children's understanding of courage. *The Journal of Genetic Psychology, 153,* 405–420.

Szagun, G., & Schäuble, M. (1997). Children's and adults' understanding of the feeling experience of courage. *Cognition and Emotion, 11,* 291–306. doi:10.1080/026999397379935

Thaler, R. H. (1980). Toward a positive theory of consumer choice. *Journal of Economic Behavior & Organization, 1,* 39–60. doi:10.1016/0167-2681(80)90051-7

Tillich, P. (1958). *The courage to be.* New Haven, CT: Yale University Press.

Walker, L. J., & Frimer, J. (2007). Moral personality of brave and caring exemplars. *Journal of Personality and Social Psychology, 93,* 845–860. doi:10.1037/0022-3514.93.5.845

Walker, L. J., & Hennig, K. (2004). Differing conceptions of moral exemplarity: Just, brave, and caring. *Journal of Personality and Social Psychology, 86,* 629–647. doi:10.1037/0022-3514.86.4.629

Woodard, C., & Pury, C. (2007). The construct of courage: Categorization and measurement. *Consulting Psychology Journal: Practice and Research, 59,* 135–147. doi:10.1037/1065-9293.59.2.135

Worline, M. C. (2004). *Dancing the cliff edge: The place of courage in social life* (Doctoral dissertation, The University of Michigan).

Part II

Basic Research and Theory

5

Courage: A Psychological Perspective

S. J. Rachman

Most people acquire remarkably few fears. Before World War II, the population and the authorities greatly overpredicted how much fear would be provoked, especially during air raids on civilian populations. For example, in 1934 Churchill warned the Commons to anticipate massive damage and casualties from repeated air attacks. He said the dangers were material, but

> no less formidable than these material effects are the reaction which will be produced upon the mind of the civilian population. We must expect . . . that at least 3 million or 4 million people will be driven out into the open country around the Metropolis. (Jenkins, 2002, p. 476)

Contrary to the virtually universal expectation that repeated air attacks would produce mass panic and very large numbers of psychiatric casualties, people endured astonishingly well (Janis, 1951). The expected panic and uncontrollable fear did not occur. As a clinician working with people who are distressed and disabled by intense fear, I was puzzled by the apparent contrast between the intense and intrusive fears of the patients and the fearlessness of people who were the victims of repeated air attacks. My curiosity about this fearlessness was enhanced by a paradox that emerged out of the introduction of behavioral methods for the treatment of abnormal fears.

Courageous Acts of Frightened People

The paradox is that in therapy clinicians urge patients to carry out acts of considerable courage, asking them to approach and engage the places or cues that frighten them and to do so frequently and for protracted periods. Clinicians expect patients to perform courageously—and they generally do. Examples of fearful people displaying courageous behavior are everyday clinical experiences made more prominent by the common use of methods in which the person is exposed to the very situations that provoke the fear. A middle-aged woman who was deeply troubled by intense, irrational fears of disease, germs, and dirt was given a course of such treatment. These deep, chronic fears had distorted and damaged all aspects of her life. She was extremely frightened of touching "unsafe" objects, eating foods that she believed were dangerous, or even touching people whom she felt were diseased. She avoided any physical contact with other people, including members of her own family, and she spent most of the day sitting in the only chair that remained safe. Even her safe chair had to be scrubbed down with powerful antiseptics each day. The treatment was described to her, and it was explained that she would have to come into direct, graded contact with the objects and people whom she felt were diseased and dangerous. After a period of hesitation, during which her fear was extremely high, she bravely chose to carry out the treatment. She made good progress during the 15 sessions, even though the first three were exceedingly difficult for her. She felt extremely frightened at times and endured unpleasant physical reactions, including profuse sweating and palpitations. After completing each of these early sessions, she was exhausted for a couple of hours. Even so, she persevered, displaying commendable courage. After 2 months of treatment she was greatly improved, her fears had subsided, and she was once again able to touch her children and other people. Her extensive avoidance behavior was reduced. Unfortunately, her courage eroded when she returned home, and she refused further help.

A severely anxious and totally housebound woman with agoraphobia provides a second clinical example of courageous perseverance. When her elderly mother fell ill and was confined to bed for 6 weeks, the patient forced herself to go out repeatedly to obtain food and medicine for her parent. She dreaded each excursion and experienced intense fear, but she persisted nevertheless.

Patients with panic disorder who fear that the palpitations they experience during excursions are a sign of an imminent heart attack, perhaps death, display courage in carrying out their therapeutic excursions. Given appropriate support and advice, agoraphobic and other extremely frightened people can be helped to endure and then overcome their fears. These patients display courage every time they carry out one of their exercises while experiencing extreme fear. Frightened people perform courageous acts.

Soldiers and Philosophers

Psychologists have displayed a strong interest in fear and comparative indifference to courage, but the concept of courage has not been neglected by philosophers and soldiers. Their lively interest in courage is illustrated by an exchange between Socrates and two generals, Laches and Nikias. He asked them how one can set about determining the nature of courage: "Young men may attain this quality by the help of study and pursuits. Tell me, if you can, what is courage?" (Plato, trans. 1953).

Peter Lang (1970), a leading psychologist in this field, expressed the new view of fear extremely well: "Fear is not some hard phenomenal lump that lives inside people, that we may palpate more or less successfully" (p. 141). He proposed a different construal, arguing that there are three components of fear: physiological arousal, subjective reactivity, and behavioral avoidance. These components are only loosely coupled and can vary independently of each other. In specific experiences of fear the three components can change at varying speeds; they can change desynchronously (Rachman, 1990). For example, during therapy the patient's physiological arousal may decline early on, followed days later by changes in avoidance. It is not uncommon for the subjective appraisal of threat to diminish last and slowest.

This construal of fear as a complex of imperfectly coupled response systems led to some novel ideas on the nature of courage. A person may be willing to approach a frightening object or situation despite feeling a high degree of subjective fear and unpleasant bodily sensations. This persistence of approach behavior in the face of subjective and physical sensations of fear suggests a definition of *courage*—to continue despite one's subjective fear; the three components of fear are desynchronous. On the other hand, approaching a potentially dangerous situation in the absence of subjective and physiological indices of fear is regarded as fearlessness, not courage.

The main sources of information about the resilience of people subjected to air raids are wartime surveys and direct observations of civilians. Information about courageous conduct comes from studies of combatants and experimental analyses of training programs designed to teach people how to carry out dangerous tasks such as dealing with explosive devices or jumping from an aircraft. A start has been made in attempting to answer the question of whether or not people can acquire courage "by the help of study and pursuits."

Most of the information is reassuring, and it appears that people *can* learn to persevere when under significant threat. Although fear reactions during or immediately after such stress are common, people apparently have the capacity to recover very quickly. People also have impressive powers of adaptation to repeated stresses and dangers. In a comparison of combat soldiers and air crews in World War II, Stouffer and others (1949) found that the airmen displayed even more courageous behavior than did the soldiers. They had higher morale than did the combat soldiers, expressed more courageous attitudes than did the combat soldiers, and won four times as many medals as did their comrades on the ground. Stouffer attributed the difference to motivation and confidence. The airmen were volunteers and said that they benefited from the high morale engendered in the small groups that constituted an aircrew. They also expressed considerable self-confidence in their flying and combat skills. Both airborne and ground combatants said that their desire to avoid letting down their comrades played a very important part in helping them to control their fear. The influence of self-confidence on courageous, or fearless, behavior is borne out by observations of combat troops in the Pacific area during World War II (Stouffer et al., 1949). Precombat ratings of self-confidence and fearlessness in battle were clearly related. Fifty-six percent of the soldiers who expressed high self-confidence before combat reported little or no fear during battle, and 62% of the soldiers who expressed little self-confidence reported a high degree of battle fear. Confidence and low fear were related, but as these figures indicate, there were exceptions. Some of the confident soldiers did experience considerable fear, and some who were lacking in confidence experienced little or no fear.

In later research on British military personnel, Cox et al. (1983) and Cox and Rachman (1983) confirmed the existence of a positive relationship between self-efficacy and low fear but encountered a few notable exceptions. Parachute training has been a fertile source of information about acquired courage. Walk (1956) asked trainee parachutists to rate their subjective fear before and after jumping from a 34-foot practice tower. Each trainee was required to jump from an exit door and drop nearly 8 feet before his fall was arrested by the straps of the parachute harness. The comprehensive training program was difficult and potentially dangerous, but a large majority of trainees passed satisfactorily. At the start of the program, most of the trainees reported at least a moderate amount of fear, but this tended to subside within five jumps. Successful execution of the required jump despite the presence of fear (i.e., courageous performance) was usually followed by a reduction of fear. The successful jumpers started the program with slightly less fear than did those who failed, but there were few differences between the groups on measures of physiological disturbance, such as sweating and tremor. The successful jumpers persevered satisfactorily in the face of moderate fear and physiological disturbances. The main difference between the successful jumpers and those who failed was in the degree of self-confidence.

A positive relationship between self-confidence and successful parachute performance was also reported in a study of 21 members of the Parachute Regiment (Rachman, 1990). The trainees who expressed low self-confidence reported significantly greater fear than did the others when they had to carry out the jumps from an aircraft. It is interesting that there was no correlation between their estimates of the dangerousness of the task and their reports of experienced fear. The successful performance of this small group of trainees was matched in a larger study by Macmillan and Rachman (1988). All 105 recruits to the same unit successfully completed their parachute training, unless it was interrupted by an injury incurred during training. In both studies, the recruits reported significant decreases in fearfulness as they passed through the training program. These declines in fearfulness were accompanied by increased levels of self-confidence.

Fearlessness

For most people, fear is a familiar emotion, and it is difficult to imagine life in which it plays no part. However, a small number of people are relatively impervious to fear. Henry Cooper, former heavyweight champion of Europe, who had a long and punishing career, said that he could not remember ever fearing anyone (Rachman, 1990). He described mild fears of flying or driving fast but was unable to think of any person or situation that had frightened or could frighten him. He had not experienced fear before or during any of his professional fights, despite having faced some of the toughest men in boxing. It seems extraordinary that repeated exposures to the punishments of boxing failed to generate any significant fear in Cooper. Moreover, he experienced none of the usual physical accompaniments of fear, such as palpitations or sweating. Henry Cooper seems to be one of those unusual people whom we can describe as being literally fearless. Like many writers before him, Mowrer (1960) linked fearlessness with courage: “May it not be,” he asked, “that courage is simply the absence of fear in situations where it might be expected to be present?” (p. 435). Fearlessness is often regarded as synonymous with courage, but on the basis of Lang’s (1970) three-component analysis of fear there is some value in distinguishing between fearlessness and courage. As well as fearlessness, or the absence of fear, we can recognize the occurrence of perseverance despite fear. This type of perseverance is a pure form of courage (Rachman, 1982).

World War II soldiers discriminated between fear that is endured and fear that is not tolerated. They made a distinction between comrades who were cowards and those who were ill, even though both showed the same symptoms of fear (Stouffer et al., 1949). The difference depended on whether the soldier had or had not made a genuine effort to resist fleeing when experiencing fear. Soldiers who were visibly upset by danger were not regarded as cowards unless they made no apparent effort to carry out their duties. If a soldier tried hard but could not perform adequately, he was regarded as a legitimate casualty. On the other hand, a soldier who exhibited the same symptoms of fear could be labeled a coward if he made no apparent effort to overcome his reactions and carry on with his tasks. "Thus men were not blamed for being afraid, but they were expected to try and put up a struggle to carry on despite their fear" (Symonds & Williams, 1979, p. 34). In many cases the medical officers found it extremely difficult to distinguish between disability and cowardice. Soldiers whose symptoms persisted long after the danger had subsided were generally regarded as being ill.

Those soldiers who displayed the most courageous behavior received the greatest admiration from their comrades. When veteran troops were asked to characterize the best combat soldiers they had ever known, fearless behavior was rated as by far the most important characteristic on which to base a judgment. The admiration of courage appears to be universal: "Courage, from whatever angle we approach it, whatever origin or purpose we assign to it, no matter what form it assumes, not even what motives underlie it, will always be a quality beloved of man" (Birley, 1923, p. 779). This admiration can even extend to courage shown by one's opponents, and as Samuel Johnson observed, "Courage is a quality so necessary for maintaining virtue, that it is always respected, even when it is associated with vice" (Boswell, 1954, p. 501).

The wartime observations and surveys, coupled with recent investigations and studies, suggest that several factors contribute to courageous behavior. Self-confidence is an important factor. Possession of the appropriate skill required to deal with the dangerous situation also serves to increase courage. A high level of motivation to succeed and a set of conditions conveniently summarized under the awkward term *situational demand* also play a part in determining courageous behavior. These demands include one's sense of responsibility to one's self and to others, the powerful effects of group membership and group morale, and the need to avoid disapproval.

Courageous behavior is promoted by courageous models. The wartime observation that children who were exposed to air raids modeled the courageous or fearful conduct of their parents has been echoed in recent years by research on therapeutic modeling for phobic patients. People are also open to the acquisition of fears by a process of modeling. In their study of combat troops, Stouffer et al. (1949) found that 40% of the troops reported significantly increased fear after observing a fellow soldier panic in battle. Fearful and courageous performance can be modeled. For many soldiers, a courageous leader was the most critical determinant of their own perseverance and ability to cope in combat conditions. Courage is "caught as men take diseases one after another and may rapidly infect the whole army" (Birley, 1923, p. 784). As with panic, so with courage: Both are contagious.

Courageous Acts or Courageous Actors?

Recognition of the fact that fearful people are capable of performing courageous acts does not rule out the existence of courageous actors. Before I address Socrates' question about whether people can acquire the "very noble quality" of courage, it is necessary to clarify the concept of a courageous actor and its relation to the distinction between courage and fearlessness.

Courageous actors are people who perform courageously more than once and in a variety of circumstances. If a person behaves courageously in one situation, does it imply that he or she will behave courageously in other circumstances? A single act of courage or one that is carried out under exceptional demands is not sufficient to describe someone as a courageous actor. In addition, courageous people are allowed only a few nonsignificant fears.

In common usage, the concept of courageous actors does not include a distinction between people who experience no fear when carrying out dangerous acts (fearlessness) and people who persevere despite their fear (courage). The case for introducing this distinction is an elaboration of the general argument that the concept of courageous actors is valid and that such actors are identifiable.

The "contagion of courage" described by military observers and the therapeutic modeling of courageous behavior kindled by clinicians are instances of the situational determination of courage. In specifiable circumstances, courage can be promoted by clinicians, research workers, firefighters, nurses, and soldiers. Courage can also be instigated by insistent demands in dangerous situations, with or without the influence of another person.

Furthermore, acts of courage can be promoted in people who are regarded by themselves and by others as timid, even excessively timid. Under the appropriate conditions, phobic patients can be helped to face and endure the objects, people, or places that elicit their worst fears. It is not necessary to be a courageous actor to carry out a courageous act.

Astronauts

Although it is not necessary to be reliably courageous, it certainly helps. Slowly accumulating evidence points to the possibility that there is a small group of people like Henry Cooper for whom courageous or fearless behavior presents few problems. The Mercury astronauts were required to carry out extremely difficult and dangerous tasks in conditions of maximal uncertainty. The seven original astronauts, all of whom were experienced jet pilots selected from the military services, were the subject of study by Ruff and Korchin (1964). They were all married men in their early 30s who had grown up in middle-class families in small towns or on farms. They were Protestant, enjoyed outdoor living, had university degrees in engineering, were of superior intelligence (mean IQ, 135), and were inclined to action. The astronauts were aware of the dangerous tasks involved in the Mercury project but regarded them as similar to tasks that they had already accomplished in flying military jets. According to the authors, the astronauts had no special wish to face danger but were willing to accept the risks demanded by their work.

During their journey, they performed their tasks with exemplary skill and success. The astronauts experienced positive and negative emotions, and exerted excellent control. Prior to their journey into space they had dealt with dangerous situations in which fear was appropriate and found that they were able to function despite its effects. The astronauts benefited from these mastery experiences and were confident that they had the skills and knowledge necessary to overcome realistic threats. They were not given to dwelling on unrealistic ones. In describing their reactions to combat, they readily admitted fear but pointed out that they were skilled pilots. These people had particular psychological competence and the resources for coping effectively with danger.

During the journey into space, they experienced remarkably little fear. Before the flights, there was little evidence of significant anxiety or elevated physiological arousal, and instead,

> the launch of a space vehicle and the flight itself often induced a feeling of exhilaration. . . . Anxiety levels had not been extraordinarily high [and] even in the instances where a possibility of death has been encountered, emotional reactions have remained within normal limits. (Ruff & Korchin, 1964, p. 216)

The astronauts felt that as a result of their intensive training and past experience, they were prepared to handle any emergency. In addition to their training and successful experiences, this small group of remarkable performers may have had the benefit of some constitutional resistance to vulnerability. Their performance on all of the tests—psychomotor, intellectual, and emotional—was well above average and their reactions under the stress of preliminary training were adaptive. It is of interest that although they had experienced fears during combat flying, by the time they had completed the specialized training, they were able to complete the space journey with minimal fear. They had undergone a transition from courage to fearlessness.

The possibility of some constitutional invulnerability in these people must be allowed, but their actual and perceived psychological competence seems to have been the factor of dominating importance. Ruff and Korchin (1964) summed up their findings: "The capacity to control emotions seems to be gained through past experience in the mastery of stress, and through confidence in training and technical readiness" (p. 218). This summary reflects the views of the astronauts themselves, who placed greatest importance on competence, and foreshadowed the concept of "perceived self-efficacy," formulated by Bandura (1977) in his explanation of therapeutic behavioral changes. The astronauts apparently felt convinced that their past experience and intensive training had prepared them to handle any emergency. The importance of training and self-confidence in promoting courageous behavior is evident in a number of military tasks, but some of these duties are so exceptional and demanding that one wonders whether they can be carried out only by people with special endowments. Rendering safe an improvised explosive device appears to be one such exceptional task, and the qualities of bomb-disposal operators are therefore of special interest. Are bomb-disposal operators courageous actors?

A Perilous Task

In an attempt to extend our understanding of courageous performance and the conditions that facilitate it, my colleagues and I carried out several studies of military bomb-disposal operators (Rachman, 1983). These soldiers are required to carry out skilled technical acts under conditions of extreme danger, in which a single error can be fatal. Bomb-disposal duty was described by Churchill as a "task of the utmost peril" (1949, p. 318). The circumstances and manner in which operators fulfill their dangerous tasks, which require the use of reasoning and technical skill under maximum and imminent threat, provide a particularly apt testing ground for some ideas on courage, particularly the notion of exceptional courageous actors.

A retrospective analysis was initially carried out on the records of over 200 British Royal Army Ordnance Corps (RAOC) bomb-disposal operators who had seen service in Northern Ireland. The major finding was that virtually all of them had performed extremely well. During a 10-year period, they dealt with 31,273 incidents.

The hazardous nature of the work is illustrated by the fact that 17 operators were killed between 1969 and 1981, and roughly one quarter of the operators received decorations for gallantry. During the period from 1970 to 1981, 73 awards were made to operators of the RAOC. They faced the greatest danger early in the bombing campaign, but with growing experience and the introduction of improved equipment, the hazards were reduced. It will be appreciated, however, that in spite of these advances, rendering safe an improvised explosive device inevitably involves danger. In light of the astonishingly large number of "incidents" that were successfully dealt with, the performance of the operators must be judged as a remarkable success. This success is all the more noteworthy for being carried out by operators who did not undergo positive selection. The major selection procedure used by the RAOC was one of negative exclusion. All ordnance personnel were expected to carry out bomb-disposal duties after completing an additional course of specialized training. Most of them (54%) were not aware at the time of joining the service that bomb-disposal work might be involved.

Dealing With Explosive Devices

The psychological significance of bomb-disposal duties is best appreciated through descriptions of some of the tasks that the operators were called on to perform. These included dealing with a bomb that had been placed inside a gasoline tanker. The operators had to locate and defuse a device that had been hidden in the cramped, dark, oily engine room of a tanker ship.

Excerpts from the specially designed daily diaries in which the operators recorded their thoughts and feelings during a tour of duty illustrate some of their experiences. Operator A dealt with one explosive device in the 1st week of his 4-month tour and said that he felt very lively and active, on duty and off. He had a busy 2nd week during which he dealt with three explosive devices and reported that he had been "slightly frightened when dealing with one of them" but remained lively and alert throughout the week. To render safe one of the devices, he had to spend a lot of time exploring the area to rule out a range of possible dangers, and as a result had worked through most of the night. On the following day he reported a slight disturbance of sleep and a confusing and disturbing dream involving bombs and violence. Having successfully completed a difficult job, he reported a large and significant increase in confidence. During the 4th week, he had to deal with two devices and one false alarm.

He remained lively, alert, and interested, and was starting to relax when off duty. Toward the end of the 4th week, he reported that "we were faced with a new type of device (a funny) but I was flexible enough to deal with it" (Rachman, 1990, p. 303). His 5th week was very busy, and he had to deal with several devices, including a number that were hidden in various parts of a large and poorly lit warehouse. "I was involved for something like 24 hours, and towards the end I was truly shattered as were the rest of the team. I had a constant worry that there was a booby-trap somewhere." However, by a gradual process of elimination, this proved not to be so.

While he was carrying out a reconnaissance phase of a suspected site, a vehicle exploded quite violently. He reported that

> precisely one minute before I was on a house roof looking down on it [and it] did not scare me at the time or during the task. However, knowing now what happened, the cab bomb inspires me to think that these trucks should be marked with a Government Health Warning.

By the end of a busy tour, his confidence was very high and he had reported little fear at any time. The only negative aspect of his tour was a number of disagreements with soldiers from a supporting regiment.

Operator B was posted to a relatively quiet area and by the 6th week he was complaining of inactivity and the lack of opportunity for exercise. Suddenly he was called out to deal with five separate explosive devices over the course of a few days. His level of alertness and confidence increased rapidly, but when the area quieted down again, he complained of his "great disappointment at not doing more work." The operators were keen to use their knowledge and special skills. This operator's experience illustrates a phenomenon that my colleagues and I encountered early in our association with the bomb-disposal service. To our surprise, the operators told us that they looked forward to the ringing of the alarm telephone so that they could go out on a task. The notion that someone can look forward to being called out to such a dangerous task, in which one's life might be at risk, can be comprehended only against a background of prolonged inactivity, restriction, and boredom. One should never underestimate the power of boredom that can be so great as to induce people to prefer exposure to great danger rather than sitting in cramped quarters watching dreary and repetitious television programs.

Operator C had an unhappy tour but performed courageously despite the fact that at times he felt extremely frightened. His mood fluctuated and he experienced periods of anger and irritability. His confidence in his ability to perform competently also fluctuated. As the tour continued, he became increasingly unhappy and lethargic, but despite all these difficulties, successfully dealt with

23 explosive devices and 23 hoaxes. It is curious that his end-of-tour report did not reflect his unhappiness, and he said that the tour had gone reasonably well and that his performance and mood had been stable throughout the tour. He stated that he had not felt fearful before or during the execution of his bomb-disposal duties, in clear contrast to his daily diary reports.

Personality or Proficiency?

Before undertaking the specialized training necessary to carry out these duties, each ordnance officer or noncommissioned officer went through a screening process in which they completed a set of psychometric tests, had a psychiatric interview and military interviews, and performed training tasks. They were then given a comprehensive and thorough course of specialized training. Fewer than 10% of the more than 200 operators who completed these tests and training in the period 1972–1980 were rejected. Of these, less than 5% were rejected on psychiatric grounds. The bold assumption underlying the selection process used by the RAOC was that virtually all of their officers and noncommissioned officers are capable of carrying out this difficult and dangerous work, provided that they are given specialized training in addition to their normal training. This apparently optimistic expectation was confirmed by events.

The psychometric information revealed that the operators were an unusually well-adjusted group of people (Hallam, 1983). On most of the psychometric tests, they scored above civilian population norms on all of those characteristics regarded as indicating psychological well-being and healthy adjustment. They did not score above the mean on any tests or subtests indicative of abnormalities or antisocial tendencies or behavior. There were very few exceptions.

The performance and attributes of operators who received ratings of "average" were compared with those who were rated as "below average" or "above average" by their commanding officers at the end of their tour of duty. There were few differences between the operators in these three categories but there was a tendency for the above average operators to be a little more calm, confident, and psychologically fit than the others. It is necessary to remember the total sample consisted of people who were unusually competent and well adjusted.

Continuing the search for markers that might indicate the existence of a select few who are capable of carrying out acts of exceptional courage that distinguish them from their fellow operators, we carried out separate analyses of decorated operators and of equally experienced and competent operators who were not decorated. To our surprise, we came across a feature that distinguished the operators who had received decorations for gallantry (Hallam, 1983; Rachman, 1990). The decorated operators were found to be slightly but significantly superior in all-around psychological health and bodily fitness. They said that they felt well in their bodies and were mentally fit and alert, even to a greater degree than their colleagues who also scored well above civilian norms. On a scale that measures hypochondriasis, almost all of the decorated operators returned zero scores. They had no bodily or mental complaints at all. It should be emphasized that all of this psychometric information had been collected well before the operators went on a tour of operations and well before the decorations were awarded.

It is worth mentioning that contrary to speculation, there is no evidence to suggest that bomb-disposal operators are psychopathic. To the contrary, their psychometric results show the 200-plus RAOC operators were emotionally stable, and the overwhelming majority was free of any psychological abnormality. Moreover, many of them were engaged in socially responsible and charitable activities. The operators who received awards for courageous or fearless behavior were, like their fellow operators, free of psychological abnormalities or antisocial propensities. Most of them had lasting and satisfactory relationships with other people.

Most of the evidence we collected in the retrospective analyses pointed to the importance of training, group cohesion, and situational determinants, but the findings on the decorated group of operators began to suggest that individual characteristics might make some particular contribution to the execution of acts of bravery. Are there courageous actors as well as courageous acts?

Training and Performance of Bomb-Disposal Operators

In a study of the effects of training we found clear evidence of a substantial increase in skill and confidence after completion of the specialized course (Hallam & Rachman, 1983). The value of the training course is emphasized by the finding that after completing it, the novices (i.e., those who had not yet carried out a tour of duty as a bomb-disposal operator) expressed approximately 80% of the confidence of the experienced operators. Put another way, the training course succeeded in taking them 80% of the way to that combination of confidence and competence that makes a successful operator. The specific value of the training is evident from the fact that before entering the course, soldiers with previous military experience in Northern Ireland unrelated to bomb-disposal duties had as little confidence in their ability to deal with explosive devices as did soldiers who had never served in Northern Ireland.

Our next investigation dealt with the adjustment and performance of the operators during a tour of duty in Northern Ireland. The most important fact is that almost all of them performed their duties successfully and without problems. They quickly adapted to the dangers of the work even though most of them had to live and work under confined and cramped, improvised conditions.

The process of adaptation was accelerated once the operator successfully carried out his first operation on a genuine device. Experience of dealing with false alarms or hoaxes made no contribution to either their confidence or their competence, but once the inexperienced operators successfully dealt with a genuine explosive device, their confidence and competence quickly rose to a level close to that of the experienced operators. Most of the operators reported feeling calm for much of the 4-month tour. Seven of the 20 operators reported no fear at any time (fearless operators). Four of the 20 had a good deal of fear and can be described as courageous performers. In general, there was a close correspondence between the ratings of self-efficacy and reported fear, but exceptions were encountered. A few operators maintained high self-efficacy ratings during the tour but nevertheless reported large fluctuations in the level of their fear.

The percentage of fearless operators is even higher than that reported by U.S. airmen who participated in a study of air-combat fears; only 1% experienced no fear during combat (Flanagan, 1948). In a comparable study by Hastings et al. (1944), 6% of the airmen were fearless. Reports from infantry soldiers indicate similarly low proportions of fearless people. Among 105 paratroop trainees 26% were classified as fearless during their training program (Macmillan & Rachman, 1988). Having experienced some fear while flying aircraft, the Mercury astronauts were almost free of fear during their trips into space, even in the most uncertain and dangerous parts of their adventure. There was little evidence of fear before the space flights. The evidence of fearless performances accumulates. A small proportion of people do display fearless behavior. Do they do so consistently?

Generality of Fearlessness and Courage

Having discovered that the decorated bomb-disposal operators rated their mental and physical health even more favorably than their equally competent and stable but nondecorated colleagues rated their own health, we decided to test the generality of this finding. In particular, we wished to determine whether operators who had been decorated for acts of gallantry would perform and react differently than would their nondecorated colleagues when given a stressful laboratory task (Cox et al., 1983). The operators were required to make increasingly difficult auditory discriminations while under threat of shock for making errors. By correctly moving a lever to the left or right in response to an auditory signal, they were able to avoid the shock, but during the final two phases of the test the auditory discrimination task was insoluble.

The comparison between the decorated and the nondecorated operators was the core of the study, but we also used the opportunity to test a few civilians and recently trained young soldiers. The subjective and psychophysiological reactions of the seven decorated operators were compared with those of seven equally experienced and successful but nondecorated bomb-disposal operators. The decorated subjects maintained a lower heart rate when making difficult discriminations under threat of shock. There were no differences between the groups in their subjective reactions or their behavioral responses. Both of these groups of operators showed significantly less fear and physiological reactivity than did the civilians, and less fear than did the young soldiers. The idea of a link between courage or fear and the heart, as determined by an unusually low heart rate in this experiment and in other research, is of course expressed in everyday terms, such as *lion-hearted* and *faint-hearted,* and the word *courage* itself is derived from the Latin for "heart."

It remained to be determined whether the stable physiological pattern identified in this experiment is attributable to military training or to constitutional factors or both. The psychophysiological difference between the decorated and nondecorated operators is unlikely to be the result solely of military training, as they shared the same training. On the other hand, the nondecorated operators and the recently trained young soldiers showed less cardiac acceleration than did the civilians, which may point to a contribution of (military) training for coping with stress. As in the psychometric study of the distinction between courageous actors and courageous acts, the experimental investigation showed that the decorated and nondecorated operators have a great deal in common, but a difference could be found.

Because the observed difference was so particular and had not been specifically predicted, a replication was necessary. Twenty-four operators were asked to participate in a close copy of the original experiment (O'Connor, Hallam, & Rachman, 1985). All soldiers who had taken part in the previous study were excluded. The fresh group of eight decorated operators had all received the George Medal or the Queen's Medal for Gallantry. A matched group of eight nondecorated operators was drawn at random from the same pool, and a third group of eight young RAOC technicians who had no operational experience was included for a second comparison. The results of the original experiment, showing lower cardiac reactivity under stress among the decorated operators, were replicated. With minor exceptions, no group differences in subjective reactions or behavioral performance were found. These results strengthen the view that it may indeed be possible to identify psychophysiological indices of fearlessness and courage.

Falklands Veterans

Is this low responsiveness to stress confined to decorated bomb-disposal operators? In an attempt to find out whether this psychophysiological pattern can be identified in other groups, the experiment was replicated on 34 members of the Parachute Regiment who were veterans of the Falklands War (Macmillan & Rachman, 1987). Sixteen had received decorations, either for a particular act of bravery or for generally outstanding behavior while on active service in the Falklands. The 18 nondecorated veterans were matched in terms of age and experience, and all had performed well on active service.

This time, we could find no difference between decorated and nondecorated soldiers. We therefore combined the two groups and compared their data with that obtained from the bomb-disposal operators. The heart rate under stress of the Falklands veterans was initially similar to that of the nondecorated bomb-disposal operators, but as the stress was increased, their cardiac reactivity resembled that of the decorated operators. Overall, the psychophysiological reactivity of the decorated and nondecorated members of the Parachute Regiment approximated that of the decorated bomb-disposal operators. Furthermore, the paratroops reported significantly less subjective anxiety before and during the stress test than had the bomb-disposal operators. The difference between these veteran paratroopers and the bomb-disposal operators may be a product of selection and training. The training of bomb-disposal operators emphasizes technical skill and the men are trained to carry out defensive duties, whereas the paratroopers are assault troops trained to be aggressive. They accept their role as an elite force and know that they may be called on to conduct offensive operations in which the likelihood of causalities is high.

These laboratory investigations provide some evidence in support of the argument that it is possible to identify a group of people who are capable of carrying out courageous or fearless acts and who also show a muted psychophysiological reaction when subjected to stress under controlled conditions. There is also evidence that they report an optimal level of functioning on self-report tests of mental and physical well-being. They appear to be unusually resilient. Evidence of cross-situational consistency in fearless or courageous behavior is beginning to emerge.

Courageous or Fearless?

To determine the viability of making a distinction between courage and fearlessness, we carried out a study of 105 recruits to the Parachute Regiment who were about to undergo parachute training (Macmillan & Rachman, 1988). Self-report measures were obtained prior to the training and again at the conclusion of the course, which they all completed successfully. A cluster analysis was carried out on 14 variables, and a three-part solution emerged. The first cluster encompassed two thirds of the sample; the recruits in this group expressed moderate optimism and moderate fear but nevertheless performed successfully. They formed a group described as courageous performers, who persevere despite the presence of fear.

One quarter of the sample fitted into the second cluster, described as the fearless performers. These soldiers were optimistic and confident, and they anticipated and reported very low levels of fear. The third cluster, comprising 7.5% of the paratroop recruits, was unexpected. The members of this group underpredicted how frightened they would be during the jumping and also underestimated how dangerous they would find the tasks. This small minority was described as "overconfident."

The fearless performers reported very little fear (14/100) during the jumping, compared with scores of 41 in the courageous group and 50 in the overconfident group. The fearless performers also had significantly lower scores on the hypochondriasis scale, which distinguished the decorated from the nondecorated bomb-disposal operators. On this measure, the fearless paratroops scored 0.7, which was significantly lower than the already very low scores reported by the other two clusters of paratroops. In addition, the soldiers in the fearless group were significantly more confident than were the other two and rated the task as being less dangerous than did members of the two comparison groups. Their actual scores are worth recording: The fearless performers were 96% confident of their ability to jump satisfactorily, and the dangerousness of jumping was rated at 20 on a 100 scale (versus 50 by the overconfident jumpers). The courageous operators predicted that they would be moderately fearful, and they were; confidence in their ability to jump satisfactorily was 58% before training and rose to 80% after completion of the jumping. They rated the training as being slightly more dangerous than expected. During the jumping, they reported a moderate amount of unpleasant bodily symptoms, at a level that was significantly higher than for the fearless jumpers.

The results of this study, viewed in the light of the earlier research, encourage the idea that a distinction can be made between fearless and courageous performers and that classifications based on this distinction are associated with the quality of performance of a demanding and dangerous task. It remains to be seen whether this type of classification is predictive of future conduct.

Can Courage Be Acquired?

Before turning to the implications of these findings on courageous and fearless actors, I can attempt a reply to the question put by Socrates, courtesy of the RAOC. Yes, it is possible for people to attain the noble quality of courage by study and training. A particularly apt example is provided by the specialized training given to the members of the RAOC that enables the great majority of bomb-disposal operators to perform their perilous tasks successfully. There is some evidence of a constitutional contribution to courageous or fearless conduct, but this does not overshadow the findings that point to the powerful influence of adequate training (e.g., the experienced operators were less fearful and less responsive to stress than were the untrained soldiers and considerably less frightened than were the civilians). The most impressive piece of evidence of the value of training arises from the justified assumption that any member of the Ordnance Corps can carry out bomb-disposal duties once he has specialized training. Several factors contribute to the performance of courageous or fearless acts. The appropriate skill required for dealing with a dangerous situation serves to increase courage, as does a general sense of self-confidence. Situational demands and support from a cohesive group also play important roles. Specific training, the provision of coping models, and the support of a small and familiar cohesive group are conditions that can be relied on to promote courageous behavior.

Young men, and not only young men, can be trained to attain the noble quality and perform courageously. The provision of graded realistic training designed to promote the required skills and to increase the person's self-confidence is a dependable way of promoting courageous behavior. The execution of courageous acts will be enhanced by the support of a tightly integrated, familiar, small group of people. I can also give a partial answer to a question that Socrates never asked. There is a small group of people who are particularly well suited to the performance of dangerous or difficult tasks by virtue of their relative fearlessness.

Concluding Observations

The research on bomb-disposal operators, assault troops, and trainee paratroops arose from an application of the three-systems concept of fear, according to which fear is best construed as a set of loosely coupled components. When the behavioral component of fear changes desynchronously in relation to the other two components, the result can be interpreted as courage. Persistence in dealing with a dangerous situation despite subjective and physical signs of fear is regarded as courageous; the person's behavior advances beyond his or her subjective behavior. People who continue to approach a dangerous situation without experiencing subjective fear or unpleasant bodily reactions are showing a concordance of the three components that define fearless behavior. Competence and confidence contribute to courageous performance, and both are strengthened by repeated and successful practice. In the early stages of training people to perform courageously, success is more likely if the person's motivation is raised. Enhanced motivation enables one to persevere, even in the face of subjective apprehension. It follows that courageous behavior, which is particularly subject to (changeable) motivational and situational influences, is likely to be less consistent than fearless behavior.

In addition to competence and confidence, situational demands contribute to the execution of courageous acts. Courageous models and social cohesiveness are also facilitative. That minority of people who remain hyporesponsive under stress are less vulnerable and better equipped to carry out dangerous acts. They probably carry out a disproportionately large number of fearless acts.

We are not in a position to attach weights to each factor, but at present it appears that the factors of confidence, competence, and demand make the greatest contribution to courageous performance. Hyperesponsiveness to stress is postulated to play a major part in fearless acts but falls short of being a necessary condition. Situational demands and confidence are thought to be important contributors to fearless behavior.

The successful practice of courageous behavior leads to a decrease in subjective fear and finally to a state of fearlessness. Courage grows into fearlessness. People who are learning to parachute from an aircraft display courage when they persevere with their jumps despite subjective fear. Veteran parachutists, having successfully habituated to the situation, no longer experience fear when jumping; they have moved from courage to fearlessness.

Our research on courage has some practical implications. The results emphasize the continuity of behavior: Fear and acts of courage are not confined to selected groups of people. Extreme fear is not necessarily a form of pathology, and all people, including the most fearful, are capable of courageous actions. People are far more resilient than our theories have implied, and even fearful patients with neurosis do not lack the potential for courageous behavior. Having several strong fears need not set a person apart from others, and it does not preclude the acquisition of skills to deal with fear. It does not preclude the performance of courageous acts.

References

Bandura, A. (1977). Self-efficacy: Toward a unifying theory of behavioral change. *Psychological Review, 84,* 191–215. doi:10.1037/0033-295X.84.2.191

Birley, J. L. (1923). The psychology of courage. *Lancet, 1,* 779–789.

Boswell, J. (1954). *The life of Samuel Johnson.* New York, NY: Modern Library.

Churchill, W. (1949). *History of the Second World War* (Vol. 2). London, England: Cassells.

Cox, D., Hallam, R., O'Connor, K., & Rachman, S. (1983). An experimental analysis of fearlessness and courage. *The British Journal of Psychology, 74,* 107–117.

Cox, D., & Rachman, S. (1983). Performance under operational conditions. In S. Rachman (Ed.), *Fear and courage in military bomb-disposal operators* (pp. 127–152). Oxford, England: Pergamon Press.

Flanagan, J. (Ed.). (1948). The aviation psychology program in the Army Air Forces. *USAAF Aviation Psychology Report No. 1.* Washington, DC: U.S. Government Printing Office.

Hallam, R. (1983). Psychometric analyses. In S. Rachman (Ed.), *Fear and courage in military bomb-disposal operators* (pp. 105–120). Oxford, England: Pergamon Press.

Hallam, R., & Rachman, S. (1983). The psychological effects of the training course. In S. Rachman (Ed.), *Fear and courage in military bomb-disposal operators* (pp. 121–126). Oxford, England: Pergamon Press.

Hastings, D., Wright, D., & Glueck, B. (1944). *Psychiatric experiences of the Eighth Air Force*. New York, NY: Josiah Macy Foundation.

Janis, I. (1951). *Air war and emotional stress*. New York, NY: McGraw-Hill.

Jenkins, R. (2002). *Churchill: A biography*. London, England: Penguin Books.

Lang, P. (1970). Stimulus control, response control and desensitization of fear. In D. Levis (Ed.), *Learning approaches to therapeutic behavior change* (pp. 256–274). Chicago, IL: Aldine.

Macmillan, T., & Rachman, S. (1987). Fearlessness and courage in paratroop veterans of the Falklands War. *The British Journal of Psychology, 78,* 375–383.

Macmillan, T., & Rachman, S. (1988). Fearlessness and courage in paratroopers undergoing training. *Personality and Individual Differences, 9,* 373–378. doi:10.1016/0191-8869(88)90100-6

Mowrer, O. (1960). *Learning theory and behavior*. New York, NY: Wiley. doi:10.1037/10802-000

O'Connor, K., Hallam, R., & Rachman, S. (1985). Fearlessness and courage: A replication experiment. *The British Journal of Psychology, 76,* 187–197.

Plato. (1953). Laches. In B. Jowett (Trans.), *The dialogues of Plato* (Vol. 1, pp. 111–129). Oxford, England: Oxford University Press.

Rachman, S. (1982). Fear and courage. *Journal of the Royal Army Medical Corps, 128,* 100–104.

Rachman, S. (1990). *Fear and courage* (2nd ed.). New York, NY: Freeman.

Rachman, S. (Ed.). (1983). *Fear and courage in military bomb-disposal operators*. Oxford, England: Pergamon Press.

Ruff, G., & Korchin, S. (1964). Psychological responses of the Mercury astronauts to stress. In G. Grosser (Ed.), *The threat of impending disaster* (pp. 144–175). Cambridge, MA: MIT Press.

Stouffer, S., & Associates. (1949). *The American soldier: Combat and its aftermath*. Princeton, NJ: Princeton University Press.

Symonds, C., & Williams, D. (1979). Clinical and statistical study of neurosis precipitated by flying duties. In E. J. Dearnaley & P. B. Warr (Eds.), *Aircrew stress in wartime operations* (pp. 9–42). New York, NY: Academic Press.

Walk, R. (1956). Self-ratings of fear in a fear-evoking situation. *Journal of Abnormal and Social Psychology, 52,* 171–178. doi:10.1037/h0042978

6

The Courage to Be Authentic: Empirical and Existential Perspectives

Cooper R. Woodard

In this chapter, I briefly review the concept of hardiness as one aspect of the authentic person, because this was the starting point for my own research on courage. I discuss early efforts to define and empirically derive a measure of courage and then more fully explore the concept of authenticity from an existential psychology perspective. The perspectives of Rollo May, Paul Tillich, Abraham Maslow, and others are considered, relative to the relationship of authenticity with courage. Finally, I suggest an alternative way of interpreting or understanding some findings that Cindy Pury and I have generated, in light of the potential meaning that may develop in people's lives should they choose the courageous route toward becoming a more authentic being.

Hardiness as a Starting Point

Tucked away in an unpublished doctoral dissertation from 1977 is Suzanne Ouellette Kobasa's first foray into what was to become the concept of *hardiness.* Interested in how certain personality variables might moderate the relationship between stressful life events and somatic or psychological illness, Kobasa (1977) explored this in a small sampling of individuals who seemed to remain healthy despite high levels of life stress. Referring to these persons almost offhandedly as "hardy," Kobasa compared them with others who tended to be physically and psychologically debilitated by similar levels of stress. In her study of more than 600 high-level male executives, Kobasa found that the hardy ones among them were more self-aware, more disposed to experience their lives as meaningful, weaker toward leadership orientations, and more likely to include the seeking out of interesting life experiences among their life goals. Like Maslow years earlier in his studies of the personality traits representative of self-actualized persons, Kobasa concluded that hardy persons possess a unique combination of personality characteristics that enable such persons to remain healthy under

I would like to express my thanks to David Wulff for his editorial assistance, ideas, guidance, and ongoing support for this chapter.

high-stress conditions. Together, these characteristics constitute the *authentic* person.

Working with Salvatore Maddi and others through the 1980s, Kobasa proposed that the core personality dimensions of hardiness consist of (a) *commitment,* an active and deeply engaged approach to self and environment; (b) *control,* the feeling that one is influential in facing life contingencies; and (c) *challenge,* the disposition to view life changes as interesting rather than a source of threat (Kobasa, Maddi, & Kahn, 1982). After reading these and later works on hardiness (e.g., Funk, & Houston, 1987; Hull, Van Treuren, & Virnelli, 1987) as well as writings on authenticity, I began wondering why courage had been left out of the hardiness equation. Courage seemed to me to be intrinsic to both hardiness and authenticity, a view shared by other researchers. In a review of hardiness research, for example, Orr and Westman (1990) suggested that courage is directly related to the control and challenge dimensions of the hardy person: "Control and challenge assess another major element of authentic being: courage. A common element of existential thinkers' views is that life is by its nature chaotic and threatening, and that persons live at their best if they react courageously" (p. 65). If courage is such a central component, would formally adding it as an empirical variable to the existing hardiness elements account for more of the somatic or psychological health variance?

Development of an Empirical Measure of Courage

In pursuing the answer to this question, I was soon faced with two problems. First, there was surprisingly little research on courage and no agreed-on definition, and second, there were no empirically derived measures of courage. To construct a serviceable definition, I started with the one offered by *Webster's New Collegiate Dictionary* (1999): "mental or moral strength to venture, persevere, and withstand danger, fear, or difficulty" (p. 226). For the purposes of my research, then, I integrated the substance of this definition with a cognitive appraisal perspective of fear, defining courage as "the ability to act for a meaningful (noble, good, or practical) cause, despite experiencing the fear associated with perceived threat exceeding the available resources" (Woodard, 2004, p. 174). This definition included the aspects of courage that I considered most salient at the time: actions toward a meaningful cause in spite of evidence of threat and corresponding fear.

For this study, we asked 10 experts in the field of psychology to write 10 statements describing circumstances that they thought would reflect courage as I defined it; other items were added, for a total of 109. Together, these items sampled a wide variety of situations related to physical, social, and psychological domains. Items were edited to ensure that all aspects of the definition were present and that the situation each item posed was sufficiently meaningful or important. Each of the 200 college-age participants in Phase 1 of the 2004 research project was asked to rate his or her agreement with the items (1 = *strong disagreement* and 5 = *strong agreement*), as well as how fearful each thought he or she would be in each particular situation (1 = *little fear* and 5 = *very high fear*). Courage scores were calculated by summing the products of the agreement scores times the fear scores, which gave equal weight to these two elements. Through a process of item reduction and factor analysis, a 31-item scale was created that appeared to have four underlying factors.

The first of these factors consisted of items related to stressful, painful, or dangerous events resulting in a positive outcome, but there were no other distinguishing themes that differentiated this collection of items from the general definition of courage. The second factor consisted of social items, in that many of the situations entailed either threats from others or benefits for others. In items loading on the third factor, the actor seemed to be acting alone, without or against a group of others, and the items of the fourth factor shared the theme of physical pain endurance. In Phase 2 of the project, 80 additional participants were recruited for the purpose of comparing courage and hardiness and assessing the validity of the scale. The courage scores, including both the multiplied version described earlier as well as scores based on the agreement responses alone, were not correlated with any of the hardiness components or a 7-item, panic-specific courage scale created by Schmidt and Koselka (2000). Furthermore, courage scores did not improve the predictive relationship of hardiness and physical illness as I had hoped.

In a follow-up research project, Cindy Pury and I undertook to refine the scale and to explore further the scale's factor structure (Woodard & Pury, 2007). We started by revisiting the definition of courage, supported by what appeared to be a sudden but welcome burst of interest in the concept of courage. We drew on recently compiled comprehensive lists of definitions of courage (Lopez, O'Byrne, & Petersen, 2003) and other burgeoning research efforts focusing on courage (e.g., Pury, Kowalski, & Spearman, 2007). Our initial discussions centered on the role of fear in courage, for we were encountering contradictory views on whether or not fear is a necessary component (Shelp, 1984). We were of the opinion, for example, that running into a burning building to rescue someone might surely be considered courageous even if the actor was not afraid. This perspective, paired with an observation by a colleague who specialized in factor analysis that multiplying willingness-to-act (WTA) ratings with fear ratings muddied the statistical waters, led us to delete fear from the courage definition. We concluded, then, that courage consists of three components: (a) the voluntary willingness to act in response to a (b) danger or threat, in order (c) to achieve an important and perhaps moral goal. Our second area of focus considered what and how many types of courage may be usefully distinguished, as the list of possible contenders was growing exponentially. It seemed that for every conceivable threat—physical, moral, vital, existential, social, psychological—there was a corresponding courage type, yet empirical evidence for each was scarce. We wondered what types of courage empirical methods could uncover, and whether participants could identify the type of threat presented in a courage-scale item and agree on the type of courage it represented. In short, were courage types related to threat categories?

To begin to answer these questions, Pury and I had 47 participants categorize the 31 courage items as threats to either social, physical, or emotional well-being. Our first goal was to determine if participants could agree on what type of threat each item represented, and our second goal was to determine if this categorization helped us to interpret the outcome of Phase 2 of the research project. Phase 2 was a repeated factor analysis of the WTA responses of the original participant pool from Woodard (2004). The fear ratings were not included in this analysis. Phase 3 of the project was to see if the factor structure from the second phase could be repeated with a new sample of 162 participants. Our results indicated that participants could categorize the type of threat of each of the 31 courage items with a fair amount of agreement (the average agreement was 77%), but this did little to help us understand the factors we found in Phases 2 and 3 of the research project. Apparently, determining the types of courage that existed was more complex than simply identifying threat types; focusing solely on the threat clearly would not suffice.

In Phase 2, we found that factor analysis of the WTA responses of the original pool of participants from 2004 again generated a four-factor solution. However, it was quite different from the structure described in the 2004 article. When we used the WTA responses only, seven items did not load greater than 0.40 on any factor, and item loadings had shifted. For Phase 3 of our project, the factor analysis on the new sample of 162 participants also produced a four-factor solution, this time with three items not loading greater than 0.40 on any factor. When the factor structure of the new sample of 162 participants was compared with the original sample from the 2004 research, 65% of the items loaded on the same factors. This version became the scale used in subsequent research, the Woodard-Pury Courage Scale–23, or the WPCS-23. Our factor structure findings suggested some moderate, although clearly not perfect, levels of consistency, and we turned to examining the content of the various factors.

For the first factor, most items related to work or employment situations, such as asking for a raise or moving to a foreign country for the perfect job. This outcome not only demonstrated a new type of "employment" courage, which we certainly did not expect, but also lessened support for a general courage factor, which had been suggested in the 2004 article. Furthermore, this factor suggested that courage type could be related to a general life context or domain. The second factor was composed of items that referred to physical pain or risk of life for political, patriotic, or religious beliefs. This finding suggested that the nature of the threat must be considered in conjunction with the outcome to determine the type of courage involved; at the same time it negated the idea of a general physical courage because other "physical" items did not load on this factor. Alternatively, the second factor may have represented a person's commitment to society's abstract principles. The items loading on the third factor entailed both social threats and socially beneficial outcomes, and each item had a distinctly moral tone. Items asked about helping others or doing the "right thing," suggesting that a type of social–moral courage may be distinguished empirically. Factor four, finally, had two possible interpretations. The three items that created this factor represented the person acting alone or independently, and the two items with the highest loadings were distinctly related to family functioning.

In partial summary, our research began to illuminate some interesting and unexpected aspects about courage. First, courage could be conceived of without fear as a component but including three other elements: (a) a voluntary action, (b) a perceived threat, and (c) an important, perhaps moral goal. We were able to generate moderately consistent factor structures without including the fear component. This result was helpful in clarifying what types of courage may exist, but it did not resolve the matter of the role of fear in courage or the question of uncertainty of outcome as a component. Second, our research suggested that there is probably not a general form of courage, and the types of courage that can be distinguished are not solely related to the type of threat presented. Thus, a typology of forms of courage based only on knowledge of threat (e.g., physical threat, therefore physical courage) is likely to be inadequate. Instead, the context or general domain of the situation may be the most salient feature of the courage type, or both the threat and the outcome working in conjunction with each other may determine the courage type.

Our findings suggested that either the type of threat (e.g., physical pain) or the type of outcome (e.g., social benefit) and the overall tone may create the courage type, or even the actor's particular situation or a domain of interest or importance (e.g., work, family) may determine a type of courage. The types of courage that could be empirically demonstrated—employment, patriotic or religion-based belief system, social–moral, and independent or family-based—appeared to be based on a complex, varied, and wide array of determinants. As a group, these types of courage and their respective contexts or determinants may represent, in theory, a fairly significant portion of what could be considered key domains of living and meaning. In other words, the extent to which these types of courage are present in any given person may indicate that person's investment in what could make life meaningful. With regard to Kobasa's existential starting point, the courageous choice to invest in that which a person finds meaningful may, in fact, be authenticity itself.

Authenticity as an Existential Perspective and Courage

There seems to be something inherently attractive, desirable, and appreciated about the term *authenticity*. For example, travelers tend to want the authentic experience when touring, buyers pay more for authentic consumer goods, and the term is considered a compliment when applied to a performer or artist. It is a term that comes to mind when one senses someone is risking being completely who he or she is, whether one is mesmerized by the striking colors of Van Gogh or listening to the piercing voice of Edith Piaf. It surfaces when one hears the openness of Carl Rogers or the flowing words of Walt Whitman. Authenticity is commonly accepted as suggesting genuineness, originality, perhaps uniqueness, and honesty or truthfulness, and is held in contrast to imitation, falseness, or fakeness. It can also have an element of pushing back or standing out in a crowd, or a more simplistic contact with true feelings or a true self that is obscured by the self people create through others and present to others.

Themes consistent with the central notion of knowing one's self date back to Greek philosophy, but such history is beyond the scope of the present chapter and may have limited relevance to the type of authenticity being considered here. In Suzanne Kobasa's early research, existential psychology provided the conceptual framework for authenticity and the foundational components of hardiness. Existential psychology is a branch of psychology that grapples with the issues of existence itself, human freedom and responsibility, and also the undeniable reality of isolation and death. As such, it presents the threats introduced by life itself, and therefore it is inextricably linked to the courage with which people live their lives. It is a unique perspective, with roots in the philosophies of Nietzsche, Kierkegaard, Beauvoir, Sartre, and, perhaps most vividly, Heidegger. It is central to the psychophilosophical writings and ideas of Rollo May, Ludwig Binswanger, James F. T. Bugental, Paul Tillich, Viktor Frankl, and Medard Boss, and it colors the writings and ideas of Abraham Maslow, Ernest Becker, Irvin Yalom, Carl Rogers, and others.

Existential psychology is a perspective that depends less on logic, reason, and scientific systems, and instead turns toward a human being's unique awareness of being and the difficult issues that ensue. Central, however, is the concept that a person exists in a perpetual dilemma, with awareness of a symbolic, conscious self that is at the same time hopelessly bound to nature and the physical world. As Becker (1973) stated,

> Man is literally split in two: he has an awareness of his own splendid uniqueness in that he sticks out of nature with a towering majesty, and yet he goes back into the ground a few feet in order blindly and dumbly to rot and disappear forever. (p. 26)

This integrated duality of a conscious self by necessity needing a physical world in order to be is captured in Heidegger's (1927/1996) concept of "being-in-the-world" or *In-der-Welt-sein,* and the closely related concept of "being there" or *Dasein.* A conscious sense of self or being is, by design, a function of and inherently bound to the physical world, the people in it, and one's true self. This entity or *Dasein*'s dilemma subsequently creates an anxiety or angst that results from a set of corollary ideas including nonbeing or nothingness or death, freedom to make choices in a contingent world, responsibility for these choices, and ultimate loneliness or isolation (Bugental, 1981). These inescapable truths of existence are commonly referred to as man's *facticity,* or *thrown* condition.

In struggling with the continual weight of one's thrown condition, each person has the option of avoiding the problem through apathy or drugs, for example, or, more commonly, seeking relief by immersing one's self to varying degrees in the mass culture, community standards, and crowd mentality that surround one. This noncourageous approach is what Heidegger termed "the they" or *das Man,* and this choice has the power and potential to "dissolve one's own Da-sein completely" (p. 119). The "they" is a dictatorship of thinking that is everywhere, an oceanic mass that is concerned mainly with a drive toward dull averageness. Heidegger (1927/1953) wrote,

> This averageness . . . watches over every exception that thrusts itself into the fore. Every priority is noiselessly squashed. . . . Everything gained by a struggle becomes something to be manipulated. . . . The care of averageness reveals . . . the leveling down of all possibilities of being. (p. 119)

When immersion in the "they" becomes a person's main mode of existence in an effort to ward off existential anxiety, that person is being inauthentic. This person becomes a dull imitation of what is around him or her—an automaton blindly operating on the instructions of others, hoping to even momentarily quell his or her ever-present angst. This person hides and turns away from his or her true self and the truth of his or her thrown condition by choosing to be "they," gladly surrendering his or her ability to choose and the associated responsibilities, and denying his or her separateness through his or her false union with *das Man*. This process immobilizes the growth and becoming process of the self.

In stark contrast, a person also has the potential for minimizing "they-ness" by courageously choosing to be who he or she truly is. A person has the option of accepting the responsibility of his or her own freedom and choosing for him- or herself, and also risking the weight of possible isolation and loneliness that comes from turning away from the "they." He or she could choose to live in this manner despite the absolutely assured nothingness that is perpetually possible, and thus embrace his or her thrown condition. This option represents the courageous choice to be authentic, the choice of risking becoming who and what one truly is. As Ludwig Binswanger (1963) stated, "By 'authentic,' we refer to those heights (or depths) which can be attained only insofar as the Dasein undergoes the arduous process of choosing itself and growing into maturity" (p. 346).

Perspectives on Authenticity and Courage

Authenticity frequently intersects with courage. Bugental (1981) clearly delineated man's existential dilemma, his thrown condition, and the subsequent sources of normal, necessary anxiety previously mentioned in this chapter. Authenticity is considered the main focus of both living and psychotherapy, a goal that can only be approximated through awareness that "confronts the existential anxieties of being . . . avoiding their distortion" (Bugental, 1981, p. 40). This continual confrontation is inescapable, a fact of life and being, leaving the person with such conscious awareness of two basic choices: facing the situation courageously or succumbing to ontic dread. The choice of courage is suggested to result in a sense of wholeness, faith in living, a sense of identity, creativity, and love, opening the opportunity for actualization of potential selves:

> Courage consists in the confronting of our limitedness within the unlimitedness of being. Courage consists in the exercising of our choice and the taking of our responsibility while recognizing that contingency can overthrow our decision and reverse our best efforts. Courage finds its finest expression in the choice to be. (Bugental, 1981, p. 26)

For Bugental, courage embodied and created the authentic mode of living by embracing the inherent threats made real by conscious awareness and risking the emergence of the true self. In contrast, the choice of dread finds its expression in "they-ness" and a turning away from the challenges of being and living. It distorts awareness of existence, denies the true self, and results in illness, powerlessness, blame, absurdity, and estrangement from the self and world.

Rollo May identified with the existential orientation, drew directly from the works of Kierkegaard, and began to bridge the gap between existentialism and both humanism and the practice of psychotherapy. The central conflicts of man included the struggle of the awareness of being against the potential of nonbeing, the challenges of freedom and responsibility, and the option of denying oneself or realizing the unique potentials of the self (May, 1960). May suggested that courage is the affirmation of the self, giving an authentic direction to these dilemmas proposed by existence and making courage a "necessary ontological corollary" (p. 687). In *The Courage to Create* (1975), he suggested that through self-affirmation and centering of the self, courage has the capacity to make all other virtues real, and make possible being and becoming. This orientation is central to the therapeutic situation, and it is in this context that not only the role of courage but also the emergence of fear is seen. Within the therapeutic relationship, the realization of how a person is living can become manifest, and the patient can decide whether he or she is actually living life, or being lived by his or her fears (May, 1953). For May, the inauthentic life is the life motivated and driven by fear.

Thompson (2006), in his discussion of authenticity within the psychoanalytic therapy situation, suggested that authenticity is marked by three primary attributes: (a) by its very nature it is unconventional, or related to the road less traveled; (b) it is the more difficult path; and (c) it is genuine in that there is an absence of "subterfuge or contrivance" (p. 142). Thompson stated that authenticity reveals one's manner of suffering, and a more difficult path results from the choice to face suffering directly, rather than thinking up ways to hide from it. This ability to cope effectively with suffering is suggested to be closely linked to the anxiety of being oneself, and together they create the "hallmarks of authenticity" (Thompson, 2006, p. 161). The pain of change, sacrifice, and suffering is a burden to be borne equally by the therapist and the patient, and reveals a relationship to courage:

> What this comes down to is that the analyst instills that capacity for sacrifice in his patients *through his own example.* This instilling is not a matter of technique that can simply be "applied" from the comfort of detaching oneself from the process, but an *act of courage* that has to be suffered, repeatedly and constantly throughout the treatment with every patient. This is why the wherewithal to endure the first kind of suffering discussed earlier in order to mitigate the second kind is what Freud, Winnicott, Bion, and Lacan had in mind when they concluded that not only life, but analysis entails suffering. Though none of them used the term, the wisdom of submitting to suffering and making use of it makes little sense without at least an instinctive awareness of the role that authenticity properly plays in all of our clinical endeavors. (Thompson, 2006, p. 173)

Thompson (2006) suggested that whether life or the therapeutic relationship is being discussed, authenticity is defined by the courage with which each person handles the inherent pain and suffering that is necessary for growth. It is not surprising that Thompson pointed out that it is Nietzsche's *Ubermensch,* or "superman," that embodied the central ideals of the authentic person. This person chooses to face the basic anxieties of living and, as a result of this act of courage, develops the capacity to live unafraid.

Paul Tillich (1952) discussed the existential orientation and courage from a historical, theoretical, and religious perspective. His classic text *The Courage to Be* (1952) contains another reference to affirmation of the self and being in that courage is "the universal and essential self-affirmation of one's being . . . the ethical act in which man affirms his own being in spite of those elements of his existence which conflict with his essential self-affirmation" (p. 3). Though he did not specify the concept of authenticity directly, Tillich discussed the anxiety that is derived from the awareness of nonbeing, and the constant pressure of this threat:

> And death stands behind fate and its contingencies not only in the last moment when one is thrown out of existence but in every moment within existence. Non-being is omnipresent and produces anxiety even where an immediate threat of death is absent. (p. 45)

He discussed the responsibility of realizing one's potential, and the importance of courageously participating in life and exercising one's freedom to make changes happen:

> Courage . . . is the act of the individual self in taking the anxiety of non-being upon itself by affirming itself either as part of an embracing whole or in its individual selfhood. Courage always includes a risk, it is always threatened by nonbeing, whether the risk of losing oneself and becoming a thing within the whole of things or of losing one's world in an empty self-relatedness. (p. 155)

Courage for Tillich was linked to faith, which represented the only reasonable answer to the hard-hitting realities of potential meaninglessness, despair, and isolation: "There is only one possible answer if one does not try to escape the question: namely that the acceptance of despair is in itself faith and on the boundary line of the courage to be" (p.175). Of the authors discussed so far, Tillich is the first to actually suggest a solution to the constant and inescapable dilemma of being. For Tillich, the concept of faith encompasses more than a personal relationship with God. It is "the existential acceptance of something transcending ordinary experience. Faith is not an opinion, but a state" (p. 173).

Abraham Maslow (1968) discussed his existential orientation in *Toward a Psychology of Being* (1968) and used the term *self-actualization* to communicate the existential notions of not only authentically becoming the true self but also living one's potentialities. In this work, one can almost immediately see the turning away from "they-ness" as a component of the becoming process of the self. The authentic person,

> by virtue of what he has become, assumes a new relation to his society and indeed, to society in general. He not only transcends himself in various ways; he also transcends his culture. He resists enculturation. He becomes more detached from his culture and from his society. (Maslow, 1968, p. 12)

In addition to minimizing the "they-ness" discussed previously by transcending culture and detaching from it, Maslow suggested the need to transcend the self. It is through this process that Maslow's representation of the authentic or actualized self crystallizes in a particular set of traits or characteristics that correspond to Bugental's sense of wholeness of identity, creativity, and love. For example, self-actualized persons can detect the fake or dishonest in people and confused or distorted realities, making their overall functioning more efficient and accurate (Maslow, 1987). They are unafraid of the unknown; display calmness even in turbulent times; lack guilt, shame, and severe anxiety; and generally accept themselves for what they are. Self-actualized persons are not defensive and dislike hypocrisy, game playing, and any attempts to impress others. They demonstrate a simple and natural spontaneity and "play down" their unconventionality so as not to hurt others, "with a good-humored shrug and with the best possible grace" (Maslow, 1987, p. 132). They are spontaneous in their own style, and develop their own style by virtue of their self-knowledge.

Self-actualized persons are problem-solvers, but the problems are generally outside of the self and not personal or internal problems. These people most often have a life mission or life task to pursue or fulfill, and are able to be solitary without difficulty. Self-actualizers are autonomous, and do not have their mind made up by their surrounding culture. Their development is dependent on their own potentialities, and they have the capacity to enjoy with fresh appreciation the basic goodness of life. These persons are ethical, creative, democratic, and often humorous, and enjoy deepened relations with others. They accept imperfections and dichotomies of the self, can be surprisingly ruthless when ruthlessness is the obvious option, and can be socially impolite when intense concentration is placed elsewhere. Finally, people who are self-actualized often may enjoy peak experiences, a goal at the very top of Maslow's well-known needs hierarchy. Suggested by Maslow (1987) to be related to the mystic experience, peak experiences are those of

> limitless horizons opening up to the vision, the feeling of being simultaneously more powerful and also more helpless than one ever was before, the feeling of great ecstasy and wonder and awe, the loss of placing in time and space with, finally, the conviction that something extremely important and valuable has happened, so that the subject is to some extent transformed and strengthened even in daily life by such experiences. (p. 137)

To summarize the preceding discussion of authenticity, existential psychology provides a basic framework: People are aware and conscious of being in relation to a physical world and the people in it, including themselves. Because of this awareness, people are also aware of nonbeing, nothingness, death, and an uncertain, contingent existence; their freedom to choose; the responsibility for their choices and living up to their potential; and their relation to but ultimate separation from others. This facticity or thrown condition is anxiety producing, and can be faced and engaged by being or becoming who one truly is, or denying and hiding from the self through social conformity. Facing the anxiety and threat of the inescapable thrown condition and choosing to become who and what one truly is, is authenticity. Authenticity is not a goal that is arrived at, but rather is a continual process or manner of living that can be chosen every day and every moment that a person experiences the ever-present awareness of being and the associated threats. The authentic choice is therefore the courageous choice to be. It is one's chosen manner of suffering, a difficult, even arduous choice to affirm the self, actively discover one's self, and take part in life in a meaningful way. This courageous choice can be fostered by a supportive atmosphere in which freedom to open to one's self is encouraged and trust in one's self is valued. The result of the authentic choice contributes to a centered sense of wholeness and identity, a spontaneous and creative manner of expression, realization of potentials internally derived from the self, and the capacity to love. The choice of authenticity, over time, creates an honest acceptance of the self, autonomous thinking that is not governed by others or culture, and the ability to invest in a life goal or mission. Most important in its relation to this discussion of courage, the choice of authenticity may generate calm acceptance of the unknown, a general lack of anxiety, and the continuing development of the capacity to live life less afraid. Diminishing anxiety and fear may be related to meaning, because when the choice is authenticity, then purpose, direction, and what is truly important to a person become clearer.

Courage, Authenticity, and the Creation of Meaning

To summarize what it means to be authentic from an existential perspective, there may be a thread of understanding, a link or set of relations that at present is not completely clear. This area may be ripe for research and further exploration. One way of understanding these concepts in relation to each other begins with the courageous nature of an authentic mode of being. Few would argue with the basic truths of the existential condition, or the perpetual threats that may evolve from the awareness of these truths. Authenticity has been suggested to be a manner of living or existing, where such existential threats are engaged rather than avoided. This corresponds with my previous discussion of empirical research, which suggested that courage had three main components: a voluntary action, a perceived threat, and an important, perhaps moral goal or outcome. According to this definition, it is clear that voluntarily choosing to engage the threats of an authentic mode of living is certainly an act of courage, with outcomes that rival and may indirectly correspond to those of the WPCS-23. The outcomes of choosing authenticity include, among other things, becoming who and what one truly is and realizing one's potential by choosing to direct one's life and take responsibility for it. It is not a single act or end point but rather a constant challenge and process, which may or may not be correlated with the situational acts of courage measured by the WPCS-23 scale.

However, how does choosing authenticity and becoming the true self create so many positive developments in the self, as well as the self's relation with the world and the people in it? What actually is happening as a result of the choice of authenticity and becoming who and what one truly is? Despite these choices, aren't people still faced with the problem of existence and resulting angst? I would suggest that the importance of choosing authenticity and undergoing the process of becoming lies in the fact that it is the only option that allows a person to answer both yes and no to this last question. The authentic mode of being is the only choice that provides an effective and productive mode of coping with one's existential dilemma because it is through the activated process of becoming who one truly is that the parallel, integral process of realizing what is important, what has value to a person as a unique being, what has meaning for a person becomes manifest. I would suggest that the value of the choice of an authentic mode of being, the courageous choice to be, is not only affirmation of the self through self-knowledge, centering, self-acceptance, and self-trust but also the discovery of what is meaningful in one's life. Guignon (2004) stated, "Only because finding your place in the scheme of things is what is truly important does it become worthwhile to assess your personal nature" (p. 13). Existential meaninglessness can be replaced with something that is worth living for, something of perhaps more value than one's own life. This discovery of meaning further reinforces the choice of authenticity as responsibility for the self is rewarded, the freedom to choose takes on added importance, and committed connections are created in the world. In a manner of speaking, this activated process or cycle of positive growth allows some degree of transcendence of the angst of one's existential condition. Peripheral, lower level, situational fears may endure, but even these may be dramatically reduced as a function of found meaning.

Consider, for example, the many outcome traits or characteristics suggested in the earlier discussion of the works of Abraham Maslow. The self-actualized person not only enjoyed the benefits of knowing and being him- or herself (e.g., efficient functioning, self-acceptance, spontaneity) but also had often found an important life mission or goal to fulfill. Maslow (1987) explained that this is not simply a preferred or chosen task; it is "a task they must do" based on responsibility, duty, or obligation, that is "concerned rather with the good of humanity in general, or of a nation in general, or of a few individuals in the subject's family" (p. 134). (I return later to the similarity of these three ideas to three of the four types of courage found in the previously discussed research.) Further, Maslow also noted that the self-actualized person was unafraid of the unknown, yet did not deny it, run from it, or try to believe it is known. Such a person was more or less uninterested in the unknown and, as noted earlier, though there was the potential for low-level fears and associated negative emotions, there was also a general lack of severe anxiety. Other authors I have discussed also noted this found meaning in the authentic person and the lessening effect on fear. One of Suzanne Kobasa's main findings regarding her hardy, high-level executives was the experience of heightened meaning in the executive's life. Rollo May viewed the authentic life as one marked by an absence of fear, and Thompson suggested that the authentic person lived unafraid and accepted existence without fear. For Rogers, the process of becoming was integral to finding what was truly satisfying, and these processes were clearly associated with fear diminishing.

If anxiety and fear diminish as meaning is realized from an authentic, courageous orientation, the relationship between courage and these two concepts should be an inverse one. Of course, the authentic, courageous choice to be is more of a basic mode of living (often in relation to anxiety), whereas choosing a courageous act is more singular and narrowed (often in relation to fear), but the inverse relationship would still likely be maintained. One rather rough way of showing support for this set of relations is through the fear levels of the various groups that took part in the research Cindy Pury and I conducted. As these groups matured and found and pursued specific and focused life missions and activities that were meaningful for them, fear levels should have diminished. As is represented by Figure 6.1, this was indeed the case.

Though I am speculating on the presence, level, and causal role of meaning in these various groups (and certainly other factors such as practice and social support mediate the WTA–fear relationship), it is possible that as a result of increased meaning, courage, or what we called *willingness to act,* increases and

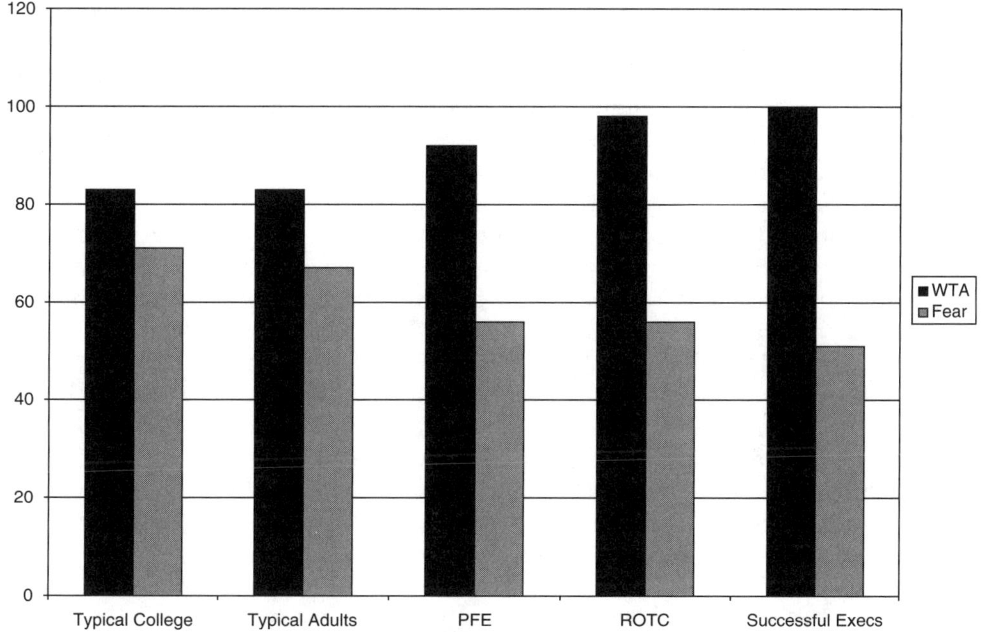

Figure 6.1. Willingness to Act (WTA) scores and fear ratings of participant groups. PFE = police, firefighter, and emergency responder; ROTC = Reserve Officers' Training Corps.

corresponding fear is diminished. This would support the notion that fear must be considered separate from courage and not an integral part of courage. One may begin by facing a threat that is highly feared, a common conceptualization of courage, but when the threat is faced, fear is diminished. When the threat is once again engaged, the act must still be considered one of courage because of the danger present in the threat. However, now the actor engages less afraid or unafraid, which is perhaps the ideal form of courage, an act, I would suggest, of a more authentic or more self-actualized person.

If the realization of meaning is the catalyst for overcoming anxiety and fear, then perhaps the types of courage found in our empirical research are, at the same time, domains of meaning. Three of the four types of courage identified in previous research—social–moral, patriotic, and family—are remarkably similar to areas noted by Maslow to be life missions or tasks chosen by self-actualizers: humanity, nation, or the subject's family. If we add to this mix employment or job-related courage (Factor 1), we now have a set of domains that may often be identified as main sources of meaning. If one were to ask where a person may find meaning in his or her life, it would not be unusual to hear responses such as "My family," "My work," "My religion," or "My relationships with other people." Meaning gives value to people's lives if they are sufficiently self-aware to know what is truly important to them, and meaning allows for a sense of belonging, so not only do people invest, but they have a sense that the domain invests in them as well. Also, consider what happens when a meaningful relationship or connection is damaged or lost, a beloved family member passes away, a job that allowed someone to do what he or she loved doing ends, someone becomes disillusioned by religion or government, or a partner or friend disappoints. These are some of the most challenging experiences in life not only because something has been lost but also because some of the meaning in one's life, a piece of one's purpose, part of one's personally valued reason for being, is diminished.

I would suggest, however, that a much sadder situation is the person who never summoned the courage to begin the development of authenticity and start the process of finding meaning in his or her life. This would truly be the life lived by fears, the life that never actually was. Granted, that first step may be the most daunting, as well as the best example of what Tillich meant by faith; who knows what people will find when they begin the process of becoming who they are, who knows if they will succeed or fail, and who knows if they will be swallowed up by nothingness and meaninglessness? However, it is ironic that if a person does not exercise courage, does not make the voluntary choice to engage the threats that are integral to existence, does not begin the process of becoming on some level, he or she almost surely will live a life of anxiety and fear, meaninglessness, and nothingness. Koestenbaum (1978) stated it in this way:

> However, the real lack of goals and meanings in a person's life is the experience of ennui, depression, unhappiness, irritability, and general dissatisfaction with life. That condition is proof that he has not yet made the decision to assume responsibility for being himself or, more specifically, responsibility for confronting evil with meaning.
>
> The fundamental archetypal decision which differentiates the person from his environment and creates him as an individual identity has not yet been made. This person is running away from dealing with this issue, and that is the source of his goallessness. The decision to be an individual has been postponed successfully, for to have a goal is to continually choose to say "yes" to oneself. (p. 270)

This central role of courage to, in Koestenbaum's words, "say 'yes' to oneself," may therefore be the single most important choice made by a person.

After surviving the horrors of Nazi concentration camps, Viktor Frankl identified meaning, or the will to meaning, as his theoretical and philosophical core. Frankl survived his experience by focusing on what was meaningful in his life (e.g., his relationship with his wife and his hopes for the future) and by accepting the responsibility to control what was left to him—his manner of suffering. For Frankl (1959), meaning was found in this suffering and courage was central to how suffering was engaged: "But there was no need to be ashamed of tears, for tears bore witness that a man had the greatest of courage, the courage to suffer" (pp. 78–79). Using these ideas, Frankl created a form of psychotherapy known as logotherapy, wherein the main goal is assisting the patient to detect or discover his or her own unique and specific meaning of life. Summoning the courage to take responsibility for fulfilling this meaning potential is proposed to be the path to happiness, as the apathy and boredom of Frankl's existential vacuum are replaced with purpose. Frankl (1964) wrote, "Meaning must not coincide with being; meaning must be ahead of being; meaning sets the pace for being. Existence falters unless lived in terms of transcendence, in terms of something beyond itself" (p. 516). Perhaps this is why courage has been considered the quality of character that truly supports all other virtues, because it opens the possibility of becoming who one is, realizing one's potentials, and lessening fear and anxiety by developing meaning in one's life. The courageous choice to be creates a path that has the potential to transcend the human dilemma and diminish fear and anxiety by helping a person realize a purpose greater than his or her self.

References

Becker, E. (1973). *The denial of death.* New York, NY: Free Press.

Binswanger, L. (1963). *Being-in-the-world: Selected papers of Ludwig Binswanger.* New York, NY: Harper & Row.

Bugental, J. F. T. (1981). *The search for authenticity.* New York, NY: Irvington.

Frankl, V. E. (1959). *Man's search for meaning.* Boston, MA: Beacon Press.

Frankl, V. E. (1964). The will to meaning. *Christian Century, 71,* 515–517.

Funk, S. C., & Houston, B. K. (1987). A critical analysis of the Hardiness Scale's validity and utility. *Journal of Personality and Social Psychology, 53,* 572–578. doi:10.1037/0022-3514.53.3.572

Guignon, C. (2004). *On being authentic.* London, England; New York, NY: Routledge.

Heidegger, M. (1996). *Being and time: A translation of Sein und Zeit* (J. Stambaugh, Trans.). Albany: State University of New York Press. (Original work published 1927)

Hull, J. G., Van Treuren, R. R., & Virnelli, S. (1987). Hardiness and health: A critique and alternative approach. *Journal of Personality and Social Psychology, 53,* 518–530. doi:10.1037/0022-3514.53.3.518

Kobasa, S. C. (1977). Stress, personality and health: A study of an overlooked possibility (Unpublished doctoral dissertation). University of Chicago, Illinois.

Kobasa, S. C., Maddi, S. R., & Kahn, S. (1982). Hardiness and health: A prospective study. *Journal of Personality and Social Psychology, 42,* 168–177. doi:10.1037/0022-3514.42.1.168

Koestenbaum, P. (1978). *The new image of the person.* Westport, CT: Greenwood Press.

Lopez, S. J., O'Byrne, K. K., & Petersen, S. (2003). Profiling courage. In S. J. Lopez & C. R. Snyder (Eds.), *Positive psychological assessment: A handbook of models and measures* (pp. 185–197). Washington, DC: American Psychological Association. doi:10.1037/10612-012

Maslow, A. H. (1968). *Toward a psychology of being.* New York, NY: Van Nostrand.

Maslow, A. H. (1987). *Motivation and personality* (3rd ed.). New York, NY: Harper & Row.

May, R. (1953). *Man's search for himself.* New York, NY: Norton.

May, R. (1960). Existential bases of psychotherapy. *American Journal of Orthopsychiatry, 30,* 685–695.

May, R. (1975). *The courage to create.* New York, NY: Norton.

Orr, E., M. (1990). Does hardiness moderate stress, and how? A review. In M. Rosenbaum (Ed.), *Learned resourcefulness: On coping skills, self-control, and adaptive behavior* (pp. 64–94). New York, NY: Springer.

Pury, C. L. S., Kowalski, R. M., & Spearman, J. (2007). Distinctions between general and personal courage. *The Journal of Positive Psychology, 2,* 99–114. doi:10.1080/17439760701237962

Schmidt, N. B., & Koselka, M. (2000). Gender differences in patients with panic disorder: Evaluating cognitive mediation of phobic avoidance. *Cognitive Therapy and Research, 24,* 533–550. doi:10.1023/A:1005562011960

Shelp, E. E. (1984). Courage: A neglected virtue in the patient-physician relationship. *Social Science 18,* 351–360. doi:10.1016/0277-9536(84)90125-4

Thompson, M. G. (2006). Vicissitudes of authenticity in the psychoanalytic situation. *Contemporary Psychoanalysis, 42,* 139–176.

Tillich, P. T. (1952). *The courage to be.* New Haven, CT: Yale University Press.

Webster's new collegiate dictionary. (1999). Springfield, MA: Merriam.

Woodard, C. R. (2004). Hardiness and the concept of courage. *Consulting Psychology Journal: Practice and Research, 56,* 173–185. doi:10.1037/1065-9293.56.3.173

Woodard, C. R., & Pury, C. L. S. (2007). The construct of courage: Categorization and measurement. *Consulting Psychology Journal: Practice and Research, 59,* 135–147. doi:10.1037/1065-9293.59.2.135

7

The Courageous Mind-Set: A Dynamic Personality System Approach to Courage

Sean T. Hannah, Patrick J. Sweeney, and Paul B. Lester

Some frame courage as an intrapersonal, subjective experience of an actor who overcomes fear to behave in a way that he or she perceives as courageous (e.g., Beck, Emery, & Greenberg, 1985; Finfgeld, 1999; Goud, 2005). Peterson and Seligman (2004) categorized such intrapersonal courage as a fairly trait-like virtue, entailing the four character strengths of bravery, persistence, integrity, and vitality, which promote "the exercise of will to accomplish goals in the face of opposition, either external or internal" (p. 199). Others frame courage as an attributional phenomenon: Observers externally attribute courage to an actor based on observers' assessments of risk, estimated presence of fear in the actor, and social norms of what constitutes a courageous act (e.g., Miller, 2000). Through this lens, courage is then attributed to an actor whose behavior meets an observer's implicit theory of courage (Rate, Clarke, Lindsay, & Sternberg, 2007) and is perceived as nonconformist, contradicting what a majority of people would do in the same situation (Deutsch, 1961; Schwan, 2004). In an empirical test, Pury, Kowalski, and Spearman (2007) indeed found discriminate validity between *general courage,* or actions that are considered courageous by a general audience, and *personal courage,* or actions that are subjectively perceived as courageous for a particular actor. Across major conceptualizations of courage, however, risk, fear, purpose, and action are key commonalities.

The study of externally attributed or general courage (Pury et al., 2007) has value in assessing social phenomena such as normative influence, social learning, and social identity processes. We certainly recognize that groups establish norms for what behaviors are considered courageous (Schwan, 2004), but we also recognize that individual members may display those behaviors without subjectively enacting or experiencing courageousness. For example, one might accomplish an act seen by others as courageous for reasons of compliance, to gain a reward, or out of sheer foolhardiness. Indeed, Rachman (1990) suggested that courageous actions can be thought of as distinct from courageous actors. Here we focus on personal courage and seek to explicate the processes and subjective experience whereby a courageous actor perceives risk, experiences fear, and overcomes fear to act toward a valued purpose or noble goal (Goud, 2005).

The need to directly address the cause of one's fear and achieve a designated purpose differentiates courage from general coping models. Coping allows a host of adaptive and maladaptive responses, such as denial or defense mechanisms that may direct one's energy away from addressing the source of threat (Moos & Schaefer, 1993). We hold that courage is by definition an adaptive process whereby one summons the internal and external resources to confront a threat, overcome fear, and act to reduce that threat. From this perspective, personal courage is foremost the manifestation of adaptive, dynamic cognitive and affective processes.

Beyond general and personal approaches to courage, taxonomies for various forms of courage have been theorized (e.g., Lopez, O'Byrne, & Petersen, 2003; Putman, 1997, 2004). These forms include social courage (Asch, 1955), moral courage (Deutsch, 1961; Kidder, 2003), physical courage or bravery (Peterson & Seligman, 2004; Rachman, 1990; Suedfeld, 1997), and psychological courage, or acting despite risks to psychological well-being (Putman, 1997). Courage is thus both dynamic and dimensional, yet we propose that the construct has been largely theorized and studied as an intact psychological resource imbued throughout an individual that he or she can call forth to meet a wide breadth of challenges as needed. We hold that a more sophisticated understanding of the dynamic processes influencing personal courage is needed to inform the development and operation of various forms of courage across contexts.

Our purpose in this chapter is threefold. First, we propose a general model explicating how various internal resources (i.e., aspects of positive psychological states and traits and core values and beliefs) and external resources (i.e., affirming normative and informational social forces) impact personal courage and moderate the relationships among risk, fear, and behavior. Second, we seek to explicate the dynamic personality structure within which courage operates with the intent of explicating what we term the *courageous mind-set* (Hannah, Sweeney, & Lester, 2007). Third, using this dynamic approach we discuss how the various dimensions of courage may differentially operate across contexts. Because of the severe lack of empirical research on courage in the literature, we make clear up front that much of this model is speculative. We seek here solely to provide a framework to guide future testing.

Introduction to the Framework

First, in our proposed analysis of personal courage we take a dynamic processing system versus trait approach to personality. We draw throughout the chapter from the work on cognitive affective processing systems (CAPS; Hannah & Luthans, 2008; Hannah, Woolfolk, & Lord, 2009; Mischel & Shoda, 1998; Shoda, LeeTiernan, & Mischel, 2002) as our primary framework for explaining the complex processes evoking courage. We use CAPS to describe how and why individuals activate and exhibit their courage in some situations and not in others. Mischel, Shoda, and colleagues (for a review, see Mischel & Shoda, 1998) showed that encoding categories, expectancies, goals, values, affects, and self-regulatory plans (what they term "CAPS units") are activated by the unique cues present in a given context, thereby producing a context-specific personality "signature." Therefore, repeated exposure to certain contexts habituates certain CAPS units and associated behavioral responses in those contexts, which can be observed as one's personality. Using this dynamic CAPS framework, we propose that courage may be variable between situations, yet may remain fairly stable within situations.

As shown on the right side of Figure 7.1, we propose that the subjective experience of courage is predicated on the perception of risk, eliciting a psychological and/or physiological fear response—and despite this response, an actor performs courageous behaviors in pursuit of a designated purpose. We hold that this risk → fear → courageous behavior linkage is moderated by the activation of a dynamic personality system; that is, discrete sets of CAPS units (Mischel & Shoda, 1998; Shoda et al., 2002) comprising encoding categories, expectancies,

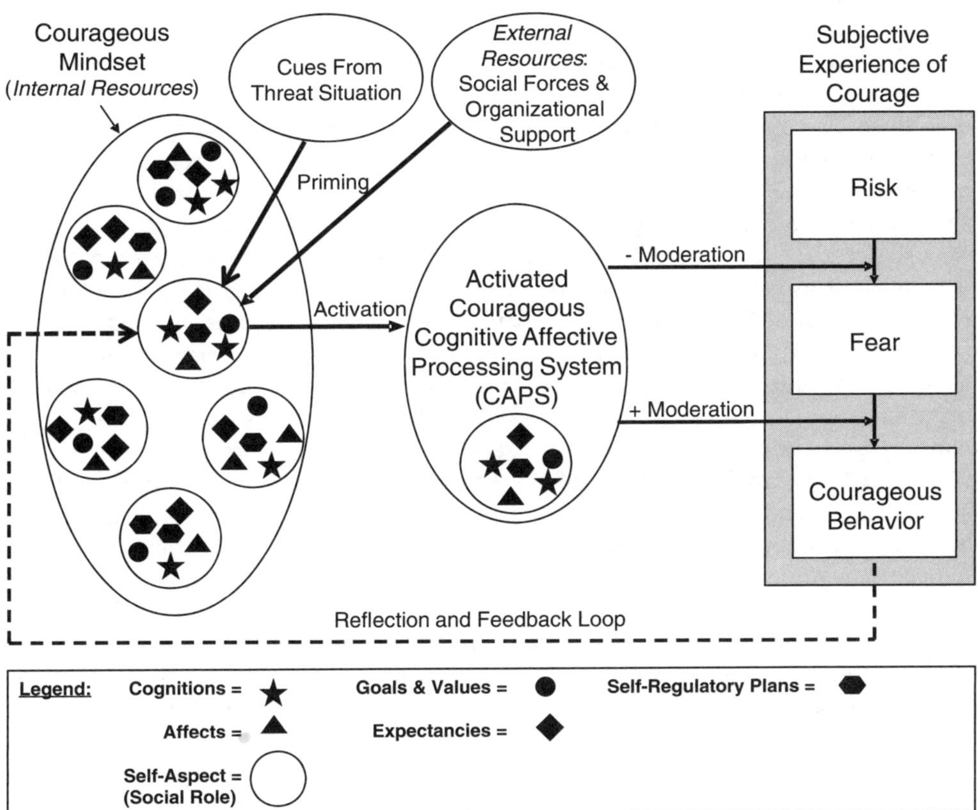

Figure 7.1. Influence of the courageous mind-set on courageous thoughts and behaviors.

goals, values, affects, and self-regulatory plans are activated when a person faces a threat. Further, on the basis of the work on self-complexity (Hannah et al., 2009), we propose, as shown in Figure 7.1, that CAPS units are structured with identity and associated with a specific self-aspect (e.g., "father as little league coach" or "leader as mentor"). When an aspect of identity is primed, it can promote more or less courageous cognitions and behaviors based on the nature of the specific CAPS units activated. For example, the activation of an identity with prosocial goals and efficacious expectancies may promote courage whereas the activation of pro-self goals and inefficacious expectancies may reduce one's courage. Further, activated encoding categories would frame the nature of the threat itself and how one conceptualizes risk.

In the center of Figure 7.1 we show an activated courageous (as opposed to noncourageous) CAPS, which would represent an activated suite of CAPS that serves to negatively (versus positively) moderate the risk → fear linkage, reducing the level of fear experienced when faced with a given risk. Such a courageous suite of CAPS would also positively (versus negatively) moderate the fear → behavior linkage by promoting courageous behaviors despite that remaining fear. This approach makes it possible that the suite of CAPS units primed in a given context may include a subset of CAPS units that moderate the risk → fear linkage, whereas another subset may moderate the fear → behavior linkage. This possibility suggests that the moderation effects can be aligned to reduce fear and increase likeliness of behavior, or they could be incongruent, in which case the more dominant or stronger influence may most predict whether courage is displayed. For example, activated CAPS units may create a perceived lack of efficacy for climbing, increasing a mother's fear of heights when her child is stuck in a tree, but other activated units may evoke goals to save her child at all costs, thus spurring action despite fear.

We propose that the activation of a courageous set of CAPS is predicated on a combination of both internal and external resources (Figure 7.1). Internal resources include factors such as positive traits, positive states, and values and beliefs that can be activated from the self-concept. External resources include social forces, such as normative and informational influence, but also levels of organizational support that prime aspects of the courageous mind-set in a given context and thereby promote courageous action. For example, group norms to "never leave a fallen comrade" might prime prosocial aspects of a soldier's self-concept, leading to courageous actions to rescue a unit member. Further, we believe organizations may promote the activation of self-regulatory plans and expectancies to engage in courageous action by increasing perceptions of a supportive context (e.g., whistle-blowers are supported versus punished). Finally, as shown by the feedback loop, we propose that through reflection, self-attributions of courageousness will further reinforce one's values and build positive states and other aspects of the self-concept, thereby bolstering the propensity to activate a courageous mind-set in the future.

The validity of this model is certainly subject to empirical testing. Our intent was to build a process model that generalizes across social, moral, physical, psychological, and other domains of courage by modeling how the unique makeup of each actor's personality system dynamically activates (or inhibits) courage within and across contexts through the activation of CAPS.

The Courageous Mind-Set as a Dynamic Personality System

Constructs such as courage are commonly assessed through self-report survey measures (e.g., Pury et al., 2007; Rate et al., 2007; Woodard, 2004). Such surveys call on respondents' retrospective memories or appraisals of prior behaviors that form their self-concept (Kihlstrom, Beer, & Klein, 2003; Markus & Wurf, 1987). If people believed that they responded to prior threats and overcame associated fears by displaying courage frequently, then when prompted, they would likely respond to survey items as their being "courageous," and observer-raters would agree. Viewing constructs such as courage as if one holds some absolute form or level, however, fails to address the underlying processes that make courage an extremely dynamic construct. Epstein (1994) stated that such

> description of surface attributes, although useful for some purposes, provides a poor basis for understanding process. If one wishes to understand what makes people tick, and what to do about their off-beat ticking, a more dynamic interactive approach capable of elucidating cause-and-effect relations is necessary. (p. 121)

In seeking to explicate the underlying complexity of the courage construct we hope to assist researchers in developing richer models of courage as well as guide experimental interventions and the development of advanced measurement techniques.

Hannah, Sweeney, and Lester (2007) first offered the term *courageous mind-set* and presented a multifactor model of personal courage. This model is taxonomic in nature, delineating how the four categories of positive traits, positive states, values and beliefs, and social forces operate to promote the courageous mind-set. Their model is also linear in nature, intending to provide basic testable hypotheses, and does not account for the rich dynamics of a personality processing system within which these constructs operate. Here we attempt to advance their model by applying its core concepts to a more dynamic CAPS framework.

We start with the position that the self-concept is central to influencing cognition, affect, and behaviors (Klein & Kihlstrom, 1986; Lord & Brown, 2004). Further, we propose that a deeper understanding of self-concept-based constructs such as courage can be gained by viewing the construct not as an intact property imbued throughout the self-concept but as a contextually tailored and "state-like"—as opposed to more trait-like—personality construct. We specifically propose that courage emerges in situ through a complex dynamic processing system (of which the self-concept is part) that includes both cognition and affect (Mischel & Shoda, 1998; Shoda et al., 2002). As the self-concept is multidimensional (Hannah et al., 2009; Markus & Wurf, 1987), we can begin to explore the state-like nature of courage and thus the variance of courageous behavior across situations.

Individual × Situation Interactionism

In their CAPS model, Mischel and Shoda (1998) proposed that "personality is construed as a system of mediating units (e.g., encodings, expectancies, goals) and psychological processes or cognitive-affective dynamics, conscious or unconscious, that interact with the situation" (p. 230). Using this dynamic approach, researchers have tied personality to goal structures (Weary & Edwards, 1994), goal pursuit (Cantor & Fleeson, 1994), and approach orientation (Higgins, 1996). Research has also linked dynamic cognition and motivation processes with action (Gollwitzer & Bargh, 1996). Through such an interactive, dynamic processing approach, Mischel and Shoda (1998) stated that the focus is

> not just on how much of a particular unit (e.g., self-efficacy expectations, or anxiety states or achievement goals) a person has, but also on how the units relate to each other within that person, forming a unique network of interconnections that function as a unified whole. (p. 237)

In a CAPS approach, units of encoding categories, expectancies, goals, values, affects, and self-regulatory plans are viewed as developed within the individual over a lifetime and are structured and interlinked in unique response to one's experiences and environment (Mischel & Shoda, 1998). Specific sets of these CAPS units, when activated, then mediate the unique cognitions and emotions experienced by a person in specific situations, thereby influencing his or her thoughts and behaviors. The set of CAPS units a person holds at any single point in his or her development, as well as the linkages between those units, form that person's current personality structure. This structure is unique to each person's experiences and how those experiences are encoded. Shoda et al. (2002) stated that it is "the number of cognitive affective units, connected to one another to form networks of associations, that distinctively characterize each individual" (p. 317). In an extension of this work, we propose that through his or her life experiences each individual forms a personality structure that is more or less likely to activate a set of CAPS that promotes courageous thought and action in the face of specific threat and fear.

In addition, a deeper understanding of a courageous personality structure may inform how different forms of courage (e.g., physical, moral, social, or psychological; Lopez et al., 2003; Putman, 1997, 2004) are activated in different situations. This is because each situation has a distinct set of stimuli that primes a distinct part of the personality structure. In sum, the courageous mind-set is a personality structure that contains a rich set of internal resources to promote courageous cognitions and behaviors across a breadth of situations.

Stable Structure yet Variable Behaviors

If the personality structure comprising the courageous mind-set described earlier is set at any one point in a person's development, then the characteristics of the contexts that person is exposed to serve as the sources of variability in courageous action. As denoted in Figure 7.1, unique cues present in each context prime a distinct CAPS. Therefore, variation in courage across situations can result from a stable personality structure. This seeming paradox explains how courage may be consistent within situations (because of repetitive exposure to similar stimuli) but variable across situations (e.g., Mendoza-Denton, Ayduk, Mischel, Shoda, & Testa, 2001; Shoda et al., 2002). For example, a firefighter may face danger regularly in fighting fires yet may not activate the courage to parachute from an airplane, even if both contexts hold equal levels of physical risk. CAPS, therefore, is clearly a Person × Situation interactionist model that is based on social information processing. More specifically, Mischel and Shoda (1998) described CAPS units as having if–then profiles or contingencies. When certain context conditions (stimulus) are experienced (*if*), a specific activation of CAPS units occurs (*then*).

What are seen as individual differences or dispositions in a dynamic processing approach (i.e., courageousness) can be explained as an outgrowth of chronic activation of certain sets of CAPS units (that promote courage) more so than others based on habitual exposure to a similar set of priming stimuli. Mischel and Shoda (1998) asserted that chronically activated units will be launched, along with other context-specific CAPS units, to form a unique situational pattern, or "signature" personality. Mischel and Shoda therefore suggested that behaviors are better predicted by viewing personality as contextualized. Indeed, some have argued that no trait survey measure is truly decontextualized (e.g., Tellegen, 1991).

Courage and Self-Construct Structure

Shoda and colleagues (2002) proposed that each aspect of the self-concept (e.g., self-as-father, or self-as-soldier) is interlinked with specific CAPS (encoding categories, affects, goals, expectations, and self-regulatory plans) that are associated with that part of one's self-concept. Therefore, we propose, for example, that one's self-conceptualization as a leader will be linked to specific CAPS units and in turn levels of courage while one's concept as a father is likely linked to a different mix of CAPS units and thus dimensions and levels of courage. As we have noted, however, such linkages are also situation-specific. Therefore, we suggest that one's self-concept as a soldier in garrison will likely have a different associated personality structure (linkages between CAPS units and associated courage) than will one's self-concept as a soldier in a combat operation. This proposition is based on the fact that the self is a multifaceted structure comprising multiple identities that are formed as individuals encode and structure their self-concept by differentiating various social roles and the attributes they possess for each of those roles (Kihlstrom et al., 2003; Markus & Wurf, 1987). The self-concept can therefore be structured as more or less complex based on this assemblage (Hannah et al., 2009). A simplified portrayal of this multifaceted self is depicted by the various self-aspects shown in Figure 7.1.

Furthermore, we know that the self-concept is normally differentiated between positive and negative semantic content that is linked to corresponding positive and negative affect (Linville, 1987; Osgood, Suci, & Tannebaum, 1957; Woolfolk, Novalany, Gara, Allen, & Polino, 1995). Thus, each separate aspect of a person's personality structure might be characterized as more or less courageous on the basis of his or her makeup and fit with the situation. When a person believes that he or she has the internal resources to act courageously in a given role and situation, we would expect CAPS units of positive encodings and self-regulatory plans to also activate linked positive affective units that promote courage. In summary, we propose that activation of courage in a given role will be based on one's structuring of internal resources associated with that role, which, when primed by the context, will activate courageous behavior. Therefore, we have argued that developing a complex self-construct with numerous self-aspects that each hold a rich suite of internal resources will increase the propensity to activate positive states such as courage across a broader range of contexts (Hannah & Luthans, 2008; Hannah et al., 2009). In summary, it is this rich personality structure interlinked to a complex self-construct that we term the *courageous mind-set.* As all people likely possess some form of courage in some situations, we conceptualize the courageous mind-set as varying in degree; that is, the personality structure of some actors promotes higher levels and dimensionality of courage across a greater breadth of contexts.

Internal Resources: A Courageous Mind-Set

Drawing from the preceding conceptualization of a dynamic versus dispositional personality processing system, we can begin to explain the development and activation of specific internal resources within individuals that promote courage. In their model of vulnerability, Beck, Emery, and Greenberg (1985) suggested that fear is experienced when the evaluation of a threat exceeds the evaluation of one's personal resources to face that threat. Here we propose that a courageous mind-set provides a personality structure that, when activated, (a) increases personal resources to reduce fear and (b) overcomes residual fear to promote courageous action. This proposal is supported in part by research on the broaden and build theory (Fredrickson, 2001) that demonstrated that, left unchecked, negative emotions such as fear narrow the scope of cognition and attention, limiting potential thought–action repertoires (i.e., a fight or flight response)—whereas positive emotions broaden such potential repertoires, facilitating action under stress.

The personality structure that we propose serves as the basis for these positive emotions is durable and accumulates over time, building personal resources to overcome narrowing effects in future stressful situations (Fredrickson, Tugade, Waugh, & Larkin, 2003). These positive emotional "stores" then operate simultaneously with and offset negative emotions during stress, creating an *undoing effect,* and "loosen the hold that a negative emotion has gained on that person's mind and body by dismantling or undoing preparation for specific action" (Fredrickson, 2001, p. 222). Fredrickson and colleagues demonstrated that positive states and traits—such as are proposed in the courageous mind-set—build personal resources to counteract narrowing of thought–action repertoires otherwise induced under stress. For example, actors with high levels of self-efficacy for a wide breadth of social skills may be able to overcome their fear and act with moral courage to confront a peer's transgression because they can envision various potential ways that they can approach and communicate with the peer in a successful manner.

Similarly, we propose that personal resources promoting personal courage include various positive states, traits, and value and belief structures. These resources may then be activated through CAPS to promote courageous action. Figure 7.2 focuses on the activated portion of the courageous mind-set (shown previously in the center of Figure 7.1) and, using the categories of Hannah, Sweeney, and Lester (2007), shows a simplified taxonomic portrayal of types of representative factors that could potentially be activated through CAPS

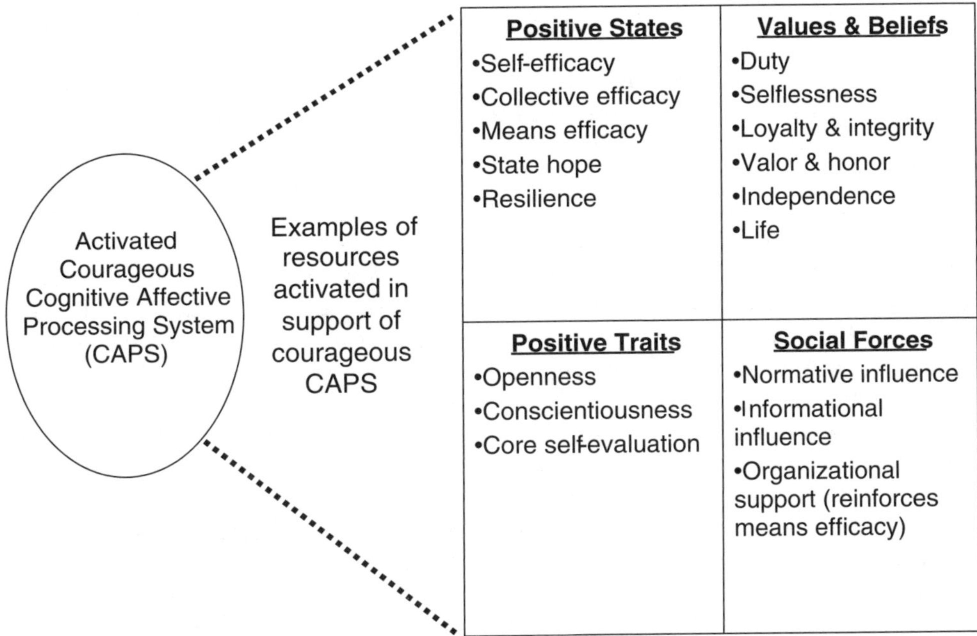

Figure 7.2. Courageous resources activated through a cognitive affective processing.

into a context-specific working self (Markus & Wurf, 1987) to promote courage. We stress, however, that this list is merely representative of the collection of factors we believe promote the activation of a courageous CAPS; others most certainly exist and will emerge as theory and empirical evidence advance. We turn now to discuss how these factors may promote the activation of courage.

Positive States

We begin our discussion by outlining the positive states associated with courage listed in the upper left quadrant of Figure 7.2. We propose that the more malleable states of efficacy (self-, collective, and means efficacy), hope, and resilience—if contained in a given activated self-aspect (i.e., social role)—play an important role in the chronic activation of CAPS units associated with courage when one is facing risks associated with that role.

SELF-EFFICACY. Cognitive structures such as self-efficacy beliefs are called on to help interpret information during stressful situations (Bandura, 1997). Self-efficacy is defined as "beliefs in one's abilities to mobilize the motivation, cognitive resources, and courses of action needed to meet situational demands" (Wood & Bandura, 1989, p. 48). Meta-analyses have shown positive links between self-efficacy, attitudes, and performance (Holden, 1992; Multon, Brown, & Lent, 1991; Stajkovic & Luthans, 1998). In addition, both Finfgeld

(1999) and Goud (2005) made theoretical links between self-efficacy and courage. Goud (2005) stated that "belief and trust in one's capabilities (i.e., confidence) is a primary force in countering fears, risks, and the safety impulse" (p. 110). These beliefs "affect whether individuals think in self-enhancing or self-debilitating ways, how well they motivate themselves and persevere in the face of difficulties . . . their vulnerability to stress and depression, and the choices they make at important decision points" (Bandura & Locke, 2003, p. 87). Actors with higher self-efficacy experience less stress and perceptions of threat when faced with fearful situations and tend to persevere better despite the threat (Bandura, 1997). Efficacy beliefs further encourage sustained goal-directed behavior (Locke & Latham, 1990), and courageous actions are typified as having an inherent goal component (i.e., the sense of a higher purpose; Goud, 2005; Tillich, 2000).

Turning toward the dynamic processing approach outlined earlier, we can understand how self-efficacy emerges within a courageous actor when certain CAPS units are activated. A given context that may require an actor to behave courageously may prime a set of encoding units that are connected to efficacy. We propose that these CAPS units help an actor define, characterize, and categorize the context as calling for courageous action. Take, for example, a military officer who debates giving an unpopular order to his or her soldiers, but clearly understands that giving the order is the "right" thing to do. This officer may activate encodings and goal structures that relate this action to several possible results, and identify second- and third-order benefits from giving the order (i.e., a better unit, better military, and mission accomplishment), resulting in a promotion versus prevention orientation toward the order (Higgins, 1996). Self-efficacy has clearly been linked to this type of human forethought and the envisioning of successful outcomes (Bandura, 1997; Carroll & Bandura, 1987). In addition, the context may prime memories within the officer of when he or she (or possibly a role model) successfully acted courageously in a similar situation. This priming in turn could result in the activation of other CAPS units associated with expectancy or self-regulation that provide confidence to the officer in the current situation.

Although the discussion of CAPS units and self-efficacy has largely focused on cognitive factors, there are clearly affective aspects as well. As previously discussed, we recognize that an individual's self-concept contains positive and negative semantic content that is connected to corresponding positive or negative affect (Hannah et al., 2009; Woolfolk et al., 1995). Although the activation of self-regulatory plans or goals promoting efficacy is largely thought of as a cognitive function, it also elicits positive affective responses (Bandura, 1997). In the context of courage, through activating efficacy, we propose actors will experience positive emotions toward taking courageous action, broadening their potential thought and behavioral repertoire. Positive affect is associated with approach strategies (Higgins, 1996) and the further development of self-efficacy (Bandura, 1997), which we hold will increase the likelihood of courage then and in the future.

Collective Efficacy. According to Bandura (1997), collective efficacy is "concerned with the performance capability of a social system as a whole" (p. 469) and is defined as "a group's shared belief in its conjoint capabilities to organize and execute the courses of action required to produce given levels of attainment" (p. 477). Among other outcomes, collective efficacy has been linked to community change (Reitzes & Reitzes, 1984), political activism (Wolfsfeld, 1986), group functioning and performance (Bandura, 1993; Gully, Incalcaterra, Joshi, & Beaubien, 2002), and group cohesion (Lee, Tinsley, & Bobko, 2002). Though the focus of this chapter is on the individual, actors' perceptions of their group's efficacy are a key component of how they formulate their own overall levels of efficacy to take on challenges (Hannah, Avolio, Luthans, & Harms, 2008). This is because though collective efficacy is believed to be an emergent construct developed via group interaction, as Bandura (2000) stated, collective efficacy beliefs are generally isomorphic and function within an actor in a process similar to that of self-efficacy and are linked to the self-concept. Indeed, Moskowitz (2005) stated that within the self-concept "exist a complex array of social identities that link an individual to various social groups" (p. 229).

Because self-identity is so closely associated with group membership, we propose that collective efficacy not only has social contagion properties but in some cases may also augment the actor's self-efficacy should his or her self-efficacy be deficient. For example, a new soldier who has limited self-efficacy beliefs could have his or her efficacy augmented by that of the collective should he or she join an elite military unit with a long history of success, high standards, and confident leadership. Therefore, we propose that actors in competent, efficacious groups will have heightened collective efficacy and that this heightened collective efficacy in turn influences activation of expectancies, self-regulatory plans, and other CAPS units promoting courage.

MEANS EFFICACY. Given that human behavior, including courageous behavior, is embedded in a social system, one must also take into consideration the actor's confidence in the resources he or she has available to assist in attaining the goal sought through his or her courageous behavior. Therefore, we propose that means efficacy, defined as an individual's belief in the quality and utility of the tools available for task performance (Eden, 2001), will also influence courageous CAPS activation. Tools are often important in successful task completion, which Eden (2001) defined as implements (e.g., equipment, computers), other persons (e.g., coworkers, followers, supervisors), or bureaucratic means (e.g., procedures, processes). For example, confidence in the quality of construction and maintenance of one's parachute should be associated with one's level of efficacy for an airborne jump. We believe that means efficacy could be quite volatile in a context calling for courage. For example, a soldier may begin a combat mission with high means efficacy because he believes that he has the best equipment, teammates, and plan; as such, these beliefs may increase the likelihood of the activation of courageous CAPS. However, this means efficacy may diminish rapidly should his weapon malfunction, team members become wounded, or the plan prove infeasible because of the combat strength of the enemy.

STATE HOPE. The dynamic CAPS model also applies to hope. According to Snyder, Rand, and Sigmon (2002), hope is a "positive motivational state that is based on an interactively derived sense of successful (1) agency (goal directed energy), and (2) pathways (planning to meet goals)" (p. 258). Therefore, as with efficacy, we propose that hope provides the courageous actor with goal-directed energy as well as promotes envisioning alternative paths to success. Extending from the broaden and build model presented earlier, we posit that increased levels of hope will promote the envisioning of broadened thought repertoires (pathways) to attend to threats and promote the focused energy to implement solutions, in turn mitigating fear and spurring courageous action. Indeed, empirical research suggests that hope reduces stress and negative affect, and also increases performance across a wide span of domains (Snyder et al., 2002).

Although hope is at times viewed as having trait-like properties, Snyder and colleagues (1996) have shown that hope does in fact take on state-like characteristics with hope varying significantly between contexts. We believe that the pathways component of hope is particularly critical to courage. As pathways entail developing potential courses of action, as well as viable alternatives, hope may (a) protect the actor through determining whether an action is in fact viable or, alternatively, foolhardy (Goud, 2005); (b) help the actor clarify what the goal or end-state of the courageous action should be; and (c) aid in envisioning successful outcomes that may activate positive affective CAPS units, which, as we previously outlined, may be linked to positive emotions and block negative emotions that may hinder action (Hannah & Luthans, 2008).

RESILIENCE. Though much of the discussion thus far has focused on the more proactive constructs that promote the activation of CAPS units associated with courage, resilience is conceptualized as being reactive to expected or current setbacks in a given context. Luthans, Youssef, and Avolio (2007) defined resilience as "the capacity to rebound or bounce back from adversary, conflict, failure, or even positive events, progress, and increased responsibility" (p. 18). Masten and Reed (2002) pointed out that resilience is a class of phenomena characterized by patterns of positive adaptation in the context of significant adversity or risk. Central to the activation of courage, resilience has been linked to overcoming stress under crisis (Fredrickson et al., 2003). Resilience is similar to *coping efficacy,* which Bandura (1989) conceptualized as one's belief that that one has the ability to overcome negative cognitions and ruminative thought to succeed in a given challenge, such as one requiring courageousness.

Because our aim here is to outline those factors that lead actors toward the activation of CAPS associated with courage, resilience may be most critical when an actor has experienced similar situations before. In short, how well actors bounced back from setbacks associated with previous courageous episodes may determine if they are willing or able to do so again. For example, some soldiers returning from war suffer from negative psychological conditions, such as post-traumatic stress disorder, whereas others do not, and findings show that soldiers who are repeatedly exposed to combat and have multiple combat tours also have a significantly higher risk of mental health problems (Mental Health Advisory Team [MHAT] IV, 2006; MHAT V, 2008), which suggests that their resilience has worn thin. We discuss the impact of reflection on courageous behavior later in this chapter, but we note here that actors likely reflect on past success or setbacks when experiencing risk and determine if they have the resiliency to bounce back from a subsequent potential setback.

Positive Traits

We now turn to the lower left box of Figure 7.2 and discuss the impact of positive traits in activating CAPS units associated with courage. We reinforce, consistent with Mischel and colleagues (Mischel & Shoda, 1998; Shoda et al., 2002), that "traits" represent chronic activations of a certain set of CAPS across situations versus a static constitution. With regard to Figure 7.1, this would occur when an individual has similar CAPS units (e.g., a core value or belief) contained across many self-aspects (social roles). Therefore, those same units would be more likely to activate across contexts and appear to be a disposition. We suggest that openness to experience, conscientiousness, and core self-evaluation traits are representative traits that would assist in the chronic activation of CAPS units associated with courage. As previously noted, these traits are far from a comprehensive taxonomy, but rather are representative traits to explain the model that we believe will influence appropriate CAPS activation when courage is called for.

OPENNESS TO EXPERIENCE. Openness to experience encompasses an actor's ability to be imaginative, nonconforming, unconventional, and autonomous (Judge, Bono, Ilies, & Gerhardt, 2002) and is related to both divergent thinking (McCrae, 1987) and creativity (Feist, 1998). Judge and Bono (2000) stated that openness to experience correlates with intelligence and that open actors tend to have high need for change. In addition, open actors are highly perceptive of the needs of others and are prone to implement more effective coping strategies (Watson & Hubbard, 1996), although the strength of this relationship tends to be somewhat mixed across studies (Lee-Baggley, Preece, & DeLongis, 2005).

A courageous act is considered by most observers to be unconventional and is the antithesis of safe behavior (Deutsch, 1961; Schwan, 2004). Given this, we suggest that highly open actors would tend to develop creative solutions in threatening situations, be more willing to take action that results in significant change, and behave in ways that are decidedly unconventional and nonconformist. In addition, open actors may also be more willing to place themselves at risk in order to provide aid to others. As such, we envision open actors as more likely to interject themselves into high-risk situations that require courage to succeed. For example, if open to experiences, the physically courageous soldier who risks his or her life to save another's may also be more likely to show morally courageous behavior when he or she speaks out against an unethical order from a superior.

CONSCIENTIOUSNESS. Conscientiousness is often associated with achievement and dependability (Judge et al., 2002). In addition, conscientiousness significantly correlates with an actor's sense of duty (McCrae, Costa, & Busch, 1986), tenacity and persistence (Goldberg, 1990), and self-discipline (McCrae, 1992). Conscientious actors are less likely to engage in avoidant behaviors (Lee-Baggley et al., 2005) and are more likely to engage in adaptive coping strategies when threatened (Vickers, Kolar, & Hervig, 1989). With respect to the type of coping strategies chosen, empirical evidence shows that conscientious actors are more likely to select an active, problem-solving strategy (Hooker, Frazier, & Monahan, 1994), which also suggests that conscientious actors are more likely to enact a promotion and approach strategy, versus avoidance (Higgins, 1996), when facing a context requiring courage.

We propose that individuals with conscientiousness structured across various aspects of their self-concept will be more prone to chronically activate CAPS units associated with courage because an actor's sense of duty, purpose, and action and his or her persistence, tenacity, and positive approach in coping with the contextual factors calling for courage are all commonalities required for courageous behavior (Goud, 2005; Peterson & Seligman, 2004). Given this, we submit that conscientious actors may feel more duty-bound to act in the face of fear because it is the right thing to do, and fear may be overshadowed by a greater sense of duty (Hannah et al. 2007). For example, what makes a firefighter run into a burning building or a soldier smother a live hand grenade with his body? Social cohesion with other members of the group likely plays a significant role in the courageous behavior, but on the basis of the previously discussed findings, we submit that conscientiousness is also an important component of the dynamic personality structure that activates CAPS units to promote such self-sacrifice and courageous behavior.

Core Self-Evaluation Traits. We propose that the core self-evaluation (CSE) traits of self-esteem, generalized self-efficacy, emotional stability, and locus of control (Judge, Locke, & Durham, 1997), if imbued across self-aspects, may further promote the chronic activation of CAPS units associated with courage. In fact, CSE traits may perhaps be uniquely linked to courageous behavior across contexts because by their very nature CSE traits are (a) self-evaluative rather than merely descriptive and (b) fundamentally core to an actor's self-concept vice, being only surface traits associated with one's self-concept (Judge et al., 1997). As such, CSE traits are considered deep personality structures that pervade most if not all behavior, suggesting CAPS units associated with CSE are therefore possessed across a breadth of self-aspects.

Within the array of individual CSE factors, Tharenou (1979) noted that individuals with high self-esteem engage in optimistic thoughts and behaviors that reinforce their self-concepts (Judge & Bono, 2001). This finding suggests that actors with high self-esteem would be more likely to behave courageously in the face of fear through motivation to maintain a positive and consistent self-concept (Lord & Brown, 2004; Swann, 1983). Judge and Bono (2001) additionally proposed that actors with higher generalized self-efficacy better cope with stress, have higher performance levels, and generally realize greater success rates. This suggests that even though actors may feel fear, they will be more likely to activate CAPS units associated with courage because they generally have a greater confidence in their ability to overcome the general threats they face. Further, empirical evidence showed that lower levels of arousal in stressful conditions have been related to courageous behavior (O'Connor, Hallam, & Rachman, 1985). This implies that actors who are emotionally stable (i.e., lack neuroticism) may tend to be more secure, steady, and confident (Judge & Bono, 2001) and less likely to ruminate over impending threats.

Finally, empirical evidence has linked locus of control, defined as the belief in one's ability to control one's environment (Bono & Judge, 2003), to courage (Shepela et al., 1999). This suggests that actors with an internal locus of control may behave courageously in part because they believe that they can master the contextual factors that may lead others not to take action. For example, military commanders with an internal locus of control may be more likely to make a courageous stand in the face of strong opposition, believing that they can make the environment (e.g., the terrain, an opposition's weakness, supplies) work in their favor.

Inner Convictions: Values, Beliefs, Goals, and Expectations

As shown in the upper right quadrant of Figure 7.2, beyond states and traits, we believe that a person's core values and beliefs are also primary internal resources that may promote courage. As the context primes the activation of various CAPS consisting of goal structures, values, and encoding categories (e.g., beliefs; Mischel & Shoda, 1998), we propose such values and beliefs will exert significant psychological pressure on an individual to behave consistently with those values. This is because salient aspects of the self create motivation to maintain positive and self-verifying behaviors (Carver & Scheier, 1998; Cropanzano, James, & Citera, 1993; Lord & Brown, 2004; Swann, 1983). Some values, beliefs, and character strengths that are shared across most societies, religions, and philosophies that we suggest will promote courageous behavior if developed in individuals include integrity and honor, valor, perseverance, vitality, love, kindness, loyalty, leadership, self-regulation, and spirituality (Peterson & Seligman, 2004).

When they are confronted with fear and while assessing potential behavior responses and probable outcomes, we propose those actors holding strong prosocial values, beliefs, and goals—as activated in CAPS—will be more likely to act with self-concordance because their core virtues provide moral strength and resiliency in meeting threats and challenges (Sandage & Hill, 2001; Shepela et al., 1999). Depending on the level of internalization, these core values and beliefs may be embedded across self-aspects as discussed earlier, with these highly salient aspects of the self increasing the likelihood that they would be activated and promote courage within and across situations where these values are at stake (Verplanken & Holland, 2002).

Furthermore, self-aspects (and associated CAPS) have strong expectations and associated self-regulatory plans that promote certain actions (Lord & Brown, 2004; Mischel & Shoda, 1998). Therefore, role expectations may influence courageous behavior. For instance, role expectations of military officers leading in combat may propel those leaders to act in a courageous manner to inspire their soldiers. This suggests social learning and social identification processes may influence courage based on the underlying personality structure developed associated with social roles (Bandura, 1977; Tajfel, 1981) as shown in Figure 7.1, such as Rachman (1990) found in his investigations of bomb-disposal operators.

External Resources: Social Influences

Next we discuss some of the representative social forces listed in the lower right quadrant of Figure 7.2 that we propose serve to promote activation of a courageous CAPS.

External Resources and Social Forces

Social expectations exert tremendous psychological pressure, greatly influencing actors' behavior choices, or even causing them to act counter to their core values and beliefs (Asch, 1955). Actors tend to conform their behavior to the expectations of others either to be liked (normative influence) or be right (informational influence; Cialdini & Trost, 1989). Some social expectations that we suggest will impact choices of behavior in fear situations come from mutual interdependence, trust, and social support with others (normative influence); attraction and commitment to a group (cohesion); identification with a group (social identity); and the influence of role models (Bandura, 1977; Kelley & Thibaut, 1978; Tajfel, 1981).

As depicted in Figure 7.1, social forces prime various CAPS units containing among other elements goals and values relating to esteem and the importance of relationships with others. These social forces can have a positive or negative effect on courageous behavior. For example, if a soldier perceives that his or her fellow comrades both value and expect him or her to behave bravely in combat, and the soldier wants to maintain his or her esteem and other positive self-evaluations, then we suggest that he or she would experience strong psychological pressure (normative influence) to behave courageously. For example, during the Civil War, soldiers viewed a lack of courage as a lack of manhood; thus, it is suggested that soldiers felt tremendous normative pressure to outwardly display bravery (Linderman, 1987). On the other hand, if soldiers witness unethical conduct by their comrades and want to maintain a connection to and status in the group, then we suggest they would experience tremendous normative influence to behave in an uncourageous manner by not confronting the unethical actor(s).

In addition, if unsure of how to behave in a fear situation, one will likely look to similar others to determine correct behaviors and likely outcomes (Bandura, 1977; Festinger, 1954). We suggest this may help explain why, in emergency situations, inexperienced people tend to look to others to determine the right behavior response (informational influence), because as a result of inexperience their CAPS structures may not have been developed to offer a readily accessible choice of action (e.g., behavioral script). For example, leaders displaying courage have been shown to have a contagion effect on followers such that followers believe they too have the capability to successfully meet the threat, which reduces their experienced fear (Worline, Wrzesniewski, & Rafaeli, 2002). Thus, we suggest that through normative and informational influence, groups with brave leaders and peers that also hold strong values such as honor, valor, and duty will be more likely to provide external resources that subsequently influence courageous action in their members.

Interaction of Inner Convictions and External Forces

Finally, we suggest that actors integrate assessments of both inner convictions and social expectations to determine optimal behavior responses. In particular, we propose that inner convictions (values, beliefs, goals, and internal expectations) and social forces interact to influence courageous behavior. On the basis of Fishbein and Ajzen's (1975) theory of reasoned action and Deutsch's (1961) model of courage, we propose that when contemplating courageous action, actors assess the outcomes (rewards or costs) of potential behavior responses in terms of meeting both their activated values, beliefs, and goals, and the perceived social expectations from referent others, subjectively weighting each outcome in terms of its importance and probability of occurrence (Fishbein & Ajzen, 1975; Kahneman & Tversky, 1979).

If the outcomes are congruent such that both inner convictions and social forces favor a courageous behavioral response, then we suggest actors will behave courageously, whereas if the outcomes are incongruent, actors must choose which factor will maximize proximal and distal outcomes (Kahneman & Tversky, 1979). We suggest that situations of incongruence test a person's character to defy the expectations of others to be true to his or her self (i.e., be authentic) or subordinate his or her convictions and conform to social expectations (Avolio & Gardner, 2005). Further, sacrificing authenticity to gain or maintain the favor of others may create "emotional labor" (Ashforth & Humphrey, 1993), further increasing anxiety and reducing perceptions of one's efficacy, which we believe will make it tougher to behave in a courageous manner. Yet, we suggest that in emergency situations, an abbreviated form of this decision calculus may occur implicitly or be bypassed. For example, research on helping behavior found that people may still assess potential costs and benefits before deciding to help others in crisis (Latané & Darley, 1970), whereas some emergency situations require individuals to act instantaneously, likely relying on habituated behavioral response repertoires or self-regulatory plans in the activated CAPS (Gioia & Poole, 1984; Mischel & Shoda, 1998). In summary, we hold that the processes through which actors process and resolve incongruence between personal and social resources will ultimately influence the extent of courage displayed.

Impact of Reflection on Building a Courageous Mind-Set

We turn now from the processes activating courage to the postbehavior reflection process denoted by the feedback loop shown in Figure 7.1, which, we hold, serves to further develop those portions of the self-construct (i.e., CAPS personality structure) associated with courage (i.e., courageous mind-set). Further, we believe that explicating this reflective and attribution process may inform how both personal and general courage are formed during social interaction.

We hold that upon performing a behavior in the presence of fear, actors will reflect on both internal and external sources of information to infer the degree of courageousness of the specific behavior (Bem, 1967, 1972; Festinger, 1954; Kelley, 1967). Internal inspection would involve a review of the goals and values and other CAPS units that were activated as well as a review of past behavior to determine if the behavior can be attributed to the self or external forces and if it is stable or unstable (Heider, 1958; Kelley, 1967, 1971). On the basis of attribution theory, we hold that actors use three types of information to attribute cause of a behavior performed in the face of fear: consensus, distinctiveness, and consistency (Kelley, 1967). Consensus information is acquired by reflecting on how other people might behave in a similar situation. Actors may determine the distinctiveness of their behavior by reflecting on how they acted in the past, and in various contexts and roles, regarding this type of fear. Actors gain consistency information by reflecting on how often in the past they behaved in a similar manner when confronted with similar fear. If actors determine their behavior had low consensus (others did not commonly perform such behavior when confronted with similar threat), low distinctiveness (the actor performs in a similar manner in different roles and contexts when faced with threat), and high consistency (the actor has time after time behaved in a similar manner when faced with a similar threat), then on the basis of Kelley's model (1967, 1971) we would expect that the actor would attribute the behavior to dispositional factors and build a self-concept imbued by courageousness.

We propose that actors may also consider role expectations to determine whether the behavior performed exceeded the reasonable expectations of the activated role or self-aspect. For example, although called heroic by the general public (i.e., general courage), many soldiers recognized for heroism state that their actions on the battlefield were not courageous and that they were just "doing their duty" (Hillis, 2008). This response may be due to social comparison because their reference group is a high-courage referent. Thus, we suggest that the degree to which the person has internalized expectations associated with a particular self-aspect associated with a given social role may greatly influence expectations of behavior and perceptions and attributions of courage.

Finally, we suggest actors may consider factors such as extreme fatigue, sickness, or extreme cold that might have hindered performance. When actors overcome inhibiting factors, research suggests dispositional attributions will be augmented (Kelley, 1967), which we suggest will strengthen personal (vs. external) attributions of courage. Further, actors may assess other plausible causes of courageous action in the environment (Kelley, 1967). For instance, an actor conducting his or her first parachute jump may try to abort because of fear but realize that once the line of jumpers starts moving toward the door of the aircraft he or she has no choice but to jump. This person may later discount internal attributions of courage. On the other hand, if an actor overcomes external factors, research suggests that he or she will tend to make dispositional attributions and, we suggest, experience feelings of courageousness (Kelley, 1967). For example, suppose this person completed his or her first parachute jump despite high winds or a sprained ankle.

Actors, however, will likely have guarded confidence in the results of internal attributions until receiving external sources of information to confirm or modify their attributions (Festinger, 1954; Kelley, 1967). Actors will likely use similar and important others to gain consensus information on how others would act in a similar situation (i.e., general courage; Bandura, 1977; Pury et al., 2007). These observers can confirm the actor's internal analysis and thus strengthen attributions of courage or, if others do not perceive the actor's behavior as courageous, perhaps weaken the actor's perceptions of courage (Kelley, 1967).

In summary, we suggest that the synthesis of the results from actors' attribution analyses will influence perceptions of courage and the extent of development of CAPS units employed in a specific situation. Returning to earlier points about social learning and state-like properties of courage, we propose that feedback (Figure 7.1) will influence the specific self-aspect and associated CAPS units activated in a given courage episode more directly than would the courageous mind-set as a whole. We do, recognize, however, that certain attributes have greater unity within the self because they are represented across various self-aspects (Hannah et al., 2009; Woolfolk et al., 1995). Therefore, some level of generalization to other self-aspects would likely occur. It is important to note, however, that individuals may be more or less "developmentally ready" based on individual difference factors such as their learning efficacy, learning (versus performance) goal orientation, self-concept clarity, metacognitive ability, and other factors that influence how they attend to, process, and store self-relevant feedback (Avolio & Hannah, 2008; Hannah & Avolio, 2009).

Implications of the Model

In viewing courage from the perspective of a courageous mind-set, we believe we can study and seek to develop courage in a more purposive and detailed manner. A CAPS approach allows assessment of the activation of specific encoding categories, expectancies, goals, values, affects, and self-regulatory plans that are activated to promote courage in certain contexts and not in others. Further, this model promotes synthesizing literature on personality structures with that of identity and self-complexity. This integration provides a framework to assess why an actor may consistently act courageously within certain contexts and not others based on the content and structure of the self. Further, by assessing the CAPS units associated with each of an actor's social roles (self-aspects), we can begin to assess how various forms of courage (e.g., physical, moral, or social) may be structured across roles.

By integrating internal resources (i.e., aspects of positive psychological states and traits and core values and beliefs) and external resources (i.e., affirming normative and informational social forces), this model incorporates context as a critical factor in the production of courage. Finally, recognizing intrapersonal self-reflection and the attribution processes that influence self-perceptions of courageousness, we can begin to advance models of courage development.

Final Thoughts

The construct of courage can be traced to antiquity (Aristotle, trans. 1987) and is popularly valued as one of the more noble virtues. As such, scholarly conversations often involve visceral responses against any perceived cheapening of courage by operationalizing it into a tangible theoretical model. This response has perhaps meant that courage has been seen up to now as a "fuzzy construct." Morality is similarly seen as an exemplary construct and often viewed as a one-dimensional, seamless whole (Jones & Pittman, 1982). Indeed, people are often viewed as moral or immoral versus "sort of moral" and we find similar dichotomizations applied to courage. While not seeking to "de-noble" the courage construct, we call for greater focus to investigate the psychological and social factors that promote such noble thoughts and behaviors in the face of fear. It is encouraging that some of the components of morality have been proposed (see Brown & Treviño, 2006; Hannah, Lester, & Vogelgesang, 2005; O'Fallon & Butterfield, 2005; Treviño, Weaver, & Reynolds, 2006), and we believe that the same can be done for courage.

We agree with Rachman (1990) that courageous actions can be thought of as distinct from courageous actors. To operationalize the internal cognitive–affective processing of such a courageous actor, we have conceptualized a model of a dynamic personality structure composing a courageous mind-set that, subject to testing, we suggest will enhance the field's understanding of courageous thoughts and behaviors across domains and contexts.

References

Aristotle. (1987). *The Nicomachean ethics* (J. E. C. Welldon, Trans.). Amherst, NY: Prometheus Books.

Asch, S. (1955). Opinions and social pressure. *Scientific American, 193,* 31–35.

Ashforth, B. E., & Humphrey, R. H. (1993). Emotional labor in service roles: The influence of identity. *Academy of Management Review, 18,* 88–115. doi:10.2307/258824

Avolio, B. J., & Gardner, W. L. (2005). Authentic leadership development: Getting to the root of positive forms of leadership. *The Leadership Quarterly, 16,* 315–338. doi:10.1016/j.leaqua.2005.03.001

Avolio, B. J., & Hannah, S. T. (2008). Developmental readiness: Accelerating leader development. *Consulting Psychology Journal: Theory and Practice, 60,* 331–347.

Bandura, A. (1977). *Social learning theory.* Englewood Cliffs, NJ: Prentice-Hall.

Bandura, A. (1989). Regulation of cognitive processes through perceived self-efficacy. *Developmental Psychology, 25,* 729–735. doi:10.1037/0012-1649.25.5.729

Bandura, A. (1993). Perceived self-efficacy in cognitive development and functioning. *Educational Psychologist, 28,* 117–148. doi:10.1207/s15326985ep2802_3

Bandura, A. (1997). *Self-efficacy: The exercise of control.* New York, NY: Freeman.

Bandura, A. (2000). Exercise of human agency through collective efficacy. *Current Directions in Psychological Science, 9*(3), 75–78. doi:10.1111/1467-8721.00064

Bandura, A., & Locke, E. A. (2003). Negative self-efficacy and goal effects revisited. *Journal of Applied Psychology, 88,* 87–99. doi:10.1037/0021-9010.88.1.87

Beck, A. T., Emery, G., & Greenberg, R. L. (1985). *Anxiety disorders and phobias: A cognitive perspective.* New York, NY: Basic Books.

Bem, D. J. (1967). Self-perception: An alternative interpretation of cognitive dissonance phenomena. *Psychological Review, 74,* 183–200. doi:10.1037/h0024835

Bem, D. J. (1972). Self-perception theory. In L. Berkowitz (Ed.), *Advances in experimental social psychology* (Vol. 6, pp. 1–62). New York, NY: Academic Press.

Bono, J. E., & Judge, T. A. (2003). Core self-evaluations: A review of the trait and its role in job satisfaction and job performance. *European Journal of Personality, 17,* S5–S18. doi:10.1002/per.481

Brown, M. E., & Treviño, L. K. (2006). Ethical leadership: A review and future directions. *The Leadership Quarterly, 17,* 595–616. doi:10.1016/j.leaqua.2006.10.004

Cantor, N., & Fleeson, W. (1994). Social intelligence and intelligent goal pursuit: A cognitive slice of motivation. In W. Spaulding (Ed.), *Nebraska Symposium on Motivation: Vol. 41. Integrative views of motivation, cognition and emotion* (pp. 125–179). Lincoln: University of Nebraska Press.

Carroll, W. R., & Bandura, A. (1987). Translating cognition into action: The role of visual guidance in observational learning. *Journal of Motor Behavior, 19,* 385–398.

Carver, C. S., & Scheier, M. F. (1998). *On the self-regulation of behavior.* New York, NY: Cambridge University Press.

Cialdini, R., & Trost, M. (1989). Social influence: Social norms, conformity, and compliance. In D. T. Gilbert, S. T. Fiske, & G. Lindzey (Eds.), *Handbook of social psychology* (Vol. 2, pp. 151–192). Boston, MA: McGraw-Hill.

Cropanzano, R., James, K., & Citera, M. (1993). A goal hierarchy model of personality, motivation, and leadership. *Research in Organizational Behavior, 15,* 267–322.

Deutsch, M. (1961). Courage as a concept in social psychology. *Journal of Social Psychology, 55,* 49–58.

Eden, D. (2001). Means efficacy: External sources of general and specific subjective efficacy. In M. Erez, U. Kleinbeck, & H. Thierry (Eds.), *Work motivation in the context of a globalizing economy* (pp. 65–73). Hillsdale, NJ: Erlbaum.

Epstein, S. (1994). Trait theory as personality theory: Can a part be as great as the whole? *Psychological Inquiry, 5,* 120–122. doi:10.1207/s15327965pli0502_4

Feist, G. J. (1998). A meta-analysis of personality in scientific and artistic creativity. *Personality and Social Psychology Bulletin, 2,* 290–309. doi:10.1207/s15327957pspr0204_5

Festinger, L. (1954). A theory of social comparison processes. *Human Relations, 7,* 117–140. doi:10.1177/001872675400700202

Finfgeld, D. L. (1999). Courage as a process of pushing beyond the struggle. *Qualitative Health Research, 9,* 803–814. doi:10.1177/104973299129122298

Fishbein, M., & Ajzen, I. (1975). *Belief, attitude, intention, and behavior: An introduction to theory and research.* Reading, MA: Addison-Wesley.

Fredrickson, B. L. (2001). The role of positive emotions in positive psychology: The broaden-and-build theory of positive emotions. *American Psychologist, 56,* 218–226. doi:10.1037/0003-066X.56.3.218

Fredrickson, B. L., Tugade, M. M., Waugh, C. E., & Larkin, G. R. (2003). What good are positive emotions in crisis: A prospective study on resilience and emotions following the terrorist attacks on the United States on September 11th, 2001. *Journal of Personality and Social Psychology, 84,* 365–376. doi:10.1037/0022-3514.84.2.365

Gioia, D. A., & Poole, P. P. (1984). Scripts in organizational behavior. *Academy of Management Review, 9,* 449–459. doi:10.2307/258285

Goldberg, L. R. (1990). An alternative "description of personality": The Big-Five factor structure. *Journal of Personality and Social Psychology, 59,* 1216–1229. doi:10.1037/0022-3514.59.6.1216

Gollwitzer, P. M., & Bargh, J. A. (Eds.). (1996). *The psychology of action: Linking cognition and motivation to behavior.* New York, NY: Guilford Press.

Goud, N. H. (2005). Courage: Its nature and development. *The Journal of Humanistic Counseling, Education and Development, 44,* 102–116.

Gully, S. M., Incalcaterra, K. A., Joshi, A., & Beaubien, J. M. (2002). A meta-analysis of team efficacy, potency and performance: Interdependence and level of analysis as moderators of observed relationships. *Journal of Applied Psychology, 87,* 819–832. doi:10.1037/0021-9010.87.5.819

Hannah, S. T., & Avolio, B. J. (2009). Ready or not: How do we accelerate the developmental readiness of leaders? *Journal of Organizational Behavior, 30,* 1–7.

Hannah, S. T., Avolio, B. J., Luthans, F., & Harms, P. D. (2008). Leadership efficacy: Review and future directions. *The Leadership Quarterly, 19,* 669–692. doi:10.1016/j.leaqua.2008.09.007

Hannah, S. T., Lester, P., & Vogelgesang, G. (2005). Moral leadership: Explicating the moral component of authentic leadership. In W. L. Gardner, B. J. Avolio, & F. O. Walumbwa (Eds.), *Authentic leadership and practice: Origins, effects, and development* (pp. 43–82). Oxford, England: Elsevier.

Hannah, S. T., & Luthans, F. (2008). A cognitive affective processing explanation of positive leadership: Toward theoretical understanding of the role of psychological capital. In L. L. Neider & C. A. Schriesheim (Series Eds.) & R. H. Humphrey (Ed.), *Research in Management: Vol. 7. Affect and emotion: New directions in management theory and research* (pp. 97–136). Charlotte, NC: Information Age.

Hannah, S. T., Sweeney, P. J., & Lester, P. B. (2007). Toward a courageous mind-set: The subjective act and experience of courage. *The Journal of Positive Psychology, 2,* 129–135. doi:10.1080/17439760701228854

Hannah, S. T., Woolfolk, L., & Lord, R. (2009). Leader self-structure: A framework for positive leadership. *Journal of Organizational Behavior, 30,* 269–290. doi:10.1002/job.586

Heider, F. (1958). *The psychology of interpersonal relations.* New York, NY: Wiley. doi:10.1037/10628-000

Higgins, E. T. (1996). Ideals, oughts, and regulatory focus: Affect and motivation from distinct pains and pleasures. In P. M. Gollwitzer & J. A. Bargh (Eds.), *The psychology of action: Linking cognition and motivation to behavior* (pp. 91–114). New York, NY: Guilford Press.

Hillis, K. W. (2008). Distinguished service cross: First Lieutenant Walter B. Jackson. *The Artillery Journal, 13, 1,* 30.

Holden, G. (1992). The relationship of self-efficacy appraisals and subsequent health related outcomes: A meta-analysis. *Social Work in Health Care, 16,* 53–93. doi:10.1300/J010v16n01_05

Hooker, K., Frazier, I. D., & Monahan, D. J. (1994). Personality and coping among caregivers of spouses with dementia. *The Gerontologist, 34,* 386–392.

Jones, E. E., & Pittman, T. S. (1982). Toward a theory of strategic self-presentation. In J. Suls (Ed.), *Psychological perspectives on the self* (pp. 231–262). Hillsdale, NJ: Erlbaum.

Judge, T. A., & Bono, J. E. (2000). Five-factor model of personality and transformational leadership. *Journal of Applied Psychology, 85,* 751–765. doi:10.1037/0021-9010.85.5.751

Judge, T. A., & Bono, J. E. (2001). Relationship of core self-evaluations traits—self-esteem, generalized self-efficacy, locus of control, and emotional stability—with job satisfaction and job performance: A meta-analysis. *Journal of Applied Psychology, 86,* 80–92. doi:10.1037/0021-9010.86.1.80

Judge, T. A., Bono, J. E., Ilies, R., & Gerhardt, M. W. (2002). Personality and leadership: A qualitative and quantitative review. *Journal of Applied Psychology, 87,* 765–780. doi:10.1037/0021-9010.87.4.765

Judge, T. A., Locke, E. A., & Durham, C. C. (1997). The dispositional causes of job satisfaction: A core evaluations approach. *Research in Organizational Behavior, 19,* 151–188.

Kahneman, D., & Tversky, A. (1979). Prospect theory: An analysis of decision under risk. *Econometrica, 47,* 263–291. doi:10.2307/1914185

Kelley, H. H. (1967). Attribution theory in social psychology. In D. Levine (Ed.), *Nebraska Symposium on Motivation* (Vol. 15, pp. 192–240). Lincoln: University of Nebraska Press.

Kelley, H. H. (1971). *Attributions in social interaction.* New York, NY: General Learning Press.

Kelley, H. H., & Thibaut, J. W. (1978). *Interpersonal relations: A theory of interdependence.* New York, NY: Wiley.

Kidder, R. M. (2003). *Moral courage.* New York, NY: Morrow.

Kihlstrom, J. F., Beer, J. S., & Klein, S. B. (2003). Self and identity as memory. In M. R. Leary & J. P. Tangney (Eds.), *Handbook of self and identity* (pp. 68–90). New York, NY: Guilford Press.

Klein, S. B., & Kihlstrom, J. F. (1986). Elaborations, organization, and the self-reference effect in memory. *Journal of Experimental Psychology: General, 115,* 26–38. doi:10.1037/0096-3445.115.1.26

Latané, B., & Darley, J. M. (1970). *The unresponsive bystander: Why doesn't he help?* New York, NY: Appleton-Century-Crofts.

Lee, C., Tinsley, C., & Bobko, P. (2002). An investigation of the antecedents and consequences of group-level confidence. *Journal of Applied Social Psychology, 32,* 1628–1652. doi:10.1111/j.1559-1816.2002.tb02766.x

Lee-Baggley, D., Preece, M., & DeLongis, A. (2005). Coping with interpersonal stress: Role of Big Five traits. *Journal of Personality, 73,* 1141–1180. doi:10.1111/j.1467-6494.2005.00345.x

Linderman, G. F. (1987). *Embattled courage.* New York, NY: The Free Press.

Linville, P. W. (1987). Self-complexity as a cognitive buffer against stress-related illness and depression. *Journal of Personality and Social Psychology, 52,* 663–676. doi:10.1037/0022-3514.52.4.663

Locke, E. A., & Latham, G. P. (1990). *A theory of goal setting and task performance.* Englewood Cliffs, NJ: Prentice Hall.

Lopez, S. J., O'Byrne, K. K., & Petersen, S. (2003). Profiling courage. In S. J. Lopez & C. R. Snyder (Eds.), *Positive psychological assessment: A handbook of models and measures* (pp. 185–197). Washington, DC: American Psychological Association. doi:10.1037/10612-012

Lord, R. G., & Brown, D. J. (2004). *Leadership processes and follower self-identity.* Hillsdale, NJ: Erlbaum.

Luthans, F., Youssef, C. M., & Avolio, B. J. (2007). *Psychological capital: Developing the human competitive edge.* New York, NY: Oxford Press.

Markus, H., & Wurf, E. (1987). The dynamic self-concept: A psychological perspective. *Annual Review of Psychology, 38,* 299–337. doi:10.1146/annurev.ps.38.020187.001503

Masten, A. S., & Reed, M. J. (2002). Resilience in development. In C. R. Snyder & S. Lopez (Eds.), *Handbook of positive psychology* (pp. 74–88). Oxford, England: Oxford University Press.

McCrae, R. R. (1987). Creativity, divergent thinking, and openness to experience. *Journal of Personality and Social Psychology, 52,* 1258–1265. doi:10.1037/0022-3514.52.6.1258

McCrae, R. R. (Ed.). (1992). The five-factor model: Issues and applications [Special issue]. *Journal of Personality, 60*(2). doi:10.1111/j.1467-6494.1992.tb00970.x

McCrae, R. R., Costa, P. T., Jr., & Busch, C. M. (1986). Evaluating comprehensiveness in personality systems: The California Q-Set and the five-factor model. *Journal of Personality, 54,* 430–446. doi:10.1111/j.1467-6494.1986.tb00403.x

Mendoza-Denton, R., Ayduk, O., Mischel, W., Shoda, Y., & Testa, A. (2001). Person X situation interactionism in self-encoding (I am . . . when . . .): Implications for affect regulation and social information processing. *Journal of Personality and Social Psychology, 80,* 533–544. doi:10.1037/0022-3514.80.4.533

Mental Health Advisory Team IV. (2006). *Operation Iraqi Freedom 05-07 Final Report.* United States Army Medical Command. Retrieved from http://www.armymedicine.army.mil

Mental Health Advisory Team V. (2008). *Operation Iraqi Freedom 06-08: Iraq; Operation Enduring Freedom 8: Afghanistan.* United States Army Medical Command. Retrieved from http://www.armymedicine.army.mil

Miller, W. (2000). *The mystery of courage.* Cambridge, MA: Harvard University Press.

Mischel, W., & Shoda, Y. (1998). Reconciling processing dynamics and personality dispositions. *Annual Review of Psychology, 49,* 229–258. doi:10.1146/annurev.psych.49.1.229

Moos, R. H., & Schaefer, J. A. (1993). Coping resources and processes: Current concepts and measures. In L. Goldberger & S. Breznitz (Eds.), *Handbook of stress* (pp. 234–257). New York, NY: Free Press.

Moskowitz, G. B. (2005). *Social cognition: Understanding self and others.* New York, NY: Guilford Press.

Multon, K. D., Brown, S. D., & Lent, R. W. (1991). Relation of self-efficacy beliefs to academic outcomes: A meta-analytic investigation. *Journal of Counseling Psychology, 38,* 30–38. doi:10.1037/0022-0167.38.1.30

O'Connor, K., Hallam, R., & Rachman, S. (1985). Fearlessness and courage: Replication experiment. *The British Journal of Psychology, 76,* 187–197.

O'Fallon, M. J. (2005). A review of the ethical decision-making literature: 1996-2003. *Journal of Business Ethics, 59,* 375–413. doi:10.1007/s10551-005-2929-7

O'Fallon, M. J., & Butterfield, K. D. (2005). A review of the empirical ethical decision-making literature: 1996-2003. *Journal of Business Ethics, 59,* 375–413.

Osgood, C. E., Suci, G. J., & Tannebaum, P. H. (1957). *The measurement of meaning.* Urbana: University of Illinois Press.

Peterson, C., & Seligman, M. (2004). *Character strengths and virtues.* New York, NY: Oxford University Press.

Pury, C., Kowalski, R., & Spearman, J. (2007). Distinctions between general and personal courage. *The Journal of Positive Psychology, 2,* 99–114. doi:10.1080/17439760701237962

Putman, D. (1997). Psychological courage. *Philosophy, Psychiatry, & Psychology, 4,* 1–11. doi:10.1353/ppp.1997.0008

Putman, D. (2004). *Psychological courage.* Lanham, MD: University Press.

Rachman, S. J. (1990). *Fear and courage.* New York, NY: Freeman.

Rate, C. R., Clarke, J. A., Lindsay, D. R., & Sternberg, R. J. (2007). Implicit theories of courage. *The Journal of Positive Psychology, 2,* 80–98. doi:10.1080/17439760701228755

Reitzes, D. C., & Reitzes, D. C. (1984). Alinsky's legacy: Current applications and extensions of his principles and strategies. In R. E. Ratcliff (Ed.), *Research in social movements, conflicts and change* (Vol. 6, pp. 31–56). Greenwich, CT: JAI Press.

Sandage, S. J., & Hill, P. C. (2001). The virtues of positive psychology: The rapprochement and challenges of an affirmative postmodern perspective. *Journal for the Theory of Social Behaviour, 31,* 241–260. doi:10.1111/1468-5914.00157

Schwan, G. (2004). Civil courage and human dignity: How to regain respect for the fundamental values of western democracy. *Social Research, 71,* 107–116.

Shepela, S. T., Cook, J., Horlitz, E., Leal, R., Luciano, S., & Lutfy, E. (1999). Courageous resistance: A special case of altruism. *Theory & Psychology, 9,* 787–805. doi:10.1177/0959354399096004

Shoda, Y., LeeTiernan, S., & Mischel, W. (2002). Personality as a dynamical system: Emergence of stability and distinctiveness from intra-and interpersonal interactions. *Personality and Social Psychology Review, 6,* 316–325. doi:10.1207/S15327957PSPR0604_06

Snyder, C. R., Rand, K. L., & Sigmon, D. R. (2002). Hope theory: A member of the positive psychology family. In C. R. Snyder & S. J. Lopez (Eds.), *Handbook of positive psychology* (pp. 257–276). New York, NY: Oxford Press.

Snyder, C. R., Sympson, S. C., Ybasco, F. C., Borders, T. F., Babyak, M. A., & Higgins, R. L. (1996). Development and validation of the state hope scale. *Journal of Personality and Social Psychology, 70,* 321–335. doi:10.1037/0022-3514.70.2.321

Stajkovic, A. D., & Luthans, F. (1998). Self-efficacy and work-related performance: A meta analysis. *Psychological Bulletin, 124,* 240–261. doi:10.1037/0033-2909.124.2.240

Suedfeld, P. (1997). The social psychology of Invictus: Conceptual and methodological approaches to indomitability. In C. McGarty (Ed.), *The message of social psychology: Perspectives on mind in society* (pp. 328–341). Malden, MA: Blackwell.

Swann, W. (1983). Self-verification: Bringing social reality into harmony with the self. In J. Suls & A. Greenwald (Eds.), *Social psychology perspectives* (Vol. 2, pp. 33–66). Hillsdale, NJ: Erlbaum.

Tajfel, H. (1981). *Human groups and social categories.* Cambridge, England: Cambridge University Press.

Tellegen, A. (1991). Personality traits: Issues of definition, evidence, and assessment. In W. M. Grove & D. Cicchetti (Eds.), *Thinking clearly about psychology: Personality and psychopathology* (Vol. II, pp. 10–35). Saint Paul: University of Minneapolis Press.

Tharenou, P. (1979). Employee self-esteem: A review of the literature. *Journal of Vocational Behavior, 15,* 316–346. doi:10.1016/0001-8791(79)90028-9

Tillich, P. (2000). *The courage to be.* New Haven, CT: Yale University Press.

Treviño, L. K., Weaver, G. R., & Reynolds, S. J. (2006). Behavioral ethics in organizations: A review. *Journal of Management, 32,* 951–990. doi:10.1177/0149206306294258

Verplanken, B., & Holland, R. W. (2002). Motivated decision making: Effects of activation and self-centrality of values on choices and behaviors. *Journal of Personality and Social Psychology, 82,* 434–447. doi:10.1037/0022-3514.82.3.434

Vickers, R. R., Jr., Kolar, D. W., & Hervig, L. K. (1989). *Personality correlates of coping with military basic training (Rep. No. 89-3).* San Diego, CA: Naval Health Research Center.

Watson, D., & Hubbard, B. (1996). Adaptational style and dispositional structure: Coping in the context of the five-factor model. *Journal of Personality, 64,* 737–774. doi:10.1111/j.1467-6494.1996.tb00943.x

Weary, G., & Edwards, J. A. (1994). Individual differences in causal uncertainty. *Journal of Personality and Social Psychology, 67,* 308–318. doi:10.1037/0022-3514.67.2.308

Wolfsfeld, G. (1986). Evaluational origins of political action: The case of Israel. *Political Psychology, 7,* 767–788. doi:10.2307/3791213

Wood, R., & Bandura, A. (1989). Impact of conceptions of ability on self-regulatory mechanisms and complex decision making. *Journal of Personality and Social Psychology, 56,* 407–415. doi:10.1037/0022-3514.56.3.407

Woodard, C. R. (2004). Hardiness and the concept of courage. *Consulting Psychology Journal: Practice and Research, 56,* 173–185. doi:10.1037/1065-9293.56.3.173

Woolfolk, R. L., Novalany, J., Gara, M. A., Allen, L. A., & Polino, M. (1995). Self-complexity, self-evaluation, and depression: An examination of form and content within the self-schema. *Journal of Personality and Social Psychology, 68,* 1108–1120. doi:10.1037/0022-3514.68.6.1108

Worline, M. C., Wrzesniewski, A., & Rafaeli, A. (2002). Courage and work: Breaking routines to improve performance. In R. Lord, R. Klimoski, & R. Kanfer (Eds.), *Emotions at work* (pp. 295–330). San Francisco, CA: Jossey-Bass.

8

What Is Moral Courage? Definition, Explication, and Classification of a Complex Construct

Silvia Osswald, Tobias Greitemeyer, Peter Fischer, and Dieter Frey

> Nothing demands more courage and character than to be in open opposition to time and mainstream, to stand up and to say aloud: No!
>
> —Kurt Tucholsky, in Frohloff (2001, p. 231)

Consider the following two instances of prosocial behavior. The first took place in Munich, Germany, January 13, 2001: About 20 Nazi skinheads harassed a young Greek and started to beat him up in a most brutal way. Five young Turks witnessed the situation and decided to intervene. Risking their own lives, they were able to save the disabled and blood-stained victim from being beaten to death. The second instance occurred in Asia: After the big tsunami wave in Southeast Asia in December 2004, more than 165,000 people lost their lives and more than one million people were made homeless by the floods. Shocked by this horrible natural disaster, people all over the world wanted to ease the victims' suffering. Thousands of volunteers went to Southeast Asia to help on the ground and in Germany, for example, more than 250 million Euros were collected in private donations to help the tsunami victims.

The young Turks and the tsunami volunteers and donors both acted prosocially and supported people who were in situations of severe distress. However, in the first situation, the young Turks had to reckon with massive negative social consequences such as being assaulted by the Nazi skinheads or at least being harassed by them. In contrast, the tsunami volunteers and donors could anticipate positive social consequences such as gratefulness from the victims and recognition from other volunteers, other donors, and the public. Thus, even if both types of actions are done in pursuit of the same goal, namely, helping persons in need, the consequences for the helper might be very different. We argue that the first kind of prosocial behavior is a typical instance of moral courage, whereas the second is more typical of helping behavior.

This chapter deals with moral courage. We seek to highlight this construct by comparing it with other prosocial behaviors, such as helping behavior and related constructs such as heroism or social control. We also include research about classical determinants of helping behavior that do not affect moral courage, followed by studies about determinants that foster moral courageous behavior. Models for moral courage as well as scales to measure it are presented. Finally, we discuss a practical implementation of our research: moral courage trainings.

Defining Moral Courage

In this chapter we use the term *moral courage* as a synonym for civil courage (see Greitemeyer, Osswald, Fischer, & Frey, 2007). Both terms refer to the German word *Zivilcourage.*[1] Moral courage is a prosocial behavior with high social costs and no (or rare) direct rewards for the actor (e.g., Bierhoff, 2002). In situations that demand a morally courageous intervention, instances of injustice happen, human rights are violated, persons are treated unfairly and in a degrading manner, or nature and cultural assets are in danger; these situations are about discrimination against foreigners or other minorities, violence and aggression against weaker individuals, sexual harassment or abuse, mobbing, or illegal business practices (Frey, Schaefer, & Neumann, 1999). Lopez, O'Byrne, and Petersen (2003) defined moral courage as "the expression of personal views and values in the face of dissension and rejection" (p. 187) and "when an individual stands up to someone with power over him or her (e.g., boss) for the greater good" (p. 187). Thus, often an imbalance of power exists with a disadvantage on the side of the person who acts morally courageously. Moral courage situations (compared with other situations that demand prosocial behavior) are also characterized by a specific social constellation: There are not only one or more victims but also one or more perpetrators who discriminate against the victim(s) or act unfairly or threateningly, and the potential helper has to deal with the perpetrators to act prosocially (Jonas & Brandstaetter, 2004). Most of the social costs moral courage entails emanate from the confrontation with the perpetrators. Greitemeyer, Fischer, Kastenmueller, and Frey (2006) defined *moral courage* as brave behavior accompanied by anger and indignation, which intends to enforce societal and ethical norms without considering one's own social costs. Social costs (i.e., negative social consequences) distinguish moral courage from other prosocial behaviors.

Hundreds of studies have addressed prosocial behavior (e.g., PsycINFO lists 428 entries from 2007 with the term *prosocial behavior* in the title), but very little research has referred to prosocial behavior with high (social) costs for the actor (i.e., the person who helps). The reason for this seems obvious, as high-cost prosocial behavior is difficult to examine in a laboratory. Indeed, it is very difficult to generate respective situations that can take place in the laboratory and do not appear artificial. Furthermore, ethical considerations prohibit an exposure of subjects to danger or to unreasonable psychological stress. Therefore, the few studies that deal with costly prosocial behavior question people ex post (e.g., Becker & Eagly, 2004; Oliner & Oliner, 1988).

---

[1]Moral courage overlaps with "bystander intervention." In our opinion, moral courage includes bystander intervention but is more broadly based.

One subtype of high-cost prosocial behavior, namely, intervening at the risk of high social costs and with no or only little hope for reward (i.e., moral courage), has been neglected for the most part. This neglect is astonishing in light of the importance of moral courage for democracy and society (Ostermann, 2004). A reason for the relatively few studies about moral courage might be that previous research and theorizing on prosocial behavior did not distinguish between moral courage and other prosocial behaviors, especially helping behavior (Batson, 1998); thus, predictors of helping behavior have also been regarded as predictors of moral courage. Recent studies and theoretical considerations, however, suggest that moral courage should be separated from other prosocial behaviors. This is treated in the following sections.

Similarities and Differences Between Moral Courage and Other Prosocial Concepts

In this section we discuss relations of moral courage to other prosocial concepts. In this connection, we focus on helping behavior, heroism, and social control.

Differences Between Moral Courage and Helping Behavior: The Role of Negative Social Consequences

As already mentioned, the anticipated negative social consequences in case of prosocial action distinguish moral courage from other prosocial behaviors. For helping behavior, positive consequences, such as plaudit or acknowledgment, can be expected. Moral courage, however, can result in negative social consequences, such as being insulted, excluded, or even attacked. Of course, helping or donating could also lead to negative consequences for the help giver (e.g., losing time or money) but not to negative social consequences. Several studies tried to prove the distinction between moral courage and helping behavior empirically. Fischer et al. (2004; see also Greitemeyer et al., 2007) investigated whether laypeople anticipate more negative social consequences of moral courage than they do of helping behavior. In a vignette study, participants read descriptions of different situations with varying negative social consequences (i.e., the perpetrators were described as very terrifying or quite harmless). Results revealed that the more severe the social consequences were, the more participants characterized the relevant behavior as moral courage (and less as helping behavior).

Subsequently, Greitemeyer, Fischer, Kastenmueller, and Frey (2006) more closely examined people's implicit theories about moral courage and compared them with implicit theories of helping behavior, because implicit theories are crucial in a decision to engage in any kind of prosocial behavior (Dweck, Chiu, & Hong, 1995). If people's implicit theories of moral courage and helping vary, then their decisions on whether to engage in moral courage will follow the application of different standards. In the first study of Greitemeyer et al. (2006), participants read a vignette in which a bystander witnessed a person in need who was threatened and attacked by an offender. Similar to the results of the already mentioned study of Fischer et al. (2004), expected negative social consequences were manipulated by varying the extent to which the offender appeared threatening. Participants learned that the actor intervened and stopped the attack, and then had to indicate to what extent they perceived the actor's behavior to be moral courage and helping behavior, respectively. Results revealed that the actor's behavior was more clearly labeled as moral courage when the offender was threatening than when the offender was not threatening. In contrast, perceptions of helping behavior did not depend on expected negative social consequences. Thus, the amount of expected negative consequences was related to the categorization of prosocial behavior as moral courage but not as helping behavior. In a second study, it was further demonstrated that in the case of offering help, participants expected more positive than negative social consequences; in contrast, in the case of moral courage, participants expected more negative than positive social consequences.

Thus, it can be concluded that people's implicit theories of moral courage and helping behavior do in fact differ and that perceptions of prosocial behavior as an act of moral courage depend on expected negative social consequences for the actor, whereas perceptions of prosocial behavior as helping behavior do not.

Moral Courage and Heroism

Moral courage shows certain similarities with heroism. Becker and Eagly (2004) defined *heroism* as taking risks "on behalf of one or more other people, despite the possibility of dying or suffering serious physical consequences" (p. 164). Regarding the possibility of suffering serious physical consequences, moral courage and heroism overlap: As already mentioned, when a person acts morally courageously he or she runs the risk of negative social consequences such as being insulted by a perpetrator; moreover, an act of moral courage can also result in physical violence by the perpetrator against the helper and thus lead to serious injuries or even to death. An important difference, however, between heroism and moral courage is that in the immediate situation (and also afterward), a hero can expect positive social consequences, such as applause or admiration. In contrast, in the immediate moral courage situation (and often also afterward) a helper cannot expect positive outcomes but rather negative social consequences, such as being insulted, excluded, or even prosecuted by one or more perpetrators. These theoretical assumptions were also investigated empirically: In a series of studies, Osswald, Greitemeyer, Fischer, and Frey (in press) demonstrated a separation of moral courage and heroism. In the first study, participants were given descriptions of different dangerous situations, and the variables of whether a perpetrator was present or not and whether social costs of the prosocial act were high or low were manipulated. Participants had to indicate to what extent they perceived the described behavior as moral courage and as heroism. Results revealed that participants clearly labeled situations with a perpetrator and high social costs as moral courage. In contrast, situations with low social costs and without a perpetrator were characterized as heroism. Further studies indicated that moral courage and heroism correspond to different moral prototypes: Moral courage was associated with the just prototype, whereas heroism was affiliated with the brave prototype (for more research about moral prototypes in general, see Walker & Firmer, 2007, and Walker & Hennig, 2004).

Moral Courage and Social Control

Another construct related to moral courage is social control (Jonas & Brandstaetter, 2004). Social control involves an intervention that curbs impolite or uncivil behavior, that is, a verbal or nonverbal communication by which individuals signal another person that they disapprove of his or her deviant, counternormative behavior (Chekroun & Brauer, 2002). For example, persons exert social control when they criticize someone who has thrown litter in a public park. Most of the empirical research about social control was conducted by Brauer and colleagues (Brauer & Chekroun, 2005; Brauer, Chekroun, Chappe, & Chambon, 2007; Chaurand & Brauer, 2002, 2005). In their studies, they regarded social control mainly as a reaction to uncivil behaviors. Uncivil behaviors are counternormative behaviors that occur in urban environments and decrease the quality of life, such as littering, failing to clean up after one's dog, urinating in public, and playing loud music in the street. These uncivil behaviors are "urban stressors" (Robin, Ratiu, Matheau-Police, & Lavarde, 2004), but they are not really serious or dangerous (Chaurand & Brauer, 2005). This is the first theoretical reasonable difference between social control of uncivil behavior and moral courage: Moral courage situations are dangerous both for the victim and for the helper. Being bullied, discriminated against, insulted, harassed, or attacked can have serious mental and physical consequences for the victim.

Social control serves to keep up and to enforce social norms because a person who violates these social norms runs the risk of receiving an angry look, a negative comment, and so on (i.e., social control; Brauer & Chekroun, 2005). Like people who show social control, people who show moral courage also want to enforce norms. One could theoretically argue that the types of norms, however, that are enforced by social control and moral courage, respectively, are different. By social control, social norms that relate to everyday living are implemented (Brauer & Chekroun, 2005). In contrast, with moral courage, ethical norms (e.g., observation of human or democratic rights) are pursued, and people stand up for a greater good (Greitemeyer et al., 2006; Lopez et al., 2003).

Because different types of norms aim to be enforced by social control and moral courage, respectively, it may be that social control and moral courage derive from different motives and values. In a recent empirical study with 65 persons (43 women), Osswald (2008) investigated whether different motives and values stand behind social control and moral courage. It could be demonstrated that social control more likely results in egoistic motives compared with moral courage ($M_{\text{social control}} = 4.41$; $M_{\text{moral courage}} = 3.79$), whereas people act morally courageously because of altruistic motives (compared with motives behind social control, $M_{\text{social control}} = 4.33$; $M_{\text{moral courage}} = 5.56$). Furthermore, compared with social control, moral courage is more strongly associated with the value of universalism (Schwartz & Boenke, 2004; $M_{\text{social control}} = 2.20$; $M_{\text{moral courage}} = 2.66$). Universalism means "understanding, appreciation, tolerance and protection of the welfare of all people and of nature" (Bardi & Schwartz, 2003, p. 1208).

So far, we have tried to separate moral courage from related constructs. In the next sections we present empirical research about classical determinants of helping behavior that do not affect moral courage followed by a description of factors that promote morally courageous behavior.

Classical Determinants of Helping Behavior and Their Failure to Predict Moral Courage

Certain classical determinants or predictors of helping behavior exist. We argue, however, that these predictors cannot simply be assigned to moral courage. Relevant experiments are reported in the next section.

The Role of Bystanders

Plenty of studies revealed that the presence of others inhibits helping behavior (for an overview, see Latané & Nida, 1981). However, in almost all studies on bystander intervention conducted to date, the bystander did not have to fear danger or severe negative social consequences in the case of intervention; the role of bystanders concerning moral courage was not yet clear. As Schwartz and Gottlieb (1976) suggested, it might be that in dangerous situations the social inhibition effect of additional bystanders is reduced by processes of a clearer emergency awareness, more arousal because of the higher need of the victim, or changed cost–reward–analysis (Piliavin, Dovidio, Gaertner, & Clark, 1981). Thus, Fischer, Greitemeyer, Pollozek, and Frey (2006) examined whether a passive bystander inhibited helping behavior but not moral courage. Participants observed a live broadcast of a cross-gender communication that allegedly took place in an adjacent room. The participants saw a woman and a man who talked with each other in a quite natural way during the first minutes. However, as time progressed, the man became intrusive, touched the woman, and started to harass her sexually. The woman, however, clearly rejected the sexual advances. She tried to escape by leaving the room, but the man blocked the exit, and a brawl started, with the woman being clearly inferior. The picture then went black. In the helping condition, the perpetrator was skinny and of small stature, whereas in the moral courage condition he was strongly built and thug-like. In the bystander condition, participants were in the presence of one additional passive bystander, whereas they were alone in the solitary condition. As a dependent measure, it was assessed how many participants tried to intervene.

In the helping condition, the classic bystander effect was replicated: More help was given in the solitary condition than in the bystander condition. In the moral courage condition, however, participants were equally likely to show moral courage in the solitary condition and in the presence of another bystander. Thus, though the probability of showing helping behavior decreased with an increasing number of bystanders, the probability of showing moral courage was not affected by the number of bystanders. In the context of dangerous emergencies, that is, in a moral courage situation, the bystander effect does not occur.

Moreover, Fischer and colleagues (2006) found out that moral courage situations faced in the presence of bystanders are recognized more quickly and less ambiguously as real emergency situations than as harmless (helping) situations. Furthermore, the costs for the victim in case of a nonintervention are also higher in a dangerous moral courage situation than in a more harmless helping situation. Thus, arousal in a moral courage situation is higher than in a helping situation and an intervention becomes more probable, independently of whether a passive bystander is present or not.

The Role of Mood

A further classical determinant of helping behavior is mood. Previous studies demonstrated that the decision to help is influenced by the mood of the potential helper. People are more likely to help others when they are in a positive relative to a neutral mood because helping others is an excellent way of maintaining or prolonging positive mood (Isen & Levin, 1972). In addition, negative, relative to neutral, mood states are shown to increase prosocial behavior because helping dispels negative mood (Carlson & Miller, 1987; Cialdini, Baumann, & Kenrick, 1981). Because moral courage situations are associated with fewer anticipated positive social consequences and more anticipated negative social consequences relative to helping situations, one may expect that showing moral courage actually worsens an actor's mood. As a consequence, whereas positive and negative mood states (as opposed to neutral mood states) can be expected to lead to more helping behavior, mood should not affect moral courage.

To test this reasoning, Niesta, Greitemeyer, Fischer, and Frey (2008) conducted three studies in which participants' mood (positive vs. negative vs. neutral mood) was experimentally manipulated and either moral courage or helping behavior was assessed. In the first study, actual behavior was recorded and results revealed that positive and to a lesser extent also negative mood promoted helping behavior. In contrast, mood did not differentially influence moral courage. In the second study, positive mood fostered the intention to show helping behavior, whereas the intention to act morally courageously was not affected. Furthermore, norm salience was shown to partly mediate the relationship between positive mood and helping behavior. The third study examined what variables beyond mood and norm salience determined moral courage. Again it was replicated that positive mood fostered helping behavior, whereas participants were comparably likely to show moral courage in each of the three mood conditions. However, it was also demonstrated that justice sensitivity, civil disobedience, resistance to group pressure, moral mandate, and anger lead to moral courage, but not to help-giving. Thus, mood as a determinant drops out, but other variables possess the potential to foster moral courage. Further determinants that promote moral courage are presented in the next section.

Factors That Foster Moral Courage

In the preceding sections we demonstrated factors that do not promote moral courage. In the following sections we seek to show variables that have the potential to foster morally courageous behavior.

The Role of Norms

The importance of social norms for promoting prosocial behavior has been demonstrated in a variety of studies (for an overview, see Cialdini, Kallgren, & Reno, 1991, or Batson, 1998). However, the prosocial behavior that was examined in the studies conducted to date did not include costs for the actor. So far, it was not clear whether norms foster moral courage as a costly prosocial behavior in a similar way. Schwartz (1977) argued that they do not because costs deactivate norms by different defense mechanisms (Schwartz, 1977; see also Tyler, Orwin, & Schurer, 1982). In two studies, Osswald, Greitemeyer, Fischer, and Frey (2008a) tested the effects of norms on moral courage. In the first study, for half of the participants prosocial norms were activated by film material, whereas for the remaining half no prosocial norms were made salient. The film material that activated prosocial norms consisted of different scenes in which people showed moral courageous behavior. The participants were then brought into a morally courage situation: They witnessed how the experimenter insulted and discriminated against a foreign student (a confederate). As a dependent measure, it was assessed whether participants intervened and defended the foreign student against the perpetrator.

Results revealed that salient prosocial norms fostered moral courage: Subjects for whom prosocial norms were activated intervened more often against discrimination than did subjects for whom no prosocial norms were made salient. Thus, when prosocial norms are salient in people's minds they are more likely to show moral courage despite possible negative social consequences. The second study shed light on mediating mechanisms: It was demonstrated that anger, awareness of the situation, and responsibility take-over (i.e., they felt more responsible to act) mediated the intention to intervene. When prosocial norms were made salient participants reported more anger, a higher awareness of the situation, and more responsibility takeover. Anger, awareness of the situation, and responsibility takeover in turn fostered the intention to show moral courage.

In summary, the results of Osswald et al. (2008a) are in line with the study of Greitemeyer et al. (2006; see earlier discussion), which already gave first hints about the importance of norms for moral courage: Prosocial norms have the potential to foster moral courage, but they have to be strongly activated in the forefront to display an effect.

The Role of Anger

In our description of moral courage, anger is an integral component: When a person acts morally courageously, he or she is in most cases angry at a perpetrator or he or she is upset because of injustice, violations of human dignity, and so on. Also, empirical results underline a close relation of anger and moral courage: Greitemeyer et al. (2006) demonstrated that moral courage situations were associated with more anger, Niesta et al. (2008) showed that anger promoted the intention to show moral courage, and Osswald et al. (2008a) found that anger (besides awareness of the situation and responsibility takeover) mediated the effect of salient prosocial norms on morally courageous behavior. Thus, anger seems to play an important role for moral courage. Anger possibly motivates or strengthens the intentions to act or the behavior itself. But what kind of anger is this? The following theoretical considerations demonstrate that a conclusive answer cannot be given yet. When people show moral courage, they stand up for a greater good and seek to enforce ethical norms without considering their own social costs, because one or more perpetrators have violated ethical norms, human rights, or democratic values. Therefore, one could guess that anger related to moral courage is about moral outrage. Moral outrage means an anger that is provoked by the perception that a moral standard (in most cases a standard of fairness or justice) has been violated (Hofmann, 2000; Montada & Schneider, 1989). However, Batson et al. (2007) recently argued that an angry reaction at unfairness is not moral outrage but rather empathic anger. In two studies, Batson and colleagues (2007) could demonstrate the existence of empathic anger but not of moral outrage. They admitted, however, that a clear distinction between the moral outrage and empathic anger is most (if not exclusively) possible by manipulation. Because the studies by Greitemeyer et al. (2006), Niesta et al. (2008), and Osswald et al. (2008a) did not manipulate but measured anger, no clear statement can be made whether empathic anger or moral outrage was assessed. The anger measured by these studies presumably includes parts of moral outrage and of empathic anger. More research is needed for a final conclusion to be drawn.

Altogether, linking anger with a prosocial behavior such as moral courage seems to be an interesting research area because in most cases empathetic or caring emotions are theoretically and empirically linked to prosocial behavior (for a review, see Batson, 1998), whereas anger has been linked to aggression and antisocial behavior (e.g., Weiner, Graham, & Chandler, 1982; Zillmann, 1988).

Personality and Moral Courage

Besides situational factors that promote moral courage, dispositional variables also play an important role. As noted earlier, Niesta et al. (2008) found justice sensitivity, civil disobedience, resistance to group pressure, and moral mandate to be conducive determinants of moral courage. In an earlier study, Kuhl (1986) demonstrated that high self-assurance, which in turn affects how difficult the situation is perceived, fosters moral courage. Hermann and Meyer (2000) also found self-assurance, self-efficacy, and social competence as well as moral beliefs and responsibility takeover to be important. In a study with more than 700 pupils, Labuhn, Wagner, van Dick, and Christ (2004) showed that the more empathy and inner ethnical contacts and the less dominance orientation pupils had, the higher was their intention to show moral courage.

Finally, in a recent study with real behavior as a dependent variable, Osswald, Greitemeyer, Fischer, and Frey (2008b) investigated the effects of different personality variables on moral courage. At a first time point, a number of dispositional variables were measured. Three weeks later, the dependent measure was assessed: Participants witnessed how an experimenter insulted and discriminated against a foreign student (a confederate). As a dependent variable it was assessed whether they intervened and defended the foreign student against the perpetrator (the data were collected in the same experiment in which we also tested the influence of norms on moral courage; see earlier section). Results revealed that the higher participants scored on the openness dimensions of the Big Five, the more likely they showed moral courage. This is an interesting result because in most studies of the relationship between personality variables and prosocial behavior the Agreeableness dimension of the Big Five was found to be related to prosocial behavior (e.g., Penner et al., 2005). Nevertheless, it makes sense that only a very slight relationship exists between agreeableness and moral courage: Being agreeable and friendly does not foster answering back a rude experimenter. On the other hand, openness to new experiences and a broad mind promote acceptance of different ways of life and of persons from other countries and cultures. It therefore seems plausible that open-minded persons are more likely to intervene against discrimination and to show moral courage. Furthermore, empathy was significantly positively related to moral courage, whereas responsibility denial was significantly negatively related. The more empathic participants were and the less they denied responsibility the more they intervened. These data are in accord with other studies and theoretical considerations (see Schwartz, 1977; Batson, 1998). Because a study by Bardi and Schwartz (2003) demonstrated a relationship between values and behavior, it was also assessed whether values might be related to moral courage. Conformity and tradition turned out to be of importance: The less central participants regarded conformity and tradition as values for their life, the more likely they were to intervene. It seems reasonable that values conformity and tradition correlate negatively with the act of intervention against discrimination. If a person esteems conformity and tradition he or she will probably not advance opposite views or argue with perpetrators.

Thus, a variety of dispositional variables have been shown to play a role in moral courage. More research is needed, however, because most of the studies conducted thus far assessed only the intention to show moral courage and not actual behavior (e.g., Kuhl, 1986; Labuhn et al., 2004).

So far, we have argued that moral courage should be separated from helping behavior and presented determinants that promote moral courage. In the next section we address the issue of whether theoretical models for helping behavior can be used to predict moral courage or whether particular models for moral courage should be established.

Classical Helping Models and Models for Moral Courage

Because implicit theories of moral courage and helping behavior differ and classic predictors of helping behavior (bystanders and mood) differently affect moral courage, it is questionable whether classical helping models such as the process models of Schwartz and Howard (1981) or Latané and Darley (1970) can simply be transferred to predict moral courage. Greitemeyer and colleagues (2006) addressed this question from an empirical point of view, and Osswald, Frey, Greitemeyer, and Fischer (2007) highlighted it in a theoretical contribution. The model of Latané and Darley (1970) consists of five different stages of making a decision to help: attention (Stage 1), emergency awareness (Stage 2), attribution of own responsibility (Stage 3), skills for helping (Stage 4), and final decision to provide help (Stage 5). Each of these stages, completed by considerations of Schwartz and Howard (1981), was examined concerning their meaning for moral courage.

For the empirical test, Greitemeyer and colleagues (2006) asked participants to describe a situation in which they had either helped someone or in which they had showed moral courage. Other participants were asked to describe a situation in which they had either failed to help or failed to show moral courage. Next, participants answered questions referring to the five stages of Latané and Darley's helping model. Results revealed that moral courage situations differed from helping situations: Moral courage situations were perceived more quickly (Stage 1) and were associated with more perceived responsibility (Stage 3) and fewer perceived intervention skills (Stage 4) than were helping situations. Regarding the decision to intervene (Stage 5), moral courage, relative to helping situations, was associated with a higher degree of expected negative social consequences, with a higher salience of societal norms, and with more evaluation apprehension, more anger, and more empathy. Furthermore, Greitemeyer et al. (2006) demonstrated that the decisions on whether to show either moral courage or helping behavior or not are differentially influenced. In other words, perceived responsibility and empathy are more important for the decision to help or not than for the decision to show moral courage or not. Thus, the helping model of Latané and Darley (1970) cannot simply be transferred to predict moral courage but has to be modified. Osswald et al. (2007), Frey et al. (2007; see also Frey & Schaefer, 2001), and Meyer (2004) proposed particular theoretical models of moral courage that we present shortly.

On the basis of the studies of Greitemeyer et al. (2006), Osswald et al. (2007) proposed a process model with steps related to the model of Latané and Darley (1970): Before a person can act with moral courage, he or she has to perceive an incident as a situation of moral courage, and he or she has to take responsibility and has to feel competent to act. Furthermore, the person should possess a variety of reaction options that he or she can promptly realize. Moral courage situations mostly happen fast and are often dangerous and quite unsettling. Therefore, fast reactions are necessary. In the model, the availability of reaction options besides self-efficacy and high self esteem as well as salience of prosocial norms, empathy, and moral outrage act as promoting factors of moral courage. As inhibiting factors, anticipated social costs, fear of being evaluated and judged, and the (mis)perception of having not enough intervention skills are proposed. Indeed, in moral courage situations people feel less competent to intervene than in other prosocial incidents.

Frey and colleagues (2006) took for their theoretical model the theory of planned behavior (e.g., Ajzen, 1985) and described variables that affect the intention to act morally courageously. Determinants of the behavioral intention are (a) situational conditions (e.g., awareness of the situation), (b) the former life of the morally courageous person (e.g., socialization), (c) personal traits (e.g., responsibility takeover), and (d) inhibiting factors (e.g., fear of being evaluated). These factors affect the intention to show moral courage which in turn influences the real behavior. The model provides good indications of which determinants may play a role for moral courage. However, it remains for the most part to be empirically tested.

In his theoretical model of moral courage, Meyer (2004) proposed four main factors that promote or inhibit moral courageous behavior: (a) social and political context, (b) situational factors, (c) personal factors, and (d) perception of the situation. All these factors consist of a variety of subsections: The social and political context includes among others the social position of the intervenor person or the form of government (democratic vs. authoritarian) under which the morally courageous person lives. Situational factors consist inter alia of the place where the situation happens and how the situation develops. Personal factors include competencies and resources such as empathy or knowledge, and motivational variables such as justice sensitivity or prosocial beliefs. Perception of the situation contains attention or evaluation of the person's own helping abilities. The model tries to specify short- and long-term determinants of moral courage, and like the model of Frey et al. (2006), it provides an interesting overview about possible influence factors. However, it also still remains to be empirically tested.

Empirical investigation is possible only with reliable measurements. Therefore, in the following section, two scales are presented that seek to measure moral courage.

Scales to Measure Moral Courage

Our research group recently developed a scale that measures the intention to show moral courage (Kastenmueller, Greitemeyer, Fischer, & Frey, 2007). The scale consists of three factors, which emerged by exploratory and confirmatory factor analyses: moral courage at the workplace, moral courage in situations of physical violence, and moral courage against racism. Validity analysis revealed that the moral courage scale, as opposed to the established helping scale of Rushton, Chrisjohn, and Fekken (1981), better predicted moral courage, whereas the helping scale better predicted helping behavior than did the moral courage scale.

Another scale that also partly measures moral courage is the Woodard-Pury Courage Scale–23 (WPCS-23; Woodard & Pury, 2007), which consists of four subscales: (a) work or employment courage; (b) patriotic, religious, or belief-based courage; (c) social–moral courage; and (d) independent courage and family-based courage. Social–moral courage seems to be the scale that is most closely related to moral courage.

So far, we have treated theoretical and empirical questions about moral courage. Research about a prosocial behavior of such importance should also have practical implications, however. In the next section we present possibilities to practically apply research results about moral courage: workshops and trainings that seek to promote morally courageous behavior.

Training Moral Courage

Moral courage is an important virtue within society. Thus, trainings, workshops, and courses that aim to promote moral courage were recently developed (see Jonas, Boos, & Brandstaetter, 2007). Moral courage is not an innate behavior but can be learned and trained. The moral courage trainings try to teach behavioral routines that can easily be recalled to foster adequate and fast reactions. For example, because it is dangerous and often not reasonable to intervene alone, participants learn in role plays how to activate other people also to help. Our research group also offers a moral courage training developed by Brandstaetter and Frey (2003) for students that goes beyond the university setting. In discussions, role plays, and group exercises, we try to work out with our participants how to react in a moral courage situation without endangering oneself. Moral courage does not refer to rushing into the most dangerous situations hoping to survive somehow. The motto of our workshop is "Small deeds instead of heroism." Already, small deeds (which are named and shown within the training, e.g., "call the police" or "inform other bystanders if you think something is happening") can have enormous effects, and the worst thing is to do or to say nothing. Presenting people with such knowledge promotes the probability that people will intervene in a critical situation because they are released of the pressure to act heroically or to work wonders. The training aims to impart practical knowledge and behavioral competencies as first aid courses do. A first empirical evaluation of our moral courage training revealed that participants perceive themselves after the workshop as more competent regarding how to react in an emergency and report more self-efficacy when faced with a situation that demands moral courage. Furthermore, after moral courage trainings, situations are recognized as an emergency more quickly and clearer, and personal responsibility to act and to intervene is fostered (Frey et al., 2007). Thus, it seems possible to train people in moral courage. However, more research, especially concerning long-term effects, is needed.

Summary and Conclusion

In this chapter, we highlighted the construct of moral courage more thoroughly. We gave theoretical outlines and empirical results showing that moral courage shares certain aspects with helping behavior, heroism, and social control. Nevertheless, moral courage also fundamentally differs from these prosocial constructs. The most important difference between moral courage and other prosocial intentions is the negative social consequences a person has to fear when acting morally courageously. Furthermore, classical determinants of helping behavior, such as mood or bystanders, do not affect moral courage, whereas other factors such as moral outrage play a role. We therefore argue that moral courage should be examined as an independent subtype of prosocial behavior and not be subsumed under prosocial behaviors such as helping behavior or heroism.

At the time of writing, our research group is working to elucidate more specific determinants of moral courage behavior and to evaluate the effectiveness of moral courage training more deeply. We constantly seek to incorporate empirical data in our moral courage trainings to improve them. Research and practice should effectively collaborate to implement moral courage more profoundly in society. Having morally courageous behavior be more common should be an important goal for every society. As noted by Franka Magnani: "The more citizens with civil courage a country has, the fewer heroes it will once need" (as cited in Frohloff, 2001, p. 230).

References

Ajzen, I. (1985). From intentions to actions: A theory of planned behavior. In J. Kuhl & J. Beckmann (Eds.), *Action control* (pp. 11–39). Berlin, Germany: Springer.

Bardi, A., & Schwartz, S. H. (2003). Values and behavior: Strength and structure of relations. *Personality and Social Psychology Bulletin, 29,* 1207–1220. doi:10.1177/0146167203254602

Batson, C. D. (1998). Altruism and prosocial behavior. In D. T. Gilbert, S. T. Fiske, & G. Lindzey (Eds.), *Handbook of social psychology* (4th ed., Vol. 2, pp. 282–316). New York, NY: McGraw-Hill/Oxford University Press.

Batson, C. D., Kenedy, C. L., Nord, L.-A., Fleming, D. A., Marzette, C. M., Lishner, D. A., . . . Zerger, T. (2007). Anger at unfairness: Is it moral outrage? *European Journal of Social Psychology, 37,* 1272–1285. doi:10.1002/ejsp.434

Becker, S. W., & Eagly, A. H. (2004). The heroism of women and men. *American Psychologist, 59,* 163–178. doi:10.1037/0003-066X.59.3.163

Bierhoff, H. W. (2002). *Prosocial behavior.* New York, NY: Psychology Press.

Brandstaetter, V., & Frey, D. (2003). Kleine Schritte statt Heldentaten [Small steps instead of heroism]. *Psychologie Heute, 7,* 67–69.

Brauer, M., & Chekroun, P. (2005). The relationship between perceived violation of social norms and social control: Situational factors influencing the reaction to deviance. *Journal of Applied Social Psychology, 35,* 1519–1539. doi:10.1111/j.1559-1816.2005.tb02182.x

Brauer, M., Chekroun, P., Chappe, B., & Chambon, M. (2007). *Within-group variability and pressures to conformity: Powerful groups are more heteregeneous and more tolerant of deviant in-group members than powerless groups.* Unpublished manuscript, University of Clermont-Ferrand.

Carlson, M., & Miller, N. (1987). Explanation of the relation between negative mood and helping. *Psychological Bulletin, 102,* 91–108. doi:10.1037/0033-2909.102.1.91

Chaurand, N., & Brauer, M. (2005). *What determines social control? People's reactions to counternormative behaviors in urban environments.* Unpublished manuscript, University of Clermont-Ferrand.

Chekroun, P., & Brauer, M. (2002). The bystander effect and social control behavior: The effect of the presence of others on people's reactions to norm violation. *European Journal of Social Psychology, 32,* 853–866. doi:10.1002/ejsp.126

Cialdini, R. B., Baumann, D. J., & Kenrick, D. T. (1981). Insights from sadness: A three-step model of the development of altruism as hedonism. *Developmental Review, 1,* 207–223. doi:10.1016/0273-2297(81)90018-6

Cialdini, R. B., Kallgren, C. A., & Reno, R. R. (1991). A focus theory of normative conduct: A theoretical refinement and reevaluation of the role of norms in human behavior. *Advances in Experimental Social Psychology, 24,* 201–234. doi:10.1016/S0065-2601(08)60330-5

Dweck, C. S., Chiu, C., & Hong, Y. (1995). Implicit theories and their role in judgments and reactions: A world from two perspectives. *Psychological Inquiry, 6,* 267–285. doi:10.1207/s15327965pli0604_1

Fischer, P., Greitemeyer, T., Pollozek, F., & Frey, D. (2006). The unresponsive bystander: Are bystanders more responsive in dangerous emergencies? *European Journal of Social Psychology, 36,* 267–278. doi:10.1002/ejsp.297

Fischer, P., Greitemeyer, T., Schulz-Hardt, S., Frey, D., Jonas, E., & Rudukha, T. (2004). Zivilcourage und Hilfeverhalten. Der Einfluss negativer sozialer Konsequenzen auf die Wahrnehmung prosozialen Verhalten [Moral courage and helping behavior: The impact of negative social consequences on the perception of prosocial behavior]. *Zeitschrift für Sozialpsychologie, 35,* 61–66. doi:10.1024/0044-3514.35.2.61

Frey, D., Peus, C., Brandstaetter, V., Winkler, M., & Fischer, P. (2006). Zivilcourage [Moral courage]. In H.-W. Bierhoff & D. Frey (Eds.), *Handbuch der Sozial- und Kommunikationspsychologie* (pp. 180–186). Göttingen, Germany: Hogrefe.

Frey, D., & Schaefer, M. (2001): Determinanten der Zivilcourage und des Hilfeverhaltens [Determinants of moral courage and helping behavior]. In H.-W. Bierhoff & D. Fetchenhauer (Eds.), *Solidarität, Konflikt, Umwelt und Dritte Welt* (pp. 93–122). Opladen, Germany: Leske und Budrich.

Frey, D., Schaefer, M., & Neumann, R. (1999). Zivilcourage und aktives Handeln bei Gewalt: Wann werden Menschen aktiv? [Moral courage and intervention at violence: When do people become active?]. In M. Schaefer & D. Frey (Eds.), *Aggression und Gewalt unter Kindern und Jugendlichen* (pp. 265–284). Göttingen, Germany: Hogrefe.

Frey, D., Winkler, M., Fischer, P., Bruckmeier, N., Gloeckner, P., Koenig, W., Mutz, D., & Spies, R. (2007). "zammgrauft". Ein Training von Anti-Gewalt bis Zivilcourage für Kinder und Jugendliche ["zammgrauft": A training ranging from anti-violence to moral courage for children and adolescents]. In K. Jonas, M. Boos & V. Brandstaetter (Eds.), *Zivilcourage trainieren! Theorie und Praxis* (pp. 139–203). Goettingen, Germany: Hogrefe.

Frohloff, S. (2001). *Gesicht Zeigen! Handbuch für Zivilcourage [Do not hide yourself! Handbook for moral courage]*. Bonn, Germany: Bundeszentrale für Politische Bildung.

Greitemeyer, T., Fischer, P., Kastenmueller, A., & Frey, D. (2006). Civil courage and helping behaviour: Differences and similarities. *European Psychologist, 11,* 90–98. doi:10.1027/1016-9040.11.2.90

Greitemeyer, T., Osswald, S., Fischer, P., & Frey, D. (2007). Civil courage: Implicit theories, related concepts, and measurement. *The Journal of Positive Psychology, 2,* 115–119. doi:10.1080/17439760701228789

Hermann, A., & Meyer, G. (2000): Was fördert, was hindert Zivilcourage? Ergebnisse einer empirischen Studie [What fosters, what impedes moral courage? Results of an empirical study]. In G. Meyer, U. Dovermann, S. Frech, & G. Gugel (Eds.), *Zivilcourage lernen. Analysen – Modelle – Arbeitshilfen* (pp. 70–85). Baden-Württemberg, Germany: Landeszentrale für politische Bildung.

Hofmann, M. L. (2000). *Empathy and moral development: Implications for caring and justice.* New York, NY: Cambridge University Press.

Isen, A. M., & Levin, P. F. (1972). Effect of feeling good on helping: Cookies and kindness. *Journal of Personality and Social Psychology, 21,* 384–388. doi:10.1037/h0032317

Jonas, K., Boos, M., & Brandstaetter, B. (Eds.). (2007). *Zivilcourage trainieren! Theorie und Praxis* [Training moral courage! Theory and practice]. Göttingen, Germany: Hogrefe.

Jonas, K., & Brandstaetter, V. (2004). Zivilcourage. Definition, Befunde, Maflnahmen [Moral courage. Definition, findings, and interventions]. *Zeitschrift für Sozialpsychologie, 35,* 185–200. doi:10.1024/0044-3514.35.4.185

Kastenmueller, A., Greitemeyer, T., Fischer, P., & Frey, D. (2007). Das Münchner Zivilcourage-Instrument (MüZI). Entwicklung und Validierung [The Munich civil courage instrument. Development and validation]. *Diagnostica, 53,* 205–217.

Kuhl, U. (1986). *Selbstsicherheit und prosoziales Handeln* [Self-assurance and prosocial behavior]. Munich, Germany: Profil.

Labuhn, A., Wagner, U., van Dick, R., & Christ, O. (2004). Determinanten zivilcouragierten Verhaltens: Ergebnisse einer Fragebogenstudie [Determinants of civil courage: Results of a questionnaire study]. *Zeitschrift für Sozialpsychologie, 35,* 93–103. doi:10.1024/0044-3514.35.2.93

Latané, B., & Nida, S. (1981). Ten years of research on group size and helping. *Psychological Bulletin, 89,* 308–324. doi:10.1037/0033-2909.89.2.308

Latané, B., & Darley, J. (1970). *The unresponsive bystander: Why doesn't he help?* New York, NY: Meredith Corporation.

Lopez, S., O'Byrne, K. K., & Petersen, S. (2003). Profiling courage. In S. Lopez & C. R. Snyder (Eds.), *Positive psychology assessment: A handbook of models and measures* (pp. 185–197). Washington, DC: American Psychological Association. doi:10.1037/10612-012

Meyer, G. (2004). Was heiflt mit Zivilcourage handeln? [What it means to act morally courageously?]. In G. Meyer, U. Dovermann, S. Frech, & G. Gugel (Eds.), *Zivilcourage lernen* (pp. 22–41). Bonn, Germany: Bundeszentrale für Politische Bildung.

Montada, L., & Schneider, A. (1989). Justice and emotional reactions to the disadvantaged. *Social Justice Research, 3,* 313–344. doi:10.1007/BF01048081

Niesta, D., Greitemeyer, T., Fischer, P., & Frey, D. (2008). *No fruit of the mood: The impact of mood on high and low cost prosocial behavior.* Manuscript submitted for publication.

Oliner, S. P., & Oliner, P. M. (1988). *The altruistic personality.* New York, NY: Free Press.

Osswald, S. (2008). *Motives and values related to moral courage and social control.* Unpublished data, University of Munich.

Osswald, S., Frey, D., Greitemeyer, T., & Fischer, P. (2007). Erarbeitung eines Prozessmodells für Zivilcourage [Development of a process model form oral courage]. In R. Frankenberger, S. Frech, & D. Grimm (Eds.), *Politische Psychologie und Politische Bildung–Analysen, Konzepte und Praxisberichte* (pp. 114–138). Schwalbach, Germany: Wochenschau.

Osswald, S., Greitemeyer, T., Fischer, P., & Frey, D. (in press). Moral prototypes and moral behavior: Specific effects on emotional precursors of moral behavior and on moral behavior by the activation of moral prototypes. *European Journal of Social Psychology.*

Osswald, S., Greitemeyer, T., Fischer, P., & Frey, D. (2008a). *Effects of social norms on high cost prosocial behavior.* Manuscript submitted for publication.

Osswald, S., Greitemeyer, T., Fischer, P., & Frey, D. (2008b). *What fosters bystander intervention in a costly situation? Predicting intervention in a discrimination situation by personality variables and values.* Manuscript submitted for publication.

Ostermann, A. (2004). Zivilcourage und Demonkratie [Moral courage and democracy]. In: R. Frankenberger, S. Frech, & D. Grimm (Eds.), *Politische Psychologie und Politische Bildung–Analysen, Konzepte und Praxisberichte* (pp. 114–138). Schwalbach, Germany: Wochenschau.

Penner, L. A., Dovidio, J. F., Piliavin, J. A., & Schroeder, D. A. (2005). Prosocial behavior: Multilevel perspectives. *Annual Review of Psychology, 56,* 365–392. doi:10.1146/annurev.psych.56.091103.070141

Piliavin, J., Dovidio, J., Gaertner, S., & Clark, R. (1981). *Emergency intervention.* New York, NY: Academic Press.

Robin, M., Ratiu, E., Matheau-Police, A., & Lavarde, A. M. (2004, July). *An evaluation of urban stressors.* Paper presented at the 18th International Association for People-Environment Studies Conference, Vienna, Austria.

Rushton, J. P., Chrisjohn, R. D., & Fekken, G. C. (1981). The altruistic personality and the self-report altruism scale. *Personality and Individual Differences, 2,* 293–302. doi:10.1016/0191-8869(81)90084-2

Schwartz, S. H. (1977). Normative influences on altruism. *Advances in Experimental Social Psychology, 10,* 221–279. doi:10.1016/S0065-2601(08)60358-5

Schwartz, S. H., & Boenke, K. (2004). Evaluating the structure of human values with confirmatory factor analysis. *Journal of Research in Personality, 38,* 230–255. doi:10.1016/S0092-6566(03)00069-2

Schwartz, S. H., & Gottlieb, A. (1976). Bystander reactions to a violent theft: Crime in Jerusalem. *Journal of Personality and Social Psychology, 34,* 1188–1199. doi:10.1037/0022-3514.34.6.1188

Schwartz, S. H., & Howard, J. A. (1981). A normative decision-making model of altruism. In J. P. Rushton & R. M. Sorentino (Eds.), *Altruism and helping behavior* (pp. 189–211). Hillsdale, NJ: Erlbaum.

Tyler, T. R., Orwin, R., & Schurer, L. (1982). Defensive denial and high cost prosocial behavior. *Basic and Applied Social Psychology, 3,* 267–281. doi:10.1207/s15324834basp0304_4

Walker, L. J., & Firmer, J. A. (2007). Moral personality of brave and caring exemplars. *Journal of Personality and Social Psychology, 93,* 845–860. doi:10.1037/0022-3514.93.5.845

Walker, L. J., & Hennig, K. H. (2004). Differing conceptions on moral exemplarity: Just, brave and caring. *Journal of Personality and Social Psychology, 86,* 629–647. doi:10.1037/0022-3514.86.4.629

Weiner, B., Graham, S., & Chandler, C. (1982). Pity, anger and guilt: An attributional analysis. *Personality and Social Psychology Bulletin, 8,* 226–232. doi:10.1177/0146167282082007

Woodard, C. R., & Pury, C. L. S. (2007). The construct of courage: Categorization and measurement. *Consulting Psychology Journal: Practice and Research, 59,* 135–147. doi:10.1037/1065-9293.59.2.135

Zillmann, D. (1988). Cognition-excitation interdependencies in aggressive behavior. *Aggressive Behavior, 14,* 51–64. doi:10.1002/1098-2337(1988)14:1<51::AID-AB2480140107>3.0.CO;2-C

Part III

Applied Research and Theory

9

Courage in Combat

Dennis McGurk and Carl Andrew Castro

Courage is resistance to fear, mastery of fear—not absence of fear.
—Mark Twain

The Battlemind Training System (Castro, Hoge, & Cox, 2006) is the cornerstone on which the U.S. Army's mental health training system is based, a system that is being widely accepted and adopted by other nations throughout the world. *Battlemind* is defined as the inner strength to face fear and adversity in combat with courage; *courage* is defined as the power to face unpleasant facts and unpleasant situations and take action despite this awareness. The battlemind model of courage attempts to explain how courage in the military (and civilian life) is developed and sustained by postulating the existence of three interactive components: courageous actions, battlemind, and sustaining forces. Furthermore, within each of these components fundamental processes are occurring that determine whether an unpleasant fact leads to bravery (courageous actions) or to cowardice (cowardly actions or inaction). Courageous actions build self-confidence and mental toughness (battlemind), which are strengthened by both interpersonal and extrapersonal forces (sustaining forces). Thus, in the battlemind model of courage, courage is a complex and dynamic force involving several interacting processes that can be developed and sustained without appealing to supernatural skills, abilities, or predispositions. Although he did not derive his view of courage from empirical evidence, Lord Moran (1945) posited that courage is not something that a person must be born with and not an inherent ability or supernatural skill that only certain special people possess. Though no new evidence has emerged to support Lord Moran's view, the battlemind model of courage builds on his perspective. The battlemind model of courage is a strength-based approach stressing a positive outlook that all service members have the strengths and abilities to be courageous and most will act courageously when in combat.

The battlemind model defines courage as the power to face unpleasant facts and unpleasant situations and to take action despite this awareness. This is a simple definition, yet it avoids the pitfall of defining courage as the absence of fear. We believe defining courage as the absence of fear hinders the intellectual and scientific understanding of courage. In the preceding quote, Mark Twain focused on the essential nature of courage reflected in the battlemind model of courage; that is, courage is not about extinguishing, eliminating, or conquering fear. Fear in combat is normal and healthy and helps ensure that service members (soldiers, marines, sailors, and airmen) and leaders do not take unnecessary risks that might result in loss of lives.

Focusing on fear in courage is too narrow because there are many possible reactions to threats or unpleasant facts other than fear that require courage to overcome. This is especially true in combat. For example, although driving down a road in Iraq or Afghanistan where there may be an improvised explosive device (IED) may inspire fear, dealing with the death of a close unit member in combat is more likely to provoke anger or sadness; yet, in both cases, the service member is still expected to carry on with the mission. Together, fear, anger, and sadness represent the three basic emotions most frequently avoided (Ortony & Turner, 1990; Parrott, 2001). Regardless of the emotional response elicited, courage is required to overcome the threat or unpleasant fact. One of the key tenets of battlemind is that service members have the strengths needed to handle the stressors of combat. The battlemind model of courage also emphasizes that all service members have courage within them and that courage is the result of character, intellect, and effort (Castro, 2006).

Combat affords the opportunity for service members to display their courage. It also provides them with an opportunity to fail. Both outcomes must be simultaneously kept in mind as we discuss courage. The opposite of courage is *cowardice*—a word that is seldom used, but one that needs to be resurrected if our discussion of courage is to have meaning. Approximately 10% of active component soldiers surveyed in Iraq in 2006 reported that their noncommissioned officers (NCOs) never displayed physical courage during their deployment and 13% reported that their officers never displayed physical courage during their deployment (Castro & McGurk, 2007b). Some of these NCOs and officers may not have had a chance to show their physical courage as a result of their job. However, 12% of soldiers reported that their NCOs never displayed moral courage during their deployment, and 13% reported that their officers never displayed moral courage during their deployment. As was the case with physical courage but probably to a lesser extent, some NCOs and officers may not have had the chance to show their moral courage. These data do not show that there are cowards serving in leadership positions in Iraq but suggest that some soldiers believe their leaders lack physical or moral courage.

This chapter expands on previous work (Castro, 2006) and includes data collected from a subsample of more than 1,000 soldiers in brigade combat teams in Iraq during 2006 (Castro & McGurk, 2007b). In addition, examples of service members displaying different components of battlemind courage are used to illustrate how service members display courage in combat. Many courageous acts are being carried out every day by U.S. service members in both Iraq and Afghanistan. The U.S. Army so highly values courage that it includes personal courage on the list of the Army's seven fundamental values (Grojean & Thomas, 2006). Although there are many stories of courage, there is very little scientific literature on courage, especially courage in combat. This chapter is one effort to address this gap in the literature. The material presented in this chapter is based on results from surveys and focus groups conducted during deployments. However, we realize that in this chapter we make strong statements about courage that are not necessarily based on empirical evidence. We base these statements on our combined experience of five combat deployments, interviews with thousands of soldiers across the deployment cycle, and more than 20 years working as uniformed research psychologists. We recognize the risk of making statements that are not based on empirical findings. Our intent is to encourage avenues of future research related to understanding courage in combat.

Battlemind Model of Courage

In response to a survey item asking about the belief that he would be injured or killed during the deployment, a soldier in one of the most dangerous areas of Afghanistan stated, "Is there a chance I will get injured or killed every time I go out on patrol? Yeah, but that doesn't keep me from going out and doing my job." This example illustrates the battlemind model of courage. The soldier faced the unpleasant fact of the possibility of injury or death, yet he went out on missions nearly every day with no mention of fear. It was not that he did not have fear; he just did not let it determine how he was going to behave. His only concern, and the motivation for his behavior, was taking care of his fellow soldiers and doing his job.

Our experience working with soldiers during and after combat leads us to believe that exhibiting courageous actions or witnessing those actions in other unit members builds self-confidence and mental toughness, the two components of battlemind. For service members in combat, self-confidence means believing in themselves and knowing that they can perform their job no matter what obstacles they may face. This is similar to the concept of self-efficacy (Bandura, 1986). We characterize mental toughness in combat as overcoming setbacks and keeping a positive outlook. Combat presents service members with mental challenges that most people will never face. At a minimum, there is separation from loved ones for long periods of time. At the worst, service members see their comrades die and may even have to pick up their buddies' body parts. Castro and McGurk (2007b) found that 42% of soldiers reported they were able to demonstrate their courage. This figure increased to 57% for soldiers who were in brigade combat teams that experienced high combat.

The battlemind model of courage consists of three primary components: (a) courageous actions, (b) battlemind, and (c) sustaining forces. The three components of the battlemind model of courage all interact. When service members in combat support their fellow unit members by actively maneuvering to effectively engage the enemy with small-arms fire (courageous action), service members may realize they have the inner strength to face personal fear and the adversity of combat with courage (battlemind). This realization in turn may lead to improved self-confidence and praise from fellow unit members (supporting forces), which may lead to service members being more likely to actively engage the enemy the next time they receive incoming fire. Thus, engaging in courageous actions leads to the development and sustenance of battlemind. As battlemind is strengthened, interpersonal and intrapersonal forces are fortified. Finally, as the sustaining forces are strengthened, courageous actions become more likely as a result of stronger courage. We now discuss each of these components in more detail.

Courageous Actions

Sergeant First Class Paul Smith, the first service member to receive the Medal of Honor in Iraq, exemplified courage. Sergeant First Class Smith was killed while leading his men against a much larger Iraqi force. He could have ordered his men to withdraw, but according to an officer who was on the scene, Sergeant First Class Smith was concerned about the safety of approximately 100 men and a medical aid station (U.S. Army, n.d.-b). His Medal of Honor citation reads:

> His actions killed 20 to 50 Iraqis, allowing the American wounded to be evacuated, saving the aid station and headquarters (as well as possibly 100 American lives). Fellow soldiers credit Smith with thwarting the advance of well-trained, well-equipped soldiers from the Special Republican Guard, which was headed straight for the 2-7 Task Force's headquarters (Tactical Operations Center), less than a half-mile away.

Sergeant First Class Smith's behavior is an outstanding example of courageous actions, the first component of the battlemind model of courage.

The courageous actions component attempts to explain the relationships between unpleasant facts and situations, adverse emotional responses, and courageous actions. The battlemind model of courage views courageous actions as synonymous with bravery and valor. The objective of all courageous actions is to overcome the unpleasant fact or situation. The emphasis on overcoming the unpleasant fact or situation represents a significant shift from other conceptualizations of courage where the entire focus is on overcoming one emotional response: fear. Indeed, both early (e.g., Rachman, 1976) and more recent (e.g., Ozkaptan, Saint, & Fiero, 2007) theories of courage focused exclusively on overcoming the fear, with little or no attention to the threat or unpleasant fact. For example, Mowrer (1960), a leading theoretician on emotion, explicitly linked fearlessness with courage: "May it not be that courage is simply the absence of fear in a situation where it might be expected to be present?" (p. 435). The U.S. Army equates courage with facing and having to overcome fear (U.S. Army, n.d.-a).

Having an absence of fear is not sufficient to lead to courageous actions. For example, a person may not have fear because of psychosis. This person may actually harm him- or herself or others by engaging in reckless actions. A service member may be so mentally worn down by combat that he or she has become numb and has no fear. The service member may be unable to engage in combat at all. Either way, neither person will engage in courageous actions. As argued earlier, however, fear is only one of many possible responses to unpleasant facts or situations. The battlemind model of courage conceptualizes courage as the bridge between threats and unpleasant facts and actions that are viewed as brave or courageous.

THREAT–ADVERSE EMOTIONAL RESPONSE PROCESS. Embedded within the courageous actions component of the battlemind model of courage is the threat–adverse emotional response process. This process begins with the threat or unpleasant fact and results in an adverse emotional response. Fear, anger, and sadness are the three primary emotional responses that arise in the presence of threats or unpleasant facts (Ortony & Turner, 1990; Parrott, 2001). The threat–adverse emotional response subprocess is recursive, whether the emotional response that ensues from the threat involves fear, anger, or sadness. For example, the perception of a threat that leads to fear may in turn lead to an increase in the perceived threat, which in turn may lead to an increase in fear, which may lead to an increase in the perceived threat, and so on. In combat, the service member may perceive the threat of sniper fire and this may lead to fear of being shot, which will lead to an increase in the perception that there may be sniper fire. Notice in this example that it is not the unpleasant fact or threat (sniper fire) per se that induces fear but the outcome (being shot) that one expects to occur as a result of the threat or unpleasant fact. Often, though, what one expects to occur in the presence of a threat, particularly when accompanied by fear, is very unlikely, and sometimes even irrational, such as with certain phobias like aerophobia, the fear of flying. Airplane flight is statistically safer than driving, but people with aerophobia may expect a horrific plane crash and not be able to fly. Many adverse emotional responses such as fear, anger, and sadness are often able to influence thoughts and behavior, causing people to believe and do things that they otherwise would not. We theorize that it is this aspect of the threat–adverse emotional response process makes it so treacherous, and is why the cycle must be broken as soon as possible.

The adverse emotional responses elicited by perceived threats or unpleasant facts and events are automatic. In the presence of the threat, the emotional response follows without requiring any action on the part of the affected individual. In certain situations, such reflexive responses can be adaptive. For example, in combat when the enemy is using improvised explosive devices (IEDs) on many roads, fear can serve to increase one's awareness of the environment and assist in identifying signs that there may be an IED, thereby increasing one's likelihood of surviving. In this case, the fear response is an advantage. However, if fear causes a person to freeze, thereby exposing him or her to enemy fire, or results in his or her refusal to assist a wounded team member because of fear of being wounded or killed, then fear in this case is a disadvantage, and that person would be seen as a coward. Similarly, a service member who is angry about losing one of his or her buddies may be more likely to fire indiscriminately into a building when taking sniper fire from that building. Thus in the latter two cases, emotional responses such as fear and anger are viewed as aversive or undesirable. However, by learning to correctly identify which emotional responses are likely to occur in specific threatening situations, soldiers can develop ahead of time the appropriate actions to take when the threatening event actually does occur. For example, training in situations where a certain level of fear is present can help link action, rather than inaction, with fear. Further, anticipating how others might respond in threatening situations can help people be more conscious of the need to act because others are not likely to do so. Again, training conducted in intact units can help with this. These remedies for responding to adverse emotional responses, however, are possible only if the emotion is brought to the level of consciousness. Training may result in actions becoming automatic, but if the emotional response is not brought to the level of consciousness, the actions would not be considered bravery. These unpleasant facts and the possible brave actions in response can take the form of moral, physical, or vital courage.

The threat–adverse emotional response process may be terminated in one of three ways: The threat is ignored, the threat ends, or the threat is confronted and action is taken. Perceiving an event as threatening or unpleasant yet ignoring it or failing to take action is a form of cowardice. A particularly damaging example is if a leader fails to defend a subordinate from unjust punishment or accusations. The leader doing nothing in this circumstance can result in decline in unit morale as well as a loss of faith in the unit leadership.

The threat might also end without any action being taken. For example, imagine you are on a combat patrol when your squad comes under machine gun attack. Without prompt action, every member of the squad will be killed. While you are formulating your plan of action, one of the men in your squad determines the location of the machine gun and throws several grenades at the machine gun site, killing all the enemy combatants. In this example, the threat was eliminated by the courageous action of someone else. However, waiting for someone else to act so you do not have to assume any risks is a form of cowardice.

The final way a threat can be ended is by confronting the unpleasant facts or situations and taking action; this is bravery. Whereas courage involves facing unpleasant facts or situations, bravery represents the behaviors that are referred to as *courageous actions*. Thus, bravery requires action directed toward overcoming the threat, and it is courage that provides the basis for the action. The greater the threat or unpleasant facts that must be surmounted, the greater the bravery required. That is why risking one's life to save a fellow service member in combat is typically viewed as a braver act than is risking one's social standing in the community by defending an unpopular politician. There are numerous examples of extremely high threat events resulting in highly courageous actions. For example, several soldiers and marines have been awarded the Medal of Honor for having placed their bodies on grenades to save the lives of their fellow soldiers or marines. Important to note, however, is that whether one is successful or not in overcoming the threat is not the issue, as there can be no doubt that assuming risks to do the right thing involves courage.

It is possible that the threat–adverse emotional response process is never activated because the threat or unpleasant fact is not perceived as threatening or harmful. That is, one can refuse to acknowledge that the unpleasant fact exists even after having been appraised of the situation. This is a form of denial, which is also a form of cowardice. For the action to be courageous, there must be an accurate perception of the threat. For example, someone with a mental disorder or an impaired intellect could not, in many cases, engage in courageous actions because he or she lacks the mental resources to appropriately assess the situation. In combat, a service member may decide that the enemy is not dangerous and refuse to take extra safety measures even if intelligence reports say large numbers of the enemy are present. This may result in the service member or other unit members being injured or killed. Another reason the threat or unpleasant fact may not be perceived as threatening is ignorance or a lack of knowledge. For example, early in the war in Iraq, insurgents placed IEDs inside the carcasses of animals. For a short time, service members did not know that this new technique was being used and they had no fear of dead animals along the side of the road. Information about this method of hiding IEDs was quickly passed among service members, and animal carcasses were avoided whenever possible.

BATTLEMIND. Engaging in courageous actions is likely to lead directly to personal growth and professional development. Similar to Finfgeld's (1999) notion of *courageous self,* the battlemind model of courage denotes that as individuals live courageously (i.e., engage in courageous actions) they experience the emergence of self-confidence and mental toughness, and they are fundamentally different from the persons they used to be. In many respects this is what we, the authors, mean when we speak of character development: that the person has changed, that personal growth has occurred. This personal growth can be seen in service members who report a new appreciation for the important things in life, such as family and friends, following a combat deployment. Four months after returning from a 15-month combat tour, one soldier reported that "coming back I've realized that I've become a more down-to-earth man and more understanding. After the war I will probably take nothing for granted" (Adler, 2008).

The term *battlemind* was coined by General Crosbie Saint (Ozkaptan et al., 2007) when he was the commanding general of the U.S. Army in Europe. Battlemind refers to one's inner strength to face fear and adversity with courage. For a service member, it is the will to persevere and win in combat, whether engaging in day-to-day contact with the enemy or filling support roles. The previously mentioned soldier in Afghanistan who said he knew there was a chance he would die on every patrol but kept doing his job is a good example of battlemind. The inclusion of battlemind in the model recognizes the fact that courageous actions are likely to lead directly to personal development. The two main factors of the battlemind component are self-confidence and mental toughness.

Self-confidence is defined from an occupational health perspective as believing that one can do one's job no matter what situation one finds oneself in. It involves the ability to take calculated risks and to handle future challenges when confronted with threats or unpleasant facts. Making such calculated decisions requires compassion, intellect, and maturity. It means taking thoughtful and directed actions that are designed to reduce or eliminate the threat or unpleasant fact instead of taking rash and impetuous actions. It involves the ability to develop multiple courses of action and select the right one. This ability is extremely important in combat, where choosing the wrong course of action may result in greater numbers of wounded or dead service members than would choosing the best course of action. As with any skill, the capacity to develop and identify the best course of action to pursue to overcome threats requires practice and effort and improves with experience. As General Charles C. Krulak (1995) said,

> You need to reach back to your moral touchstone to ensure that who you are and what you stand for is as large a part of your professional reputation as your ability to drive tanks, lead troops, fly helicopters or draft an overlay.

Similarly, Ozkaptan et al. (2007) reported that

> the warrior intuitively knows the integrity of his leaders, will assure that they will have the courage of their convictions, the boldness and strength to take chances, and most fundamentally to do the right thing (honor) under the stress of battle. (p. 55)

We define mental toughness as not quitting when setbacks occur. Setbacks are a part of combat. Bad things happen in war, up to and including having unit members killed. Nearly 60% of soldiers surveyed in Iraq in 2006 reported they had a member of their unit become a casualty, and 70% said they knew someone seriously injured or killed (Castro & McGurk, 2007b). Mental toughness means being able to continue with the mission when these setbacks occur and keep a positive mental outlook. As an example, in Iraq in 2006, nearly 50% of the soldiers surveyed who stated that they had a unit member injured or killed reported medium to very high personal morale (Castro & McGurk, 2007b).

SUSTAINING FORCES. Numerous factors may sustain, facilitate, or enhance courageous actions. These factors are located within the sustaining forces component of the battlemind model of courage. The two broad categories of sustaining forces are intrapersonal and interpersonal variables (Finfgeld, 1999).

Intrapersonal variables include enabling values and experiences of successful coping in the face of threats and unpleasant facts. The idea that there are values that ensure courageous actions is not new. For example, wisdom and temperance have been associated with courage (e.g., Welton, 1922). Within a military environment, enabling values such as discipline, intellect, subordination, fairness, brotherhood, and trust is probably a good place to begin a systematic investigation into how values sustain courageous actions. Ozkaptan et al. (2007) provided an excellent discussion of enabling values and their role in the development of courage.

Successfully confronting unpleasant facts is also a sustaining force for engaging in courageous actions in the future. As Porter (1888) stated, "The moral influence of the prestige which comes from past success does much towards developing courage" (p. 253). The battlemind model of courage posits that service members who have experienced success when facing unpleasant facts and situations will develop a belief that they will be successful in coping with future difficulties. In addition, taking action can have the positive effect of distracting the service member from his or her fear. Past success with action-oriented coping strategies directed at reducing or eliminating the unpleasant fact provides support for future courageous behavior, as compared with passive strategies involving ignoring or avoiding the unpleasant fact. In fact, we propose that overcoming past failures of courage (cowardice) is just as important for sustaining future courageous actions because failures in courage can decrease self-confidence and increase the likelihood to fail to act courageously in the future. Leaders may also aid in helping service members overcome past failures by supporting them, encouraging success, and setting up a situation in which those service members can succeed.

Interpersonal variables include role models and gestures of support. Role models are critical for developing and sustaining courageous actions. As

Ozkaptan et al. (2007) noted, leaders personify the values of the organization, transmit those values, and ensure the values are disseminated throughout the organization. In addition, courageous leaders as role models are important for developing other courageous leaders. Subordinate leaders will learn how to be courageous by following the example set for them by more senior leaders. Without role models, courage is likely to remain an abstract concept that has no effect on the organization. An example of role modeling is provided in the 1919 Medal of Honor citation of First Lieutenant George Robb (cited in Ozkaptan et al., 2007):

> Displaying wonderful courage and tenacity at the critical times. . . . His example of bravery and fortitude and his eagerness to continue with his mission despite severe wounds set before the enlisted men of his company a most wonderful standard of morale and self-sacrifice. (p. 9)

Gestures of support can be thought of as means of encouragement or incentives and include actions such as telling someone "good job" and giving monetary rewards, promotions, or awards. Gestures of support are extremely helpful when service members are confronted with threatening situations or unpleasant facts. Although gestures of support are not absolutely necessary for courageous actions to occur, they are certainly necessary for the creation of an environment that fosters courageous behaviors. Providing gestures of support is the responsibility of leaders within an organization. We strongly believe that leaders should not tolerate the ridiculing or minimizing of courageous actions. In units where soldiers reported their NCOs often or always embarrassed them, 65% reported having low or very low morale compared with 40% in units where NCOs never or sometimes embarrassed soldiers (Castro & McGurk, 2007b). Gestures of support should communicate a sense of respect and admiration for the individual confronting the threat. Oftentimes, courageous actions require personal sacrifices, and these sacrifices should be acknowledged publicly and privately. Courageous actions should be rewarded. In the military this typically involves the awarding of medals or promotions.

The objective of these types of recognition is to encourage other unit members to also engage in courageous actions. When a service member is awarded, it improves his or her self-esteem and this may lead to more courageous acts. This area needs further research. Courage, like fear, is contagious (see Worline, 2004). Although most service members who perform courageous acts are not generally motivated by the desire for an award, others who see the courageous individual receiving an award may not only want to emulate that service member but may also have more respect for and loyalty to the unit leaders who give the awards. Service members will gladly follow those leaders who have promoted and recognized their personal growth (Ozkaptan et al., 2007).

The way in which punishment is administered when service members have made a mistake can also develop or impede courage. First, there must be clear expectations and standards of behavior for all service members as well as clear expectations of punishment for violating the standards (Ozkaptan et al., 2007). To develop courage, leaders must ensure they focus on the service member's action and not attack the service member's character. When a leader publicly embarrasses a service member, that leader sets up a zero-defect climate that does not encourage initiative and self-confidence, two hallmarks of courage.

Intrapersonal and interpersonal sustaining forces can influence each other to either facilitate or hinder courageous actions. Role models and gestures of support can facilitate and encourage the development of enabling values and successful coping strategies even in the absence of prior courageous behavior. In addition, soldiers anecdotally report that when a soldier fails to act courageously on the battlefield, his or her self-confidence and self-esteem are adversely impacted, especially if he or she is a member of a unit in which courageous behaviors are highly esteemed. Reports from mental health providers in Iraq indicate that many soldiers who seek mental health care do so as a result of their perception of failing to act in a courageous manner on the battlefield. This clearly is an area that requires further research. Supportive leadership can provide the shamed soldier with another opportunity to redeem him- or herself. In this case, supportive leadership can right the negative consequences of previous cowardly behavior. Conversely, the absence of role models and a unit climate that does not encourage and reward courageous behaviors will not facilitate courageous actions and can even cause their extinction. It is for this reason that prior courageous actions are not sufficient by themselves to ensure future courageous actions.

Multilevel Forces

The battlemind model of courage loops from the courageous actions component where bravery occurs to the battlemind component where character development takes place, to the sustaining forces component, and so on. The overall flow of the model is unidirectional and circular. However, the interpersonal forces that sustain courageous behavior are found at numerous levels that are mutually reinforcing. This makes the battlemind model of courage dynamic in that external factors can influence courageous actions. At the individual level, unit members can foster a courageous environment by recognizing and praising courageous actions that they observe in each other. Leaders can also foster an environment where courageous behaviors occur by serving as role models and by directly rewarding those unit members who display courageous behaviors, both physical and moral. The military organization fosters a courageous environment by clearly communicating the importance of courage and how courageous behaviors will be recognized, rewarded, and inculcated into the military culture. We believe that this must be done for displays of moral as well as physical courage. For example, it is very rare that a leader gets awarded for standing up for one of his or her service members who has been wrongly accused. However, this kind of moral courage can lead to courageous actions by all members of the unit.

Data From Iraq

In the following two sections we use data collected from a subsample of more than 1,000 soldiers in brigade combat teams in Iraq during 2006 (Castro & McGurk, 2007b) to describe several aspects of courage in combat. In the first section we discuss moral versus physical courage. Following that, we use data from Iraq to explore the relationship between courage and mental health.

Moral Versus Physical Courage

The U.S. Army defines personal courage as "our ability to face fear, danger, or adversity (physical and moral)" (U.S. Army, n.d.-a). With physical courage, it is a matter of enduring physical duress and risking personal safety. Every day in Iraq and Afghanistan many service members endure the duress of working 14-hour days in heat or cold, sometimes 7 days a week. They risk their personal safety every time they leave their forward operating base. There is no shortage of displays of physical courage among the men and women who are in the units that are doing the fighting in Iraq and Afghanistan. Moral courage entails facing adversity when confronted with the choice to do the right thing, even if it may not be popular or it may harm one's career. Moral courage begins at an early age, cultivated by the family and in schools (Ozkaptan et al., 2007). Just as with physical courage, there are many opportunities for displays of moral courage in Iraq and Afghanistan. Leaders sometimes may have to tell their higher commanders that their unit is receiving too many missions even though this may not curry favor with those higher commanders. More extreme displays of moral courage include service members choosing to not injure or kill noncombatants (the right choice) instead of expressing their anger over losing unit members by injuring or killing noncombatants (the wrong choice).

Most people may think only of physical courage when talking about courage in combat. However, moral courage is also an important factor in whether wars are won or lost. Moral courage should not be ignored when discussing courage or when training leaders. Like Ozkaptan et al. (2007), we believe that both moral and physical courage are signs of a service member's character and vital to both leaders and individual service members' effectiveness in combat. Similarly, moral courage too may be viewed as an ongoing struggle because numerous decisions in one's daily life require actions that may be viewed as unpopular or threatening to one's job or livelihood. It is this aspect of moral courage, that it is constant and ongoing, that has led many to claim it as the superior form of courage. According to Ozkaptan et al., moral courage is the building block of physical courage and they use the term *courage* to mean both physical and morale courage. The U.S. Army differentiates between physical and moral courage, but is there evidence other than definitional that real meaning is obtained by making this distinction?

One area that we evaluated in the study mentioned previously (Castro & McGurk, 2007b) was the effect of leaders displaying moral or physical courage on soldiers' reports of mental health. Although both moral courage and physical courage in leaders are highly correlated, their relationship to soldiers' mental health is different. These differences will be explored in greater detail later.

It has been proposed that there are three types of courage (Lopez, O'Byrne, & Petersen, 2003). In addition to physical and moral courage, there is also a third type of courage, vital courage. Vital courage may be defined as carrying on with life while enduring a long-term illness or injury such as dealing with an amputation resulting from combat. Finfgeld (1999) referred to the chronically ill as engaging in an ongoing, neverending struggle. However, in many ways, this ongoing struggle with life-long injuries is synonymous with the courage of endurance by means of which service members at war survive, albeit on a much shorter timeline, when they are called on time and time again to risk their lives in service to their country (Hynes, 1997). Vital courage is an even more important issue with the number of service members who were wounded while serving in Iraq or Afghanistan. As of February 2008, more than 29,000 service members have been wounded; over 1,000 of those are amputees (Fischer, 2008). Many of these men and women deal with chronic pain, loss of their livelihood, and the stigma of being labeled handicapped. Another important but less visible example of vital courage is evident in those service members who have mental health problems such as posttraumatic stress disorder (PTSD) and seek treatment in spite of possible psychological stigma (i.e., being seen as weak) and organizational barriers (i.e., transportation to treatment is not available). This concept is similar to what Putman (1997) referred to as psychological courage. Putman defined psychological courage as the strength to confront and work through mental health problems.

The Buffering Effect of Courage on Soldier Mental Health

Research has shown that the level of combat experienced by a service member is the primary stressor related to mental health outcomes (Castro & McGurk, 2007b). Courage can be viewed as a protective measure against the effects of combat experience on many measures of mental health and well-being, including morale, anger, and posttraumatic stress. Ozkaptan et al. (2007) hypothesized that service members who can manage or control their fear have less risk of developing battle fatigue. In addition, courage may lead to service members experiencing a more positive effect of their deployment. To test these hypotheses (see Figure 9.1), we conducted regressions using courage as a moderator of the relationship between combat experiences and the previously mentioned mental health outcomes and positive effect of the deployment (Castro & McGurk, 2007b). Gender and rank were controlled for in the analyses. Personal courage was measured by asking service members whether "during this deployment, I was able to demonstrate my courage." Responses ranged from *Never* to *Five or more times.* We found that personal courage accounted for unique variance in all of the outcomes: Those who reported they had displayed their courage had higher morale, less anger, fewer symptoms of posttraumatic stress, and more positive effects of their deployment.

Similarly, courageous leaders may be thought to "protect" the service members who make up their unit by creating a climate that reduces the effects of combat. Consistent with this, Worline (2004) reported a similar finding in business environments. Ozkaptan et al. (2007) hypothesized that leaders' displays of courage help maintain a service members' fortitude. We tested this by conducting regression analyses using both NCO and officer physical and moral courage as moderators of the relationship between combat and measures of unit climate. NCO and officer physical and moral courage were measured with one-item questions that were asked of junior enlisted soldiers only. The questions were "In your unit, NCOs are viewed by soldiers as having physical courage"; "In your unit, officers are viewed by soldiers as having physical courage"; "In your unit, NCOs are viewed by soldiers as having moral courage"; and "In your unit, officers are

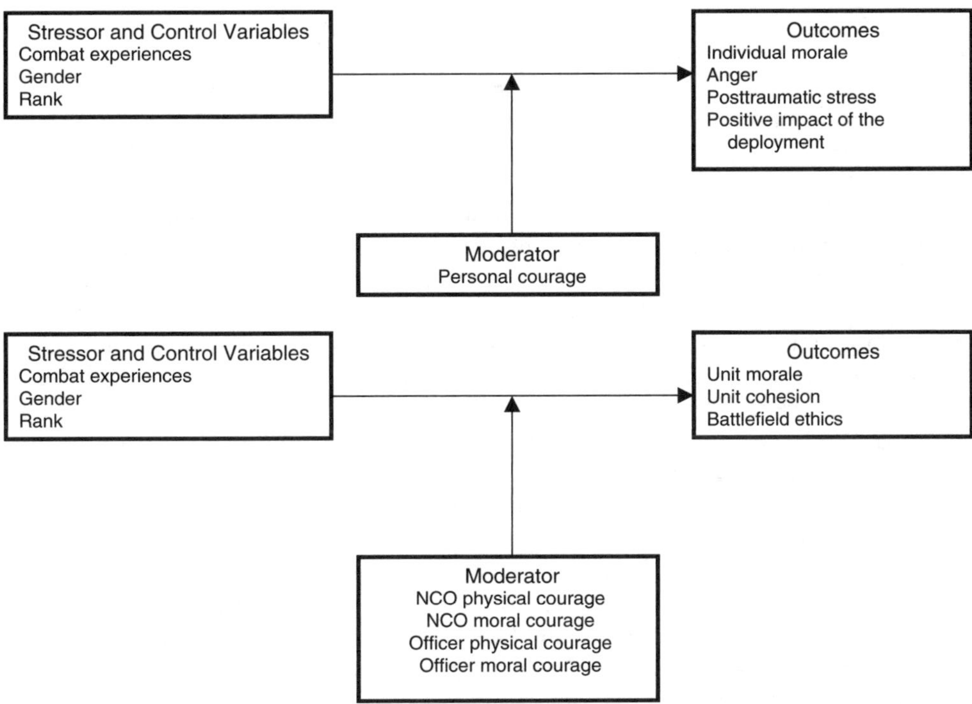

Figure 9.1. Analyses model. NCO = noncommissioned officer.

viewed by soldiers as having moral courage." Responses ranged from *Never* to *Always*. The analyses evaluated the buffering effect of NCO and officer courage on the effect of combat on unit morale and unit cohesion while controlling for gender, rank, and soldier personal courage. NCO and officer moral courage accounted for unique variance in unit morale. When soldiers rated their NCOs and officers positively, the negative effect of combat on morale was less than for those soldiers who rated their leaders less positively. However, only NCO physical and moral courage accounted for unique variance in unit cohesion (Castro & McGurk, 2007b). Where officers may have spent time with individuals and therefore affected their morale, the finding of no relationship between officer courage and unit cohesion may be due to NCOs spending much more time with the junior enlisted soldiers while conducting group activities and therefore having a greater effect on unit cohesion.

Battlefield Ethics

Battlefield ethics is defined as how service members think about combatants and noncombatants and how they act toward both groups during combat operations. The Mental Health Advisory Team IV (Castro & McGurk, 2007a) conceptualized battlefield ethics in four domains: (a) attitudes, (b) training, (c) reporting, and (d) behaviors. Attitudes included items such as "all non-combatants should be treated as insurgents"; training items included "I received training in the proper treatment of non-combatants"; reporting items included "I would report a unit member for mistreatment of a non-combatant"; and, finally, behavior items included "physically hit/kicked a non-combatant when it was not necessary."

By exhibiting either physical or moral courage, courageous leaders can set a unit climate in which service members know they cannot commit battlefield ethical violations. We tested this by comparing rates of ethical violations, defined as "damaging/destroying private property when it was not necessary" or "hitting/kicking non-combatants when it was not necessary," among soldiers who reported their units had NCOs and officers who exhibited physical and moral courage. The only significant predictor was NCOs exhibiting moral courage. When soldiers reported their NCOs exhibited moral courage, a significantly lower number reported that they committed ethical violations. Reports of NCO physical courage and both officer physical and moral courage were not related to whether soldiers committed ethical violations. This pattern may be the result of soldiers expecting their NCOs to show physical courage and the fact that far fewer officers are with the soldiers in situations where ethical violations may occur. Compared with NCOs, a higher percentage of officers never leave the base camp and therefore would not have the opportunity to commit ethical violations or for their subordinates to see them commit violations.

Prescription for the Development of Courage

In the following section, we describe the role of the organization, group, leaders, and individual in developing courage. In addition, we discuss a controversial subject: the development of the opposite of courage, cowardice. Finally, we show how the battlemind model of courage is applicable outside the military.

Role of the Organization

It is our belief that the best way for the military to assist in developing courage is by conducting hard, realistic training that involves a controlled level of fear and uses intact units. This would also apply to other organizations (i.e., law enforcement and firefighters) in which fear is a part of the job. For organizations that do not have fear as part of their profession, the training should be realistic and involve pressure to perform such as placing time demands on participants. As previously mentioned, service members often report that their training kicked in when they faced stressful situations. That is why it is so important for training to be realistic. As previously mentioned, training involving a controlled level of fear helps soldiers associate fear and actions to reduce that fear. Finally, this type of training may develop cohesion, which can have a positive effect on unit members' well-being. When intact units train together, cohesion is nurtured, and it will continue to grow while the unit is deployed.

Ozkaptan et al. (2007) correctly described training as the glue that holds units together.

Two training methods for reducing fear and developing courage are stress inoculation and stress desensitization training (e.g., Kellett, 1982; Rachman, 1976). Stress inoculation training through virtual reality or situational training is not the solution. This type of training may help service members do their jobs under stress but no studies have shown that it prevents fears, PTSD, or any other adverse outcomes, nor does it directly build courage. The flawed logic of stress desensitization is that fear in combat is viewed as a phobia. The falsity of this logic was clearly articulated over 100 years ago (Porter, 1888). Phobias are irrational fears; being afraid in combat is not irrational. Combat is dangerous; fellow soldiers are injured and killed in combat. This is why procedures designed to treat phobias will not be effective in handling fear in combat. The fact that soldiers on their third or fourth deployment were at significantly higher risk than were soldiers on their first or second deployment for mental health problems and work-related problems (Office of the Surgeon, 2008) provides actual proof that this "stress inoculation" approach does not work.

Role of the Group

Unit-level attributes such as cooperation, communal will, and the resulting comradeship can increase individual courage (Ozkaptan et al., 2007). Cooperation, which is defined as service members being together and working together, can be developed by having units train together. Communal will occurs when service members work together for a common goal and develops when training requires teamwork to achieve goals.

Comradeship is the result of cooperation and communal will. According to Ozkaptan et al. (2007), comradeship is the deep emotional bond among service members that is formed in combat and can last a lifetime. Comradeship results in subordination of the self and elevation of the group's goals. Comradeship can increase individual courage by (a) the mere presence of fellow service members, (b) the sense of immortality when the group survives, and (c) communal will (Ozkaptan et al., 2007). Many service members have expressed the adage that they do not fight for their country—they fight for the man to their left and the man to their right. In the Iraq study (Castro & McGurk, 2007b), soldiers in high-cohesion units were more likely to have demonstrated their courage than were soldiers in low-cohesion units.

Role of the Leaders

A leader's responsibility is to develop fortitude in his or her subordinates, and this is best done during training (Ozkaptan et al., 2007). This fortitude in the face of danger is what General Saint originally called *battlemind.* It is a state of mind that can be developed by good training. Service members must have confidence in their leaders' competence as well as their loyalty.

Leaders must remove incompetent subordinate leaders as well as service members who do not meet standards. Fear, like courage, is contagious and can destroy a unit. Good leadership can help a unit achieve its mission as well as improve the quality of life of unit members. Kolditz (2007) postulated that good leadership is especially important in in-extremis situations, that is, in dangerous settings. Combat is a very dangerous setting, for both the leader and the led. Leaders in the military must risk their own lives in combat just as their subordinates do (Ozkaptan et al., 2007). One requirement of a good leader, whether in peacetime or in combat, is that he or she display courage. The best way to create courageous service members is by leaders displaying courage at every opportunity that presents itself. As previously mentioned, subordinate leaders will learn how to lead by following the example set for them by more senior leaders.

Alternatively, cowardly leaders can have a detrimental effect on a unit. A soldier in Afghanistan reported that a behavioral health provider refused to go on a convoy because of fear for his safety. This was viewed as an act of cowardice considering that all other service members were required to go on convoys when told to do so. When the word got out that this provider refused to go on the convoy, he lost all credibility with the service members he was supposed to support, and the majority refused to see him. Those who wanted to speak to a behavioral health provider decided to wait until another provider was available and that sometimes took weeks. As a result, the unit suffered because service members who had mental health problems did not get the help they needed. Displays of cowardice by any leader must not be allowed.

Role of the Individual

Courage is not about faith or religious beliefs. It is not about finding God. Religion, as well as other spiritual belief systems, can be helpful to the extent that it gets service members to face up to the tough facts and do the right thing. In some cases, a service member's faith may lead to increased courage because of a belief in eternal life (Ozkaptan et al., 2007). In addition, faith can lead to increased courage through the belief that a "higher power" will protect the service member from harm. Prayer during combat can lead to increased courage through contemplation and focusing of consciousness (Ozkaptan et al., 2007).

"Discipline mitigates the effects of fear" (Ozkaptan et al., 2007, p. 28). Service members who are highly disciplined will react automatically instead of freezing when faced with a fearful situation. Many service members in Iraq and Afghanistan reported they went on "autopilot" during fearful events. They said their training kicked in and they reacted automatically. The automatic nature of the response during combat is what allows service members to make split-second decisions that may be lethal to the enemy. In addition, discipline may lead to greater courage by counteracting negative fear reactions such as abandoning a position or comrades. A popular saying provides comfort to service members: "Leave no one behind." Service members are taught that they will not be left by their fellow unit members and they should ensure they never leave one of their unit members behind. Believing that no one will be left behind may provide comfort to service members because they can be sure that someone is looking out for them as they look out for others.

Development of Cowardice

As was mentioned in the introduction, the word *cowardice* is seldom used, but we feel it is necessary in any discussion of courage. The prescription of developing cowardice is the opposite of developing courage and also consists of three primary components: (a) cowardly actions by individuals or leaders, (b) giving in to fear, and (c) sustaining negative forces. The three components all interact. When a service member in combat lets his or her fellow unit members down by failing to effectively engage the enemy with small-arms fire, or a leader does not set a good example by leading from the front (cowardly actions), this may result in service members giving in to their fear of combat (giving in to fear); this is turn will lead to unit members losing their confidence or leaders not recognizing acts of moral and physical courage (supporting forces), which will lead to the service member being less likely to actively engage the enemy next time he or she receives incoming fire. When service members or leaders engage in cowardly actions, it leads to the destruction of battlemind. As battlemind is weakened and fear reigns, interpersonal and intrapersonal forces need to be fortified to regain battlemind. If this does not occur, and the sustaining forces do not reverse the course, cowardly actions become more likely.

Applicability of the Battlemind Model of Courage Outside the Military

Battlemind is the service member's inner strength to face fear and adversity in combat with courage. By definition, battlemind is focused on combat. However, the strengths that allow service members to handle the challenges of combat are also applicable to those who never engage the enemy and to those who are not deployed, and are relevant to organizations outside the military. Challenges due to facing unpleasant facts and situations are present in all aspects of life and in every work environment. Therefore, having self-confidence and mental toughness when faced with these challenges will help in any environment. In other high-risk organizations outside the military (e.g., law enforcement, firefighters), physical courage and, in some cases, vital courage, may be very important. However, moral courage is important for all people in all situations.

Conclusion

The battlemind model of courage asserts that courage is not about fear; it is about facing unpleasant facts and situations and taking action despite this awareness. Combat challenges service members with many unpleasant facts and situations in which to display their courage, and most service members and their leaders show both moral and physical courage. Unfortunately, a significant number of service members are also forced to display vital courage. Vital courage is the strength to carry on with life while dealing with permanent injuries such as amputation(s). The battlemind model of courage explains that courage is the result of the interaction of courageous actions, battlemind, and sustaining forces such as role models and gestures of support. Courage is developed within the individual but affected (potentially positively or negatively) by the organization, the group, and their leaders. Within the individual, courage may be influenced by such things as the person's religion and self-discipline. Data from Iraq demonstrate the importance of both individual courage and courageous leadership in terms of soldier well-being and battlefield ethics. However, more research on courage and courageous leadership is needed to further define and identify the processes and how courageous leaders may be developed.

References

Adler, A. B. (2008). [Transition strategies and soldier behavioral health following combat deployment]. Unpublished raw data.

Bandura, A. (1986). *Social foundations of thought and action: A social cognitive theory.* Englewood Cliffs, NJ: Prentice-Hall.

Castro, C. A. (2006). Military courage. In T. Britt, A. Adler, & C. Castro (Eds.), *Military life: The psychology of serving in peace and combat* (Vol. 4, pp. 60–78). Westport, CT: Praeger.

Castro, C. A., Hoge, C. W., & Cox, A. L. (2006). Battlemind training: Building soldier resiliency. In *Human dimensions in military operations – Military leaders' strategies for addressing stress and psychological support* (pp. 42-1–42-6). Meeting proceedings RTO-MP-HFM-134, Paper 42. Neuilly-sur-Seine, France: RTO.

Castro, C. A., & McGurk, D. (2007a). Battlefield ethics. *Traumatology, 13,* 24–31. Retrieved from http://tmt.sagepub.com/cgi/content/abstract/13/4/24

Castro, C. A., & McGurk, D. (2007b). The intensity of combat and behavioral health status. *Traumatology, 13,* 6–23. Retrieved from http://tmt.sagepub.com/cgi/content/abstract/13/4/6

Finfgeld, D. L. (1999). Courage as a process of pushing beyond the struggle. *Qualitative Health Research, 9,* 803–814.

Fischer, H. (2009). *United States military casualty statistics: Operation Iraqi Freedom and Operation Enduring Freedom.* Congressional Research Service Report for Congress. Retrieved from http://www.fas.org/sgp/crs/natsec/RS22452.pdf

Grojean, M. W., & Thomas, J. L. (2006). From values to performance: It's the journey that changes the traveler. In T. Britt, A. Adler, & C. Castro (Eds.), *Military life: The psychology of serving in peace and combat* (pp. 35–59). Westport, CT: Praeger.

Hynes, S. (1997). *The soldier's tale.* New York, NY: Penguin.Kellett, A. (1982). *Combat motivation: The behavior of soldiers in battle.* Boston, MA: Kluwer-Nijhoff.

Kolditz, T. A. (2007). *In extremis leadership: Leading as if your life depended on it.* San Francisco, CA: Jossey-Bass.

Krulak, C. C. (1995, November). Military courage. Speech presented at the Command and General Staff College, Fort Leavenworth, Kansas.

Lopez, S., O'Byrne, K. K., & Petersen, S. (2003). Profiling courage. In S. Lopez & C. Snyder (Eds.), *Positive psychological assessment: A handbook of models and measures* (pp. 185–197). Washington, DC: American Psychological Association.

Office of the Surgeon Multi-National Force-Iraq, Office of the Command Surgeon, and Office of the Surgeon General United States Army Medical Command. (2008). *Mental Health Advisory Team (MHAT) V.* Retrieved from http://www.armymedicine.army.mil/reports/mhat/mhat_v/mhat-v.cfm

Moran, L. (1945). *The anatomy of courage.* Boston, MA: Houghton Mifflin.

Mowrer, O. H. (1960). *Learning theory and behavior.* New York, NY: Wiley.

Ortony, A., & Turner, T. J. (1990). What's basic about basic emotions? *Psychological Review, 97,* 315–331.

Ozkaptan, H., Saint, C. E., & Fiero, R. S. (2007). *Conquering fear: Development of courage in soldiers and other high-risk occupations.* Available from http://lulu.com/ebsi

Parrott, W. (2001). *Emotions in social psychology.* Philadelphia, PA: Psychology Press.

Porter, H. (1888, June). The philosophy of courage. *Century Magazine,* 246–254.

Putman, D. (1997). Psychological courage. *Philosophy, Psychiatry, & Psychology 4.1,* 1–11.
Rachman, S. J. (1976). Courage, fearlessness and fear. *New Scientist, 44,* 271–273.
Rachman, S. J. (1984). Fear and courage. *Behavior Therapy, 15,* 109–120.
Saint, C. E. (1992). Battlemind guidelines for battalion commanders. *United States Army, Europe, and Seventh Army Training Manual.* Heidelberg, Germany: U.S. Army Europe.
U.S. Army. (n.d.-a). *Soldier life: Living the Army values.* Retrieved from http://www.goarmy.com/life/living_the_army_values.jsp#courage
U.S. Army. (n.d.-b). *Official citation.* Retrieved from http://www.army.mil/medalofhonor/smith/citation/index.html
Welton, J. (1922). *Groundwork of ethics.* London, England: Clive.
Worline, M. C. (2004). Dancing the cliff edge: The place of courage in social life. *Dissertation Abstracts International: Section B: Sciences and engineering, 65*(2B), 1016. (UMI No. 3122074)

10

Developing Courage in Followers: Theoretical and Applied Perspectives

Paul B. Lester, Gretchen R. Vogelgesang, Sean T. Hannah, and Ted Kimmey, Jr.

Although interest in courage has recently grown among both practitioners and researchers, little is known about how courage is developed (Goud, 2005). Gaining an understanding of the process of how individuals become courageous is especially important to military, public safety, and other communities that operate in harm's way because moral, social, or physical courage, or a combination of all three, is often necessary to meet organizational goals within the high-risk, high-stakes environments in which these communities typically operate. In addition, recent large-scale financial scandals in both the for- and nonprofit sectors suggest that the development of moral and social courage could be important for organizational survival. It is fortunate that several of these organizations appear to clearly understand the importance of courage. For example, courage is a codified core value of both the U.S. Army and Navy, and it, or one of its components (e.g., bravery), is highlighted in the values of the Federal Bureau of Investigation, the U.S. Marshals Service, the U.S. Secret Service, the New York Fire Department, the French Foreign Legion, and the Israeli Defense Force.

It is interesting that, in many of these organizations, individuals tend to discount the courageousness of their actions (Worline, Wrzesniewski, & Rafaeli, 2002), belying the subjective nature of courage (Hannah, Sweeney, & Lester, 2007). For example, though a bystander may witness the actions of firefighters or police officers and conclude that the acts were courageous, there is a tendency for members of these organizations to simply state that they "were just doing their job" or that they "did what anyone would" in that particular situation. This suggests that those individuals occupying social roles in which displays of courage are expected may not necessarily believe that their actions are courageous. Rachman (1990), for example, held that self-conceptualizations of their role propel soldiers to act in a courageous manner. This suggests that courage is connected to one's identity and therefore is influenced through social learning processes and during the socialization process. This phenomenon highlights one of the many complexities organizations face in the development of courage in that attributions of courage appear to be context-specific.

Nevertheless, the questions remain: Can courage be developed? If so, how is it developed? Sekerka and Bagozzi (2007), Goud (2005), Worline, Wrzesniewski, and Rafaeli (2002), and others have called for inquiry into the developmental processes of courage. Until now, however, little theoretical or empirical work has explored these developmental processes of courage. Saint Thomas Aquinas is credited with the proposition that courage could be instilled not through school or faith but rather through preparing oneself daily to face fears by cultivating one's judgment and valuing the humanity of others (Worline, Wrzesniewski, & Rafaeli, 2002). Rachman (1990) clearly disagreed with this notion and went as far as saying, "Yes, it is possible to attain the noble quality of courage by study and training" (pp. 311–312). Miller (2000) took a more direct approach and stated that "courage is one of those things that can only be properly attained by doing it. To get courage, be courageous" (p. 26).

As pointed out by Hannah, Sweeney, and Lester (see Chapter 7, this volume), courage is defined as "an adaptive process whereby one summons the internal and external resources to confront a threat, overcome fear, and act to reduce that threat." These authors suggest that courage is statelike and that these internal and external resources are open to development. Hannah and colleagues also suggest that the development of courage stems from introspective reflection processes regarding one's actions when faced with past threats, and as such is driven by the individual.

In this chapter, we propose that courage can indeed be developed, and our intent here is to explore that process. However, we do not wholly subscribe to the notion that a person will learn a particular skill set that directly leads him or her to show courage. Instead, specific skills serve only to increase the probability of success while taking on a courageous act and may serve as a factor in one's decision-making process. For example, members of the Federal Bureau of Investigation's Hostage Rescue Team (HRT) undergo extensive marksmanship training. However, the fact that members of the HRT can accurately fire a weapon is not what makes them courageous; on the contrary, being able to do so is merely a "tool of the trade" that may confirm that they can successfully be courageous. We submit that HRT members and others of their ilk are courageous because they regularly and voluntarily place themselves in situations of high personal risk where, bolstered by skills, they act courageously.

This is not to say, however, that the link between skills, knowledge, and abilities and courage is not an important one. For example, Lord and Hall (2005) argued that skills are linked to deeper knowledge structures related to the self-concept. They specifically proposed that skills develop from proactive efforts to seek out experiences relevant to one's self-concept, and that the self may provide a critical structure for benefiting from such experiences. Building off our notion that courage is influenced by self-conceptualizations formed from one's social roles, we suggest that the pursuit of skills, knowledge, and abilities that promote courage under threat conditions may also be socially related. This may add further explanation to Rachman's (1990) notion that some individuals are more suited to be courageous than are others (e.g., based on personality or other individual differences), yet individuals also socially learn to become courageous based on the influence of others.

We begin our discussion of the development of courage by first presenting the benefits that individuals and organizations gain by developing courage in others. Later, we take a social learning perspective and explore the processes by which individuals learn to become courageous via exposure to courageous role models and mentors. Given the premium that many of the organizations noted previously place on leadership, we end this chapter by examining how certain leader behaviors, such as those linked to the tenets of transformational leadership (Avolio, 1999), may also provide methods for individuals to become courageous.

Why Learning to Be Courageous Matters

A discussion of developing courage in others begs the question of whether courage should be developed in others and, if so, what is the value in doing so? We feel that these questions are certainly valid, and our response is yes, courage should be developed, and the value in doing so is significant to both individuals and organizations. Developing courage in others can lead to individuals who are better suited to adapt to and overcome fear to achieve organizational goals, especially in organizations in which the necessity of courageous action may be part of the organization's mission or a natural by-product.

Benefits to the Individual

Developing courage in individuals serves to build their agency and breadth of responses to potential threats as well as their ability to activate encoding categories, expectancies, goal structures, values, affects, and self-regulatory plans to approach goals when challenged.

BOLSTERING INDIVIDUAL AGENCY. The inherent value of courage becomes clearer when one examines the impact it has on flight responses (Frijda, 1986). Worline, Wrzesniewski, and Rafaeli (2002) pointed out, courage "allows us to dampen our immediate response to danger, halting the flight response in order to evaluate the proper course of action" (p. 297). This suggests that through enhancing agency, individuals will establish a broader behavioral repertoire available to them to respond to threats. In light of this dampening of the flight response, perhaps the greatest benefit of developing courage in others is its impact on bolstering human agency.

Bandura (2001) identified the four core features of human agency, or the capacity to exercise control over one's life: intentionality, forethought, self-reactiveness, and self-reflectiveness. Each of these, we suggest, has a reciprocal relationship with the development of courage. First, *intentionality* suggests that acts of agency are done deliberately. Evidence shows that intentionality is a hallmark of courage insofar as courageous action is undertaken by free choice and to achieve a designated purpose (Szagun, 1992); though in some situations the alternative to courageous action may not be acceptable (e.g., death), the choice does in fact exist. Second, *forethought* suggests that people anticipate likely consequences of their actions and select courses of action that they think will produce desired outcomes and avoid detrimental ones. Forethought is consistent with the definitions of courage described previously from an evaluative standpoint given that a courageous actor must assess the threat and determine a course of action to eliminate the threat (Hannah, Sweeney, & Lester, 2007; Worline, Wrzesniewski, & Rafaeli, 2002; see also Chapter 7, this volume). Third, *self-reactiveness* is the ability to self-motivate and self-regulate thoughts, emotions, and behaviors. Self-reactiveness is inherent in a context calling for courageous action because the actor must be motivated as well as able to regulate his or her thoughts and behaviors in the presence of fear to pursue his or her goal. Indeed, members of organizations where courage is habitually activated (e.g., elite military organizations, fire and police departments) repeatedly rehearse drills under stress to increase their abilities to self-regulate under intense challenges—a form of "stress inoculation." Finally, *self-reflectiveness* is the ability to review past behavior to determine the adequacy of one's thoughts and actions. As outlined by Hannah, Sweeney, and Lester (2007; see also Chapter 7, this volume), taking courageous action spurs reflection insofar as the actor makes a post hoc assessment of the circumstances leading to the action, the behavior during the action, and the outcome of the action. When all these are taken together, it appears that taking courageous action and, by extension, developing others to be courageous, has direct linkages to the exercise of human agency and likely the probability that one will take courageous action in the future as one works through an evaluative process of each component of agency described here.

BOLSTERING A COURAGEOUS COGNITIVE AFFECTIVE PROCESSING SYSTEM. In addition, Hannah, Sweeney, and Lester (see Chapter 7, this volume) draw on the work of Mischel and Shoda's (1998) cognitive affective processing system (CAPS) model and suggest that personal resources such as self-efficacy (Bandura, 1997), state hope (Luthans, Youssef, & Avolio, 2007; Snyder, Rand, & Sigmon, 2002), and resilience (Hannah & Luthans, 2008; Masten & Reed, 2002) can be developed to form what they refer to as courageous CAPS. These personal resources then activate encoding categories, expectancies, goals, values, affects, and self-regulatory plans to promote courage when a threat is faced. Following the courageous act, the individual reflects on the event to verify the threat assessment, the subsequent action, and the outcome of the action. Should the assessment be positive, the actor's self-efficacy, state hope, and resilience will likely further increase, albeit incrementally and perhaps in an unstable or temporary fashion given the statelike qualities of each personal resource. Rachman (1990) and Goud (2005), however, suggested that one can "practice" for courage through "moral and physical 'toughening'" (p. 111), which suggests that perhaps the gains in personal resources such as self-efficacy, state hope, and resilience realized by a courageous action can become stable if they are habitually activated. For example, a new platoon leader's self-efficacy in leading a combat patrol may spike after the successful completion of the first mission, but he or she likely cannot sustain that confidence unless he or she experiences success again and again, forming more generalized courage.

Benefits to the Organization

Little has been written on the cascading or diffusing impact that courageous individuals have on the organization. In line with Worline and colleagues' theory (2002), we also believe that developing courageous individuals can influence the agency of other organizational members, thereby increasing a collective sense of organizational agency. In addition, we assert that courage can have a positive impact on both organizational innovation and performance.

BOLSTERING ORGANIZATIONAL AGENCY. In a qualitative study on courage, evidence showed that 83% of the stories told by the participants were interpersonal and that "people feel a strong emotion when behavior is outside normative bounds" (Worline, Wrzesniewski, & Rafaeli, 2002, p. 302). Worline and colleagues contended that organizational members who witness others' courageous behavior will be more likely to personally act courageously when called on to do so in the future. Although we agree with this notion and discuss it at greater length later from a theoretical standpoint, quantitative evidence has yet to establish a clear link between one's current behaviors and subsequent courageous behavior in others. What is clearer, however, is the impact that courageous action has on members' organizational agency. Worline and colleagues found many cases in which an individual who witnessed a courageous act had higher levels of self-efficacy, a sense of organizational ownership, and a willingness to be engaged in work; in short, seeing courage first-hand had an empowering effect on employees and made them want to work harder for their organization. We believe that through social learning, courageous behaviors will result in an emergent, collective phenomenon of organizational agency.

INCREASING ORGANIZATIONAL INNOVATION. Research by Lee and colleagues (2001) alludes to the impact of role models and leadership in developing courage. These studies present evidence that organizational performance is negatively impacted in two scenarios, both when managers fail to explicitly state that mistakes would be forgiven and when employees were punished for making mistakes. In both cases, employees were less likely to experiment with a new software system and, by extension, new business ideas failed to materialize. In contrast, employees who worked for managers who were explicit in their willingness to underwrite mistakes and withhold punishment tended to be more innovative. This suggests that in situations where evaluative pressure is high, individuals have a diminished sense of agency and are less likely to show courage because they fear retribution from their leader should their courageous behavior fail. Such pressures, through reducing agency and courage, stunt learning, hampering an organization's ability to succeed in today's dynamic, competitive, and often global markets. Evidence shows, however, that leaders can set the organizational conditions at the individual, team or social network, and organizational levels for learning and innovation to occur through establishing a culture of knowledge exploration and empowerment (Berson, Nemanich, Waldman, Galvin, & Keller, 2006; Hannah & Lester, 2009).

AUGMENTING ORGANIZATIONAL PERFORMANCE. In addition, we suspect that courage is inherently and inextricably related to the performance of all organizations, and foremost those where acts of social, physical, or other forms of courage may be part of an individual's job description, as seen in the public safety (e.g., police, fire, and emergency medical departments) and national defense fields (e.g., military, intelligence, foreign services). This is admittedly also an empirical question that warrants research. However, one would be hard pressed to imagine members of the military, with a mission of fighting and winning a nation's wars, or members of a police force, with a mission of protecting and serving a community, failing to show courage at some level given the inherent risk and fear involved in warfare and policing. In sum, we feel that courage is central to organizational success and that it is imperative to determine the processes that allow courage to develop within both individuals and organizations.

Social Linkages to Developing Courage in Others

Social learning theory (SLT; Bandura, 1977), subsumed under the umbrella of social cognitive theory (SCT; Bandura, 1986), is perhaps one of the most influential and widely known theories that inform how individuals learn. We propose that concepts within both SLT and SCT provide a road map for developing courage in others. SLT describes how a person could spontaneously increase his or her courage through environmental stimuli, whereas SCT offers a road map for a more systematic method of development. Next, we provide a brief review of the key concepts of these theories and suggest how the concepts are directly related to the development of courage.

Unstructured Development of Courage

Bandura (1977) suggested that individuals learn new information and behaviors by observing others. The three social learning and social cognitive concepts that are most germane to the present discussion on courage are as follows: (a) individuals can learn through observation (Bandura, 1973); (b) attentional, retentional, reproduction, and motivational processes impact this process; and (c) enactive mastery, role modeling, vicarious learning, social persuasion, and physiological and emotional arousal each have a significant impact on the process of developing courage.

OBSERVATIONAL LEARNING. Though the tenets of SLT have been widely studied and the theory has extensive empirical support, several factors must be present for observational learning to take hold. According to Bandura (1977), social learning cannot occur unless the individual has sufficient attentional processes, has the ability to retain what he or she learned, is able to reproduce the observed behavior, and possesses sufficient motivation to reproduce the behavior. Related to courage, successful displays of skills and abilities during a significant experience such as combat would likely trigger deep reflection and alter the deeper structures of the self-concept (Lord & Hall, 2005), such as those related to a soldier's conceptualization of his or her level of physical courage.

In light of the attention–retention–reproduction–motivation linkage, what is clear is that, as in most learning, the burden of learning to become courageous is borne largely by the individual. However, a role model could also play an important role in developing courage by setting the conditions that bolster these factors by providing those individuals with demonstrated organizational scripts and relevant training and development. Borrowing concepts from SCT and, more specifically, the self-efficacy literature, we next describe how models can systematically influence these factors.

Systematic Development of Courage

Role models are an important part of creating a systematic courage development program within an organization. Drawing on the learning mechanisms set out in SCT and the self-efficacy literature (enactive mastery, vicarious learning, social persuasion, and physiological and emotional arousal), we provide a method by which the development of courage can be institutionalized.

MASTERY EXPERIENCES. Time and again, empirical research has shown that successful past or current personal performance enhances future performance (e.g., Bandura, 1997, 1991, 1982). Here, we suggest that repeated exposure to situations that elicit some level of fear and require action do in fact lead to an individual developing courage. In addition, we suggest that a mentor or leader can purposively create these task challenges and provide guidance and feedback to the individual to develop his or her courage.

Bandura (2000a, 2000b) proposed two major types of mastery: guided and cognitive mastery modeling. Guided mastery is defined as instructive modeling to gain specific skills and knowledge, guided perfection of those skills, and the transference of those skills back to the individual's place of work. Though we stated earlier that learning a specific skill set does not alone make one courageous, having skills relevant to the given situation does enhance goal attainment, self-efficacy, and means efficacy, which bolster one's self-concept and resulting displays of courage. In light of this, guided mastery's link to developing courage may be viewed as providing an individual with a given skill set or personal resources (Hannah, Sweeney, & Lester, 2007) that he or she can call on when placed in a situation calling for courageous behavior, and a role model can be of benefit in teaching and reinforcing those skills.

This phenomenon underscores the importance of training and development prior to a high-threat condition. Research on high-reliability environments has shown that individuals are more successful at completing complex tasks under intense pressure when the organization prepared those individuals with behavioral scripts for action (Zohar & Luria, 2003). For example, soldiers in basic training learn battle drills, which are immediate actions taken when initial contact is made with enemy forces (e.g., react to contact, react to an ambush); typically, these skills are taught by drill sergeants. Once the soldier leaves basic training, these skills are honed and reinforced at the soldier's unit by members of his or her chain of command during combat training where they also build means efficacy and collective efficacy in the team. When placed in actual combat, the soldier can call on his or her self- and means efficacy for battle drill skills to promote physical courage as required.

Whereas guided mastery focuses on hands-on experience, cognitive mastery modeling is concentrated on teaching individuals how to mentally rehearse and think in a reasoned and decision-oriented manner to reach sound conclusions and performance (Bandura, 1997). An individual gains cognitive mastery by observing a model formulating effective decisions and implementation steps, then visualizing his or her own performance in a similar task. Cognitive mastery modeling has applications to developing courage in individuals insofar as it strengthens what Hannah, Sweeney, and Lester (2007) referred to as a courageous mind-set, or the interaction of positive states, traits, personal values, and social forces that reduce the level of fear experienced when faced with risk. We suggest that this form of modeling assists an individual in clarifying personal values and in performing an evaluative function that assesses the social forces that impact future courageous behavior. For example, cadets at the United States Military Academy live under an honor code that states "A Cadet will not lie, cheat, or steal, or tolerate those who do," which suggests that living under this code requires moral courage. Cadets are introduced to the honor code within days of arriving at the academy and several times per year participate in discussions about the code that are led by fellow cadets and faculty members. These experiences often focus on how to identify a breach in the code, how to confront an individual thought to have committed an honor violation, the importance of upholding the underlying values of the code, and the moral courage it takes to live under the code (e.g., choosing the harder "right" over the easier "wrong"). In addition, many cadets take part in practical exercises where they role play confronting someone who has committed an honor violation. Armed with the knowledge gleaned from these discussions and practical exercises, cadets are better prepared to uphold the tenets of the honor code in part because they know that others have faced challenges in doing so, they understand how those challenges were addressed, and they have practiced doing so. When faced with a similar situation in real time, these cadets have cognitively rehearsed and understand their options in addressing the moral dilemma.

VICARIOUS LEARNING. As suggested earlier, another method that a role model may use to develop courage in others is vicarious learning. Vicarious learning is most effective when individuals observe competent, relevant role models successfully performing a given task (Bandura, 1997). Research suggests (see Bandura, 1996, 1997; Stajkovic & Luthans, 1998) that the impact of vicarious observation on an individual is predicated on the similarity between the individual and the role model on task-specific characteristics, the similarity between what the individual observed versus what he or she currently faces, and the quality of how the task is portrayed by the role model. In addition, Bandura (1977) pointed out that the individual's attributions of credibility, prestige, and trustworthiness in the role model are also critical given that positive attributions would likely make the salience of the modeled behavior greater.

SOCIAL PERSUASION. Role models can also employ social persuasion and positive feedback to develop courage in others. The impact of verbal persuasion and feedback on attitude change is well established in the literature (e.g., Eagley & Chaiken, 1998, 1993). Here, we propose that regular, systematic counseling and coaching could be used to increase an individual's self-attributions of courage if the role model chooses to focus on courage as a discussion topic. In addition, these sessions tend to serve as an affirmation function in that they allow the individual and role model to discuss personal values (Johnson, 2007), which become a central focus in promoting courage as individuals seek to obtain goals in line with their values (Goud, 2005; Sandage & Hill, 2001; Shepela et al., 1999). Here, the role model has an opportunity to reinforce to the individual that courage, regardless of form, is important to his or her personal as well as the organization's performance.

In organizations in which risk is commonplace, individuals may feel compelled to act courageously out of fear of becoming ostracized and placed in an outgroup (Cialdini & Trost, 1998; Hogg & Abrams, 2001). Further, empirical work by Tesser (1988) and Festinger (1954) has shown that the positive performance of others, in this case the courageous behavior of others, can actually enhance or damage self-esteem depending on how closely the individual's behavior matches that of the model. By extension, should a mismatch exist that is not favorable toward the individual, the resulting dissonance could drive the individual to show courage when the next opportunity to do so becomes available. For example, if a young police officer fails to act courageously while issuing a high-risk arrest warrant but witnesses a more seasoned partner or peer (i.e., the model) showing courage in the same instance, then the police officer may actively seek out opportunities to show courage to "prove" him- or herself.

In hierarchical organizations, in which rank and experience are salient, it may be easier for organization members to identify a role model. Research suggests, however, that effective role models are those who are proximal to and similar to the individual on task-specific characteristics and other factors (Bandura, 1996, 1997; Stajkovic & Luthans, 1998). This finding suggests that members should look to those with expertise, tenure, or some other relevant skill set to recognize potential role models.

Physiological and Emotional Arousal. The final method we propose for developing courage is physiological and emotional arousal. The self-efficacy literature has made clear linkages between physiological and emotional arousal and performance (Bandura, 1997). Sources of arousal can be perceived as either positive or negative by the individual experiencing it. For example, some individuals may find indicators of arousal to be energizing, whereas others may see arousal as a sign of vulnerability or stress and associate such stress with a lack of confidence and high anxiety (Bandura, 1997; Hannah & Luthans, 2008). In addition, individuals also interpret their physiological state such as health issues and overall well-being in calculating their ability to perform (Bandura, 1997), which suggests that individuals who are able to control their anxieties may view themselves as healthier and better suited for tasks calling for physical courage. This notion is alluded to in the recent posttraumatic stress research by the U.S. Army, which suggests that repeated exposure to high-risk environments such as combat can lead to individuals with a heightened, sustained arousal level (i.e., anxiety) and a diminished capacity to perform in subsequent exposure to those environments (Mental Health Advisory Team [MHAT] V, 2008).

Individuals may choose to show courage because they make an emotional connection to what role models say or do. As Bandura (1997) suggested, this connection could be explicit (e.g., volunteering for the Peace Corps after seeing President Kennedy's call for action: "Ask not what your country can do for you, but what you can do for your country") or implicit (e.g., joining the military after watching the inspirational Saint Crispin's Day speech from the play *Henry V*). In any event, it is important to note that without the proper guidance and mentorship, extreme forms of arousal can lead to poor decision making and foolhardy behavior (Goud, 2005). It must also be noted that evidence in regard to physical bravery (specifically when examined in bomb-disposal operators) shows that lower levels of physiological arousal in high-stress conditions were related to courageous behavior (O'Connor, Hallam, & Rachman, 1985). As such, we suggest that models can certainly manipulate an individual's emotional and physiological arousal state by understanding what motivates the individual.

Summary of Social Learning

In this section, we outlined how concepts embedded within social learning and social cognitive theories impact how an individual learns and develops to become courageous. We examined SCT and explained how role models can manipulate mastery experiences, vicarious learning, social persuasion, and physiological and emotional arousal to develop courage in others. Next, we operationalize these concepts by showing two mechanisms whereby role models can develop courage. First, we outline how the mentor–protégé relationship provides a fertile field for developing courage. Later, we outline the transformational leader's (Bass & Avolio, 1990) role in developing courage in followers.

Mentoring Toward Courage

The mentor–protégé relationship, in its purest form, is a very close, enduring relationship that is transformative for both parties. According to Johnson (2007), the mentor–protégé relationship offers an opportunity for self-exploration, identity transformation, and social and emotional support. We suggest that because of this close relationship, the protégé has a significant freedom of inquiry to explore what it means to be courageous. Given the previous discussion of social learning's role in the development of courage, we propose that the mentor–protégé relationship offers an excellent opportunity for the development of courage. For purposes of this chapter, we use the characterization of mentorship by Collins (1994):

> . . . an interpersonal helping relationship between two individuals at different stages of their professional development. The mentor—the more professionally advanced of the two—facilitates the development and advancement of the protégé—the junior professional—by serving as a source of social support beyond what is required solely on the basis of their formal role relationship. (p. 413)

Existing mentorship research suggests that the functions of a mentor can be grouped into three categories—career, psychosocial, and role model functions (Johnson, 2007; Kram, 1985; Russell & Adams, 1997)—and, on the basis of the previous social learning discussion, the latter two may be the most germane to developing courage. In the next sections, we outline how a few mentorship behaviors, out of Johnson's (2007) taxonomy, may develop courage in others.

Psychosocial Functions

According to Kram (1985), the mentor's psychosocial function serves to promote and strengthen the professional identity, competence, and self-esteem of the protégé. The psychosocial mentorship behaviors that may best develop courage within a protégé include the following:

- *Teach and train.* Mentors often assist in developing skill sets in protégés that may be called on during courageous action and may assist in goal attainment. Doing so will likely enhance the protégés' sense of competence, self-esteem, and self-efficacy. In line with Lord and Hall (2005), because of their expertise, mentors have deep structures, or the ability to understand and articulate the deeper, more principled factors of a context in which courage may be called for (e.g., highlighting how personal values were primed in a given situation that resulted in courageous behavior). Consistent with the ideas of Hannah, Sweeney, and Lester (see Chapter 7, this volume), these deep structures help formulate and sustain one's identity as a courageous person when contextual cues prime that aspect of the self. Within the mentor–protégé relationship, elucidating these deep structures reinforces the notion that, in certain contexts, moral, social, or physical courage could be needed.
- *Challenge by encouraging risk taking.* Throughout our discussion thus far, the linkage between fear, risk taking, and courage has been clear. Here, the mentor plays an important role in providing "permission" to take prudent risks and engage in mastery experiences by explaining to the protégé the inherent benefit of doing so.
- *Clarify performance expectations.* Mentors can go beyond the daily work expectations (e.g., job description) and explain their expectation that the protégé show moral, social, and perhaps even physical courage should the organization need it. Doing so also provides a greater understanding of role expectations within the organization.
- *Provide encouragement and support.* A critical task mentors perform is providing the encouragement and support (i.e., social persuasion and psychological arousal) for the protégé to develop. We see this encouragement and support as critical for developing courage given that the protégé may not understand how to overcome the fear and attain his or her goal or may not be able to overcome the fear alone.
- *Deliver feedback.* As discussed in the Social Linkages section of this chapter, feedback is critical to development both in altering the self-concept of the courageous actor and in his or her cognitive modeling of the task requirements required to perform courageously. We submit that protégés need this feedback as they make incremental development steps toward being courageous.

- *Constantly affirm.* Along with the feedback, the mentor serves an affirmation role, essentially telling the protégé that showing courage is important for personal, professional, and organizational growth and performance. Furthermore, affirmation diminishes imposter syndrome within a protégé, reducing levels of self-doubt about his or her worthiness to be in a specific job, school, or program of study (Johnson & Ridley, 2004), which can also have a negative impact on courageous behavior.

Role Model Functions

Russell and Adams (1997) and Johnson (2007) pointed out that by performing as a role model, the mentor serves as both a personal and professional exemplar to the protégé. Though we have provided an overview of role modeling previously in this chapter, a few specific behaviors warrant further discussion.

- *Be an intentional role model.* Johnson (2007) stated that "to mentor is to model" (p. 59). As such, he suggested that mentors must intentionally model the behaviors they wish the protégé to learn. Though modeling courage before a protégé may prove challenging for the mentor, especially given that opportunities to do so may be rare, the mentor should understand the positive impact that doing so can have on the protégé.
- *Encourage socialization to the profession.* Perhaps one of the greatest hurdles to developing courage in a protégé is his or her understanding of where and how one is expected to show courage in a given profession. Johnson (2007) stated that "your protégés need you to help them forge an attitude of personal responsibility for their role in a profession; they must establish a commitment to behave ethically and morally, to develop *deep pride in the profession*" (p. 63), which is also echoed by Bruss and Kopala (1993), who suggested that mentors have an obligation to transmit their personal and professional values.
- *Self disclose.* Because the road to becoming courageous is ripe for self-doubt and hesitation, a mentor may use self-disclosure to develop courage in a protégé. The mentor can provide personal stories about instances in which he or she hesitated or failed to show courage and how the issue was resolved. In addition, self-disclosure shows that the mentor cares about the protégé and his or her courage development and encourages similar disclosures from the protégé, promoting more transparent developmental interactions. Doing so likely will establish the salience of the protégé becoming a courageous individual and accelerate his or her development.
- *Offer counsel.* In parallel to self-disclosure, the mentor should be available to offer advice about courage should the protégé seek it. Through active listening and clarification of concerns, the mentor can assist the protégé in identifying the potential courses of action available to the protégé in a situation calling for courageous action.

Summary of Mentoring

In this section, we established that the mentor–protégé relationship offers an excellent venue for developing courage in others. In addition, we outlined specific psychosocial and role modeling behaviors that may assist a mentor in doing so. However, there is one important postscript: We agree with Johnson's (2007) statement that "mentorships are extremely beneficial, yet all too *infrequent*" (p. 22; emphasis added). The mentorship literature suggests that the costs (e.g., time and effort) and relational obstacles often lead to formal mentorship being rare (Dickinson & Johnson, 2000; Ragins & Scandura, 1994). Furthermore, these mentorships may be informal and therefore out of the organization's purview. Given that most individuals are members of some form of organization, be it in their professional or personal life, we outline in the next passage that quality organizational leadership, and specifically transformational leadership (Bass & Avolio, 1990), can also lead to the development of courage in others, when mentorship is not an option.

Role of Transformational Leaders in the Development of Courage in Followers

Although it is possible that individuals can develop their courage through any personal or impersonal connection, we suggest that transformational leadership behaviors may be the most effective method by which organizational leaders can implement a systematic development program focused on developing courage in its members. Empirical research supports the idea that transformational leadership has many positive influences on organizational outcomes, such as both subjective and objective measures of performance, performance beyond expectations, creativity, and openness to change, while also showing an increase in agency by diminishing social loafing and stress (e.g., Bass & Riggio, 2006; Judge & Piccolo, 2004; Jung, Chow, & Wu, 2003; Kahai, Sosik, & Avolio, 2003; Waldman, Javidan, & Varella, 2004).

Research suggests that transformational leaders positively affect followers through four specific types of behavior: intellectual stimulation, individual consideration, idealized influence, and inspirational motivation (Bass & Avolio, 1990, 1993). Transformational leaders "help followers grow and develop into leaders by responding to individual followers' needs through empowering them and by aligning the objectives and goals of the individual followers with those of the leader, the group, and the larger organization" (Bass & Riggio, 2006, p. 3). In summary, transformational leaders seek to positively transform followers versus merely influencing them to perform. More specifically, they develop followers into leaders themselves.

Over the past 4 decades, empirical research has determined through studies of monozygotic twins that the majority of leadership abilities (about 70%) are able to be developed through contextual factors and skills gained from leadership role attainment, disconfirming the original belief that leaders are born with innate leadership traits (Arvey, Rotundo, Johnson, & McGue, 2006; Avolio & Hannah, 2008; Avolio & Yammarino, 1990; Bass & Riggio, 2006; Rose, 1995).

Transformational leadership theory prescribes behavioral competencies that individuals can develop throughout their lives, through both life experiences and a personal commitment to enhancing one's leadership capacity (Conger & Kanungo, 1988). Further, research has found that these behavioral competencies not only are available to leaders at the highest levels of society and organizations, but can also be attained by leaders at all levels who have the commitment to become a better leader (Bass & Avolio, 1990).

We suggest that the evolution of the construct of courage will follow the same path as our understanding of leadership, moving away from the notion of courage as a rare phenomenon (Miller, 2000) toward the notion that courage can be developed in any individual who is committed to becoming courageous.

Transformational Leadership and the Development of Courage

SLT, as outlined earlier, explains that individuals learn in part by observing others. Further, empirical evidence supports the idea that transformational leaders serve as idealized role models from whom followers observe and learn (Bass & Riggio, 2006). Thus, we suggest that if a transformational leader is courageous and exhibits or verbalizes that courage in various ways, followers may learn from and emulate that behavior and over time adapt a courageous mind-set. This mind-set may lead to a positive enhancement of the follower's personal attributions of courage, manifesting in the exhibition of future courageous behaviors.

As stated previously, research demonstrates that common outcomes of transformational leadership behaviors are follower development and performance (Bass & Avolio, 1990). For instance, Dvir, Eden, Avolio, and Shamir (2002) suggested that transformational leaders exhibit charismatic behaviors, arouse inspirational motivation, provide intellectual stimulation, and treat followers with individualized consideration. These behaviors transform their followers, helping them to reach their full potential and generate the highest levels of performance. Furthermore, research suggests that "leaders and followers go beyond their self-interests or expected rewards for the good of the team and the good of the organization" (Bass & Avolio, 1993, p. 118). There is also a strong influence from norms that have been adopted and adapted over the organization's history (Bass & Avolio, 1993). When a culture of transformation exists, it may be that individuals within that culture are constantly testing their own personal boundaries, which alone may be viewed as an act of courage as well as a source of continuous courage development.

To more specifically explain and support our proposal that transformational leaders promote the display and development of courage in followers, we focus on the four specific categories of transformational behaviors (Bass & Avolio, 1993, 1990): intellectual stimulation, individual consideration, idealized influence, and inspirational motivation.

INTELLECTUAL STIMULATION. The first component of transformational leadership creates intellectual stimulation in followers. Transformational leaders enact questioning behaviors and encourage creative and innovative thoughts in followers (Bass & Riggio, 2006). Leaders encourage new ideas by creating an atmosphere wherein followers are not fearful of ridicule or scorn for having a bad idea. Furthermore, followers are encouraged to try different methods for completing tasks, which can expand an individual's repertoire of possible courageous behaviors.

When leaders create an environment without fear of reprisal and encourage their followers to question the status quo and experiment with different processes to complete tasks, we suggest that they are creating an environment that fosters courage by decreasing followers' perceived fear of offering new and different options. Although it would seem to be more courageous for a follower to offer innovations and critiques in a less forgiving environment, it is also less likely that those deviations from the norm would be expressed. Behaviors that stimulate the intellect of followers could support the overall development of courage by forcing them to consider their personal boundaries, and by persuading them to advance beyond those borders. Courage is by definition unconventional, contradicting what a majority of people would do in the same situation (Deutsch, 1961; Hannah, Sweeney, & Lester, 2007). Therefore, as much as intellectual stimulation enhances the follower's efficacy for trying new things or having innovative thoughts, we suggest leaders who use this method will accelerate the development of courage in those followers. Organizations with transformational leaders create this environment of intellectual stimulation and innovation by allowing their employees time and resources to try new and interesting things.

INSPIRATIONAL MOTIVATION. The next set of behaviors discussed in transformational leadership theory has to do with inspirational motivation. Inspirational motivation provides followers with the challenge and motivation to confidently succeed at shared tasks. Bass and Steidlmeier (1999) suggested that the inspirational appeals of transformational leaders tend to focus on the best in people—"on harmony, on charity and good works" (p. 5). Transformational leaders empower followers, yet research suggests that empowerment involves more than increasing participation.

Though there is no known empirical evidence specifically linking inspirational motivation and courage development, military history is replete with anecdotal examples of soldiers taking courageous actions because they were inspired to act after witnessing the courageous actions of their peers and leaders. A powerful example is that of the soldiers serving under Colonel Robert Gould Shaw, commander of the African American 54th Massachusetts Volunteer Infantry during the American Civil War. During the Battle of Battery Wagner in South Carolina on July 18, 1863, Shaw's soldiers hesitated in their charge in the face of heavy Confederate fire. Seeing this, Shaw rallied his soldiers by personally charging a parapet and yelling "Forward, 54th!"; his soldiers followed up the parapet and fought valiantly. Though Shaw was killed along with more than a hundred of his soldiers, the actions of the 54th were widely heralded as helping to increase African American enlistment and bringing the war to an end sooner. In sum, the soldiers saw what Shaw was doing and followed his lead.

Inspirational motivation also serves as an enabling function that can result in a transformation of the person, which some have argued is a critical link in the development of followers into leadership roles (e.g., Avolio & Luthans, 2006; Kanungo & Mendonca, 1996). Bass and colleagues (1987) suggested that transformational leaders motivate and inspire followers by making things not only important but also challenging. Aligned with earlier discussion of the importance of arousal in courage development, leader inspiration often results in enthusiasm and optimism in followers (Bass & Riggio, 2006). Bass and Riggio (2006) went on to state that "leaders get followers involved in envisioning attractive future states; they create clearly communicated expectations that followers want to meet and also demonstrate commitment to goals and the shared vision" (p. 8). With regard to Colonel Shaw, his actions identified his goal (going over the parapet and victory), he clearly communicated his expectations ("Forward 54th!"), and his behavior suggested that he too was committed to the end-state (showing physical courage in the face of the enemy). This ultimately resulted in the physically courageous behavior of his followers.

INDIVIDUALIZED CONSIDERATION. A transformational leader takes the time necessary to learn about and understand each follower with whom he or she works, creating individualized consideration (Bass & Riggio, 2006). As both potential and desire for growth vary by individual, the transformational leader adjusts his or her expectations and challenges for each follower, motivating each individual to strive toward reaching the height of his or her capabilities. Furthermore, individualized consideration allows the leader to understand the different methods by which he or she can create the conditions of motivation for each follower to more appropriately prompt courage development in each follower.

In this manner, leaders could learn the specific fears or difficulties a follower may have, and then devise a method by which that follower could confront those fears in a developmental manner. Not only is the leader serving as an example to the follower by being an active listener, but the leader is also compelling the follower to pursue enactive mastery by creating specific tasks that are meant to build the personal resources (e.g., skills and efficacy in those skills) to clear barriers. Further, through such individualized focus, leaders can target the persuasion techniques as well as calibrate the level of emotional and psychological arousal that best promotes courage in followers. In sum, individualized consideration allows for another aspect of SLT to envelop the follower in the pursuit of developing courage. Returning to the example of Colonel Robert Gould Shaw, we see an example of individualized consideration that allowed his troops to be remembered as extremely courageous. He and his battalion of freed slaves were facing death if they were captured by the enemy as well as dealing with a bureaucracy in the Union Army that would not put them into battle. However, he witnessed the desire in his troops to serve their country and to serve as examples to generations of African Americans, and he lobbied for the mission to launch the attack on Fort Wagner. He harnessed that desire and sense of collective agency to conduct what many concluded was a suicide mission, because he knew his soldiers were seeking more than victory—they were seeking glory.

IDEALIZED INFLUENCE. Idealized influence is the concept that the leader is foremost a role model and is idealized as a "possible self" to followers (Bass &

Riggio, 2006; Lord & Brown, 2004). In some cases, the transformational leader emphasizes teamwork and promotes ethical policies within his or her organization (Howell & Avolio, 1992). These leaders are admired, respected, and trusted by followers, and are believed to have extraordinary capabilities that contribute to continued success. Bass and Riggio (2006) stated that "Followers identify with the leaders and want to emulate them; leaders are endowed by their followers as having extraordinary capabilities, persistence, and determination" (p. 6).

In the end, transformational leaders who exhibit idealized influence have high self-efficacy and are willing to take risks (Bass & Riggio, 2006), in part because they draw on their expert leadership skills (Lord & Hall, 2005). Transformational leaders are historically known for their ability to ensure confidence and efficacy in their followers by inspiring them and being positive exemplars of behavior, and also by creating a transformational culture (Bass, 1985). Further, transformational leaders hold high standards of moral and ethical conduct, which will directly and positively influence the values and beliefs of their followers (Hall, Johnson, Wysocki, & Kepner, 2002).

Transformational leaders are role models of the appropriate behaviors that foster courage development because they tend to do what is good for the organization and put themselves at risk for the good of the organization (Bass & Steidlmeier, 1999). Choi and Mai-Dalton (1999) suggested that this example of self-sacrificial leadership relates directly to transformational leadership in that leaders might exhibit self-sacrificial behavior, defined as "inspirational and exemplary behavior that becomes of particular importance when the followers' commitment is essential for effective organizational performance" (pp. 397–398), to build trust, to earn the acceptance of followers, to be role models, or to demonstrate loyalty to the company. They further suggested that self-sacrificial leadership will facilitate individual and organizational adaptations to changing environments, and followers will intend to imitate the leader's behaviors. Within a collective context, building trust, loyalty, and acceptance between the leader and follower could compel a follower to act courageously because the follower may see the leader as a "future self" (Lord & Brown, 2004; Lord & Hall, 2005), which we discuss later.

In light of this, it is clear that Choi and Mai-Dalton's (1999) position gets at the very nature of courage (self-sacrifice) and transformational leadership and the resultant behavior of followers. The researchers found that self-sacrificial leadership and transformational leadership used in combination positively influenced followers, who subsequently intended to imitate and follow the example of the leader. Self-sacrifice by the leader, then, exemplifies the organizational member's ideal behavior.

Building on this notion, a substantial amount of research has supported the linkages between the environment and its role in priming different aspects of the self, thus influencing an individual's thoughts and behavior (e.g., Bargh, Chen, & Burrows, 1996; Lord & Brown, 2004). Applied to leadership, a pattern of findings has emerged from research on the self-concept, suggesting that leaders do have an enormous influence over various aspects of a subordinate's self-concept (Lord, Brown, & Freiberg, 1999). For example, Lord and Brown (2004) proposed that effective leadership will "be directly proportional to the degree to which leaders are able to prime relevant aspects of a subordinate's self-concept" (p. 73). Building on this research, we suggest that idealized transformational leaders will serve as role models for their followers' behaviors as well as influence the development of each follower's self-concept.

When followers alter their own self-concepts and self-identity to better match those of the courageous leader, we propose that they will be more likely to enact courageous behaviors because they have altered their belief system to include courage as a core self-aspect. Research suggests that such core self-aspects are highly salient and powerful in driving cognition and behaviors (see Hannah, Woolfolk, & Lord, 2009). Furthermore, the transformational culture that the leader creates allows for social persuasion and normative influence to become an important component in the social development of courage. As all members of the organization witness the self-sacrificial behaviors of the leader, many will emulate those behaviors, just as Colonel Shaw's leading of the charge inspired emulation by his troops.

Summary of Transformational Leadership and Courage

In summary, we suggest that through intellectual stimulation, individual consideration, idealized influence, and inspirational motivation, transformational leaders serve as role models for courageous behavior, intellectually stimulate their followers to push beyond boundaries and encourage them to question the status quo, and inspire followers to be courageous, which leads to the further development of courage in those followers.

Conclusion

The development of courage in individuals and collectives is perhaps central to organizational development and performance. Indeed, it is difficult to imagine how an organization can succeed over the long term without individuals who are willing to take risks to challenge the status quo (i.e., social courage), demand ethical behaviors (i.e., moral courage), explore new challenging opportunities (i.e., entrepreneurial courage), risk self-esteem to pursue new challenges that may result in failure (i.e., psychological courage), and if the situation calls for it, be willing to place themselves in harm's way for the greater good (i.e., physical courage). Despite the importance of courage in organizations, research on courage development is scarce. In this chapter, we took initial steps to explore the social linkages to developing courage in others. Via observational learning and other concepts of social learning and social cognition, we determined that developing courage is not only possible but also a responsibility of leaders. We built a case for the extensive influence that mentors and transformational leaders can have on developing courage. Though theoretical contributions at this early point in developing a framework of courage development are important, we readily recognize that most of what we proposed here is subject to empirical testing and feel that doing so is critical to gaining a better understanding of human and organizational development and performance.

References

Arvey, R. D., Rotundo, M., Johnson, W., & McGue, M. (2006). The determinants of leadership role occupancy: Genetic and personality factors. *The Leadership Quarterly, 17,* 1–20. doi:10.1016/j.leaqua.2005.10.009

Avolio, B. J. (1999). *Full leadership development: Building the vital forces in organizations.* Thousand Oaks, CA: Sage.

Avolio, B. J., & Hannah, S. T. (2008). Developmental readiness: Accelerating leader development. *Consulting Psychology Journal: Practice and Research, 60,* 331–347. doi:10.1037/1065-9293.60.4.331

Avolio, B. J., & Luthans, F. (2006). *The high impact leader: Moments matter in accelerating authentic leadership development.* New York, NY: McGraw-Hill.

Avolio, B. J., & Yammarino, F. J. (1990). Operationalizing charismatic leadership using a levels-of-analysis framework. *The Leadership Quarterly, 1,* 193–208. doi:10.1016/1048-9843(90)90020-I

Bandura, A. (1973). *Aggression: A social learning analysis.* Englewood Cliffs, NJ: Prentice-Hall.

Bandura, A. (1977). *Social learning theory.* Englewood Cliffs, NJ: Prentice-Hall.

Bandura, A. (1982). Self-efficacy mechanism in human agency. *American Psychologist, 37,* 122–147. doi:10.1037/0003-066X.37.2.122

Bandura, A. (1986). *Social foundations of thought and action.* Englewood Cliffs, NJ: Prentice-Hall.

Bandura, A. (1991). Social cognitive theory of self-regulation. *Organizational Behavior and Human Decision Processes, 50,* 248–287. doi:10.1016/0749-5978(91)90022-L

Bandura, A. (1996). Ontological and epistemological terrains revisited. *Journal of Behavior Therapy and Experimental Psychology, 27,* 323–345. doi:10.1016/S0005-7916(96)00049-3

Bandura, A. (1997). *Self-efficacy: The exercise of control.* New York, NY: Freeman.

Bandura, A. (2000a). Cultivate self-efficacy for personal and organizational effectiveness. In E. A. Locke (Ed.), *Handbook of principles of organizational behavior* (pp. 120–136). Oxford, England: Blackwell.

Bandura, A. (2000b). Exercise of human agency through collective efficacy. *Current Directions in Psychological Science, 9,* 75–78. doi:10.1111/1467-8721.00064

Bandura, A. (2001). Social cognitive theory: An agentic perspective. *Annual Review of Psychology, 52,* 1–26. doi:10.1146/annurev.psych.52.1.1

Bargh, J. A., Chen, M., & Burrows, L. (1996). Automaticity of social behavior: Direct effects of trait construct and stereotype activation on action. *Journal of Personality and Social Psychology, 71,* 230–244. doi:10.1037/0022-3514.71.2.230

Bass, B. M. (1985). *Leadership and performance beyond expectations.* New York, NY: Free Press.

Bass, B. M., & Avolio, B. J. (1990). The implications of transactional and transformational leadership for individual, team, and organizational development. *Research in Organizational Change and Development, 4,* 231–272.

Bass, B. M., & Avolio, B. J. (1993). Transformational leadership and organizational culture. *Public Administration Quarterly, 17,* 112–122.

Bass, B. M., & Riggio, R. E. (2006). *Transformational leadership* (2nd ed.). Mahwah, NJ: Erlbaum.

Bass, B. M., & Steidlmeier, P. (1999). Ethics, character, and authentic transformational leadership behavior. *The Leadership Quarterly, 10,* 181–217. doi:10.1016/S1048-9843(99)00016-8

Bass, B. M., Waldman, D. A., Avolio, B. J., & Bebb, M. (1987). Transformational leadership and the falling dominoes effect. *Group & Organization Studies, 12,* 73–87. doi:10.1177/105960118701200106

Berson, Y., Nemanich, L. A., Waldman, D. A., Galvin, B. M., & Keller, R. T. (2006). Leadership and organizational learning: A multiple levels perspective. *The Leadership Quarterly, 17,* 577–594. doi:10.1016/j.leaqua.2006.10.003

Bruss, K. V., & Kopala, M. (1993). Graduate school training in psychology: Its impact upon the development of professional identity. *Psychotherapy (Chicago, Ill.), 30,* 685–691. doi:10.1037/0033-3204.30.4.685

Choi, Y., & Mai-Dalton, R. R. (1999). The model of followers' responses to self-sacrificial leadership: An empirical test. *The Leadership Quarterly, 10,* 397–421. doi:10.1016/S1048-9843(99)00025-9

Cialdini, R., & Trost, M. (1998). Social influence: Social norms, conformity, and compliance. In D. T. Gilbert, S. T. Fiske, & G. Lindzey (Eds.), *Handbook of social psychology* (Vol. 2, pp. 151–192). Boston, MA: McGraw-Hill.

Collins, P. (1994). Does mentorship among social workers make a difference? An empirical investigation of career outcomes. *Social Work, 39,* 413–419.

Conger, J. A., & Kanungo, R. N. (1988). *Charismatic leadership in organizations.* Thousand Oaks, CA: Sage.

Deutsch, M. (1961). Courage as a concept in social psychology. *Journal of Social Psychology, 55,* 49–58.

Dickinson, S. C., & Johnson, W. B. (2000). Mentoring in clinical psychology doctoral programs: A national survey of directors of training. *The Clinical Supervisor, 19,* 137–152. doi:10.1300/J001v19n01_08

Dvir, T., Eden, D., Avolio, B. J., & Shamir, B. (2002). Impact of transformational leadership on follower development and performance: A field experiment. *Academy of Management Journal, 45,* 735–744. doi:10.2307/3069307

Eagly, A. H., & Chaiken, S. (1993). *The psychology of attitudes.* Dallas, TX: Harcourt Brace Jovanovich.

Festinger, L. (1954). A theory of social comparison processes. *Human Relations, 7,* 117–140. doi:10.1177/001872675400700202

Frijda, N. H. (1986). *The emotions.* Cambridge, England: Cambridge University Press.

Goud, N. H. (2005). Courage: Its nature and development. *The Journal of Humanistic Counseling, Education and Development, 44,* 102–116.

Hall, J., Johnson, S., Wysocki, A., & Kepner, K. (2002). Transformational leadership: The transformation of managers and associates. *University of Florida Institute of Food and Agriculture Sciences,* 1–3.

Hannah, S. T., & Lester, P. B. (2009). A multilevel approach to building and leading learning organizations. *Leadership Quarterly, 20*(1), 34.

Hannah, S. T., & Luthans, F. (2008). A cognitive affective processing explanation of positive leadership: Toward theoretical understanding of the role of psychological capital. In L. L. Neider & C. A. Schriesheim (Series Eds.) & R.H. Humphrey (Ed.), *Research in management: Vol. 7. Affect and emotion: New directions in management theory and research* (pp. 8–42). New York, NY: Information Age.

Hannah, S. T., Sweeney, P. J., & Lester, P. B. (2007). Toward a courageous mindset: The subjective act and experience of courage. *The Journal of Positive Psychology, 2,* 129–135. doi:10.1080/17439760701228854

Hannah, S. T., Woolfolk, L., & Lord, R. (2009). Leader self-structure: A framework for positive leadership. *Journal of Organizational Behavior, 30,* 269–290. doi:10.1002/job.586

Hogg, M. A., & Abrams, D. (2001). *Intergroup relations.* Philadelphia, PA: Psychology Press.

Howell, J. M., & Avolio, B. J. (1992). The ethics of charismatic leadership: Submission or liberation? *The Academy of Management Executive, 6,* 43–54.

Johnson, W. B. (2007). *On being a mentor.* Mahwah, NJ: Erlbaum.

Johnson, W. B., & Ridley, C. R. (2004). *The elements of mentoring.* New York, NY: Palgrave-MacMillan.

Judge, T. A., & Piccolo, R. F. (2004). Transformational and transactional leadership: A meta-analytic test of their relative validity. *Journal of Applied Psychology, 89,* 755–768. doi:10.1037/0021-9010.89.5.755

Jung, D., Chow, C., & Wu, A. (2003). The role of transformational leadership in enhancing organizational innovation: Hypotheses and some preliminary findings. *The Leadership Quarterly, 14,* 525–544. doi:10.1016/S1048-9843(03)00050-X

Kahai, S., Sosik, J. J., & Avolio, B. J. (2003). Effects of leadership style, anonymity, and rewards on creativity-relevant processes and outcomes in an electronic meeting system context. *The Leadership Quarterly, 14,* 499–524. doi:10.1016/S1048-9843(03)00049-3

Kanungo, R. N., & Mendonca, M. (1996). Corporate leadership in the context of liberalization in India. *The Social Engineer, 5,* 114–136.

Kram, K. E. (1985). *Mentoring at work: Developmental relationships in organizational life.* Glenview, IL: Scott Foresman.

Lee, F. (2001). The fear factor. *Harvard Business Review, 79,* 29–30.

Lee, F., Edmondson, A. C., Thomke, S., & Worline, M. (2004). The mixed effects of inconsistency on experimentation in organizations. *Organization Science, 15,* 310–326. doi:10.1287/orsc.1040.0076

Lord, R. G., & Brown, D. J. (2004). *Leadership processes and follower self-identity.* Mahwah, NJ: Erlbaum.

Lord, R. G., Brown, D. J., & Freiberg, S. J. (1999). Understanding the dynamics of leadership: The role of follower self-concepts in the leader/follower relationship. *Organizational Behavior and Human Decision Processes, 78,* 167–203. doi:10.1006/obhd.1999.2832

Lord, R. G., & Hall, R. J. (2005). Identity, deep structure and the development of leadership skills. *The Leadership Quarterly, 16,* 591–615.

Luthans, F., Youssef, C. M., & Avolio, B. J. (2007). *Psychological capital: Developing the human competitive edge.* New York, NY: Oxford University Press.

Masten, A. S., & Reed, M. J. (2002). Resilience in development. In C. R. Snyder & S. Lopez (Eds.), *Handbook of positive psychology* (pp. 74–88). Oxford, England: Oxford University Press.

Mental Health Advisory Team V. (2008). *Operation Iraqi Freedom 06-08: Iraq and Operation Enduring Freedom 8: Afghanistan final report.* Office of the Surgeon Multinational Force - Iraq, Office of the Command Surgeon, Office of the Surgeon General – United States Army Medical command. Retrieved from http://www.armymedicine.army.mil/reports/mhat/mhat_v/mhat-v.cfm

Miller, W. I. (2000). *The mystery of courage.* Cambridge, MA: Harvard University Press.

Mischel, W., & Shoda, Y. (1998). Reconciling processing dynamics and personality dispositions. *Annual Review of Psychology, 49,* 229–258. doi:10.1146/annurev.psych.49.1.229

O'Connor, K., Hallam, R., & Rachman, S. (1985). Fearlessness and courage: Replication experiment. *The British Journal of Psychology, 76,* 187–197.

Rachman, S. J. (1990). *Fear and courage.* New York, NY: Freeman.

Ragins, B. R., & Scandura, T. A. (1994). Gender differences in expected outcomes of mentoring relationships. *Academy of Management Journal, 37,* 957–971. doi:10.2307/256606

Rose, R. J. (1995). Genes and human behavior. *Annual Review of Psychology, 46,* 625–654. doi:10.1146/annurev.ps.46.020195.003205

Russell, J. E. A., & Adams, D. M. (1997). The changing nature of mentorship in organizations: An introduction to the special on mentoring in organizations. *Journal of Vocational Behavior, 51,* 1–14. doi:10.1006/jvbe.1997.1602

Sandage, S. J., & Hill, P. C. (2001). The virtues of positive psychology: The rapprochement and challenges of an affirmative postmodern perspective. *Journal for the Theory of Social Behaviour, 31,* 241–260. doi:10.1111/1468-5914.00157

Sekerka, L. E., & Bagozzi, R. P. (2007). Moral courage in the workplace: Moving to and from the desire and decision to act. *Business Ethics. European Review (Chichester, England), 16,* 132–149.

Shepela, S. T., Cook, J., Horlitz, E., Leal, R., Luciano, S., & Lutfy, E. (1999). Courageous resistance: A special case of altruism. *Theory & Psychology, 9,* 787–805. doi:10.1177/0959354399096004

Snyder, C. R., Rand, K. L., & Sigmon, D. R. (2002). Hope theory: A member of the positive psychology family. In C. R. Snyder & S. J. Lopez (Eds.), *Handbook of positive psychology* (pp. 257–276). New York, NY: Oxford University Press.

Stajkovic, A. D., & Luthans, F. (1998). Self efficacy and work-related performance: A meta analysis. *Psychological Bulletin, 124,* 240–261. doi:10.1037/0033-2909.124.2.240

Szagun, G. (1992). Age-related changes in children's understanding of courage. *The Journal of Genetic Psychology, 153,* 405–420.

Tesser, A. (1988). Toward a self-evaluation maintenance model of social behavior. In L. Berkowitz (Ed.), *Advances in experimental social psychology* (Vol. 21, pp. 181–227). New York, NY: Academic Press.

Waldman, D. A., Javidan, M., & Varella, P. (2004). Charismatic leadership at the strategic level: A new application of upper echelons theory. *The Leadership Quarterly, 15,* 355–380. doi:10.1016/j.leaqua.2004.02.013

Worline, M. C., Wrzesniewski, A., & Rafaeli, A. (2002). Courage and work: Breaking routines to improve performance. In R. Lord, R. Klimoski, & R. Kanfer (Eds.), *Emotions at work* (pp. 295–330). San Francisco, CA: Jossey-Bass.

Zohar, D., & Luria, G. (2003). Organizational meta-scripts as a source of high reliability: The case of an army armored brigade. *Journal of Organizational Behavior, 24,* 837–859. doi:10.1002/job.216

11

Understanding the Role of Courage in Social Life

Monica C. Worline

Work has become one of the primary theaters for the drama of human life, and although people may not always recognize it, what is most important about a person is often at stake in the workplace. Describing this "theater" of modern work, Whyte (1994) wrote:

> In work, the stakes are dramatically high. You can be fired today, this very moment. Your company can go under. Even if it seems as invulnerable as the Titanic, you may be busily and efficiently rearranging the deck chairs even as it disappears beneath the waves. Loutish and brutal takeover specialists may break in through the back door, take over the company, break it up, and sell it off for breathtaking personal gain. Your husband may hate your job and ask you to give it up, your wife may leave you because of your unstoppable, Faustian worship of career. Like drama, everything is at stake and everything can happen, and real human souls are living at the center of it all. (p. 20)

The real human souls living at the center of it all are the focus of this chapter. The fields of business and organizational psychology rarely conceive of work in this manner, as a theater for the human soul (Frost, 2003; Rozin, 2001). Instead, the most typical representations of work organizations appear as economic or statistical abstractions, hindering the development of a dramatic sensibility that would help explain how "we play out our lives as part of a greater story" (Whyte, 1994, pp. 18–19). Greek society had theater at its center as a way of working through the dramas, tragedies, and comedy of human collective life. Because the world lacks an agreed-on venue for working through people's lives together, these dramas, tragedies, and comedies often play themselves out through the workplace. Truly understanding organizations requires engagement with the whole human drama, where at any moment one may be fired or promoted, downsized or reorganized, raided or merged. In these settings, the individual is at risk and the collective is easily neglected—these are settings that call for courage.

In this chapter, I make an argument that when work organizations foreground the omnipresent tensions between individual life and collective life, courage becomes a crucial part of the workplace. Understanding courage as it plays a role in collective life requires looking deeply into the patterns of activity that repeat themselves throughout organizing. To situate courage within workplaces and to help build an understanding of its role in social life, I draw on foundational studies from three scholars who are central in the development of social and organizational psychology: Solomon Asch, Philip Zimbardo, and Stanley Milgram. The purpose in revisiting these fundamental findings in social psychology is to renew an understanding of the vital importance of social conformity, deindividuation through social roles, and obedience to authority, each of which is part of the heart of organizing and is central to the idea of courage in organizations.

Building on a foundation of research that shows the multiple ways in which people are beholden to social situations, scholars of courage can construct new answers to questions about what happens in a social system when conformity fails, when role expectations are disrupted, or when authority is challenged. I argue that the most common forms of courage in the contemporary workplace are deeply related to these three well-studied moments in social life. Courage in organizations happens in the form of resisting conformity, seizing individual responsibility regardless of role, and challenging authority. Revisiting the fundamental studies related to these moments helps increase the knowledge base regarding the organizing dynamics of courage. In this chapter, I explore these expressions of courage as well as the psychological and social consequences that result when people do things such as standing out from their peers at work to represent what they feel to be right, stepping into responsibility for an error instead of eluding blame, or speaking up against a manager or a vice president or a CEO to say what they know to be true. Such instances show the vital importance of courage in contemporary workplaces and point to its role in the broader welfare of social life.

Revisiting Asch: Conformity in Contemporary Workplaces

You enter a room in a jumble of coats and backpacks, everyone trying to move through the door at the same moment. Stashing your jacket on a hook on the wall, you wait until a smiling young woman comes into the room. She calls names one-by-one until only two seats are left, and then finally you are called. You take your place in a half-circle of people, looking at a blank screen in the front of the room. The smiling young woman tells you that you will all be participating in a perception study. Part of the study involves judging the length of lines printed on cards. “Select the shortest line,” she says. You look at the card, easily picking the shortest line and marking your answer sheet. Next, she says, she wants all of you to look at the screen as she dims the lights. On the screen appear three lines, very similar to those that were on the cards. This time, she instructs, please select the shortest line and say the number of the shortest line aloud when it is your turn. “We will start here,” she says, pointing to the opposite end of the semicircle. As you look at the screen, the line numbered 1 takes almost the whole length of the wall, line 2 appears only half as long as line 1, and line 3 takes just a fraction of the space on the wall, and is obviously the shortest. Looking down at her clipboard, the young woman marks the first answer as a voice calls out: “Line 2.” She points to the next person in line, who answers: “Line 2.” She marks her clipboard and looks at the next person: “Line 2.” You glance around the semicircle—do they see it from a different angle? It is close to your turn to speak. Do they see something that you do not? The smiling young woman looks up at you. Which line is the shortest?

This situation is a dramatization of one of the classic laboratory setups for studies of social conformity (see Asch, 1956). Asch's studies showed that in a setup similar to the one described here, people would agree that Line 2 was actually the shortest about 33% of the time, disregarding their personal knowledge (Line 3 was in fact the shortest). This finding was not due to a difference in perception, however. On their individual worksheets the same people would correctly identify the shortest line at least 98% of the time (Asch, 1956). Asch concluded that people will often conform to what their peers are doing in a strong social situation like this one. It seems better to go with the crowd than to stand out, at least in a laboratory where a person knows he or she is under observation by experimenters with clipboards.

One might hope that when the stakes are higher than just line-length judgments or laboratory outcomes, Asch's findings would be mitigated. Writing about a contemporary corporate setting, Whyte (2002) told a story that begins with a setting very similar to Asch's laboratory setup: Executives sit around the table in a corporate boardroom, asked to give their opinion on a plan for restructuring the firm. One vice president, sitting near the end of the table, knows that the plan is supported by the CEO, but he feels that it would be devastating in its effects on the organization. The vice president listens as one by one his colleagues sitting around the table agree to the proposed benefits of the plan. Most of the other executives, the vice president notices, are obviously uncomfortable, but one by one each agrees to support the restructuring. The vice president suspects that they do not believe what they are saying. When it is his turn to speak, though his mind is crying out that he does not believe in this plan or its supposed benefits, he hears himself go along with the positive evaluations and agree to its implementation. Though he later told Whyte that it was one of the most distressing moments in his career, this vice president behaved just like one of Asch's (1956) research participants, disregarding his personal knowledge, values, and better judgment to go along with the emerging consensus of the group and to remain as one of the team in the eyes of the CEO.

Revisiting Zimbardo: Deindividuation in Contemporary Workplaces

Imagine it's a sunny Sunday morning, a police car pulls up in front of your home, and two police officers stride confidently to knock on your front door. Answering their knock, you are ordered to surrender yourself to police custody; you are to be taken via police escort to participate in a study of how people become socialized into prison roles. Though you volunteered for this study and will be paid for your time, you were not quite expecting to be handcuffed and put in the back of a police car to arrive at the research site (Zimbardo, 2007, pp. 26–39). The well-known Stanford prison experiment began just this way.

On the 1st day of the simulated prison experiment, the guards, who were also study volunteers, taught the prisoners rules, such as referring to fellow prisoners only by number, participating in all prison activities, remaining silent, and obeying all orders from guards. As a few days passed, the guards' orders became more and more demeaning and abusive. Near the end of the study, after only 5 days in the simulated roles, one guard ordered the prisoners to bend over, putting their nude buttocks in the air, and then ordered other prisoners to stand behind them and "hump" them like camels, simulating sodomy. The principal experimenter, Philip Zimbardo (2007), confessed that he himself was carried away by the situation, being trapped in his role as overseer of the prison. Of this final incident, he wrote:

> It is hard to imagine that such sexual humiliation could happen in only five days, when the young men all know that this is a simulated prison experiment. Moreover, initially they all recognized the "others" were also college students like themselves. Given that they were randomly assigned to play these contrasting roles, there were no inherent differences between the two categories. They all began the experience as seemingly good people. Those who were guards knew that but for the random flip of the coin they could have been wearing the prisoner smocks and been controlled by those they were now abusing. They also knew that the prisoners had done nothing criminally wrong to deserve their lowly status. (p. 172)

Zimbardo's simulated prison conditions went on for only 5 days, yet those 5 days of strong role pressure still haunt social psychologists with the clear demonstration that simulated situations with strong roles become all too real for those who participate in them.

In light of such strong role pressure resulting in deindividuation and violent, harmful behavior in only 5 days of the prison study, it should not be surprising that workplace roles exert similar pressures on people who often become, in Zimbardo's words, "perpetrators of evil" (think, perhaps, of leaders of Enron such as Jeffrey Skilling; see McLean & Elkind, 2003) or "zombie-like followers" who go along with wrongdoing in organizations almost without realizing it and certainly without feeling culpable (for a description of such mindless everyday employee corrupt behavior at Enron, see Fishman, 2002, and more generally in organizations, Jackall, 1988).

Revisiting Milgram: Obedience in Contemporary Workplaces

Imagine yourself walking into a room full of sophisticated-looking electronic equipment, most of which is strange to you. The man who greets you is wearing a long white lab coat, similar to one a doctor would wear. He is cordial, offers a strong handshake, and asks you to sit down, which you do willingly. Without realizing it, you have already begun to obey. The man in the long white coat explains that you will be filling the role of teacher in this study of how people learn. To fulfill your role as teacher, you will need to read out pairs of words, push levers at certain times, and then let go of the pressure at certain times. Another man, who arrived at the same time as you did, is seated in a chair next to you, looking a bit uncomfortable. As you watch with curiosity, the man in the white coat explains to this other man that he will play the role of learner in this study and attaches electrodes to the man's skin. The electrodes, you learn, are under your control as the teacher. You must shock the learner when he makes a mistake.

This is the well-known laboratory setup that formed the basis for many of Milgram's (1974) studies of obedience. The research subject was assigned the role of teacher and seated in front of a long instrument panel. The teacher was instructed to shock the "learner" (who was a research confederate) each time he made a mistake in memorizing and reciting pairs of words. As the learner exhibited greater and greater signs of distress from the shock, the teacher would often suggest to the man in the white coat that there was something wrong. Each time, however, the man in the white coat would insist that the teacher continue, saying, "You must go on." In approximately 65% of cases, the teacher did.

Perhaps the most shocked person in the room was Milgram himself. Still grappling with the horrors of World War II and the Nazi regime, Milgram (1974) predicted that Americans, with their strong culture of individualism and history of pioneering self-reliance, would act differently than the German populace had under authority figures who demanded that they inflict pain on others. In reality, however, on average across many variations in the study, 60% of the "teachers" in Milgram's studies continued to shock another human being in distress when ordered by an authority figure, even when they were experiencing great discomfort themselves and wanted to stop the experiment.

In the social institutions that shape much of contemporary life, hierarchy is the most common form of organization and deference or obedience to those in authority is a strong norm (Goffman, 1956; Weber, 2002). Just as Asch's findings echo in the boardrooms of modern corporations or Zimbardo's findings resonate through Enron and the other all-too-numerous corporate scandals of the 21st century, Milgram's laboratory findings can be seen to be alive and well in contemporary workplaces. In a study of instances of courage in high-technology workplaces, Sandy[1] gave me this description of her workplace:

> The group I worked with was managed by people who picked up a failure and magnified it. The work environment did not foster an atmosphere of taking courageous stands, with the result that workers watched out for themselves and did not seek to rock the boat. To be courageous was to stand out; not in anyone's long-term career interests. I felt disempowered, unappreciated, stifled, and paranoid.

Organizations are systems of authority and social control, and leaders or managers often demand obedience from those in their workplaces, even when that obedience perpetrates wrongdoing or works to the detriment of the overall organizational productivity and purpose.

[1]All quotes are taken verbatim from research transcripts. However, all names and identifying information have been disguised to protect the confidentiality of research participants. Names reported in this chapter are pseudonyms.

Where, Then, to Look for Courage?

Many scholars have relied on the findings of Asch (1956), Zimbardo (2007), and Milgram (1974) to understand fundamental organizational behavior, easily citing instances in workplaces that look a lot like the classic studies of conformity, deindividuation through social roles, and blind obedience to authority. Organizations rely on the ability to create order through the formal establishment of groups, roles, and status, as well as reinforce order through informal social reification of group membership, role expectations, and status norms (Weber, 2002). Given that these aspects of social psychology are firmly established as part of the basis for organizing, where, then, does one look to find courage in the workplace?

I suggest that it is necessary to revisit these classic studies in social psychology to ask about the people who did not go along with the demands of strong situations. What about those who did not give the wrong answer in Asch's conformity studies? What about the people who resisted the roles in Zimbardo's prison, especially the outsider, Christina Maslach, who was instrumental in ending the study? What about the people who did not continue on with the shocks under Milgram's paradigm? Asch (1956) was largely silent about what allowed people to resist conformity. Beginning with an image of stark individuality and nonconformity as his null hypothesis, in effect, Asch was surprised by how many people did not act on their individual knowledge or judgment. Those who conformed thus became the subject of research attention. As with Milgram's (1974) accounts of his work in many variations on the basic laboratory setup, his attention was flowing to those who exhibited obedience to authority, rather than examining what enabled those who resisted the demands of the authority figure. Zimbardo (2007) described the important role of an outsider who pointed out to him that as an experimenter he was responsible for creating suffering and that he too had been blinded by his role. Courage in the workplace will be found by looking to these same moments of social life but with different eyes. As positive psychology has suggested, what creates the good in human life is not necessarily simply the opposite of the bad (e.g., Seligman, 2003). These studies point research toward an examination of moments when conformity does not rule the day, when people are awakened from their zombielike role execution and take individual responsibility for what is happening around them, or when they stand up to authority that violates their integrity or the integrity of others. These are moments when courage will be found in organizations.

Understanding Courage as Action in Context: Constructive Opposition to Duress

In some versions of his numerous studies of obedience, Milgram (1974) asked people how they would imagine themselves behaving in the experiment. No one predicted that they themselves would proceed all the way to the end of the shock generator. In making predictions about other people's behavior, participants suggested that only a lunatic fringe of society would progress all the way to the end. Milgram asserted that these predictions from participants, and the dramatic difference between the predictions and the ensuing actual behavior, suggested a deeply embedded assumption in the American (or Western; see, e.g., Markus & Kitayama, 1991) psyche, which might be described like this:

> Unless coerced by physical force or threat, the individual is preeminently the source of his own behavior. A person acts in a particular way because he has decided to do so. Action takes place in a physical-social setting, but this is merely the stage for its occurrence. The behavior itself flows from an inner core of the person; within the core personal values are weighed, gratifications assessed, and resulting decisions are translated into action. (Milgram, 1974, p. 31)

In thinking about obedience to authority, both Milgram (1974) and his subjects underestimated the power of their involvement in the physical–social setting. Something similar happened with Zimbardo's (2007) prisoners and guards, who deluded themselves into thinking that their behavior toward other prisoners did not matter or that their depravity was warranted by their role. Because organizational settings are so powerful, theorizing about courage as an aspect of the workplace must take people's involvement in the organization seriously.

In the remainder of this chapter, I offer reports on an empirical study of courage in work contexts as a way of generating theory about courage in social life. This theoretical perspective takes involvement in physical–social life as a primary aspect of courage. This perspective helps scholars see courage not just as an aspect of psychology or individual judgment, but as a distinctive pattern of action in context. This perspective offers new ways of conceptualizing courage as it is lived out in everyday work, and also offers insight into the role of courage in protecting and expanding the possibilities inherent in social organization.

Involvement in Social Life

Anders, one of the research respondents in my studies of courage among knowledge workers, suggested the following about himself and his highly trained engineering coworkers:

> Yes, we often tend to be like sheep when massed in groups; often agreeing with the people in charge when in our hearts and minds we know that it isn't the best or right way.

In this quote Anders reveals the prevalence of conformity—sheep massed in groups—and obedience—agreeing with the people in charge—in contemporary work. I refer to this propensity for individuals to be caught up in the physical–social circumstances of organizations, exemplified by Asch's, Zimbardo's, and Milgram's experiments, as *involvement in social life,* defined as the fluid and largely unconscious participation of humans in the dynamics, tensions, and inner logics of organizing (Worline, 2004). Involvement in social life is often unarticulated and becomes almost invisible to actors because their involvement is infused with feeling (Sandelands, 2003) and ruled by preconscious thought (e.g., Bargh & Chartrand, 1999). Accounts of courage in work organizations often call attention to how one member of the group is able to stand apart from the expected going-along that characterizes involvement in the flow of organizing. Consider this example from Habir, a semiconductor engineer:

> I was once on a technical talk by one of my colleagues. During the talk, he raised one point that led to an argument. All product managers and leads were present, and they are all on one side. That guy argued endlessly and made his superiors accept his valuable point.

Habir singled out his colleague as courageous for his willingness to stand his intellectual ground, going against the tide of conformity. Eileen, who worked in a software development group, pointed out how an individual can accept responsibility that goes beyond his or her role, and how this expression of courage often challenges nonconscious involvement in organizations:

> An account manager stood up to management with an anticipated problem associated with a policy change. . . . The proposal was immediately shot down as non-team play. However within two weeks the impact was surfaced by customers affected [by the policy], and a solution very like the one proposed by the account manager was put in place.

Eileen saw courage in the account manager's willingness to accept individual responsibility and draw attention to a problem, though he could have just gone along with the status quo. Note that Eileen singled this act out as courageous, even when the action did not have a good result for the individual or the organization. Courage at work is related to what other scholars have called social courage or moral courage (see Sekerka, Bagozzi, & Charnigo, 2009; Woodard & Pury, 2007). Against a backdrop of conformity, role deindividuation, and obedience to authority, which become expected forms of involvement in the workplace, the findings of this research suggest that nonconformity, individual responsibility, and principled dissent of various kinds, when undertaken in service of the good of the organization, are two of the most widespread forms of courage at work.

Individuation

Involvement in social life stands in contrast to a second concept, individuation, which is necessary to understand the form and role of courage in social life. The individual actor, standing against forces that threaten to overrun the social good, is the most familiar image associated with courage. In Eileen's story, that actor is an account manager who takes responsibility rather than going along with the other faceless, zombielike followers who wait for the problem to escalate into a customer-service crisis. Even in the language that Eileen chose we see the structure of individuation; the account manager is construed as separate and identifiable as opposed to a monolithic "management" that is arrayed against him.

Individuation is a form of development that involves taking the dynamics of social life into the self (Sandelands, 2003; Viorst, 1986). Individuation as one of the elements of courage in organizations comes out in this general description from interview data with a customer service manager:

> Each time I see someone step up to the plate and take responsibility for something that went wrong, I see that as courage. And when I take responsibility for my part in something going wrong or askew I feel a mixture of fear and courage.

Through individuation, people become unique and separate mental, emotional, and physical beings, and yet they are also deeply connected to their social worlds and responsive to social life (Brothers, 1997; Langer, 1962; Sandelands, 2003). Relational psychology and clinical psychology suggest that individuation and differentiation is a crucial but taxing life-long project (Schnarch, 1998; Viorst, 1986). Studies such as Zimbardo's (2007) point out how easily people can fall prey to deindividuation, however, sometimes simply by adopting masks or wearing uniforms. Theories of courage as an element of social life must take into account both the fact of individuation and its limited and partial nature. Through individuation, people gain the capacity for internally driven, self-determined, agentic action (Sandelands, 2003; Vallacher & Wegner, 1989). Because of the partial nature of individuation, people also have a strong inclination and ability to direct individual action toward their understanding of the collective good (Sober & Wilson, 1998). When people use their capacity for individuality as a way to protect or advance their sense of the common good, people understand this pattern as courageous. Look for this pattern of the opposition of individuation and involvement in this story from Carl:

> I started in a small business unit. The employees in this business unit came from an acquisition several years previously. I had only been in the unit a couple of months when a decision was made to close the unit. My manager knew that I didn't have the tenure or awareness of people at headquarters, and made a huge effort to market me to many there. My manager wasn't supposed to act on his inside knowledge that our office would be closed. His outrage with this policy and awareness that I had just moved my family several thousand miles drove him to break the rules on my behalf. His actions could have resulted in disciplinary action or termination for him. There was a lot of downside and little upside potential. . . . His action reinforced that I need to approach all business activities with no fear—always do the right thing.

Carl concluded his account of his manager's courageous opposition to a company policy by suggesting that he has become more willing to do what he thinks is right in the organization. Carl's sense that this was the right thing for his manager to do bolstered his sense of possibility for individuated action and made him feel more able to make decisions that reflect his sense of what is right. This pattern bears itself out across the stories in this study.

Constructive Opposition

Understanding courage as it unfolds in social systems hinges on two of the concepts explored earlier—individuation and involvement in social life—and on their being in a particular relationship to one another, a relationship I term *constructive opposition.* In Carl's story, a boss opposed an organizational policy to honor the life of his group. The manager, sensing duress to his employees from the impending closure of their unit, acted in constructive opposition to the flow of involvement the policy demanded. I use these patterns from the data to theorize that courage appears in the constructive opposition between the manager and the expected flow of involvement in work life, and this pattern of constructive opposition remedies duress in the workplace, setting things right when they go askew.

Individual activity is usually directed in accord with ongoing projects that are always happening in social systems. At times, people become aware of their involvement in ongoing projects that are contrary to their values or desires, as when Whyte's (2002) vice president heard himself agreeing to a plan that he knew would be damaging to the organization. The instances in which members of a group become aware of their involvement and its contrast to their individual sensibilities become interesting to scholars of courage. As Zimbardo (2007) noted, when people lose their individuation, they become highly susceptible to influence by others and by the social context. However, when people retain their individual sensibilities they are less susceptible to losing themselves to dehumanized behavior and more able to resist unwanted influences. Courageous action hinges on the possibility for a group member to call on his or her individuation and detach from the collective to redirect activity and sometimes to exhibit behavioral disobedience or even challenge the organizational system altogether (Milgram, 1974; Zimbardo, 2007). I propose that courage in social life is manifest in these moments when people draw on their capacity for individuation and act in opposition to the flow of involvement in social life.

Consider the pattern of constructive opposition in a story told by Randy, a member of a large software development group:

> Recently I was in a meeting in which a peer told a vice president [VP] that our product road map was fatally flawed due to our chronic under-estimation of schedules. This was courageous due to the nature of the VP and the implicit statement that the VP was behind these schedule issues. . . . This could have been a very career limiting move, yet it was a statement that everyone in the room (other than the VP) agreed with.

Randy found his peer's action courageous in part because the peer was standing out as an individuated member of the group. In addition, however, Randy's peer expressed a thought and feeling that others in the group had but were unable or unwilling to articulate. This action of voicing an issue that is unspoken in a group is important because it is one common way that people recognize oppositional action as constructive. Randy differentiates constructive opposition like that of his peer from self-aggrandizing or grandstanding behavior, in which his peer might be calling attention to himself to curry favor with the vice president or to look smart. What makes Randy's peer courageous is the way that his individuated action is attuned to people's sense of what needs to happen to advance the collective good.

Remedying Duress

A final theoretical element that emerges from these data relates to the sense of advancing the collective good touched on in Randy's story. To fully understand the role of courage in social life, one needs to understand how individuated action becomes attuned to or aligned with collective interests. Randy suggested that his colleague is courageous because he is responding to what I theorize as *duress* in the organization. Duress is a felt or intuited threat to the dynamism of a social system (Worline, 2004). Duress registers in members of an organization as people come to feel that "something is not right." As with the visibly discomposed executives around Whyte's (2002) boardroom table, people register the dynamics of social life and feel when something is going wrong. When heeded, such duress serves to align the individual with the collective, acting as a trigger for courageous action. This kind of trigger is apparent in a story taken from the data offered by Natalia, a member of a start-up software company:

> A colleague questioned the complete product line and direction of the product. He was a software developer with less than two years of experience. He told our manager (I later met the Chief Technology Officer directly) that the technology was all wrongly focused. . . . I had some doubts about the product and technology being used, but I never questioned it openly. He prepared well, had data and articles, reviews, market research to back up his claim. He did this just a month-odd before the company went IPO.

Natalia suggested that her colleague was courageous because he was responding to duress in the organization, duress that is also reflected in Natalia's nagging doubts about the product and technology. Natalia did not act on her doubt, but when she observed her colleague, who used his individuated agency to skillfully articulate these doubts to senior managers of the organization, she recognized her own sense of danger to the organization reflected in her colleague's concerns. Duress appears in Whyte's (2002) story of the silent vice president, who had a sense that the CEO's plan would be devastating to the organization. His courage failed when he failed to respond to that duress by finding a means of constructive opposition to the plan. What if the vice president in Whyte's story, rather than remaining silent, had confidently raised his voice to address the assembled board and describe the destruction the plan would unleash? I predict that we, as observers of courage in the world of work, would have a different sense of him, and he would have a different sense of himself.

Courage Changes the Possibilities in Social Life

Michaela, a general manager of a semiconductor design firm, described an experience of courage at work that draws attention to a feeling of duress that triggers one member of the general manager group to engage in constructive opposition to the flow of involvement:

> Every quarter, all of the design center general managers meet and the vice president grades us on five metrics and tells us we must improve. After

> five quarters, one general manager stepped up and created a weekly forum for all of us to actually start working on our problems. [This seemed courageous to me because] it was a shared responsibility divided among so many people, [so] why be the one to figure out how to fix it? We are all busy enough.

Michaela's account of courage in her workplace describes a fellow general manager who responded to the duress created by inertia in the organization by taking responsibility for pushing the organization forward. Again, observers can recognize a moment of individuation amidst the deindividuation created by the role expectations and division of labor. Michaela's account made the duress palpable when she indicated that for five successive quarters the general managers had been failing their review. However, despite repeated failure, the press of involvement in other aspects of the workplace kept the general managers from acting on what they knew needed to be done. Duress spurred by the lack of responsibility and action threatened the organization. The act of courage changed the threat, however, remedying the duress by interrupting the deindividuation contributing to the diffusion of responsibility (Darley & Latané, 1968; Zimbardo, 2007). In so doing, this expression of courage changes the organization, which is one theoretical insight provided by Michaela's story.

Michaela's story does not end with the organizational change, however. The experience of courage in her workplace changed what Michaela thought and felt about her work and her capacity for individuated action. In her words:

> [This experience] makes me want to look for these opportunities. [This one action has prompted] several business process improvements [that] have been made, shared, and are planned.

These data reveal that when someone stands in constructive opposition to the flow of involvement to remedy duress, observers feel it and know it as courage. The data also support the finding that the more that people are exposed to actions like this, the more capable they become of taking similar actions (Nemeth & Chiles, 1988). Through her participation in the organization, and by witnessing one member who was able to summon the strength and energy to act apart from the flow of involvement in ways that remedied the duress, Michaela's sense of the possibilities for what she could accomplish in her work changed. In theory, then, the expression of courage at work is tied to employees' sense of what is possible in the organization.

Sometimes people are equipped with the knowledge, resources, confidence, and ability to stand against the flow of involvement. Much of the current work in psychology focuses on understanding the conditions under which people will act in these situations (see, e.g., Pury, Kowalski, & Spearman, 2007). The data reported in this chapter suggest that witnessing such actions, even if one is not the actor, is an important aspect of courage in social life because the expression of courage is related to people's sense of what is possible in social systems (Nemeth & Chiles, 1988). In one of a very few studies that look at the development of courage across social situations, Nemeth and Chiles (1988) reported that those who are exposed to one person who resists conforming and agreeing to a majority opinion will be more likely to resist conforming or going along with the majority opinion in the next situation. For these research participants, being exposed to someone who does not conform changes that person's sense of what is possible in his or her behavior. This finding is echoed in the current research. Recall Carl, earlier, witnessing his manager's opposition to a company policy that would harm employees. By witnessing his manager's courage, Carl felt himself become more capable of acting courageously.

This dynamic of courageous action changing the possibilities in a social system is echoed in a story by Hannah, a human resources (HR) representative in a large corporation:

> An employee relations incident was investigated and the decision was made to terminate this temporary employee. The decision involved HR, legal, the temporary staffing group, and the manager—it was unanimous. The issue of whether to classify the temp as eligible vs. ineligible [for benefits] was not unanimous. All but the temporary staffing group rep (TSG) thought ineligible. After much debate, we ended up classifying the person as eligible in accordance with the temporary staffing group rep. The TSG rep stood alone in the face of massive pressure and held fast to her ideals. In addition, her arguments were persuasive and passionate enough to convince the rest of the people involved to change their minds. . . . [After this incident] I'm less likely to completely close off options until all angles are examined. I'm also more willing to stick firmly to an ideal when necessary.

Hannah recognized the effect of hearing the TSG representative make a persuasive case about the right course of action. Her participation in this instance of courage in the organization impacted her own sense of how and when to act on what she thinks is right.

The concept of possibility in philosophy relates to a perception that something is conceivable ("Possibility," 1989)—in particular, that something agrees in intuition and feeling with the conditions of one's experience of social life (Buchanan, 1927). Piaget (1987) suggested that reality appears as being necessarily as it is given—in other words, people take what is happening to be the only thing that can happen. This way of perceiving social reality makes the creation of possibility in social systems crucial. The fact that people perceive reality as necessarily given suggests that people don't often, of their own accord, think of doing things contrary to the flow of involvement in social life. However, through the experience of someone else's action, a different reality may be found, as Hannah did from the TSG representative's nonconformity.

Because of the fact of individuation, not all of our realities and experiences are the same. Group memberships or boundaries often make a difference in terms of one's individuation and capacity for action. In the Stanford prison study, Zimbardo (2007) credited an outsider, Christine Maslach, with being able to see what was happening from a different perspective and speaking out about it, thereby courageously disrupting the dehumanization and deindividuation that had taken over in the study. People bring different psychological and social resources to their experience of work. This variation in training, emotions, relationships, skill, group memberships, and other resources increases the likelihood that someone will think of a way to constructively oppose duress. As they do, their action changes what seems possible for everyone else.

Recall Natalia's story of her colleague who challenged the start-up company's technology, just a few months before their initial public offering (IPO). In regard to that situation, Natalia said:

> My feeling about "upper management knows everything" changed. I learned to ask good question[s] and prepare supporting data. In my workplace, management acknowledged that the technology and product line needs revisiting and a number of reviews and follow-up assignments . . . followed.

Natalia found her organization changed through the expression of courage, and her own thinking about her role and her relationship to management changed as well. Of course, not every story of the expression of courage at work ends with successful organizational change, nor with successful individual outcomes. Sometimes people who call attention to wrongdoing are fired (e.g., see Jackall, 1988); sometimes those who challenge authority are sidelined or demoted (Glazer & Glazer, 1989). It is important to note that the pattern of constructive opposition to remedy duress holds true regardless of the "outcome" of the pattern of action. The expression of courage shapes what is perceived to be possible in a social system, even when it is "unsuccessful courage," to use the words of Larry, a software designer. Larry told a story in which an expression of courage was met with disdain:

> Through multiple interactions with numerous customers, this person developed requirements and a solution/product design for using our technology to solve complex business process analysis, design, definition, implementation, and maintenance. This person presented the product idea and design to direct management. Although not accepting of the idea, the manager coached this person on approaches and sent her off to try again. After two more failed attempts, she went to the vice president, 3 levels up, and tried again. This person was convinced that she had identified a real opportunity for revenue generation. She worked hard to justify her position and back it up with facts and analysis. She did not give up, and finally bypassed all barriers to get her idea heard. Her ideas and approach were rejected, and the rejection was very public. Unfortunately this somewhat killed the innovative spirit of everyone reporting to this VP. A story of unsuccessful courage.

The courage that Larry saw in his coworker inspired his respect, regardless of the success of the outcome. The expression of courage also suggested to others in the organization that they could be more innovative. However, those shifts in possibility were offset by a nonaccommodating managerial response to this expression of courage, which narrowed people's sense of the possibility for change in the organization. Larry's story suggests the importance of leadership responses to courageous action as an important and understudied aspect of courage in social life. Theoretically, then, one can infer from the data presented here that both the expression of courage and its reception in a social system are crucial to creating organizations that inspire rather than stifle possibilities for change.

Asch, Zimbardo, and Milgram Revisited

It is curious that Milgram (1974) drew very few conclusions about the minority of people who did not proceed all the way through his experiments on obedience. Revisiting Milgram's studies through the lens of positive psychology (e.g., Seligman, 2003), however, showed me that it might be useful to study those who express dissent as closely as those who obey have been studied. What enabled 40% of people to refuse to participate when most succumbed to the pressure of the experimenter's authority? The authors in this volume have begun doing work that will help psychologists and organizational members better answer that question. Contributing to that growing understanding, I suggest that a starting point for a reexamination of Milgram's participants involves attending closely to the pressures of involvement in the physical–social situation. What kind of involvement is demanded by Milgram's study? What is the sense of duress created by Milgram's study design, and how do people come to recognize it? As people come to sense duress in the study, what are the kinds of personal experiences and social or psychological resources that participants draw on to act in a strongly individuated manner to constructively oppose those pressures? Asking and answering questions like these will help deepen the knowledge base regarding courage and its role in such things as principled dissent (Graham, 1986), prosocial rule-breaking (Morrison, 2006), and other forms of prosocial opposition to authority (Morrison & Milliken, 2000; Schwan, 2004).

Rorty (1988) commented that courage as an emotional experience requires an oppositional attitude. By revisiting social conformity studies from Asch (1956) and role deindividuation studies from Zimbardo (2007), I found that this oppositional attitude is necessary for courage at work. It appears in Larry's story of unsuccessful courage as a press for innovation—a press that goes in opposition to the ideas of management. It appears in Hannah's story of passionate minority influence from a TSG representative in an HR decision. It appears as a creative voice in Natalia's story of her colleague who disagreed with an entire product line just a few months before its launch. Some have suggested that this capacity for opposition to the collective is a danger of individualism (Rorty, 1988; Sandelands, 2003), and yet it is clear that individual agency expressed in response to duress can be directed toward the collective good.

Thus, in instances of the expression of courage in social life, this oppositional attitude and individual agency must be harnessed and employed in ways that are aligned with the collective good. What enables such opposition to the pressures of conformity? Though Asch (1956) drew few conclusions about what enabled his study participants to resist conforming to their peers, Nemeth and Chiles (1988) suggested that having witnessed such nonconformity is important to the development of this form of courage. Workplaces need people who will speak in the midst of strong pressures to remain silent (Morrison & Milliken, 2000). Workplaces need people who will offer new ideas in the midst of pressures to do what everyone else is doing—not only for the sake of changes in the organization, which do flow from the expression of these forms of courage, but also for the sake of expanding what others in the organization think is possible (Worline, 2004). One of the roles of courage in social life is to provide members with the capacity to resist the stifling pressures of conformity.

Conclusion

I began by looking to the workplace as a site of contemporary theater, where human dramas play out and call on people to make decisions and take actions in relation to their most sacred values and cherished beliefs. Revisiting classic social psychological studies by Asch (1956), Zimbardo (2007), and Milgram (1974) offered a reminder that much of one's behavior does not stem from the inner core of the person, or from the conscious weighing of values and preferences, but rather from one's involvement in these workplace dramas. People often underestimate the power of this involvement, taking for granted that they will act as independent, individuated selves. Understanding the role of courage in social life entails remembering the powerful role of involvement in social life and seeing it in relation to the difficulty of independent, individuated action.

In forgetting the power of involvement in social life, one forgets the lesson of the Cowardly Lion in the beloved children's tale, *The Wizard of Oz* (Baum, 1956; Nathanson, 1991). The Cowardly Lion, who is afraid of everything, including his own shadow, sets out to see the wizard to find courage. As the Cowardly Lion and his friends travel the yellow brick road, the story teaches that to find courage is really to find one's place in a vibrant social life. The Cowardly Lion discovered the essence of courage not by meeting the wizard, and not even by acting particularly heroically, but rather by not giving up on his place with his friends when they needed him. Courage is not simply something inside the Cowardly Lion, and not simply something that can be bestowed by the wizard; courage is the moment when the Cowardly Lion feels afraid and turns to run away from the fearsome castle (involvement in the flow of social life), but stops himself (individuation) and faces the wicked witch (duress) to rescue his friends (constructive opposition that remedies duress). The wizard bestows the Cowardly Lion with a medal of honor, a symbolic recognition of the moment of courage that readers have witnessed.

In theory, courage has an important role in social systems because it is a protective response to threats to collective dynamism. In this chapter, I have presented empirical evidence to show theoretical inferences about courage in social life as represented by a very particular pattern of activity that unfolds when a person attempts to remedy duress by employing the capacity for individuated action in constructive opposition to ongoing involvement in social life. Courage takes on the quality of a virtue in almost all cultures (Lash, 1995; Robinson et al., 1962) precisely because it is a moment of crucial consequence to collective vitality. Because of its importance to collective life and its ability to align individuated action with the collective good, courage becomes remarkable and celebrated (Goode, 1978). In this way, the role and importance of courage in workplaces and in broader social life cannot be explained only by understanding the psychology of the individual; it also requires a perspective on activity and an understanding of the pressures of involvement and the precise pattern of constructive opposition to involvement in ways that remedy duress. A review of hundreds of accounts of courage from mid- and low-level employees in organizations suggests that new ways of understanding courage are needed to help elaborate its role in people's collective life. By adopting a grounded theoretical perspective on courage as constructive opposition that remedies duress, one can come to understand the manifestation of courage as an exquisitely patterned and delicate form of organized activity, one with tremendous import for the vitality of social life.

References

Asch, S. E. (1956). Studies of independence and conformity: A minority of one against a unanimous majority. *Psychological Monographs, 70*(9), 70–81.

Bargh, J., & Chartrand, T. (1999). The unbearable automaticity of being. *American Psychologist, 54,* 462–479. doi:10.1037/0003-066X.54.7.462

Baum, L. (1956). *The Wizard of Oz.* Chicago, IL: Rand McNally.

Brothers, L. (1997). *Friday's footprint: How society shapes the human mind.* New York, NY: Oxford University Press.

Buchanan, S. (1927). *Possibility.* New York, NY: Harcourt Brace.

Darley, J. M., & Latané, B. (1968). Bystander intervention in emergencies: Diffusion of responsibility. *Journal of Personality and Social Psychology, 8,* 377–383. doi:10.1037/h0025589

Fishman, C. (2002, April). What if you'd worked at Enron? *Fast Company,* 58.

Frost, P. J. (2003). *Toxic emotions at work.* Boston, MA: Harvard Business School Press.

Glazer, M. P., & Glazer, P. M. (1989). *The whistleblowers: Exposing corruption in government and industry.* New York, NY: Basic Books.

Goffman, E. (1956). The nature of deference and demeanor. *American Anthropologist, 58,* 473–502. doi:10.1525/aa.1956.58.3.02a00070

Goode, W. (1978). *The celebration of heroes: Prestige as a social control system.* Berkeley: University of California Press.

Graham, J. W. (1986). Principled organizational dissent: A theoretical essay. *Research in Organizational Behavior, 8,* 1–52.

Jackall, R. (1988). *Moral mazes: The world of corporate managers.* New York, NY: Oxford University Press.

Langer, S. K. (1962). *Philosophical sketches.* Baltimore, MD: Johns Hopkins University Press.

Lash, J. (1995). *The hero: Manhood and power.* New York, NY: Thames and Hudson.

Markus, H., & Kitayama, S. (1991). Culture and the self: Implications for cognition, emotion, and motivation. *Psychological Review, 98,* 224–253. doi:10.1037/0033-295X.98.2.224

McLean, B., & Elkind, P. (2003). *The smartest guys in the room: The amazing rise and scandalous fall of Enron.* New York, NY: Penguin.

Milgram, S. (1974). *Obedience to authority.* New York, NY: Harper & Row.

Morrison, E. (2006). Doing the job well: An investigation of pro-social rule breaking. *Journal of Management, 32*(1), 5–28. doi:10.1177/0149206305277790

Morrison, E., & Milliken, F. (2000). Organizational silence: A barrier to change and development in a pluralistic world. *Academy of Management Review, 25,* 706–725. doi:10.2307/259200

Nathanson, P. (1991). *Over the rainbow: The Wizard of Oz as a secular myth of America.* Albany: State University of New York Press.

Nemeth, C., & Chiles, C. (1988). Modeling courage: The role of dissent in fostering independence. *European Journal of Social Psychology, 18,* 275–280. doi:10.1002/ejsp.2420180306

Possibility. (1989). In *Oxford English dictionary* (2nd ed). (2003). Retrieved from http://www.oed.com

Piaget, J. (1987). *Possibility and necessity* (H. Feider, Trans.). Minneapolis: University of Minnesota Press.

Pury, C., Kowalski, R., & Spearman, J. (2007). Distinctions between general and personal courage. *The Journal of Positive Psychology, 2*(2), 99–114. doi:10.1080/17439760701237962

Robinson, H. S., Wilson, K., & Picard, B. L. (1962). *The encyclopaedia of myths and legends of all nations.* London, England: Kaye & Ward.

Rorty, A. O. (1988). *Mind in action: Essays in the philosophy of mind.* Boston, MA: Beacon Press.

Rozin, P. (2001). Social psychology and science: Some lessons from Solomon Asch. *Personality and Social Psychology Review, 5*(1), 2–14. doi:10.1207/S15327957PSPR0501_1

Sandelands, L. (2003). *Thinking about social life.* Lanham, MD: University Press of America.

Schnarch, D. (1998). *Passionate marriage: Love, sex, and intimacy in emotionally committed relationships.* New York, NY: Holt.

Schwan, G. (2004). Civil courage and human dignity: How to regain respect for the fundamental values of western democracy. *Social Research, 71*(1), 107–116.

Sekerka, L., Bagozzi, R., & Charnigo, R. (2009). Facing ethical challenges in the workplace: Conceptualizing and measuring professional moral courage. *Journal of Business Ethics, 89,* 565–579. DOI10.1007

Seligman, M. E. (2003). Positive psychology: Fundamental assumptions. *American Psychologist, 16,* 126–127.

Sober, E., & Wilson, D. (1998). *Unto others: The evolution and psychology of unselfish behavior.* Cambridge, MA: Harvard University Press.

Vallacher, R., & Wegner, D. (1989). Levels of personal agency: Individual variation in action identification. *Journal of Personality and Social Psychology, 57,* 660–671. doi:10.1037/0022-3514.57.4.660

Viorst, J. (1986). *Necessary losses.* New York, NY: Simon & Schuster.

Weber, M. (2002). *The Protestant work ethic and the spirit of capitalism* (P. Baehr & G. Wells, Trans.). New York, NY: Penguin.

Whyte, D. (1994). *The heart aroused: Poetry and the preservation of the soul in corporate America.* New York, NY: Currency Doubleday.

Whyte, D. (2002). *Crossing the unknown sea: Work as a pilgrimage of identity.* New York, NY: Riverhead Books.

Woodard, C., & Pury, C. L. S. (2007). The construct of courage: Categorization and measurement. *Consulting Psychology Journal: Practice and Research, 59,* 135–147. doi:10.1037/1065-9293.59.2.135

Worline, M. (2004). *Dancing the cliff edge: The role of courage in social life.* Unpublished dissertation, University of Michigan.

Zimbardo, P. (2007). *The Lucifer effect: Understanding how good people turn evil.* New York, NY: Random House.

Part IV

Conclusion

12

The Future of Courage Research

Cynthia L. S. Pury, Shane J. Lopez, and Melinda Key-Roberts

This chapter on the future of courage research begins with a sketch of the types of courage that aspiring and novice researchers can identify and examine in media happenings and pop culture. Next, we consider the future of courage by examining the past. Scientific research about why people behave badly has often ignored the individuals who were strong of character. We briefly revisit some best-known psychological experiments and call for a reexamination of the outlier data and explore the progress made in the research outlined in this volume. Finally, we chart a course for future courage research that will demystify this cardinal virtue.

Courage All Around Us

Although courage is considered a universal virtue, it lacks a universally agreed upon definition. As suggested in this volume, aspects of courage include intentionality or freedom of choice, pursuit of a worthy goal, perception of personal threat or fear of a situation, and the willingness to take risks when the outcome is unknown. Building on the various components of courage, researchers have proposed different types of courage. The most common forms include physical, moral, and vital or psychological courage (Lopez, O'Byrne, & Petersen, 2003; Pury, Kowalski, & Spearman, 2007; Putman, 1997; see also Chapters 1 and 2, this volume). Each type is associated with different risks and difficulties and understanding these forms can help aspiring and novice researchers begin to examine courage in daily life. "Knowing it when you see it" is where a courage researcher begins his or her development. Then, qualities of the courageous person and act need to be carefully considered.

Physical courage, for example, involves bodily risk or difficulty. This form of courage is epitomized by Wesley Autry, the man who dove onto subway tracks in New York City after a stranger fell into the path of an oncoming train. Autry's actions typify physical courage in that the physical risks he assumed were aimed at preventing harm to someone else. Moral courage involves standing up for what is right in the face of disapproval. It is associated with risk to one's image and can include rejection, loss of rights, or termination of privileges. Individuals with moral courage make choices that benefit the common good rather their own interests. They are characterized by authenticity and integrity, qualities demonstrated by Sherron Watkins when she blew the whistle on Enron's illegal accounting practices. Finally, vital courage is the courage to thrive in the face of serious illness, and psychological courage is the courage to face doubt, uncertainty, and a risk to one's own emotional well-being for growth. Unlike physical and moral courage, which are needed to face external threats and difficulties, these types of courage are needed to tackle personally challenging situations involving risks to one's own well-being. Icons of vital courage include Christopher Reeve, who lobbied for people with spinal cord injuries following an accident that left him confined to a wheelchair. An icon of psychological courage is Temple Grandin, who stepped outside of the small comfort zone she inhabited as a person with Asperger's disorder to attend college, then to attend graduate school, then to build a successful career as an animal behavior specialist, writer, and speaker.

Have you witnessed physical courage in the past month? Can you think of a local politician who has demonstrated this form of the virtue? One place to start looking for actions that have been awarded the accolade of courage is the local, national, or international news media. Perhaps because of the inspiring qualities outlined by Worline (see Chapter 11), stories of courage are abundant in the news. Just before this chapter was written, the national news in the United States had been dominated by the dramatic actions of Richard Phillips, the captain of a cargo ship that had been attacked by pirates. Phillips offered to become a hostage to prevent another attack on his ship. After several days being held captive aboard a lifeboat, Phillips was rescued by Navy SEAL sharpshooters, whose own courage was praised (Radia & James, 2009). At about the same time, Susan Boyle, an average-appearing middle-aged woman who had spent decades caring for her parents, became an overnight Internet sensation via her audition for a British TV talent show. Her efforts to follow her dreams to become a famous singer were called courageous by many (e.g., Bregman, 2009). Elements of both physical and moral courage are present in the Phillips story, whereas Boyle's story exemplifies psychological courage.

However, as Pury and Starkey (see Chapter 4) noted, there may be a difference between the qualities that lead to the accolade of courage and the qualities of a courageous action seen from the actor's vantage point. For instance, think of times when you believe you overcame fear or other limitations for a noble reason—do you consider those actions courageous?

In psychology, the "what is" question often is followed by the "can it be changed" question; that is true for courage. To answer the question "Can courage be learned?" one should consider the relationship between fear and courage. With moral courage, for example, it is known that a number of emotional elements, including fear, are frequently associated with courageous action. The relationship between fear and courage is particularly complex (for more complete discussions of this issue, see Pury, Kowalski, & Spearman, 2007, and Chapters 3, 5, 6, 7, and 9, this volume).

If illogical fear hinders courageous action, then interventions designed to reduce fear may be particularly effective in enhancing courageous behavior. Exposure therapy is one way to target the amount of fear felt in a given situation, thus increasing the likelihood of acting courageously. This therapy requires participants to purposefully face a feared situation, remaining in the situation until feelings of anxiety subside. Repeated exposure to the feared stimulus eventually leads to habituation or a sense of boredom. However, as McGurk and Castro (see Chapter 9) pointed out, fear in combat (and other objectively dangerous situations) is really quite logical and thus approaches designed to deal with illogical fear may not work. Instead, techniques designed to give people automatic and adaptive responses when fear is felt may be better suited to these objectively dangerous situations.

Because exposure therapy requires repeated successful contact with a feared condition and training adaptive responses provides a more active type of mastery experience, the means of reducing or coping with fear may also be an effective means of increasing self-efficacy. Self-efficacy is a sense of confidence in one's ability to act in an effective manner and is primarily affected by past successes (both direct and indirect). In addition, the ability to influence self-efficacy via vicarious experience makes it an ideal target of interventions designed to enhance courageous action (see, e.g., Chapter 10).

When faced with an urgent situation, individuals frequently experience the physiological changes of the fight-or-flight response. As discussed in the prior paragraph, reducing fear may lessen the likelihood of fleeing from a risky situation. In contrast, increasing anger may help prepare an individual to face difficult circumstances. Feeling angry may facilitate courageous action by decreasing the perceived risk and increasing the perceived likelihood of a desired outcome (Lerner & Keltner, 2001). It may also be associated with a greater sense of moral rightness, one of the features of courageous action (Pury, 2008). In 2003, Lerner, Gonzalez, Small, and Fischhoff explored the impact of induced anger by asking their subjects to describe what made them most angry about the terrorist attacks of September 11, 2001, and then to describe the single thing that made them most angry in detail. Participants in the study who wrote about the events in an angry way were more optimistic about the reduced likelihood of future terrorist attacks on the United States than were participants who were asked to write about the events in a fearful way. Although caution is warranted when inciting anger, this study highlights the role increased anger may play in outcome expectations and the probability of a courageous response. Anger clearly plays a naturally occurring and facilitating role in moral courage when the target of the anger is the true opponent (see Chapter 8, this volume). However, when the anger is misdirected at innocent bystanders, such as noncombatants in a military operation, resisting the urge to act on this emotion may be what courage requires (see Chapter 9). Thus, anger may play a role in facilitating courage in some situations while hindering it in others; at this point it appears that the target of the anger is the key, although this has yet to be confirmed in empirical research.

Altering the risks associated with courageous action, through training, practice, and planning, is another theoretically likely means to increase courageous behavior (Pury, 2008). Intense specialized training has the added benefit of reducing emotions known to hinder courageous action (Rachman, 1990; Chapter 2, this volume). Although training programs aimed at increasing physical courage (e.g., training firefighters to rescue people from burning buildings) are more prevalent than are those attempting to target vital, moral, or civil courage, programs directed at these other forms of courageous action are beginning to emerge. For example, Osswald et al. (see Chapter 8) reviewed their current training program intended to inspire civil courage.

Knowledge of those factors that either hinder or facilitate courageous action is an important first step in moving toward increasing courageous action. Interventions designed to increase courage may be influenced by common elements found in most of the modern definitions of the word (i.e., intentionality, facing risks, facing uncertainty, and a worthy goal) as well as the emotional states frequently associated with courage (i.e., fear, anger, and confidence). Though courses aimed at increasing courageous action are springing up, more research is needed to assess the effectiveness of such programs.

Learning About Courage From the Past (and Into the Future)

Classic psychological experiments have revealed how good people turn evil (Zimbardo's Stanford prison study) and inflict pain (Milgram's pain study) as a result of the subtle pressures of authority, and why other people stand by and watch them do it. It is understood why people succumb to fear. Yet, little is known about how people rise to the occasion and defend what they believe in or why they fight for the rights of others. Maybe if Zimbardo (2007) or Milgram (1974) had been looking for the defiant participants, those who faced their fears and did the "right" thing, the science of courage would be more robust today.

Why do good people stay good (behave well) rather than turn evil? That question does not get as much attention as Zimbardo's "good people turn evil" headline, yet it may be more important to know how to withstand the pressures and situational ambiguity than that many are transformed by it. The students who wanted nothing to do with the prison study and the soldiers who distanced themselves from the work of a select few in the former prison of Abu Ghraib have stories to tell. Courage researchers need to chronicle those accounts.

Monica Worline (see Chapter 11) posed a question about the Milgram study that could be answered via some historical work and data sleuthing: "What enabled 40% of people to refuse to participate, whereas most succumbed to the pressure of the experimenter's authority?" (The fact that 40% of Milgram's participants did not succumb to the conditions of the experiment was news to the first author, who had always assumed until reading the original study that only a small minority of participants refused to mistreat fellow participants.) Though Worline contended that understanding social factors may explain why people behave badly and behave well, the explanations for the lack of conformity need to be explored further.

There is much to learn about courage hidden in old studies about fear and conformity. There also is a demand for knowledge about the courage that will manifest itself in the future. What is specifically needed are long-term studies of groups of people that probably will be called on to be courageous in the future. Little is known about the characteristics of people who will one day be courageous. Work with the military or civil first responders might allow for studies of service people at the beginning of their training, with yearly follow-ups and extensive examinations of the subset of individuals who demonstrated courage in the line of duty.

The Future of Courage Research: Where We Are and Where We Are Going

A review of the major themes in the chapters of this volume suggests many likely directions for the content of courage research. The social effects of observing courageous or cowardly action were discussed by multiple authors (including Chapters 2, 7–11). The effects of observation include, but are not limited to, its role in leadership. As described by these and other authors (e.g., Nemeth & Chiles, 1988), courage can be contagious, as can cowardice. In light of one of psychology's basic observations about human behavior—that negative information outweighs positive information—is cowardice more contagious than courage? Or is the inspiring nature of observing courage in action (see Chapter 11) strong enough to overcome cowardice's example? What features of the social environment make the contagion of courage or cowardice more likely?

A second major theme of these chapters is the search for shared features of all types of courage (see, e.g., Chapters 2, 3, 4, and 9). The building consensus seems to be that all acts of courage involve a desirable, important, and morally relevant goal that is intentionally pursued by the actor despite risk, threat, or other unpleasant facts. Because courage involves possible negative outcomes for the actor, fear may be involved (see the earlier discussion). Because courage involves performance, self-efficacy may be involved. Multiple chapters in this volume provide theory and empirical evidence on the importance of self-efficacy for courage (see, e.g., Chapters 5, 7, 8, and 9), and we believe that the link between self-efficacy and courage is one that deserves fuller exploration and increased empirical study.

Types of courageous acts are also a common theme, with multiple authors describing unique properties of the major types of courage: physical, moral, psychological, and vital (see, e.g., Chapters 1, 2, and 8). Of these, physical courage appears to be the prototype for courage, with moral courage falling close to the prototype and psychological and vital courage further from the prototype (see, e.g., Chapters 1 and 2). Is this because physical and moral courage share universally valued goals and universally feared risks (see, e.g., Chapter 4)? Other, more specific types of courage are discussed in these chapters as well, including entrepreneurial courage (Chapter 10), military courage (Chapter 9), existential courage (Chapter 6), bad courage (Chapter 4), and foolish courage (Chapter 4). The extent to which the differences between these types can be explained by differences in the content of the shared features of risks and goals has yet to be fully explored.

Although the subjective states of fear and confidence or efficacy are common themes of current research, several chapters suggest two other subjective states of interest: anger and duty. Anger may play a very context-specific role in courage: To date, it has been discussed only as part of moral courage (see Chapter 9), but the role it plays varies. Although theoretically anger can be used to increase confidence and courage (see Chapter 8, and previous discussion in this chapter), it also may be one of the unpleasant facts that a solder in combat needs to deal with appropriately to avoid needless civilian casualties (Chapter 9). Duty or obligation also appears as a theme of several chapters (e.g., Chapters 6, 7, and 8) and are themes the first author has heard mentioned many times by her own research participants. As with courage, duty or obligation has rarely been investigated by psychologists (86 hits in a PsycINFO keyword search conducted on the entire database on April 30, 2009), although the sense that one is obligated to take action is crucial for understanding ethical conduct. Further research into anger, duty, and other subjective states beyond fear and confidence is required.

Identity is also raised in several chapters (e.g., Chapters 1, 2, 6, and 7). Observing courage changes the social landscape (Chapter 11); does taking courageous action change the actor? If there are changes, do they depend on the actor's reflection (Chapter 7)?

Finally, the most common theme of the chapters, indeed the subtext of all of the chapters in the volume, is the way in which courage can be changed. Can courage be increased? Can all types of courage be increased? Can undesirable types of courage be decreased (see, e.g., Chapter 4)? Doing so will require three things: an understanding of the working parts of courage, techniques to alter those parts, and outcome measures of courage to see if the techniques worked. Much of this volume and the other existent work on courage is beginning to flesh out these working parts. Although a complete answer has not been arrived at, a consensus appears to be coming into focus. That consensus includes not only common features of all courageous actions but also context- or brand-specific features of particular types of acts, such as morally courageous acts (see, e.g., Chapter 8).

A true understanding of courage, however, requires a model of the process by which someone comes to take a courageous action (Chapter 4). The chapters in this volume contain several explicit and implicit models of the process of courageous action in general (e.g., Chapters 5, 7, and 10) and in specific types of courage (e.g., Chapters 6, 8, 9, and 11). As these models are refined and others developed, an understanding of how courage works can be used to alter its course.

The true test of any modification technique depends on the development of valid outcome measures to determine whether it did what it was designed to do, which brings us full circle to the definition of courage. What does it mean to be courageous? What actions can be observed that would lead (trained) raters to say "yes, that was courageous" and to determine how courageous it was with reliability? What individual differences markers should researchers look for in people who have successfully increased their courage? How can researchers measure how courageous someone feels? Answering any of these questions requires that the crucial work of developing a consensus definition continue. Although we see excellent agreement that courage involves worthy goals pursued despite risk, other questions remain. One of the biggest questions is the extent to which courage has a narrow definition, limited to the pursuit of universal and extremely good goals despite universal and very high risks, versus a broader definition that includes the pursuit of more personally relevant goals despite individual risks (see, e.g., Chapters 4 and 9).

We encourage researchers to continue to examine these important questions and, in doing so, to develop the outcome measures needed to determine if various attempts to teach (good) courage are working. A set of ideal outcome measures will enable researchers to observe courage over the course of an afternoon or a lifetime, in undergraduate laboratory participants as well as in field samples. The challenges of finding such measures may be daunting: The most prototypical courageous actions involve levels of risk and importance of action that exceed typical ethical boundaries for laboratory work; longitudinal studies are difficult and time consuming to complete; and though some key features of the construct, such as risk and meaningful goal, are agreed on, others, such as fear, anger, and magnitude of risks and goals, are far from settled. However, we believe that the long-term gains of understanding and cultivating one of humanity's key virtues will be worth the effort.

References

Bregman, P. (2009, April 22). *Commentary: Why we're fascinated by Susan Boyle.* Retrieved from http://www.cnn.com/2009/SHOWBIZ/Music/04/22/bregman.boyle/

Lerner, J., Gonzalez, R., Small, D., & Fischhoff, B. (2003). Effects of fear and anger on perceived risks of terrorism: A national field experiment [Electronic copy]. *Psychological Science, 14,* 144–150. doi:10.1111/1467-9280.01433

Lerner, J., & Keltner, D. (2001). Fear, anger, and risk. *Journal of Personality and Social Psychology, 81,*146–159.

Lopez, S., O'Byrne, K., & Petersen, S. (2003). Profiling courage. In S. J. Lopez & C. R. Snyder (Eds.), *Positive psychological assessment: A handbook of models and measures* (pp. 185–197). Washington, DC: American Psychological Association. doi:10.1037/10612-012

Milgram, S. (1974). *Obedience to authority.* New York, NY: Harper & Row.

Nemeth, C., & Chiles, C. (1988). Modeling courage: The role of dissent in fostering independence. *European Journal of Social Psychology, 18,* 275–280. doi:10.1002/ejsp.2420180306

Pury, C. L. S. (2008). Can courage be learned? In S. J. Lopez (Ed.), *Positive psychology: Exploring the best in people: Vol. 1. Discovering human strengths* (pp. 109–130). Westport, CT: Praeger Publishers.

Pury, C. L. S., Kowalski, R. M., & Spearman, J. (2007). Distinctions between general and personal courage. *The Journal of Positive Psychology, 2,* 99–114. doi:10.1080/17439760701237962

Putman, D. (1997). Psychological courage. *Philosophy, Psychiatry, and Psychology, 4,* 1–11.

Rachman, S. (1990). *Fear and courage* (2nd ed.). New York, NY: Freeman.

Radia, K., & James, M. (2009, April 12). *Captain's dramatic rescue is 'going to make a great movie'.* Retrieved from http://abcnews.go.com/print?id=7318145

Zimbardo, P. (2007). *The Lucifer effect: Understanding how good people turn evil.* New York, NY: Random House.

Index

About the Editors

Cynthia L. S. Pury, PhD, is an associate professor of psychology at Clemson University. Trained as a clinician specializing in anxiety disorders, she comes to courage research with a background in cognitive theories of emotion, particularly fear and anxiety. Her current research focuses on developing a psychological model of courage, with the ultimate aim of developing courage-promotion strategies for use in clinical, counseling, medical, and organizational settings. She teaches positive psychology, personality, abnormal psychology, and research methods.

Shane J. Lopez, PhD, senior scientist in residence, is an architect of the Gallup Student Poll. A measure of hope, engagement, and well-being, the Student Poll taps into the hearts and minds of American students to determine what drives achievement. Dr. Lopez is also the director of the annual Gallup Well-Being Forum, which convenes scholars, leaders, and decision makers to discuss health care and global well-being. He also serves as the research director for the Clifton Strengths School. Dr. Lopez has published more than 100 articles and chapters and seven books, including *Positive Psychology: Exploring the Best in People* and *The Encyclopedia of Positive Psychology.* With C. R. Snyder, he published *Positive Psychology: The Scientific and Practical Explorations of Human Strengths,* which won the Sage Press Book of the Year Award; *Positive Psychological Assessment: A Handbook of Models and Measures;* and *The Handbook of Positive Psychology.* He is a licensed psychologist, a fellow of the American Psychological Association, and an educational advisor for *Discovery Television.*